F.C.Muther

Robert Owen and the Owenites in Britain and America

The Quest for the New Moral World

Robert Owen and the Owenites in Britain and America

The Quest for the New Moral World

J. F. C. Harrison

Professor of History, University of Wisconsin

London: Routledge and Kegan Paul

First published 1969
by Routledge and Kegan Paul Ltd
Broadway House, 68–74 Carter Lane
London E.C.4

Printed in Great Britain
by Alden & Mowbray Ltd, at the Alden Press, Oxford

SBN 7100 6035 1

Contents

Illustrations

Preface

During the six years that this book has been in the making I have incurred many obligations. First and foremost is my debt to the Department of History and the Graduate School of the University of Wisconsin for granting me the time and financial support necessary for research and writing. I am also indebted to the Social Science Research Council for a faculty research fellowship in 1963–64, and to the American Philosophical Society for a summer grant in 1967. To Miss M. B. C. Canney and her assistants in the Goldsmiths' Library, University of London, I owe special thanks for their kindness and patient help extending over many months.

Mr H. L. Beales, formerly Reader at the London School of Economics and Political Science, University of London, first introduced me to many of the characters in this book, and has, as always, generously shared with me his unrivalled knowledge of social movements in the nineteenth century. My colleague, Professor William R. Taylor, gave me valuable advice at a crucial stage of the writing, and I owe a great deal to my collaboration with him at the University of Wisconsin in recent years. Professor Harold Perkin of the University of Lancaster read the whole manuscript and gave me the benefit of his expert editorial experience. Successive research assistants relieved me of much of the burden of research routine, especially in connection with the bibliography, and I wish to thank them all: Eileen M. Yeo, Robert D. Storch, Barbara A. Frankle, Robert T. Orrill and David A. DeGiustino.

In the collection of material scattered widely throughout Britain and America I received help and kindness from all sorts of people. Members of the Owen family were most generous and I would like to thank Mrs Jane Blaffer Owen, Mr Kenneth Dale Owen, Miss Joyce Mann, and Miss Helen Elliott, of New Harmony, Indiana; and Baroness Eleanor Perenyi of Stonington, Connecticut, for hospitality and information. At New Lanark the General Manager and staff of the Gourock Ropework Company generously gave me access to their records and took time out to show me the mills and village. I have relied heavily upon the services of many libraries and in particular would like to thank the Librarians and staffs of the following: Manchester Central Library, Birmingham Public Library, Central Library (Leeds), British Museum (Bloomsbury and Colindale), Robert Owen Museum (Newtown, Wales), Library of the

PREFACE

Cooperative Union (Manchester), Motherwell Public Library, National Library of Scotland, International Institute of Social History (Amsterdam), Burgerbibliothek (Bern, Switzerland), Wisconsin State Historical Society, Memorial Library (University of Wisconsin), Illinois Historical Survey, and New Harmony Workingmen's Institute. Among individual correspondents who have helped me are Mr Alfred Plummer, Mr John Sever and Mr D. Caradog Jones.

Lastly, my wife Margaret has typed and retyped the manuscript, and has patiently shared with me the frustrations as well as the joys of producing this book.

J. F. C. H.

Madison, Wisconsin

Acknowledgements

The author wishes to thank the following for their help in providing photographs and granting permission for the use of material in the plates shown: British Museum, London (29, 30), National Portrait Gallery, London (4, 6, 7), National Library of Wales (26), University of London Library (13, 15, 22, 27, 31, 32, 40), State Historical Society of Wisconsin (5, 19, 20, 23, 33), Indiana Historical Society Library (18), Manchester Public Libraries (28), Manchester University Press (2), Gourock Ropework Company Ltd (1, 3), and Mr Colin Franklin (24).

Introduction

Since every book is in some degree an intellectual or spiritual biography, it will perhaps make this one clearer if its origin is briefly told. It began as a study in the history of early English socialism. Dissatisfaction with the standard interpretations, most of which date from the 1920s and 1930s, prompted a detailed study of the writings of Robert Owen and the school of Owenite socialists, from which it was soon apparent that only by a much broader approach than had been used hitherto would it be possible to examine the significance of Owenism. The material could not be made meaningful nor the questions which arose from it answered unless the scope and terms of the enquiry were extended. This had to be done in several directions, with the result that the book became an experiment in the writing of comparative social and intellectual history. More specifically it became an analysis of socialist institutions and ideas within the total framework of an early industrial society in Britain and an agricultural, frontier society in America.

The historiography of Owen and the movement associated with his name has gone through several stages. Within two years of his death in 1858 a book-length biography of Owen appeared, and the 1860s produced two more studies published in London and Philadelphia.[1] None of these was based on intimate knowledge of Owen or the movement and all relied heavily on Owen's autobiography. The first attempt at interpretation of Owen's work came from cooperators.[2] Thanks to the efforts of George Jacob Holyoake,[3] the indefatigable publicist of the British consumers'

[1] William Lucas Sargant, a Birmingham manufacturer, published his *Robert Owen and His Social Philosophy* in 1860. The next two biographies were Frederick A. Packard, *Life of Robert Owen* (Philadelphia, Pa., 1866); and Arthur John Booth, *Robert Owen, the Founder of Socialism in England* (London, 1869).

[2] John Colier Farn, who had been an Owenite social missionary, published an article in 1864 in which he already saw Owenism in historical perspective as the forerunner of later cooperative efforts. 'The First, Second and Third Cooperative Movements', *The Cooperator*, September 1864.

[3] Holyoake produced a short pamphlet, the *Life and Last Days of Robert Owen* in 1859; but his chief writings on Owenism are *Sixty Years of an Agitator's Life* (2 vols., London, 1892); *Bygones Worth Remembering* (2 vols., London, 1905); and *History of Cooperation in England* (2 vols., London, 1875–79). These are a mine of information about the personalities in the movement but have to be used with caution because he was often inaccurate in details. The only other account of Owen and Owenism by a participant is Lloyd Jones, *Life, Times and Labours of Robert Owen*, ed. William Cairns Jones (2 vols., London, 1889–90), which is disappointingly uninformative.

cooperative movement, Owen was presented as the Father of Co-operation, and the inspirer of secularism and other social reform movements of the 1860s and 1870s with which many old Owenites were associated. Holyoake was notoriously unreliable on detail, but he had the great advantage of having known Owen well and he had been active in the Owenite movement. The Fabians at the end of the century took over the cooperators' view and developed it further.[1] They found in Owen a sympathetic though misguided reformer and in Owenism a native socialist theory which owed nothing to Marx. For their part the Marxists, through the spread of Marx and Engels's works in English in the 1890s, popularized the epithet 'utopian' as a derogatory label for Owenite socialism.[2] A second generation of Fabian historians, with some assistance from Marxists, in the inter-war period integrated Owen into the history of the British working-class movement, and this has been the usual treatment of Owenism in recent years.[3] Owen has been accorded a niche in the standard histories of British labour and socialism, and Owenism is seen as a link in the continuous chain which stretches from 1789 to the present-day Labour movement.

In America the emphasis has been different. Here Owenism has been treated as part of the communitarian tradition by historians from John Humphrey Noyes to Professor Arthur Eugene Bestor. The standard accounts present it as an episode in the quest for utopia or an aspect of 'freedom's ferment'.[4] New Harmony, Owen's first community in America, has also exercised a continuing fascination for essayists, novelists and writers of semi-serious history.[5] For historians of American labour

[1] The Fabians—Frank Podmore, B. L. Hutchins, Sidney and Beatrice Webb, Graham Wallas, J. L. and Barbara Hammond, C. E. M. Joad—all wrote on Owen.

[2] Chiefly Marx and Engels, *Communist Manifesto* (1848), and Engels, *Socialism, Utopian and Scientific* (1880), both issued in many cheap editions in English after 1888.

[3] Notably by G. D. H. Cole, *Robert Owen* (London, 1925, repr. 1965); *A Short History of the British Working-Class Movement, 1789–1947* (London, revised edn., 1948); and his introduction to his edition of Owen, *A New View of Society and Other Writings* (London, 1927).

[4] John Humphrey Noyes, *History of American Socialisms* (New York, 1870, repr. 1961); George B. Lockwood, *The New Harmony Movement* (New York, 1905); Alice Felt Tyler, *Freedom's Ferment* (1944, repr. New York, 1962). However, all previous work is largely superseded by Arthur Eugene Bestor's thorough and scholarly study, *Backwoods Utopias: the Sectarian and Owenite Phases of Communitarian Socialism in America, 1663–1829* (Philadelphia, Pa., 1950). Attempts to include Owenism in some general concept of utopia have produced little insight and have usually over-emphasized the quaint and curious: e.g. W. H. G. Armytage, *Heavens Below: Utopian Experiments in England, 1560–1960* (London and Toronto, 1961); Everett Webber, *Escape to Utopia: the Communal Movement in America* (New York, 1959).

[5] Some of the better works of this type are included in the bibliography. For a recent example of this genre see William E. Wilson, *The Angel and the Serpent* (Bloomington, Ind., 1964).

Owenism is a warning example of what can happen to working men if they allow themselves to be misled by intellectual reformers instead of concentrating on job-conscious trade unionism.[1]

Now all of these interpretations are valid facets of the Owenite story, but each is only partial. None of them is adequate to comprehend the whole of the Owenite record, putting the British and American material together, and seeking the relationship of Owenism to the two different societies. The most widespread interpretations, which present Owen and his work as part of the consumers' cooperative or working-class movement syndrome, are particularly unsatisfactory. They do not accord with the tone or feel of much of what Owen wrote and said and did; they largely ignore the significance of Owenism and the Owenites except in so far as they were theoretical socialists; and they distort the chronology of Owenism by over-concentration on a few selected years. The working-class movement approach to Owenism is too constricting to make full use of the sources, and is based on certain narrow assumptions about the nature of social history, the relation of ideas to society and the process of social change. If we set aside the various partial interpretations (that is, Owenism as an aspect of this or that social or intellectual development in one particular country) the central feature of Owenism is the dual nature of its role in two such different societies as early nineteenth-century Britain and America. That contemporaries should have considered Owenite ideas and institutions relevant in these two very different contexts is the starting point for new questions and new approaches. Instead of asking what Owenism contributed to the making of the English working class, or how it related to American frontier conditions and westward expansion, we have to examine the points of contact or similarity in British and American social experience which made Owenism acceptable in certain situations. The research area is sufficiently small and well-defined to serve almost as a microcosm of Anglo-American society, so that through a comparative, or, more accurately, a relational, approach questions of a wider significance than the specifics of social reform may be raised. In fact in this context Owenism becomes a contemporary comment on Anglo-American civilization in the early nineteenth century.

The working out of an interpretation along these lines calls for something more than a purely institutional and biographical method. The role of institutions and personalities cannot be assessed without some wider social, intellectual and psychological reference. Most traditional liberal

[1] John R. Commons, *et al., History of Labour in the United States* (New York, 1936); Selig Perlman, *Theory of the Labor Movement* (New York, 1928, repr. 1948).

accounts of movements such as Owenism have been imprisoned within the confines of some implicit version of the doctrine of progress and the reformer himself has been presented as simply a far-seeing man who responded to the problems of society more unselfishly and intelligently than his fellow men; he was, as we say, ahead of his time. Now this last phrase begs the whole question of historical interpretation, and the liberal theory of social change is inadequate for an assessment of Owenism in terms of the total culture of an age. In the following pages two methods have been used to try to break new ground: the employment of some techniques from intellectual history, and experiment with comparative approaches.

Speculation on the pedigree of Owen's ideas is not new. Whether he 'borrowed' his ideas from Rousseau, Bentham and Godwin, or was influenced by contemporaries in Manchester, has been discussed in his biographies with somewhat inconclusive results. Perhaps a more profitable approach is to consider Owenism as part of the whole complex of ideas of the late eighteenth and early nineteenth centuries. The hypothesis underlying this is that the ideas of a period are contained within a framework and have a certain unity based on common assumptions and attitudes. Owenism thus becomes a cluster of social ideas drawn from several sources united within an overall intellectual boundary. In this context both the originality and limitations of Owen's ideas become apparent.

The second method—comparative study—has long been familiar in other social sciences and in literature, but is still rare in history. Although historians have sometimes made allusions to parallel developments outside their particular topic of study, these have usually been incidental insights, bright ideas thrown off in passing, and not followed up very far. Again, historians have frequently made judgements (as for instance on the uniqueness or otherwise of an institution) which imply comparative knowledge, without being aware of, or making fully explicit the assumptions of their statements. In the analysis of the Owenite movement three types of comparative treatment seem likely to be fruitful. First and most obvious is the trans-national comparison between Britain and America, and to a lesser extent between England and Scotland. Area studies of Owenism in the different regions of Britain also invite this approach. Second is the technique of comparable personalities. In order to establish the uniqueness or ordinariness of Owen and his followers it is necessary to compare them with contemporary figures who were in a similar situation. Given two philanthropists with basically the same social position and ideology, why does one become an Owenite and the other not? Third, and most difficult is the use of comparative concepts and techniques from other social sciences. In establishing the role of Owenism in the new industrial civilization of the early nineteenth century some help may be obtained from sociological concepts and from the comparative study of ideological systems. None of these three methods is without its weaknesses and difficulties, but it is in the nature of experiment that risks have to be taken. Moreover the general plight of academic history today is such that the historian is surely justified in seeking help wherever he can find it, for history is no less than the study of man and society in the dimension of time.

The general result of these methods has been to extend the interpretation of Owenism beyond what has been customary in standard histories in Britain and America. The story has been extended in time— backward into the eighteenth-century Enlightenment, and forward into the post-1848 period. It has been extended in space to cover both Britain and the United States. And it has been extended in discipline to include intellectual history and a more broadly defined social history. Some parts of the story will of course be familiar, particularly the career of Owen. Nevertheless since his life forms a central thread running throughout the book it will be convenient to summarize it here by way of introduction. Just as Marx protested that he was not a Marxist, so there was the perennial problem of the differences between Owen and his followers. But the logical starting point is the founder and not the disciples.

Robert Owen's life (1771–1858) falls into six main periods, each characterized by a dominant interest or theme.[1] The first, 1771–99, extends from his boyhood in Newtown, Montgomeryshire, where as the son of an ironmonger and saddler, he had but a few years of schooling before being apprenticed to a draper in Stamford, Lincolnshire. He left home at the age of ten, and after three years moved from Stamford to London, still in the drapery business. About 1788 he arrived in Manchester, a friend having secured for him a position in a draper's shop. He

---

[1] The most useful biography of Owen is still Frank Podmore, *Robert Owen: A Biography* (2 vols., London, 1906). It may be supplemented with G. D. H. Cole, *Robert Owen*; and Margaret Cole, *Robert Owen of New Lanark, 1771–1858* (London, 1953). All biographical accounts of Owen rely heavily on his autobiography, *Life of Robert Owen, Written By Himself* (2 vols., numbered I and IA, London, 1857–58), since there is no other source for his early life. The main collection of his correspondence, the Owen papers, Manchester, begins in 1821, which is where the autobiography ends. These manuscripts may have been collected for a second volume of the autobiography which Owen did not live to complete.

B

did not stay there long, but formed a partnership with John Jones, a machine maker, and with borrowed capital set up as a manufacturer of cotton spinning machinery. From there he moved into the cotton spinning business, and after managerial experience became a partner in the Chorlton Twist Company. The successful young cotton spinner did not spend all his time in the counting house but entered into the cultural life of Manchester, making friends and acquaintances in particular through the Literary and Philosophical Society. In 1799 he and his partners acquired the New Lanark Mills in Scotland from David Dale and at the same time Owen fell in love with Dale's daughter, Caroline. The pair were shortly married and in 1800 Owen went to live at New Lanark.

The period of Owen's life from 1800 to 1824 was in many ways his most splendid. A vigorous young man at the height of his powers, he was sole manager and dominant partner of the largest cotton spinning establishment in Britain. In these years he made New Lanark a model factory, acquired a large fortune, and raised a family of seven children. Owen's career was one of the big success stories of the early industrial revolution. About 1812, however, Owen began to show signs of departure from the usual pattern of an industrialist's life. His emphasis on schemes of education and social welfare for the employees became more and more pronounced, and he began to talk of extending these ideas to society at large. After the ending of the Napoleonic Wars he became increasingly absorbed in his plans for the reconstruction of society and his social criticism became more radical. At first he was listened to with respect, and gained support in high places. But when he went on to attack basic institutions of society such as the family and the churches sympathy in this quarter ebbed away. By 1824 he concluded that progress along this particular road of social reform was likely to be slow and frustrating, and that a fresh start might be rewarding. In the summer of 1824 he decided to leave New Lanark and go to America to found a community.

Owen's American or communitarian phase lasted only five years (1824–29), but was crucial for him in several ways. It marked the end of his long association with the world of business, for he never went back to New Lanark. It established his reputation as a radical social reformer and attracted disciples in two continents. He sank practically the whole of his fortune in a village and estate at New Harmony, Indiana, and transferred his family (though not his wife) to America, where they became citizens. The community of New Harmony did not flourish as he had hoped, and the experiment came to an end in 1827. After toying with the idea of a community in Mexico Owen returned to England, considerably poorer in pocket but not in conviction and enthusiasm.

On his return he discovered that his social schemes, which were now called socialism, had attracted support among working men, who were anxious to adapt them to their needs. Owen found himself drawn into the British working-class movement, which for five years (1829–34) was dominated by Owenite theories. A climax was reached in 1834 when Owen was for a few months at the head of a great national federation of trade unions and was the acknowledged leader of the working classes. The sudden collapse of this federation ended the fourth period of Owen's life.

In 1835 Owen was sixty-four, but still very energetic and hard working. His wife had died in 1831 and all his children were in America. His life's fortune was tied up in New Harmony, which he made over to his sons in return for a modest annuity. He lived simply and frugally in London, devoting his whole time and energies to the promotion of his 'new view of society'. The period from 1835 to 1845 was marked by the development in Britain of a sectarian organization of Owenites in which Owen played the role of patriarch. He wrote and lectured continually, and supported another attempt at community building at Tytherly in Hampshire. The closing of this community and the ending of the chief Owenite journal, the *New Moral World*, brought to an end this phase of his career.

He was now (1845) an old man but still very spritely, and as ever an inveterate traveller. He revisited the United States, and was on hand in Paris to observe the events of the 1848 Revolution. A constant stream of writing poured from his pen. Much of it was a repetition of his earlier work, but it also included his autobiography which is in many ways the most attractive of all his books. In his last years he took up spiritualism, and claimed to be in communication with people who had helped him in his early days. His final effort was an attempt to address the annual meeting of the newly formed National Association for the Promotion of Social Science in 1858, but he was unable to go on with his speech. A few days later he died in Newtown, his birth-place which he had not seen for over seventy years.

A bare chronicle of dates and details does not of course do justice to this remarkable man. In the pages that follow his ideas and activities, interwoven with those of his followers, are presented as part of the world in which he lived. He sought to control that world, to make it a better place to live in, and his name became an inspiration to later social reformers. Discussion of Owen in terms of success or failure does not form part of this book, and his epitaph was written many years ago.[1] Our theme begins with the origins of Owen's thought and an account of his first followers.

[1] On the Owen memorial in Kensal Green cemetery, London. It reads: 'He originated and organised infant schools. He secured a reduction of the hours of labour for women and children in factories. He was a liberal supporter of the earlier efforts to obtain national education. He laboured to promote international arbitration. He was one of the foremost Englishmen who taught men to aspire to a higher social state by reconciling the interests of capital and labour. He spent his life and a large fortune in seeking to improve his fellow-men by giving them education, self-reliance and moral worth. His life was sanctified by human affection and lofty effort.'

Philanthropic Origins

Philanthropic Origins

The phrenologists agreed that Owen's bump of benevolence was unusually large.[1] *Visitors to New Lanark, impressed by the mills and disarmed by Owen's charm, praised his practical benevolence and enlightened philanthropy.*[2] *To a whole generation after 1815 he was 'Mr Owen, the Philanthropist' or 'the benevolent Mr Owen'. His name was everywhere linked with successful, paternalistic schemes for improving the lot of the poor, and in this role he at first gained the support of the Duke of Kent and influential members of the landed interest and the business world. Several of the most important of his early followers were men of this stamp. Philanthropy was a basic motif in the pattern of Owenism.*

1 The Dimensions of Poor Relief

Owen's Plan for the reorganization of society (soon for the salvation of the world) matured rapidly between 1816 and 1820. His philanthropic endeavours had first been directed to improving working and living conditions at New Lanark, then to educational reform and the restriction

[1] His head was examined by George Combe who reported on it in the *Phrenological Journal*, I (1823–24), 235–7; and by Spencer T. Hall who included Owen in his *Biographical Sketches of Remarkable People* (Burnley, 1881), pp. 275–8. Robert Dale Owen also commented similarly on his father in *Threading My Way* (London, 1874), p. 66.

[2] John Griscom, the Quaker professor of chemistry at Columbia College, New York, visited Owen at New Lanark and his description in *A Year in Europe* (2 vols., New York, 1823), II, 373–93, was typical of many such visitors' accounts. Mr Toogood, the 'co-operationist' and 'philanthropist' in Thomas Love Peacock's *Crotchet Castle* (London, 1831) was a caricature of Owen.

of child labour in factories. The 'distress' which followed the peace of 1815 turned his attention to problems of the unemployed. In the Fourth Essay of *A New View of Society* he suggested a reform of the Poor Laws (which, he thought, under the guise of aid to the distressed encouraged idleness and crime) and a programme of public works to provide employment where necessary on road and canal construction. By the summer of 1816 public concern at the widespread nature of distress caused the Association for the Relief of the Manufacturing and Labouring Poor, headed by the Duke of York and the Archbishop of Canterbury, to convene a public meeting in London, at which Owen was invited to speak. He elaborated his remarks in the *Report to the Committee of the Association for the Relief of the Manufacturing and Labouring Poor*, which was then referred in March 1817 to Sturges-Bourne's Select Committee of the House of Commons on the Poor Laws. The *Report* diagnosed the cause of unemployment as a combination of the effects of peace and the spread of machinery. 'The war was a great and most extravagant customer to farmers, manufacturers, and other producers of wealth. . . . And on the day on which peace was signed, this great customer of the producers died.'[1] Wartime demand had stimulated a vast increase in productive capacity through the introduction of machinery: 'thus our country possessed, at the conclusion of the war, a productive power which operated to the same effect as if her population had been actually increased fifteen- or twenty-fold'.[2] The two factors of decreased demand and increased productive power led to a depreciation in the value of human labour which was, argued Owen, the cause of the present distress. His remedy was the creation of self-supporting communities of about 1200 persons, with accommodation arranged in a parallelogram of buildings, and provision for all the educational and social needs of the inhabitants. Here, in the form of an improved method of relieving the unemployed, was the first presentation of Owen's famous Plan.

Not surprisingly, the Plan found little favour with the economy-minded Select Committee. Owen therefore turned elsewhere for support, and throughout 1817 carried on a large-scale publicity campaign, using press, pamphlets and public meetings to great effect. However, as the propaganda expanded so also did the range of his expectations. In July 1817 he was still protesting: 'I merely ask to be permitted to relieve the

---

[1] Owen, *Life*, I, 124.

[2] *Report on the Poor* (1817) in *Life*, IA, 54-5. Owen republished his most important writings up to 1821 in vol. IA of his autobiography, and quotations are hereafter taken from this source and cited as Owen, *Life*.

poor and working classes from their present distress.'[1] The next month he told a meeting in the City of London Tavern that his fondest hope was to be able to retire to such a 'happy village'. By September he was using millennial language and equating his plan with the emancipation of mankind: the Villages of Unity and Mutual Cooperation were now to include all classes, not just paupers. Owen's publicity drive was successful to the point of attracting criticism of, as well as support for his ideas, and so through the necessity of defining his economic position more fully he was led to a mature formulation of his plan in the *Report to the County of Lanark*, submitted in May 1820. The details of the Villages of Cooperation were as in his earlier proposals, but now embedded in a theory of cooperative socialism and prophetic utterance. Owen's Plan, which had begun as a method of unemployment relief, emerged as a scheme for the thorough reorganization of society.

This development in Owen's social thinking was not for some time clearly apparent to his contemporaries, who, like William Thompson, first thought of Owen's Plan as 'an improved system of pauper management'.[2] Nor was this surprising in view of the extent to which early Owenism was nurtured in the soil of poor relief. The context of Owen's schemes of practical philanthropy was the Poor Law problem as inherited from the late eighteenth century and aggravated by the impact of the Napoleonic Wars. Under the umbrella of the Poor Laws was subsumed a complex of socio-economic issues and decisions of social policy. From the 1780s to 1834 no subject was more prolific of pamphlets, books and homilies. Every country parson felt qualified to prescribe his nostrum for the cure of rural pauperism; political economists, social reformers and country gentlemen all held emphatic views on the 'Poor Law question'; while successive governments managed to avoid anything so controversial as a comprehensive reorganization of the system.

Superficially the Poor Law question was a matter of relief. Disagreement arose over who the recipients should be and what form the assistance should take in an England where rapid economic and social change was making the existing Poor Laws irrelevant and unworkable. In a rural society, where the poor were taken for granted, the periodic need to help them beyond the extent of normal Christian charity created something of

---

[1] *A Further Development of the Plan* . . . in *Life*, IA, 77. The relevant statements by Owen on poor relief are all contained in appendix I of this volume.

[2] William Thompson, *Labor Rewarded* (London, 1827), p. 98. John Minter Morgan, *Hampden in the Nineteenth Century* (2 vols., London, 1834), I, 104, complained that if the *Quarterly* or *Edinburgh Review* had deigned to notice Owen's views 'they had commented upon the scheme as belonging to the question of the Poor Laws'. Cf. also Griscom, *op. cit.*, II, 391.

a dilemma. As Bernard Mandeville put it in his *Fable of the Bees* (1714), 'the poor have nothing to stir them to labour but their wants, which it is wisdom to relieve but folly to cure'. From Elizabethan times the responsibility for looking after its own poor was laid squarely upon each parish, under the direction of the Justices of the Peace. The Poor Law Act of 1601 provided Overseers of the Poor who were to levy a poor rate for the relief of the sick, aged and unemployed. With the spread of enclosures after 1760 and the rise in food prices during the French Wars the number of poor to be relieved increased rapidly, and the poor rates jumped accordingly. In 1775 they had amounted to less than £2 million, by 1801 they had doubled, and in 1818 were nearly £8 million and provoked loud protestations from the rate-payers. In many districts the practice of granting outdoor relief to unemployed labourers had grown up, and in 1795 this became semi-regularized as the 'Speenhamland system'. It was the intention of the Justices at Speenhamland to help the poor by ensuring that each family had a minimum income calculated according to the price of bread and number of dependants, but the effect was to subsidize low wages out of poor rates. The system was adopted widely in the southern counties, and was held by orthodox political economists to be largely responsible for rural pauperization.

It was at this point—the cause of pauperization—that disagreement began, whence it soon became clear that much more than questions of relief were under discussion. From a common starting point of lamentation over the burdensome level of the poor rates, each commentator drew from his own experience or reflection a different interpretation of the problem. For some it was basically a problem of labour mobility and the creation of a free labour market; for others the distress was due to 'the abridgement of labour' and the problem was how to cope with the new machinery; yet others thought in terms of population growth and the need to counteract the 'vulgar errors' arising from ignorance of the 'natural' laws of the wages fund; and to some, Poor Law problems meant the exercise of charity and the maintenance of stable personal relationships within a community. The language, concepts, and attitudes of the Poor Law question were drawn from economics and moralistic religion; and when writers expressed their views on the question they revealed the fundamentals of their social philosophy. By and large they divided into two broad categories—those committed to a 'hard' line Poor Law policy, which finally triumphed in 1834, and those who favoured a 'soft' line and opposed the New Poor Law. The former, although originating with Pitt and some other landed politicians, became especially identified with the political economists, and represented the dominant middle-class commercial and industrial attitude to problems of the poor. The latter was a traditional, squirearchical approach whose logical outcome was Speenhamland.

Into this dichotomy Owenism fitted uneasily. By background and interest Owen belonged to the hard line school, for it was in the cotton industry, centred on Manchester and Glasgow, that the problems of labour in early industrialism were first encountered. Yet he rejected the normal industrialist's views on Poor Law policy, and elaborated a Plan which was more akin to the paternalistic concern of the landed gentry for 'their' people. His object was not to destroy the protection afforded by the old Poor Laws in order to create a free labour market for a competitive society, in which workers would be treated simply as hands.[1] Rather, he sought to draw upon a traditional sense of community concern to provide conditions of security and independence for the poor. Because of Owen's position on the Poor Law question his early followers included some of those who in spirit were most opposed to the values of commercial civilization, the rural gentry.

Owen's appeal to an older moral economy probably owed something to his Scottish experience. Poor relief in Scotland was much more limited than in England, being restricted to those who were permanently unable to provide for themselves.[2] The able-bodied poor did not qualify for assistance, nor were poor houses provided except in a few large towns. As a result, Scottish poor rates remained low and there was no equivalent of the Speenhamland system of doles. The harshness of Scottish parochial poor relief was in theory and practice mitigated by the operation of agencies of 'moral economy', whose function was to foresee and prevent, and in the first instance relieve, indigence. In a small-scale, largely rural society a parochial system based on close personal relationships was deemed adequate for dealing with the problems of poverty. The family, the church and the school provided a series of interlocking neighbourhood institutions which took care of the aged, the sick, the orphans and those temporarily without work. From 1812 this system became increasingly inadequate, and to deal with the post-war distress schemes of direct assistance to the unemployed had to be worked out in Edinburgh and Glasgow. A Committee for the Relief of the Labouring Classes, established in Edinburgh in 1815, organized relief through public works, and

[1] This process is analysed in Karl Polanyi, *Origins of Our Time: the Great Transformation* (London, 1944). A valuable revision of the economic aspects of the old Poor Law is Mark Blaug, 'The Myth of the Old Poor Law and the Making of the New', *Journal of Economic History*, XXIII (1963), 151–84.

[2] For this para. I have drawn upon Laurence James Saunders, *Scottish Democracy, 1815–1840: the Social and Intellectual Background* (Edinburgh and London, 1950), pp. 192–230.

some municipal funds were added to the contributions of private philanthropists. The committee was careful to emphasize its temporary role and reluctant to institute any precedent which might develop in the direction of the English pattern. Talk of preserving the Scot's traditional independence could easily become humbug when used by an employer to limit relief to unemployed workers. But the strengths of the traditional moral economy—family obligation, recognition of the poor as persons, community interest and concern—were sufficiently genuine to make it seem worth while to try to translate them from their pre-industrial setting to meet the needs of an urbanized commercial society.[1] Owen's Plan, which was notable for its compassion for the poor and its emphasis on community values, was in certain respects not far removed from this concept of a moral economy. It provided the context in which the committee of Scottish gentry received his *Report to the County of Lanark* in 1820. By contrast, the English version of the older moral economy—of which the Speenhamland policy was a dwindling expression—had virtually expired in the 1790s, though old-fashioned J.P.s continued to think along paternalist lines.

Poor relief was the starting point for many philanthropists though but few of them travelled as far along the road of social analysis as Owen. The measure of his achievement and the nature of the philanthropic element in Owenism can best be brought into high relief by a comparison with other contemporary philanthropists. To contrast Owen and his early followers with the classical political economists such as Malthus, Torrens or Senior only points up well-known differences of attitude towards the poor and their problems. In order to establish more precisely the uniqueness or otherwise of the Owenite position it is necessary to use rather more refined methods of comparison. What is required is not a black and white contrast, but various shades of intermediate grey. Were there, for example, business men and manufacturers with a similar background to Owen's, who set out with the same interests and objectives, reached some of the conclusions, but yet did not become Owenites? If so, how did they come to be in partial agreement with Owen and at what point did they feel compelled to diverge? Two such examples, both of whom knew Owen and his work but were by no means Owenites, may be considered.

The first was Patrick Colquhoun (1745–1820).[2] He was a Scots

---

[1] See Thomas Chalmers, *The Christian and Civic Economy of Large Towns* (3 vols., Glasgow, 1821–26).

[2] Biographical details from 'Iatros' [Grant David Yeats, son-in-law of Colquhoun], *Biographical Sketch of the Life and Writings of Patrick Colquhoun, Esq., Ll.D.* (London, 1818); and James Cleland, *Annals of Glasgow* (2 vols., Glasgow, 1816).

merchant, closely familiar with the cotton industry and its problems, who served for three successive years as Lord Provost of Glasgow and founded the Glasgow Chamber of Commerce in 1783. Through his activities as a lobbyist for the cotton industry he settled in London, where in 1792 he was appointed stipendiary police magistrate, and soon developed into an active philanthropist. His experiences as a magistrate led him to an investigation of poverty and distress in London, and thence to sociological analysis: 'the statesman', he wrote, 'will ponder the chart of society'.[1] Owen was immensely impressed by Colquhoun's mature work, *A Treatise on the Wealth, Power and Resources of the British Empire* (London, 1814), which provided the Owenites with statistics on which to base their socialist analysis of distribution (in the same way as Ricardo provided them with the basis for a socialist theory of value). In his *Treatise on the Police of the Metropolis* (London, 1795) Colquhoun described the variety and extent of crime in London, and concluded that the only sure, long-term remedy for it was a general amelioration of popular manners and habits. A consideration of wider social problems was therefore his next task, and in *A Treatise on Indigence* (London, 1806) he examined 'the national resources for productive labour' and put forward 'propositions for ameliorating the condition of the poor and increasing the comforts of the labouring people'.

After the usual statistics showing the massive increase in paupers and poor rates since the 1770s, Colquhoun drew a distinction (derived from his friend Bentham) between poverty and indigence. Poverty he defined as 'that state . . . in society where the individual has no surplus labour in store, and, consequently, no property but what is derived from the constant exercise of industry'.[2] This is the normal condition of the majority of the people and is wholly desirable, since without it there would be no labour and therefore no wealth created. Poverty is the necessary basis of the riches, refinements and comforts of the wealthier classes in a civilized nation. Indigence, by contrast, is 'the state of anyone who is destitute of the means of subsistence and is unable to labour to procure it to the extent nature requires'. This is 'the condition in society which implies want, misery and distress', and is the evil to be combated. Certain types of indigence—insanity, blindness, old age and infirmity—are irremediable, and should receive permanent support. A second category of indigence is that which arises out of involuntary unemployment or temporary sickness: this is remediable and worthy of support. The third type of indigence is caused by vicious and immoral habits and idleness, and since

---

[1] Patrick Colquhoun, *A Treatise on Indigence* (London, 1806), p. 166.
[2] Quotations in this para. are from *Indigence*, pp. 7–9.

it is culpable should not be assisted. Colquhoun was much concerned that the second category should be helped. These were labouring people who through no fault of their own had fallen on hard times, and whose need was for a 'prop' until they could once more raise themselves from indigency to poverty. The great fault of the existing Poor Laws, argued Colquhoun, was that they blurred the distinction between different categories of need: 'the barrier between these two conditions in society [indigence and poverty] is often slender, and the public interest requires that it should be narrowly guarded'.

From this distinction between indigence and poverty Colquhoun deduced the need for a policy of enlightened social welfare, to be administered centrally on Benthamite principles. He saw the connection between crime and indigence: if the poor are debased their morals will be corrupted, and hence they cannot be expected to 'be regular, sober, frugal or industrious'. But, unlike Owen, he did not formulate any general doctrine of the paramount influence of circumstances. Similarly his conception of the role of education stopped short of Owen's total commitment. In 1803 Colquhoun established a school in Westminster for 300–400 children and he advocated a Board of Education to provide a national system of education for the poor. Yet the limits of his vision were set by the monitorial system, which was cheap and efficient: 'a limited education, suitable to the condition of the poor, [is] all that is necessary. Everything beyond a mere channel for conveying religious and moral principles would be mischievous and utopian.'[1] He did not see the causes of distress as lying beyond the Poor Laws and the Act of Settlement: substitute a central Pauper Police Department under a Board of Commissioners for the obsolete parochialism of the Elizabethan Poor Law, remove settlement restrictions to ensure the 'full circulation of labour', and indigence would largely disappear. The 'utopianism' of Owen was that he went beyond the relief of indigence; he proposed to do away with poverty as well, which was truly 'mischievous'.

From the same stable as Colquhoun and Owen came another socially concerned manufacturer, John Kennedy (1769–1855). He was born in Scotland, apprenticed as a machine maker in Chowbent, Lancashire, and in 1791 became a partner in a Manchester firm of textile machine makers and mule spinners. He was thus an exact contemporary of Owen, with whom he was on friendly terms as a brother cotton spinner in Manchester.[2]

---

[1] Quotations in this para. are from *Indigence*, p. 140.

[2] John Kennedy, *Miscellaneous Papers, on Subjects connected with the Manufactures of Lancashire* (Manchester, 1849), pp. 73–4; Owen, *Life*, I, 212. Kennedy's biography is outlined in the *D.N.B.*; Samuel Smiles, *Industrial Biography* (London, 1863), pp. 317–23; and

Kennedy's views on the Poor Laws, as set forth to the Manchester Literary and Philosophical Society in 1819, were considerably different from those usually associated with Lancashire industrialists intent on creating a free market economy.[1] He concluded that the existing system of parochial poor relief, when properly administered, was perfectly sound, and infinitely superior to the arrangements in Scotland and Ireland which, he alleged, resulted in begging and vagrancy. Kennedy postulated a fundamental sympathy in a prosperous country between the higher, middle and lower classes, to the extent that 'supposing the lower order to advance a certain number of degrees in the enjoyments and comforts of life, the middle and higher classes will make a similar ascent, each preserving its original distance from the others, and vice versa'. The vast increase in the national wealth during the previous fifty years he attributed to the enterprise of the whole community and ultimately to the labour of the lower classes, who were motivated by a desire for comforts, which when once enjoyed they were loath to give up: 'among the lower orders it may . . . be safely affirmed that industry can only be found where artificial wants have crept in, and have acquired the character of necessaries'. A prosperous working class also created a home market, which would grow as their standard of living increased. *Pace* Malthus, prudential restraint operated not where there was want and misery, but 'where a certain degree of comfort and luxury is enjoyed, and where the sacrifice of those comforts must be the inevitable consequence of an indiscreet marriage'.

To Kennedy parochial relief was a necessary means of maintaining the 'community' of the lower classes during times of distress. It would prevent them from being broken, physically and morally, by want. This they had a right to expect, 'for the poor-rate is to them a capital indirectly arising out of their own former labour, and upon this capital they have a claim, until, by the revival of trade, their industry and activity are again called forth unimpaired'. In times of depression the lower orders inevitably suffer more than the middle and higher classes, and it is reasonable to expect that if the peace of society is to be preserved there should be some 'sacrifice of property to the exigencies of the needy'. The expense of poor rates is but a small price to preserve the English poor from degradation. Kennedy was well aware that such conclusions

[1] 'An Inquiry into the Effects produced upon Society by the Poor Laws. (Read before the Literary and Philosophical Society of Manchester, March 5, 1819)', in *Miscellaneous Papers*, pp. 26–39, from which quotations in this and the following paragraphs are taken.

William Fairbairn, 'Brief Memoir of the Late John Kennedy, Esq.', *Memoirs of the Manchester Literary and Philosophical Society*, 3rd series, I (1861).

were 'not those which promise to become most popular'; but he refused to believe that poor relief was simply a bounty to idleness and imprudence. Like Owen, and for similar reasons, he was opposed to a hard line Poor Law policy. He realized what the social cost of an early industrial economy could be, and feared the atomizing effects of a policy of *laissez faire*. But he was not thereby led to reject competitive society, only to seek to mitigate it by philanthropy within the bounds of poor relief.

The examples of Kennedy and Colquhoun suggest that Owen was by no means alone among philanthropists in finding the problem of poor relief the gateway to social investigation and the formulation of programmes of social reform. Some elements of Owen's Plan were familiar enough to be considered as not peculiar to him; and conversely he and his followers could agree with many features of non-Owenite schemes of Poor Law reform. Under the umbrella of the Poor Law question there was ample room to accommodate the Owenites along with many others. It was only when Owenism moved outside this shelter that it became truly distinctive—and suspect. Until that time 'Mr Owen the Philanthropist' and his friends were within the limits required for a sympathetic hearing.

The problems of poor relief, while providing a main outlet for the practice and development of philanthropy, also raised the question of a correct definition of philanthropy. By the late eighteenth century the ancient Christian idea of charity was usually expressed by the more fashionable term benevolence. Theoretically the 'principle of benevolence' was applicable to rich and poor alike, though in practice it could mean for the poor little more than contentedness and a cheerful disposition, whereas for the rich 'active benevolence' meant involvement in good works for the benefit of the poor. Such practical benevolence or philanthropy (as it was also called) occupied a border land between religion and economics. One moment the aspiring philanthropist was assured: 'the benevolent feelings are in unison with Heaven, and not only tend to the comfort of our present existence, but will doubtless be productive of the highest gratification in a future state';[1] the next he was warned on no account to confuse indiscriminate almsgiving with scientific, discriminating philanthropy as advocated by the political economists. Benevolence as inherited from the eighteenth century was an individual obligation towards those in need, and the ideal of philanthropic patronage died hard. Even when societies or committees were formed to organize philanthropic effort, they were usually dependent upon a few individuals with a well-developed social conscience. However, the problems raised

[1] [William Allen], 'On the Duty and Pleasure of Cultivating Benevolent Dispositions', *The Philanthropist*, I (1811), 6.

1. New Lanark today

2. Strutt's Milford Mills, Derbyshire

by massive rural pauperization and industrial unemployment put the traditional concept of benevolence to the test, and soon showed its possibilities and limitations.

The tone of a new approach to philanthropy was set by Sir Thomas Bernard (1750–1818), a lawyer and baronet who had been educated at Harvard while his father was Governor of New Jersey and later of Massachusetts Bay. 'Let us', declared Bernard, 'make the inquiry into all that concerns the poor, and the promotion of their happiness, a science.'[1] The Society for Bettering the Condition and Increasing the Comforts of the Poor, which he founded in 1796, was an attempt to apply the principles of 'experimental philosophy' to the state of the poor. The series of *Reports* which Bernard edited for the Society contained accounts of every type of good works from simple schemes for the distribution of soup, coals or milk to institutional provision through schools, hospitals, libraries and friendly societies. Through the collection of hard facts, as opposed to 'cumbrous theories', conclusions for future action could be drawn.

Despite these scientific pretensions the ingredients of philanthropy between 1790 and 1840 were a strange mixture of old and new. Deeply ingrained was the distinction between the deserving and the undeserving poor, of whom only the former were to be helped. The difficulty was that the customary distinction between the two became ever more difficult to make. Traditionally the sick, aged and orphans were the deserving cases, while vagabonds, idlers and out-of-works were to be punished by the harsher sections of the Poor Laws. The appearance of large-scale unemployment and under-employment broke down this convenient distinction, and faced philanthropists with a more complex task. They admitted the deserving nature of much distress: the problem was how to relieve it without offending against the canons of political economy. In the concept of 'enlightened' philanthropy an answer was found. Institutions to help the poor should wherever possible be self-supporting, and the role of philanthropy limited to pump priming. Any scheme that might encourage pauperization was ruled out of court. It was also desirable that philanthropic ventures should be essentially conservative of the existing social structure and should serve as antidotes to radical agitation. Almost by definition the philanthropist was an individualist and therefore a bulwark against the meddling interference of government. Behind all his

[1] Thomas Bernard, 'Preliminary Address to the Public, 27 April 1797', *Reports of the Society for Bettering the Condition and Increasing the Comforts of the Poor* (5 vols., London, 1798–1808), I (1798), ii–iv. For this Society see also Robert Southey, *Essays, Moral and Political* (2 vols., London, 1832), I, 191–2; and George Jacob Holyoake, *Self-Help a Hundred Years Ago* (London, 1888). The most recent study is David Owen, *English Philanthropy, 1660–1960* (Cambridge, Mass., 1964).

C

efforts was a strong sense of social conscience, the idea that he had a duty to help the poor.[1]

Owen's original Plan was well within the bounds of enlightened philanthropy. In the Second Essay of *A New View of Society* he counselled the smallest possible amount of change adequate to secure immediate objectives, and added:

For some time to come there can be but one practicable . . . reform, which without danger can be attempted in these realms; a reform in which all men and all parties may join—that is, a reform in the training and in the management of the poor, the ignorant, the untaught and untrained . . . among the whole mass of British population; and a plain, simple, practicable plan which would not contain the least danger to any individual, or to any part of society, may be devised for that purpose.[2]

By means of this Plan the poor would be enabled to become independent and self-supporting; crime would be prevented and the poor rates reduced. Owen expected—and largely received—the approbation of his brother-philanthropists. He originally dedicated the First Essay of *A New View of Society* to William Wilberforce on the grounds that no one 'appears to have more nearly adopted in practice the principles which this Essay develops than yourself'. William Allen, the Quaker philanthropist, who had recently become one of Owen's partners and who had not yet quarrelled with him over religious issues in the New Lanark schools, praised *A New View of Society* and commended Owen for carrying out his experiment without waiting for government initiative.[3] The sociological approach recommended by Bernard and practised by Colquhoun found favour with Owen, and in the Fourth Essay of *A New View* he suggested governmental surveys to collect social statistics. He referred to the experiences of the pauper colonies at Fredericksoord in Holland, and also to the work of Count Rumford in Bavaria. Above all, New Lanark was presented as a model of enlightened philanthropy—a highly successful enterprise in which benevolence was combined with 5 per cent on capital.

Few of Owen's original doctrines as set forth in *A New View of Society* were far from the sentiments of contemporary philanthropists. Even his doctrine of circumstances, which later gave such offence to Christian opponents, at first appeared nothing untoward. It was difficult for anyone

---

[1] Dr John Epps, 'the Christian phrenologist', recorded of his father, a well-to-do Calvinist who lived in Kent, 'A prominent idea of my father's was that of the duty devolving on us to give employment to the poor instead of alms'.—Mrs [Ellen Elliott] Epps, ed., *Diary of the Late John Epps, M.D.* (London, [1875]), p. 35.

[2] *A New View of Society*, in Owen, *Life*, I, 285.

[3] *Philanthropist*, III (1813), 102.

with practical experience of working among the poor not to see the stunting effects of environment. Crime and immorality were widely recognized to be closely associated with bad physical conditions. Theological pessimism about human nature prevented Evangelicals from subscribing to Owen's complete doctrine, but many were prepared to recognize a partial truth in what he said about the formation of character. William Allen, in reviewing *A New View of Society* in 1813, denied any conflict with religion on the grounds that 'the character to which . . . [Owen's] doctrine wholly refers is the worldly character, not the religious'.[1] Moreover the petition 'lead us not into temptation' in the Lord's prayer is an implicit acknowledgement of the strength of circumstances in inducing men to sin.

If Owen's doctrines could be accommodated (perhaps set aside as harmless idiosyncrasies) there was little in his practical suggestions that was not sufficiently familiar to be acceptable as praiseworthy philanthropy. He was recognized as of the same genus as Count Rumford (1753–1814), the American-born inventor and benefactor, whose House of Industry and other social experiments at Munich in Bavaria were widely quoted.[2] Owen himself was intrigued to discover from Francis Place that the 'New View of Society' had been largely anticipated by John Bellers, a seventeenth-century philanthropist, in his *Proposals for Raising a Colledge of Industry* (London, 1696).[3] A variety of experiments and suggestions for allotments, cultivation of waste lands, cottage building and industrial schools appeared between 1790 and 1848, often under the title of Home Colonies.[4] William Allen initiated such a scheme at Lindfield, Sussex in 1825;[5] and John Gurdon of Assington, Suffolk, conducted an agri-

---

[1] *Philanthropist*, III (1813), 115.

[2] Amongst others by Owen himself: see *Mr Owen's Proposed Arrangements for the Distressed Working Classes . . . consistent with . . . Political Economy, in three letters to Mr Ricardo* (London, 1819), pp. 34–5. For Rumford see Benjamin Count Rumford, *Essays, Political, Economical, and Philosophical* (3 vols., London, 1796); Jason Clark Easton, 'The Social and Economic Reforms of Count Rumford in Bavaria' (unpublished Ph.D. thesis, University of Wisconsin, 1937); and W. J. Sparrow, *Knight of the White Eagle* (London, 1964).

[3] Reprinted by Owen in 1818. Owen, *Life*, IA, appendix L.

[4] There is a large literature on this subject, e.g. William Allen, *Colonies at Home; or, the Means for Rendering the Industrious Labourer independent of Parish Relief* (new edn., Lindfield, Sussex, 1832); Rowland Hill, *Home Colonies: Sketch of a Plan for the Gradual Extinction of Pauperism and for the Diminution of Crime* (London, 1832); E. J. Lance, *The Cottage Garden; or, Farmers' Friend: Pointing out the means of making the Earth serviceable to the Rich and Poor, by giving Employment to Capital and Labour on all Sorts of Land* (London, 1832).

[5] In addition to Allen, *Colonies at Home*, see *Life of William Allen, with Selections from his Correspondence* (3 vols., London, 1846–7). There was also a 2-vol. American edition, Philadelphia, 1847.

cultural cooperative society for labourers from 1830 until the 1860s.[1] All such schemes had at least two features in common: their object was to make the poor self-supporting, and they depended upon an individual philanthropist for their initiation and guidance. The extent to which Owenism remained part of this tradition, even when combined with other, socially radical principles, was shown in 1840 when Owen, William Galpin and Frederick Bate formed the Home Colonization Society to raise funds for the Queenwood community. Nowhere was the philanthropic heritage stated more clearly than in the sub-title of Owen's pamphlet, *Self-Supporting Home Colonies* (London, 1841): 'a development of the principles and plans on which to establish Self-Supporting Home Colonies; as a more secure and profitable investment for capital, and an effectual means permanently to remove the causes of ignorance, poverty and crime; and most materially to benefit all classes of society; by giving a right application to the now greatly misdirected powers of the human faculties, and of physical and moral science'.

Most of these philanthropic schemes had an agricultural bias, and this was true whether they were intended for the relief of industrial workers or rural labourers. Although in theory the union of manufacturing and farming was praised, in practice it proved extremely difficult to do more than cultivate a little land and perhaps pursue a few hand crafts which did not require elaborate machinery. A fad which found its way into several schemes for home colonies was spade husbandry. In the *Report to the County of Lanark* Owen proposed that all cultivation of the soil should be by the spade instead of the plough. This he justified on the grounds of a greatly increased yield per acre, and cited the evidence of William Falla, a nurseryman of Gateshead.[2] As a method of providing work for the unemployed spade husbandry had the obvious advantage of employing the maximum number of labourers, but to Owen this aspect was only incidental. His main arguments were that cultivation by the spade was superior on practical scientific grounds, and would also require a change in social relationships. There was also something of the feeling that working on the land to produce food was a basic, even noble occupation

---

[1] Descriptions of the Assington cooperative experiment were reprinted in several places: see reports in Arthur John Booth, *Robert Owen* (London, 1869), pp. 159–63; *Chambers' Journal*, 13 February 1869; *Coventry Herald*, 20 March 1863. A later experiment is described in William Lawson, Charles D. Hunter, *et al.*, *Ten Years of Gentleman Farming at Blennerhasset, with Cooperative Objects* (London, 1874).

[2] *Report to the County of Lanark* in Owen, *Life*, IA, 271–6, 314–20. Allen, *Colonies at Home*, advocated spade husbandry; and the *New Harmony Gazette*, 5 July 1826, quoted a letter from Thomas Robinson of Leeds confirming the claims of Falla and Owen for it. Poor Abram Combe's fatal illness was precipitated by his spade digging at Orbiston.

which was morally superior to manufacturing in towns. It also demonstrated to the satisfaction of Owenites that labour was clearly the source of all wealth. The conception of Owenism as a variety of Home Colonization was one reason why among the early Owenites appeared a fair number of squires, including a following in Ireland. They were attracted to Owen as a philanthropist whose Plan offered a solution to the problems of rural pauperization and poor relief with which they were faced on their estates.

The circle of active philanthropists in Regency and early Victorian Britain was not very large, since the necessary requirements as reflected in the careers of the men mentioned above were stringent. First, an active social conscience motivated by religious or humanitarian notions was necessary. Second, an ample fortune, either inherited or acquired in business before middle age, had to be on hand. Third, having decided on an early retirement or semi-retirement the would-be philanthropist had to devote himself virtually full time to the problems of practical benevolence, acquiring thereby an almost professional expertise. This small group of men were all known to each other. They sat on one another's committees, subscribed to each other's causes and quoted each other in their pamphlets and reports. Beyond them was a wider philanthropic public to whom they appealed—members of the aristocracy and business community, who might be persuaded to subscribe to schemes for the relief of distress or general improvement of the condition of the poor. The first Owenite organization, the British and Foreign Philanthropic Society for the Permanent Relief of the Labouring Classes, founded in 1822, was of this type, as also was the Hibernian Philanthropic Society formed after Owen's lectures in Dublin the following year.[1] An impressive collection of aristocratic patrons, a committee of philanthropic M.P.s, bankers and industrialists, together with a subscription list headed by wealthy friends and neighbours of Owen, launched the British and Foreign. The Hibernian supporters were somewhat less eminent, but included local gentry under the leadership of Lord Cloncurry. From these and later circles of enlightened philanthropy came support for Owen's plans.

[1] *Proceedings of the First General Meeting of the British and Foreign Philanthropic Society for the Permanent Relief of the Labouring Classes; held . . . the 1st of June 1822* (London, 1822). For Irish Owenism see British and Foreign Philanthropic Society, *A Report . . . explanatory of Mr Owen's Plan for the Relief of Ireland . . .* (Dublin, 1823); *New Harmony Gazette*, 10 May 1826; and cuttings from Dublin newspapers for 1823 in Jane Dale Owen, Scrapbook.

2 Owenite Philanthropists

For convenience of analysis the Owenite philanthropists can be grouped into four main categories. First, a Scottish element attested the local influence of New Lanark: Archibald James Hamilton of Dalzell, Abram Combe of Edinburgh and Captain Donald Macdonald. Second was a group of Irish landowners: William Thompson, Captain O'Brien and John Scott Vandeleur, together with a Belfast physician, Dr Henry McCormac, and Anna Wheeler. Third, Owen always had a group of wealthy followers in London and the southern counties: John Minter Morgan, William Devonshire Saull, William Galpin and Frederick Bate. Fourth, in America Owenism had support from philanthropists such as William Maclure, Jeremiah Thompson, and the richer members of the New Harmony 'Boatload of Knowledge'. There was also a fifth group of persons who were friendly to Owen and willing to invest money in his schemes but who were not Owenites. Such were the Rathbones of Liverpool, the Strutts of Derby, Isaac Lyon Goldsmid the London banker, and the New Lanark partners after the reorganization of 1813–14. Some of the members of these groups can be considered in roles other than that of philanthropist; for others the evidence of their Owenite activity is only minimal. But for three of them philanthropy was the key to their association with Owen and his theories—Arthur James Hamilton, the radical laird; John Minter Morgan, the Christian Owenite; and William Maclure, scientist and educator.

In 1820 Owen's reputation as a philanthropist stood high in Lanarkshire. He was on friendly terms with the leading men of the county and was assured of a respectful hearing for his plans of social amelioration. Some of the local gentry, while nervous of his religious views and sceptical of his social theories were sympathetic to his practical proposals for tackling distress. One neighbour, however, was prepared to commit himself further. Archibald James Hamilton (1793–1834) was the son and heir of General John Hamilton, the laird of Dalzell and Orbiston, an estate some ten miles from New Lanark.[1] After what he described later as

---

[1] The main source for his life is an unpublished autobiography entitled 'The Soldier and Citizen of the World, with Reflections on Subjects of Intense Interest to the Happiness of Mankind' in the Hamilton Papers, Motherwell Public Library. This is a typescript copy (3 vols.) of an original which has not been located, and there is also a MS. Diary relating to the Peninsular War and Waterloo. This collection also contains MS. letters, accounts, notebooks, memos. and pamphlets of A. J. Hamilton, Robert Owen, Abram Combe and others connected with the Orbiston community. Some of this material (then in the possession of the Hamilton family) appears to have been used by Alex. Cullen, *Adventures in Socialism* (Glasgow and London, 1910).

a 'useless' education Hamilton went into the army at the age of eighteen and saw service as a lieutenant with the Fourth Dragoons in the Peninsular War. At Waterloo he was with the Scots Greys in the bloodiest part of the battle. From his war experiences he emerged very critical of the army, its commander-in-chief, and the whole business of war. He retired from his regiment and determined to devote himself to agriculture. The 'massacre' of Peterloo and a visit to France in 1819 deepened his radical and republican tendencies, and the following year he and his sister, Lady Anne Hamilton, were attendants on Queen Caroline during her trial.[1] From his letters and papers he appears as a handsome, dashing young squire, usually in debt and full of schemes for raising money. During his short life he spent a good deal of time on the Continent, partly on account of ill-health. His liberal sympathies were expressed in support for political reform and opposition to churches and priests, and his radical friendships stretched from Brougham to Cobbett.[2] He was a romantic and quoted from Byron and Thomas Moore (Lallah Rooke). He met his death as a result of a feud with his neighbour.[3]

Hamilton was attracted to Owenism in the first instance through his role as an improving landlord. He studied agriculture theoretically and experimented with methods of soil cultivation at Dalzell. Like Owen, he was much impressed by the agricultural methods of Thomas Coke of Norfolk and was present at the Holkham sheep shearing—a series of private agricultural shows at which Coke popularized new methods to large gatherings of farmers, aristocracy and reformers.[4] Owen's Plan, as developed in the *Report to the County of Lanark*, contained elements of the philosophy of agricultural improvement: even the apparently backward step of spade husbandry was justified in scientific terms. To the gratification of the fashionable interest in agricultural science Owenism added

---

[1] [Lady Anne Hamilton], *The Authentic Records of the Court of England for the Last Seventy Years* (London, 1832).

[2] MS. letter, William Cobbett to A. J. Hamilton, 23 October 1832, Hamilton Papers; William Cobbett, *Tour in Scotland* (London, 1833), pp. 204–16.

[3] Letter, George Combe to John Minter Morgan, 17 March 1834, George Combe's letterbook, Combe Papers. The feud developed when the Duke of Hamilton agreed to let A. J. Hamilton cut a new road through one of his (the Duke's) fields, but stopped him when work began. Both sides then sent men to contest the road by force and the Duke's men drove in great stakes to block the road. Hamilton went out at night with a party of men to remove these stakes and as a result of these exertions was taken ill and died.

[4] R. N. Bacon, *A Report of the Transactions at the Holkham Sheep-Shearing* (Norwich, 1821). This contains Owen's speech in reply to a toast to him and also a paper he read after the event entitled 'An Attempt to explain the Cause of the Commercial and Other Difficulties . . .'. See also the *Economist*, 11 August, 1 September 1821; and Owen, *Life*, I, 218–25.

opportunities for practical philanthropy. The combination was likely to evoke a sympathetic response from progressively minded gentlemen farmers. In the case of Hamilton, who was already a radical reformer and freethinker, this sympathy soon developed into enthusiasm, and he became, in Owen's words, 'one of the most ardent admirers of the New Views in principle and practice'.[1]

In an attempt to relieve distress in the parish, Hamilton first experimented with the 'cottage system', by which he granted long leases of land for the purpose of cottage building. Attached to each cottage was a small holding, sufficient to keep a cow, grow potatoes and raise other crops. The experiment was not successful as the tenants were mostly weavers who were not enthusiastic for outdoor labour. Hamilton therefore turned to Owen, whom he had first met in 1816 and whose essays on the *New View of Society* he had subsequently read. Owen had condemned the cottage system as perpetuating the evils of an individualist society and therefore greatly inferior to his proposed cooperative villages.[2] After Owen's *Report to the County of Lanark* had been submitted to a general meeting of the county on 1 May 1820, it was referred to a committee of the sheriff and six local gentlemen, who reported back in November. At this meeting a proposal from Hamilton was read. He offered an estate of 500–700 acres at Motherwell on perpetual lease for a grain rent, 'with a view to facilitate the formation of an establishment on Mr Owen's plan'.[3] The County was to advance up to £40,000 to provide the necessary capital and Hamilton offered to superintend the institution with Owen's assistance. But the scheme did not meet with the approval of Owen, who objected to Hamilton's suggestion that it would also serve as the county bridewell. Another meeting of Lanarkshire gentry, including Hamilton, was held in April 1821 to consider further Owen's *Report*, and it was agreed to petition both Houses of Parliament. In June the *Report* was duly brought before the House of Commons and the House of Lords and on each occasion the motion to examine Owen's Plan in detail was defeated. Hamilton's offer of the land at Motherwell remained open, and with Owen's approval he proposed a new scheme for starting a community.[4] Capital was to be raised by 2000 shares of £25 each, and the proprietors were to receive 5 per cent on their stock. A committee of management

---

[1] Owen, *Life*, I, 239.
[2] *Address at the City of London Tavern . . . August 21, 1817*, in Owen, *Life*, IA, 112–14.
[3] *Ibid.*, IA, 313.
[4] *Prospectus of a Plan for Establishing an Institution on Mr Owen's System in the Middle Ward of the County of Lanark* (n.p., n.d.). This was reprinted as an appendix to later editions of the *Report to the County of Lanark*. See also the *Economist*, I (1821), 141–4.

was to consist of equal numbers of representatives of the shareholders and settlers, and ultimately the shareholders would be repaid their original sum by the settlers who would then become sole proprietors. The scheme was to begin as soon as 1500 shares had been subscribed, but despite publicity in Lanarkshire and in the Owenite *Economist* the appeal met with little response.

The following year (1822) the Motherwell scheme was adopted by Owen's new organization, the British and Foreign Philanthropic Society. Hamilton was a member of the committee of the Society and one of its largest supporters with a promised subscription of £5000. The essentially philanthropic and agricultural framework of much Owenite thought at this time was reflected in the title of the organization and the speeches and resolutions at its first general meeting in June 1822.[1] The committee was at pains to reassure the members that the plan was neither visionary nor irreligious but an acceptable practical solution to the problems of poor relief and unemployment. Rule II of the Society defined its objects as 'the permanent relief of the labouring classes, by forming communities for mutual interest and cooperation, in which by means of education, example, and employment, they will be gradually withdrawn from the evils induced by ignorance, bad habits, poverty and want of employment'. The community was not to exceed five hundred persons at first and was to be 'essentially agricultural', with manufactures to be added later. Buildings were to be planned as a square, with communal arrangements for domestic chores. As before, management was to be handed over to a committee of working members when the capital was repaid, but until then control would remain with the shareholders. Subscriptions were solicited for a parent establishment at Motherwell, which would serve as a model community and a training centre for teachers to be employed in the promotion of new communities. Owen proposed that £100,000 be raised to launch the scheme, and over £55,000 was subscribed. But there the total stuck, and after a few months the Motherwell proposal had to be quietly abandoned.

In the meantime Owen, accompanied by Hamilton and Captain Macdonald, went over to Ireland, where he received a warm welcome from local gentry and clergy in many parts of the country. He climaxed his campaign with a series of lectures in the Rotunda, Dublin, in March and April 1823, after which was formed the Hibernian Philanthropic Society, 'for carrying into practice the plans of Mr Owen as they apply

---

[1] Details in this paragraph are from *Proceedings of the First General Meeting of the British and Foreign Philanthropic Society for the Permanent Relief of the Labouring Classes* (London, 1822); and *Robert Owen's Journal*, I–IV (1850–52).

to the amelioration of the condition of the working classes in Ireland'.[1] Support came from the same quarters as in England and for the same reasons: Owenism was taken to be primarily a plan for remedying working-class distress by means of agriculturally orientated philanthropy. General concern at the 'distressed condition of Ireland' was being voiced throughout 1822–23, and Owen's Plan was but one among several enquiries, reports and suggestions.[2] Like its English counterpart, however, the Hibernian Philanthropic Society did not manage to start any practical activity on the land, though as a result of its memorial to a Select Committee of the House of Commons for Relief and Employment of the Poor in Ireland, Owen was invited as a witness and his Plan was considered at length by the committee.

The efforts in Lanarkshire and the proceedings of the two Philanthropic Societies demonstrated a considerable measure of support for Owen's Plan among enlightened gentry and industrialists to the extent of promising fairly large subscriptions. But beyond this there was no response. For Owen's more deeply committed followers this presented a tantalizing situation, and left them with two broad courses open: either they could continue to follow Owen's leadership and support whatever practical suggestions he came up with next, or they could attempt an experiment by themselves, with or without Owen's blessing. Captain Donald Macdonald chose the first course, and accompanied Owen to America when he left in October 1824. Captain Robert O'Brien, who had induced Owen to visit Ireland, and who had been a main supporter of the Hibernian Philanthropic Society, preferred to experiment nearer home, and joined the Orbiston community. In this he followed the lead of Hamilton who, with Abram Combe, was the prime mover in the establishment of this first Owenite community in Britain.

After he had become interested in Owen's views Hamilton was stimulated to attend courses at Edinburgh University and during the winter of 1821 studied natural and moral philosophy, chemistry and natural history. In Edinburgh he also came under the influence of George Combe, and for a time was much impressed by phrenology. Like many Owenites Hamilton never completely rejected this early enthusiasm, but by 1824 was convinced that phrenology 'as a matter of speculation is very well,

---

[1] *Dublin Journal*, 9 May 1823, cutting in Jane Dale Owen, Scrapbook. Also Robert Owen, *Report of the Proceedings . . . in Dublin* (Dublin, 1823); *Report of the British and Foreign Philanthropic Society . . . explanatory of Mr Owen's Plan for the Relief of Ireland* (Dublin, 1823).

[2] See Hibernicus, *Practical Views and Suggestions on the Present Condition and Permanent Improvement of Ireland* (Dublin, 1823); and *Report of the Committee for the Relief of the Distressed Districts in Ireland . . . 7th May 1822* (London, 1823).

but can never be of any practical utility'.[1] He collaborated with Abram Combe and Captain Macdonald in the Edinburgh Practical Society and later commented wryly that it was a pity this Owenite experiment had neglected phrenology when selecting its storekeeper, a religious man who stole the funds.[2] Hamilton's association with Abram Combe in 1821 led to their collaboration four years later in the Orbiston community experiment. 'There being no prospect of a projected establishment of one of Mr Owen's villages of cooperation at Motherwell in Lanarkshire being carried into effect', wrote Hamilton in his autobiography, 'Mr Abram Combe of Edinburgh matured a plan by which a society might commence upon the old system and gradually get into the new, as soon as it was found that the minds of the members became adapted to the change.' The subscribers to the Motherwell scheme were canvassed, and with the support of several of these philanthropists Abram Combe began operations in March 1825. Hamilton made available to the community his family estate of Orbiston, a 290-acre site about a mile west of the Motherwell lands. He went to London with Combe and exhibited a model of the proposed community before the members of the London Cooperative Society, but after the launching of the scheme he did not play a very active part in its affairs. Ill health compelled his absence abroad, and in any case he did not wish to interfere in the community, believing that the settler-members should work out their own salvation.

The premature death of Abram Combe in 1827 deprived the community of effective leadership and led to its winding up. Hamilton was then engulfed in the debts of the community, and for the next five years was engaged in recriminative arguments and harassed by creditors. He retained his Owenite convictions to the last, and believed that the collapse of the community was due mainly to Abram Combe's death and the 'bad times' of 1825–26. Although the particular experiment was abandoned, 'no one … abandoned the principles of the system then attempted to be established, the truth of which every event that occurred tended to confirm'.[3]

This was also the sentiment of Henry Jones, a retired naval officer from Devonshire. He had promised a £5000 subscription to the British and Foreign Philanthropic Society, and also supported the Orbiston community. On its demise he collected a party of Scottish emigrants and sailed for Ontario where he established the Owenite colony of Maxwell in 1827–28.[4] Another of Hamilton's acquaintances, whom he had met in

[1] MS. letter, Hamilton to George Combe, Dalzell, 6 March 1824, Combe Papers.
[2] Hamilton, Autobiography.
[3] *Ibid.*
[4] John Morrison, 'The Toon o' Maxwell—an Owen Settlement in Lambton County, Ont.', Ontario Historical Society, *Papers and Records*, XII (1914), 5–12.

Ireland, was General Robert Brown of County Wexford. He too had been a subscriber to the British and Foreign and the Hibernian Philanthropic Societies, and in 1826 was actively planning a community on his property.[1] Brown, Jones, O'Brien, Macdonald and Hamilton were all officers in the army or navy, who were attracted to Owenism through a desire to play the role of improving landlord and philanthropist. There were aspects of Owen's character and the regime at New Lanark which perhaps appealed to the soldierly mind. Other contemporaries besides Cobbett commented on the similarity between factories and barracks, and a sympathetic visitor to New Lanark reported that 'the discipline employed by Mr Owen resembles, to a certain degree, that of a commander in chief of an army'.[2] Owen's relations with his workers was through a hierarchy of subalterns, who managed the various departments in the mills, and this was the pattern which his soldierly admirers had in mind when they planned their communities. Like Owen, they were imbued with a strong combination of 'benevolence and inclination to ordain and rule'.[3]

Hamilton's commitment to Owenism, however, went beyond the paternal benevolence of his fellow-squires for whom Owenism was a method of dealing with problems of poor relief and rural distress or a solution to the Irish problem. To Hamilton Owenism was also an ideological conviction.[4] Neither his political radicalism nor his belief in Owenite communitarianism was shaken by his experiences: in 1832 he presented himself (unsuccessfully) as parliamentary reform candidate for the county of Lanark, and at the third Cooperative Congress was appointed trustee to select land for a community. His fellow-trustees were William Thompson and John Minter Morgan, both leading Owenite philanthropists. But Hamilton did not live to participate further in communitarian projects.

Among the committee members and main subscribers to the British and Foreign Philanthropic Society was a London philanthropist, John Minter Morgan (1782–1854). With an ample fortune inherited from his father (a London wholesale stationer) and a great admiration of Owen he

---

[1] MS. letter, Donald Macdonald to Hamilton, Edinburgh, 19 July 1826, Hamilton Papers.

[2] Henry Grey Macnab, *The New Views of Mr Owen of Lanark Impartially Examined* (London, 1819), p. 127.

[3] Obituary, *Daily News*, 19 November 1858; also reprinted in Harriet Martineau, *Biographical Sketches*, new edn. (London, 1877), p. 307.

[4] He wrote a series of letters to the *Glasgow Chronicle* which earned him the enmity of William M'Gavin, editor of the *Protestant*. See William M'Gavin, *Letters on Mr Owen's New System* (Glasgow, 1823), and *Fundamental Principles of the New Lanark System Exposed. . . .* (Glasgow, 1824).

was excellently cast for the role of Owenite philanthropist. He was among the first to defend Owen's views and subsequently wrote popular expositions of Owenism. He was a subscriber to the Orbiston community and a trusted adviser at the Cooperative Congresses in the 1830s. In his later years he became well known for his tireless advocacy of his plan for a Christian community. There was little that was original in his writings, and he was remarkable to contemporaries chiefly through his ability to reconcile Owenite beliefs with membership of the Church of England.

Because of the paucity of biographical detail it is difficult to trace Minter Morgan's early steps towards Owenism with certainty.[1] It is possible that a reading of Gibbon first awakened doubts about the truth of revealed religion and led to a questioning of contemporary Christian professions. He did not lose his faith, but became convinced of the need for a more strenuous exercise of Christian charity in social action. The 'pleasures of benevolence' soon superseded his earlier love of the study: 'the truths recently elicited in the progress of moral science had opened a wide field for immediate practical exertion, in which the most important benefits might be secured'. His reading of Dugald Stewart's *Elements of the Philosophy of the Human Mind* and Owen's *New View of Society* provided an intellectual preparation for this activity. He was also influenced by Dr Charles Hall, a West country physician, whose anti-capitalist book *The Effects of Civilisation* (London, 1805) was reprinted by Minter Morgan in his Phoenix Library series in 1849. In August 1817 he attended Owen's meetings in the City of London Tavern and 'heard the grand but simple outline of society promulgated. There I recognized as a foundation the principles of universal justice, and hailed the dawn of mental emancipation'. The new convert lost no time in proclaiming the New Views, and under the pseudonym of Philanthropos published his *Remarks on the Practicability of Mr Robert Owen's Plan to Improve the Condition of the Lower Classes* (London, 1819).

This tract was a faithful reproduction of Owen's views as formulated in 1817. Starting from the position that the state of the poor was the most pressing problem of the times, Minter Morgan diagnosed the cause of this to be the 'depreciation in the value of manual labour',[2] occasioned by the widespread introduction of machinery. In a properly constituted

---

[1] It is probable that parts of his *Hampden in the Nineteenth Century* (2 vols., London, 1834) are autobiographical; the quotations in this para. are taken from vol. 1.

[2] This and the following quotations are from Philanthropos [John Minter Morgan], *Remarks on the Practicability of Mr Robert Owen's Plan to Improve the Condition of the Lower Classes* (London, 1819).

society, he argued, machinery would be a blessing, but in contemporary Britain it caused only unemployment. There was no prospect of any permanent improvement in the demand for labour, and legislation (for example, to regulate wages) was no longer feasible. Hence, argued Minter Morgan, 'the unemployed poor must now be placed in a situation where they will be removed from the misery arising from the fluctuations or continued depression in the value of labour'. The only practical method of achieving this was for them to support themselves by agriculture, which was what Owen's plan for villages of mutual cooperation would enable them to do. Once the poor had tasted the blessings of community life they would not willingly revert to the old system, and so it was necessary to think in terms of permanent communities. The beauty of the plan was that it would not upset the stability of society. It would be effected 'not by depriving the rich of their possessions, but by giving industrious habits, employment and religious instruction to the poor'.

Only on the last point did Minter Morgan depart from Owen's teaching. He regretted Owen's 'attack upon Faith' but set it aside as irrelevant to the evaluation of the Plan, which was not basically antagonistic to Christianity. Owen's doctrine of character formation, he argued, took account of differences between individual temperaments, and it was undeniably true that a large part of men's views was derived from their surroundings. Education at present was insufficient to counteract the total influence of society. But since Christian virtues could be produced by environmental factors in youth (that is, by a truly Christian education), Owen's Plan could be an instrument for the spread of 'true Christian benevolence'. By such arguments Minter Morgan assured himself that Owenism was in fact 'the offspring of Christianity'.

The need for some such assurance was very real if Owenism was to be made acceptable as philanthropic benevolence. Owen's anti-clericalism, combined with the heretical implications of the Essays on the Formation of Character (which could be held to deny moral accountability and original sin), constituted a stumbling-block for Evangelical Christians. The subject was continually debated throughout the history of the Owenite movement, but the argument seldom advanced much beyond the position reached in 1819–21, namely, that practical Owenism produced the same desirable results as 'true' (practical) Christianity, and that theoretical or dogmatic difficulties should therefore be ignored.[1] Minter Morgan's distinctive contribution to Owenism was that he confronted this difficulty as early as 1819 and established the precedent that a

[1] See the discussion between correspondents ('Tyro', 'Philo-Justitia', 'Overton' and 'Philadelphus') in the *Economist*, II (1821).

Church of England philanthropist could also be an Owenite. The ideal of the Owenite philanthropist was elaborated in his *Hampden in the Nineteenth Century* (1834), where the hero, a young man possessed of an income of £2000 a year left him four years previously by an uncle, has 'a heart overflowing with benevolence united to a strong sense of justice'.

More widely known than this manual of Owenite philanthropy was Minter Morgan's popularization of Owenism, *The Revolt of the Bees*, which went through five editions between 1826 and 1849, and was serialized in the *Cooperative Magazine*. The title (reminiscent of Bernard Mandeville's *Fable of the Bees*, 1714) referred to a simple allegory by which Minter Morgan described the consequences of the introduction of private property and competition and the theories of the political economists. Like *Hampden* it was fanciful and romantic in form, and drew widely upon authors of the Scottish Enlightenment as well as Bacon, Helvetius and of course Owen. Minter Morgan consistently rejected Malthus's views, and reproached the orthodox political economists for their social blindness and arrogance.[1] He was by no means unaware of Owen's faults, and was prepared to distinguish between what he considered was the essence of Owen's original plan and later accretions or personal idiosyncrasies.[2]

For twenty years Minter Morgan was prepared to go along with Owen, to support his projects and to defend his views. But from 1840 he drifted away from the main Owenite body and concentrated his efforts on his own organization, the Church of England Self-Supporting Village Society.[3] His plan was to win support for a Christianized version of Owenite communities. As J. M. Ludlow, the Christian Socialist, put it, 'He adopted Mr Owen's views as to the formation of village communities, only would put a Church and a clergyman into each, and then call it a "Church of England Self-Supporting Village" '.[4] The movement was approved by several members of the aristocracy, including Lord John Manners, and by the Bishop of Norwich. Active support came from the Hon. William F. Cowper, M.P., James Silk Buckingham, and the Rev. E. R. Larken, as well as from socially minded clergymen in various parts

---

[1] Also in John Minter Morgan, *The Reproof of Brutus* (London, 1830). Morgan elaborated his general views in a series of letters under the pseudonym 'Philanthropos' in the *Crisis*, 24 May–25 August 1832.

[2] *Hampden*, II, 102–6.

[3] See John Minter Morgan, *Religion and Crime* (London, 1840), *The Christian Commonwealth* (London, 1845), *Letters to a Clergyman* (London, 1846), *The Church of England Self-Supporting Village* (London, 1850).

[4] *Economic Review*, III (1893), 486.

of the country.[1] From 1846 the movement became caught up in the general enthusiasm for Association, and the salon at Minter Morgan's London house was frequented by social reformers of the stamp of the Howitts, Mrs Gaskell, Emerson and January Searle.[2]

Although on the important question of religion Minter Morgan differed from his friend and fellow-philanthropist, the free-thinking A. J. Hamilton, in other respects their interpretations of Owenism were similar. They both first came to Owen's Plan thinking of it as a solution to the problems of poor relief, and after they had widened their horizons they still regarded it as an exercise in gentlemanly philanthropy.[3] Their ideas of community were set in an agricultural mould, and they strongly resented the values of industrialism—hence Minter Morgan's diatribes against the political economists and Malthus in particular. As philanthropists they each had a radical twist which alarmed their more orthodox friends. In Minter Morgan this took the form of an anti-capitalist critique derived from Charles Hall and Owen, in Hamilton it emerged as political reform radicalism. In both instances their Owenism was worn with a difference: the bond between them was a common heritage of philanthropy.

In America Owenite philanthropy assumed a somewhat different hue from its counterpart in Britain. The Poor Law problem in its English form did not exist in the States, nor was squirearchical paternalism appreciated except in parts of the South. American philanthropy stemmed from other roots, usually either evangelical or radical, and this was reflected in the type of philanthropic support which American Owenism attracted. Thus on the one hand was Jeremiah Thompson, a wealthy Quaker merchant and shipowner of New York, who supported both New Harmony and Nashoba;[4] on the other was William Maclure (1763–1840), philanthropic radical and deist.[5] What there was not room for in

---

[1] Details are given in Armytage, *Heavens Below*, pp. 209–33.

[2] Spencer T. Hall, *Biographical Sketches of Remarkable People* (Burnley, 1881), p. 207. Further details of this circle of social reformers are given in J. F. C. Harrison, *Social Reform in Victorian Leeds: the Work of James Hole, 1820–1895* (Leeds: Thoresby Society, 1954).

[3] As an indication of Minter Morgan's later paternalistic attitudes see his translation of Louis Napoleon Bonaparte, *Extinction of Pauperism* (London, 1847).

[4] Frank Thistlethwaite, *America and the Atlantic Community: Anglo-American Aspects, 1790–1850* (New York, 1963), pp. 13–15, 53, 189; Herbert Heaton, 'Yorkshire Cloth Traders in the United States, 1770–1840', Thoresby Society, Leeds, *Miscellany*, vol. XXXVII, pt. 3, no. 88 (April 1944), 225–87.

[5] The main source for biographical details of Maclure is Samuel George Morton, *A Memoir of William Maclure, Esq.* (Philadelphia, Penn., 1841). Modern accounts of his work are W. H. G. Armytage, 'William Maclure, 1763–1840: a British Interpretation', *Indiana*

3. New Lanark in 1825

4. The benevolent Mr. Owen (by W. H. Brooke, 1834)

the American environment was Owen's type of paternalism; as Maclure sagely observed: 'the materials in this country are not the same as the cotton spinners at New Lanark, nor does the advice of a patron go so far'.[1] The careers and interests of Owen and Maclure were very similar, and their ultimate disagreement after an initially enthusiastic collaboration may be explained as well by differences in the role of philanthropist in Britain and America as by differences in personality or educational policy.

Born in Ayr, Scotland, William Maclure made a fortune as a merchant, and in the late 1790s decided to move to Philadelphia and become an American citizen. He then retired from commerce to devote the rest of his life to the philanthropic pursuit of his two enthusiasms, science and education. In 1809 his reputation as a natural scientist was established by the publication of his pioneer geological map of the United States, which he extended and revised in 1818 after further geological researches. This work brought him into contact with naturalists such as Charles Alexandre Lesueur, Thomas Say and Gerard Troost, and into correspondence with leading scientists such as Benjamin Silliman of Yale. Maclure was president of the Academy of Natural Sciences in Philadelphia from 1817 to 1840, and first president of the American Geological Society in 1819. He was both a benefactor of these institutions and a distinguished member as a scientist in his own right.

Maclure's educational interests alternated with his scientific work. Contemptuous of his own classical education ('launched into the world as ignorant as a pig of anything useful'[2]) he discovered in Pestalozzi's school at Yverdon, Switzerland, a system which conformed to his notions of 'a rational education'. Subsequent visits to Yverdon strengthened his faith in Pestalozzianism, which he endeavoured to propagate in America and Spain. He persuaded Joseph Neef, one of Pestalozzi's teachers, to

[1] Letter, Maclure to Mme Fretageot, 25 September 1826. Bestor, *Maclure–Fretageot Correspondence*, p. 371.

[2] Letter, Maclure to Benjamin Silliman, 19 October 1822. *Ibid.*, p. 293.

Magazine of History, XLVII (1951), 1–20; C. A. Browne, 'Some Relations of the New Harmony Movement to the History of Science in America', *Scientific Monthly*, XLII (January–June 1936), 483–97; Harvey L. Carter, 'William Maclure', *Indiana Magazine of History*, XXXI (1935), 83–91; J. Percy Moore, 'William Maclure: Scientist and Humanitarian', American Philosophical Society, *Proceedings*, XCI (1947), 234–49; and Arthur Eugene Bestor, Jr., ed., *Education and Reform at New Harmony: Correspondence of William Maclure and Marie Duclos Fretageot, 1820–1833* (Indiana Historical Society, *Publications*, vol. XV, no. 3; Indianapolis, 1948). Also useful is Charles Orville Burgess, 'The Educational State in America: Selected Views on Learning as the Key to Utopia, 1800–1924' (unpublished Ph.D. thesis, University of Wisconsin, 1962) which has sections on Maclure and New Harmony.

establish a school in Philadelphia in 1806, and guaranteed it financially. Later he enabled two more Pestalozzian teachers, Madame Fretageot and William S. Phiquepal, to leave France and settle in Philadelphia.

This patronage of science and education was the practical expression of Maclure's general social philosophy. 'He aimed', wrote his earliest biographer, 'at reforming mankind by . . . the cultivation of the mind.'[1] But his philanthropy was rooted not in general Christian benevolence, nor in problems of the relief of the poor, but in a robust democratic radicalism. Whether he emigrated to America because of his radical principles or developed his radicalism as a result of his American experiences is not clear, but certainly his philanthropy coincides with that period of his life when he rejected his past, including that symbol of aristocratic tyranny, Britain. By the time he came to formulate his *Opinions on Various Subjects*[2] his main concern was with 'the cake of liberty', and his analysis of social and political problems was in terms of 'the trinity of property, knowledge and power'. He argued that power (and therefore liberty) is dependent on property, and an equality of property is necessary to secure equal liberty for all. The only effective safeguard of equality is knowledge: 'the division of property divides knowledge, and the division of property and knowledge divides power. The nearly equal division of knowledge will equalise both property and power.'[3] Education (or the diffusion of knowledge) was thus basic to his plans for social improvement, and he never tired of reiterating the Baconian maxim that Knowledge is Power.

Such a passion for education would alone have been sufficient to ensure Maclure's interest in Owen's Plan. Add to this a common language of business and similar Enlightenment beliefs in deism and environmentalism, and the result was Maclure's description of Owen as 'the only man in Europe who has a proper idea of mankind and the use he ought to make of his faculties'.[4] The two men had met in July 1824 at New Lanark, and when Maclure learned of Owen's arrival in America a few weeks later he enthusiastically welcomed him. Maclure did not at first think of joining forces with Owen, despite the urgings of Madame Fretageot in Philadelphia. In the fall of 1825, however, he decided to

[1] Morton, p. 29.

[2] William Maclure, *Opinions on Various Subjects, dedicated to the Industrious Producers* (3 vols., New Harmony, Indiana, 1831–38). These essays originally appeared in the *New Harmony Gazette* and the *Disseminator*, and the earliest of them was written at Paris in 1819.

[3] *Opinions*, I, 199.

[4] Letter, Maclure to Mme Fretageot, 10 September 1824. Bestor, *Maclure–Fretageot Correspondence*, p. 309.

support the New Harmony venture and, moreover, brought with him the distinguished 'boatload of knowledge' which set out down the Ohio river early in December. The keelboat was named, appropriately enough, 'Philanthropist', and among its forty passengers were the naturalists Say and Lesueur, and the Pestalozzians Madame Fretageot and Phiquepal. At this stage (and especially since reading John Gray's *Lecture on Human Happiness*) Maclure thought that he had found a synthesis of his social philosophy in Owenism.

So substantial were Maclure's contributions in three main directions at New Harmony that he may almost be considered a co-founder with Owen. First, his large financial investment made him the owner of part of the village, and he was virtually joint patron of the experiment.[1] Second, the reputation of New Harmony as a centre of scientific research and publication, which lasted long after the ending of the social experiment, was due to Maclure. He persuaded Say, Lesueur and Troost to make New Harmony their headquarters, and Owen's sons continued in the same tradition. It was Maclure's library, equipment and collections of natural history that provided the necessary basis for scientific teaching and research. Third, the practical success of the schools at New Harmony was the work of a small band of Pestalozzian teachers—Madame Fretageot, William Phiquepal and Joseph Neef—whom Maclure supported; and the School of Industry was the result of his special concern to provide 'useful' as opposed to 'ornamental' education.

Because its aim was to be self-supporting as well as practical the school of industry was an institution much favoured by philanthropists on both sides of the Atlantic. The formula of 'physical labour . . . combined with moral and intellectual culture'[2] which Maclure applied in his agricultutal school at Alicante in Spain was typical of other philanthropists, including Owen, who were impressed by Fellenberg's work at Hofwyl in Switzerland. Pestalozzianism (particularly as set forth in the popular *Leonard and Gertrude*) suggested the feasibility of social improvement through education and enlightened benevolence, using the village community as the unit of reform. Maclure's basic philosophy already included a strong distrust of all central authority in government and a corresponding conviction that the smaller the community the happier and more efficient it would be.[3] In the idea of an Owenite community at New Harmony Maclure's hopes of social betterment seemed most likely to find their

[1] Estimates of the size of Owen's and Maclure's investments in New Harmony are given in Bestor, *Backwoods Utopias*, pp. 191, 198.
[2] Morton, p. 18.
[3] *Opinions*, I, 78, 83.

realization. And indeed, despite his quarrel with Owen and the failure by 1827 of all Owen's attempts to organize the community successfully, it was Maclure's work at New Harmony which flourished in the 1830s and proved to be its most lasting legacy.

Yet Maclure was an unusual sort of philanthropist. Just as John Griscom of New York was puzzled as to how to reconcile Owen's theories with his philanthropy ('that such sentiments should be found in union with . . . practical philanthropy . . . is a circumstance which has seldom occurred in the history of civilisation'[1]), so contemporaries were embarrassed by the unorthodox principles which were at the root of Maclure's benevolence.[2] The *Opinions* contained not only condemnations of 'king-craft and priest-craft' but scepticism about all revealed religion. To this infidelity was added a permissive attitude towards sexual intercourse between unmarried persons. Labour, asserted Maclure, is the basis of all wealth, and inequality (of property, knowledge and power) is the main cause of social conflict. The political economy of Ricardo, Malthus and McCulloch should be called the science of 'the production and destruction of wealth', since it unduly favours the interest of the 'land proprietors, priests and governors' and assumes a static relationship between existing social classes. Maclure's philanthropy was an attempt to change the conditions in which the producers of wealth (the labouring classes) remained impoverished while the non-producers (aristocrats, clergy and politicians) grew rich. The key to this change was education: an equal distribution of knowledge would lead to equality of power. Unless this peaceful method of social change were adopted the labouring classes would seize the 'pick-axe of revolution'.

This philosophy of social reconstruction was far removed from the usual concept of philanthropy in either Britain or America, so much so that Maclure came to the conclusion that philanthropy was inadequate to raise the working classes and that in the long run improvement could only be effected by working-class self-help. Commenting on the failure of communitarianism by 1828 he thought that this was because the promoters of communities had not had any pecuniary interest in their success; and the motive of 'moral gratification' in benefiting one's species was incomprehensible to the labourers for whose benefit the scheme was intended.[3] Since the pursuit of happiness through enlightened self-

---

[1] Account of a visit to New Lanark in 1819, in Griscom, *A Year in Europe*, II, 382.

[2] As his friend and biographer, Dr Samuel Morton, sententiously observed when discussing the failure of Maclure's schemes of social reform, 'what Religion itself has not been able to accomplish, Philosophy will attempt in vain'—Morton, p. 29.

[3] *Opinions*, I, 98–9.

interest is the root of human motivation ('all our morality should be founded on the immovable rock of well understood self-interest') it seemed to Maclure that at times philanthropy and benevolence were but cloaks to disguise real motives such as egotism and self-conceit. Philanthropy had become so closely identified with the rich and privileged, and with the churches, that it was no more than a disguise for perpetuating their superiority over the mass of the people.

By the 1830s Maclure had come to reject the label of philanthropist, and talked the language of Jacksonian democracy. He had travelled beyond Owen's paternalistic position but continued to play the role of wealthy benefactor from his retirement in Mexico. Maclure explained his association with Owen on purely practical grounds, but he shared so many of Owen's basic attitudes and assumptions that he was, intellectually, an Owenite. Even after his break with Owen in 1827 he protested his continued belief in cooperative socialism: the experience of New Harmony vindicated the 'System' and condemned only Owen's mode of executing it. Fundamentally he was perhaps a better Owenite than Owen himself, for he realized more clearly how great was the gulf between the old immoral and the new moral worlds. After Maclure had left New Harmony he was visited in Mexico by Owen, who characteristically enthused on how Birkbeck, Brougham and other liberal reformers in Britain were prepared to support him. On which Maclure commented: 'I have been trying to show him how far his system is in advance of any of theirs, and what an immense chasm . . . lies between his radical cure of all evils and the partial remedy of . . . other reformers in both church and state; . . . this moral chasm ought to be considered as a physical ditch drawn round the old castle of ancient prejudice . . . fortified by all the instruments of defence invented by all the talent and acumen of both church and state for many centuries.'[1]

In Britain and America the philanthropists formed an influential group in the Owenite movement. By virtue of their wealth, education and articulateness they occupied positions of leadership in the communities and other Owenite institutions. They were for the most part able men and of some status in society at large. The type of work they were engaged in—practical philanthropy—was widely approved among the affluent classes from dukes to merchants. Why then did Owenite philanthropists gain such meagre support and Owenite institutions wither so quickly, as compared with other philanthropic causes which crusaded successfully in the early nineteenth century? Sunday schools, anti-

[1] Letter, Maclure to Mme Fretageot, 28 January 1829. Bestor, *Maclure–Fretageot Correspondence*, pp. 403–4.

slavery and temperance—all aiming at far-reaching social reconstruction under philanthropic leadership—established organizations much more stable and widespread than Owenism. In part the difference arises because Owenism was more than philanthropy, which was not an encompassing framework but only one strand interwoven with others such as community, millennialism and anti-capitalism. More significantly, Owenite philanthropy was predominantly secular. It was antagonistic towards the religion of evangelical Christianity and the faith of political economy. Consequently it found no favour with the dominant school of philanthropy as represented by William Wilberforce in England or the Tappan brothers in the United States. Owenite philanthropy was part of an earlier tradition, rooted in the humanistic values of the Enlightenment. Utility or the pursuit of happiness was its starting point, not the saving grace of Christ Jesus. The use of millennial language or professions of Christianity by individual Owenites did not change the general secular image of Owenism. In an age of intensive evangelical religion the Owenites stood condemned as infidels, and their philanthropy was therefore discountenanced.

The Definition of Socialism

The Definition of Socialism

Probably the best-known image of Robert Owen is as 'the father of English socialism'. He and his followers have received attention as the main English school of utopian socialists, predecessors, together with their Saint-Simonian and Fourierist contemporaries, of Marx and Engels. Owenism as a body of social thought has usually been presented as a variety of pre-Marxian socialism, with emphasis on its economic doctrines and critique of capitalism.[1] But the record of early Owenism, especially in America, suggests that this reading of events is to some extent a distortion. During the one hundred and forty years of its history the term socialism has undergone several changes of meaning, and when it was first used by the Owenites it connoted something different from what it did in the later nineteenth and twentieth centuries.[2] To see what the Owenites meant when they talked of socialism it is necessary to peel away several layers of subsequent usage and interpretation.

The word socialist first appeared in the London Cooperative Magazine *of November 1827, where a writer referred to the 'Communionists or Socialists', but it was not widely used by Owenites until the mid-1830s. In the 1820s Owenites used phrases such as the 'new view of society', the 'social system' and 'cooperation'. By 1840 socialism was virtually synonymous with Owenism; so much so that when Marx and Engels came to write their* Manifesto *in 1847 they could not call it a Socialist Manifesto but had to resort to the alternative title of Communist.[3] The label socialist was adopted*

[1] E.g. G. D. H. Cole, *Socialist Thought: The Forerunners, 1789–1850* (London, 1953); Max Beer, *History of British Socialism* (London, 1919, new edn. repr. 1948).

[2] The definitive examination of this is Arthur E. Bestor, Jr., 'The Evolution of the Socialist Vocabulary', *Journal of the History of Ideas*, IX (1948), 259–302.

[3] Friedrich Engels, Preface dated 30 January 1888, to Karl Marx and Friedrich Engels, *Manifesto of the Communist Party*, authorized English translation (London, 1934 edn.), p. 7.

by the Owenites because it stressed what they felt was the core of their doctrine: socialists were those who emphasized a social, as opposed to an individual, approach in all fields of human endeavour—including, though not
limited to economic organization. Earlier terms in the vocabulary of social
reform, such as radical or agrarian, were inadequate to distinguish the new
doctrines: the Owenites (who disliked eponymous labels such as Owenian or
Owenite) therefore appropriated to themselves the title of socialist. (One
learned Owenite social missionary with a classical background traced the
word socialism to 'the Latin socialis or socialibis, signifying friendly', and
concluded that this was a most apt name for the followers of Owen who were
animated by the purest principles of charity and good will to their fellow-
men.[1])

Posterity has fastened upon the socialism of the Owenites the adjective
'utopian', and the three schools of Saint-Simon, Fourier and Owen are
usually classified together as the Utopian Socialists. Owen and his followers
were always sensitive to charges of being impractical visionaries, and went
to some lengths to protest their bona fides as successful men of the world who
had little time for the 'mere closet theorist'.[2] If the disparaging epithet
utopian had come only from conservative critics it might have been successfully
rebuffed. But in 1837 Jerome-Adolphe Blanqui in his History of Political
Economy in Europe applied the term utopian economist to Owen and
Fourier. When Marx and Engels discussed Saint-Simon, Fourier and Owen
in a section of the Communist Manifesto devoted to 'Critical-Utopian
Socialism and Communism' the tone was set for most subsequent discussion,
culminating in Engels's pamphlet Socialism, Utopian and Scientific
(1880).[3] The many cheap editions in English of these Marxist works after
1888 served to perpetuate as a description of pre-Marxian socialism a term
that originated as a criticism by contemporary polemicists. Marx and
Engels commended Owen and the other utopian socialists for their attack
upon 'every principle of existing society', but condemned them for failure to
realize the significance of class antagonisms. The 'utopian' element in
Owenite socialism was that which prevented it from supporting revolutionary
class action.

The Owenites rejected the term utopian,[4] and their socialism cannot be

---

[1] James Napier Bailey, Monthly Messenger (London, 1840), no. 1, pp. 1–2.
[2] Report to the County of Lanark, in Life, IA, 281. Cf. also New View of Society, in Ibid.,
I, 271.
[3] Louis Reybaud, Études sur les Reformateurs contemporains (Paris, 1840) also linked
ideas of utopia with his study of Saint-Simon, Fourier and Owen.
[4] As early as 1819 Minter Morgan in Remarks on the Practicability of Mr Owen's Plan,
p. 40, had felt it necessary to defend Owen against 'the epithet of a Utopian Politician'.
However, Josiah Warren named his Ohio community 'Utopia' in the 1840s (Noyes,

analysed by the canons considered appropriate after the rise of modern socialism in the 1880s. Owenite socialism was 'the true social or cooperative and communional system',[1] a blend of communitarian theory, anti-capitalist economics and a science of society. These three elements made up the main part of the doctrines of Owenism and together gave it distinctive characteristics as a philosophy of social reform.

1 The Idea of Community

When Owenites spoke of their 'communional system' they had several ideas in mind. In the first place they were referring to a general concept of community which they felt was essential for satisfactory human relationships in any society. The absence of such community was diagnosed by Owen as the chief ill of British society in the period 1814–19: society was fragmented and turned against itself. In his efforts to restore harmony to society Owen became a socialist and was led to condemn all institutions which 'individualized' man. Second, the communional system for many Owenites meant the holding of property in common and the abolition of individual ownership. Owen's position on this issue was not completely consistent, nor did he maintain the same views at different periods in his career. His followers similarly advocated varying degrees of communism, some wanting complete equality and community of goods, others content with a less absolute scheme. Third, there was an active belief in communitarianism as a method of social reform. Society was to be radically transformed by means of experimental communities, and this was regarded as a valid alternative to other methods of effecting societal change such as revolution or legislation.[2] In Britain and America there were traditions of community upon which the Owenites could draw in support of these three aspects of their communional system.

On both sides of the Atlantic Owenite thinking on community (as on much else) started from the principle of human happiness. In almost every Owenite book and pamphlet the pursuit of happiness was taken as

[1] Editorial, *Cooperative Magazine*, II (1827), 3.

[2] 'The whole arrangements form one grand moral as well as economical experiment', wrote William Thompson, arguing the case for community as a social experiment. *Inquiry into the Principles of the Distribution of Wealth* (London, 1824), p. 427.

History of American Socialisms, pp. 97–8), and the Bradford Owenite, Samuel Bower, wrote *The Peopling of Utopia* (Bradford, 1838) and *Sequel to the Peopling of Utopia* (Bradford, 1838). Cf. also John Francis Bray, *A Voyage from Utopia*, ed. M. F. Lloyd-Prichard (London, 1957), written in 1840–41 'our being's end and aim',[1] and right and wrong defined in terms of increasing or diminishing happiness. An early Owenite tract by John Gray, often quoted in Britain and America, was entitled *A Lecture on Human Happiness* (London, 1826); and when the London Cooperative Society drew up a plan for a community in 1825 they felt it necessary to begin with the preamble that 'happiness is the true object of human exertions'.[2] In America the Declaration of Independence lay conveniently to hand, so that the Philadelphia Owenite printer, Langton Byllesby, could begin his treatise with the famous quotation by Thomas Jefferson.[3] Yet Owenites observed that despite this universal pursuit of happiness, happy individuals were rare, and society was plagued by economic distress and social misery of unprecedented magnitude. Happiness, in fact, was virtually impossible in present society. Only in community, so the argument ran, would it be possible to realize the prime goal of happiness for all men. 'It appears to be indisputable', concluded George Mudie, editor of the *Economist*, 'that all men pursue happiness; and that happiness can only be attained by the possession of abundance, and by the cultivation of the physical, moral and intellectual powers . . . and that the proposed societies [i.e. communities] offer the only means of giving abundance, and intellectual and moral excellence, to all mankind.'[4]

For Owen 'utility, or the greatest happiness principle' was fundamental to all his thinking. As Max Beer put it, 'Bentham's formula is Owen's premise'.[5] It appeared in simple form in the Third Essay of the *New View of Society* and, more sophisticatedly, in the Third Part of the *Book of the New Moral World* (1836–44). Thirteen conditions necessary for individual happiness were laid down, ranging from health of body and mind (Owen recognized psychosomatic illness), full education and freedom of thought and expression, to a society whose institutions are in unison with the law of nature. But basically Owen declared happiness to be the end of living in the sense that happiness is a condition of man's self-realization as a complete human being. He did not envisage happiness as the seeking or attainment of pleasure, but rather as some 'rational' form of living. Like most theories of hedonism Owen's theory of happiness presented certain logical difficulties. While psychologically happiness

---

[1] Robert Dale Owen, *An Outline of the System of Education at New Lanark* (Glasgow, 1824), p. 12.

[2] *Articles of Agreement . . . by the London Cooperative Society, for the Formation of a Community . . .* (London, 1825), p. 3.

[3] Langton Byllesby, *Observations on the Sources and Effects of Unequal Wealth* (New York, 1826, repr. New York, 1961), p. 25.

[4] *Economist*, I (1821), 338–9.

[5] *History of British Socialism*, I, 163.

is primary and fundamental, ethically it is derivative. Owen attempted to account for moral issues in non-moral terms: the aim of conduct was to be simply a subjective state of feeling (happiness). Realizing that ethically this was inadequate, Owen coupled it with a belief that man should live for others as well as for himself; the individual has a duty to live for the happiness of the greatest number, and in so doing he will also promote his own highest happiness. Hedonism was thus in effect abandoned, and Owen was left with a theory of ethics which was inconsistent.[1] In his failure to satisfy critics on this point, however, he was in no worse position than any of his Utilitarian friends and contemporaries. However incomplete as a theory of individual morality the doctrine of happiness might be, as the psychological base for a theory of society it was widely attractive to all shades of radicals and reformers. They quoted Bentham to the effect that 'the happiness of the greatest number is the only legitimate object of society'—to which the Owenites added their claim that only in a 'system of general cooperation and community of property' could this greatly desired end be attained.[2]

In Britain the communitarian element of Owenism had several roots. Men who were interested in community for different reasons found grounds for sympathy with the Owenite movement. When Owenites talked in terms of communitarianism they were using language which was fairly widely intelligible. The number of squires and Scots and Irish landowners who were among Owen's early supporters has already been noted.[3] A paternalist rural tradition provided a favourable seeding ground for Owenite community ideas as a solution to agricultural distress and problems of improved husbandry. Home colonies could be interpreted in terms of scientific benevolence as well as Owenite communitarianism. Without ascribing too much to conservative ideas of the organic nature of English society, the Tory tradition of an Old England which was a genuine community provided welcome material for Owenite apologists. Robert Southey was quoted approvingly;[4] and Tory-

[1] For a general critique of hedonism and utilitarianism see F. H. Bradley, *Ethical Studies* (London, 1876, 2nd edn., 1927), Essay III.

[2] *Cooperative Magazine*, I (1826), 3–5.

[3] P. 26 above. Cf. also Owen's own model of a pre-industrial age in which landed proprietors were motivated by feelings of social responsibility and their workers enjoyed a sense of membership in a larger family unit. *Observations on the Effect of the Manufacturing System* (London, 1815), in Owen, *Life*, IA, 40.

[4] Especially his *Sir Thomas More: or Colloquies on the Progress and Prospects of Society* (2 vols., London, 1829), on which Minter Morgan probably modelled his *Hampden in the Nineteenth Century* (1834). Southey was also associated earlier (1794) with Samuel Taylor Coleridge in a plan for a 'pantisocracy' on the Susquehanna river in Pennsylvania, near to a community settled by the English republican refugees, Joseph Priestley and Thomas Cooper.

Radicals of the stamp of William Cobbett and Richard Oastler (though they held no brief for Owen) popularized a critique of industrial society based on the myth of an older, happier England. It is significant that Owen's severest critics were not (with the exception of Churchmen) generally Tories but Whig-Radicals. A curious echo of this squire-archical tradition is found in the settlement of the English Prairie, Illinois, where Morris Birkbeck developed a frontier village for English immigrants with strong community overtones.[1] Birkbeck's prairie was settled in 1817–18. Seven years later his neighbours across the Wabash river were the Owenites of New Harmony, and there was a constant intermingling of the inhabitants of the two settlements.

The Tory tradition of community was matched in Britain by an in-digenous working-class culture of collectivism. In the later eighteenth century a network of friendly societies, burial clubs and trade societies attested the strength of this 'ethos of mutuality'.[2] Methodism reinforced it, with the language of brotherhood and the essentially neighbourhood institution of the chapel. In 1842 there was still visible a sign over the Owenite cooperative store in Sowerby Bridge, Yorkshire, taken from Isaiah: 'They helped everyone his neighbour, and said one to another, "Brother, be of good cheer".' The threat or challenge to this tradition from the impact of industrialism provided the ground for alliance with Tory-Radicalism.

This sense of the loss of community was expressed by contemporaries in several forms. For Thomas Carlyle it was a consequence of the Gospel of Mammonism: 'We call it a Society; and go about professing openly the totalest separation, isolation. Our life is not a mutual helpfulness; but rather, cloaked under due laws-of-war, named "fair competition" and so forth, it is a mutual hostility.'[3] The new industrial order in England was not a true society because it lacked the necessary characteristics of whole-ness, unity and stability. Instead it offered only fragmentation, loneliness and strife. Karl Marx described much the same phenomena as alienation. Under machine capitalism the worker becomes a mere commodity, and

[1] George Flower, *History of the English Settlement in Edwards County, Illinois, founded in 1817 and 1818 by Morris Birkbeck and George Flower*, ed. E. B. Washburne (Chicago, 1882); Morris Birkbeck, *Notes on a Journey in America, from the Coast of Virginia to the Territory of Illinois, with Proposals for the Establishment of a Colony of English* (Phila-delphia, 1817); Edwin Erle Sparks (ed.), *The English Settlement in Illinois. Reprints of Three Rare Tracts on the Illinois Country* (London and Cedar Rapids, Iowa, 1907). Cf. also C. B. Johnson, *Letters from the British Settlement in Pennsylvania* (Philadelphia, 1819) for an account of a community of English professional people.

[2] E. P. Thompson, *The Making of the English Working Class* (London, 1963), p. 423, and chap. 12 for a full examination of working-class 'community'.

[3] Thomas Carlyle, *Past and Present* (London, 1843), bk. III, chap. 2.

his work is meaningless to him, being only a means to other ends. He becomes, in fact, alienated from the product of his labour, and, in due course, alienated from himself and from his fellow-men.[1] He is denied that community with others which is essential for each individual to cultivate his gifts in all directions. This was also what Owen had in mind when he described society as artificial and atomized, and saw his task as the restoration of harmony to the world. George Mudie lamented 'the decay of the social principle' and the loosening of 'the bonds of society'.[2] Harmony was the keynote of the New Moral World, in sharp contrast with the discord of existing society, and Owenites found in music the fullest development of the harmonic ideal. Paul Brown, Josiah Warren and other American communitarians found in music a science of sound, a rational means to the harmonization of mankind.[3] Neither the Owenites nor their contemporaries were able to define the problem of community in psychological terms, but they realized that the implications of industrialism could not be confined to physical changes. Owenism took account of the uniqueness of industrial society and sought to explain what industrialism was doing to the lives of ordinary people by reference to the concept of community.

A very different aspect of community, stemming not from the Tories or the working men but from middle-class industrialists, was also associated with Owenism. This was the idea of community as an instrument of industrial relations. Early factory owners were faced with acute problems of labour shortage and labour discipline, and community provided a solution to some of these difficulties. New Lanark was created by Owen's father-in-law, David Dale, who built the first mill there in 1785.[4] He found that while water power from the Falls of Clyde was cheap and plentiful, labour from the sparsely populated countryside was scarce; and Glasgow (24 miles) and Edinburgh (30 miles) were too far away for convenience. In 1791 he hit upon a partial solution of this problem. Two hundred emigrants to America from the Isle of Skye were left destitute in Greenock when their vessel was driven in by bad weather. Dale offered them immediate employment, which the greater part of them accepted.

[1] Karl Marx, *Economic and Philosophical Manuscripts* (1844), in *Early Writings*, trans. and ed. T. B. Bottomore (New York, 1964), pp. 120–34.

[2] *Economist*, I (1821), 61–2.

[3] T. D. Seymour Bassett, 'The Secular Utopian Socialists', chap. 5, in Donald Drew Egbert and Stow Persons, *Socialism and American Life* (2 vols., Princeton, N.J., 1952), I, 196–7.

[4] Details are from Sir John Sinclair, Bart., *Statistical Account of Scotland* (21 vols., Edinburgh, 1791–99), XV (1795), 34–48; and Thomas Bernard, *Reports of the Society for Bettering the Condition . . . of the Poor*, II (1800), 363–8.

To encourage further recruitment to New Lanark he built houses for two hundred families, and advertised in the Western Highlands: 'Families from any quarter possessed of a good moral character, and having three children fit for work, above nine years of age, are received—supplied with a house at a moderate rent, and the women and children provided with work.' (Poor widows with families were particularly encouraged: 'the greater number of children the woman has, she lives so much the more comfortably; and upon such account alone she is often a tempting object for a second husband'.)[1] The other means of overcoming the labour shortage was the employment of apprenticed pauper children. In 1795 they accounted for 275 of the 1500 inhabitants of New Lanark, and by 1800 the number was 500. Between 1785 and 1797 a total of nearly 3000 children was employed in the mills. Discipline among these children was maintained by long hours of work (6 a.m. to 7 p.m. with half an hour for breakfast and one hour for dinner) and by filling in their scanty leisure with schooling in the evenings and religious worship and instruction on Sundays. But the problem of adult Highlanders was more intractable, and Owen claimed later that when he arrived at New Lanark there was still considerable drunkenness, anti-social behaviour and poor work-habits. Nevertheless, he saw in the community, imperfect as it was, a method of dealing with problems of industrial relations which he had already encountered in the mills in Manchester. The model factory was the germ of Owen's communitarianism.

An interesting speculation is whether Owen would have become a communitarian had he not been a cotton spinner. The idea of the factory colony or community was closely associated with the early machine textile industry, which not only pioneered the technological changes of the first Industrial Revolution but also developed new forms of social organization. New Lanark was by no means unique. David Dale established similar mills and village at Stanley near Perth in 1785, and the Strutts at Belper and Milford, and Arkwright at Cromford did likewise.[2] In New England the textile industry until 1814 developed along similar lines—in small rural mill hamlets, dependent upon water power, and containing houses for the workers and basic community institutions. Even after the textile industry had entered its second phase of steam-driven town factories it retained distinctive community features, as at Lowell in the 1830s and 1840s and Saltaire in the 1850s. A pattern of community development crystallized out of the technological needs of

---

[1] Sinclair, pp. 40–1.
[2] R. S. Fitton and A. P. Wadsworth, *The Strutts and the Arkwrights, 1758–1830* (Manchester, 1958), chap. 8.

5. William Maclure

6. The Social Father.
Robert Owen in 1851

7. Joanna Southcott (by William Sharp, 1812)

the industry and the paternalistic social ethic of the proprietors. 'Must the whole world be converted into a cotton factory?' protested William Hazlitt in his criticism of Owen's plans.[1]

Just as the Cotton Kingdom stretched from America to Lancashire and the Clyde, so the concept of community was nurtured on both sides of the Atlantic. In America, moreover, there were other soils in which communitarianism could grow, notably religious sectarianism, and from this tradition the Owenites profited in several ways. Many of the millennial sects were also communitarian: the Ephrata Community, the Moravian Brethren, the Separatists of Zoar, Jemima Wilkinson's New Jerusalem, the Mormons.[2] With two of the communitarian sects—the Shakers and the Rappites—Owen and his followers were particularly familiar. The communal system of the Shakers ('Gospel Order') emerged from pragmatic experience rather than from an original theory of collectivism. Their withdrawal from the world in order to live a life free from sin had social and economic consequences leading towards communal life. The discipline needed to break down private family life and strengthen celibacy likewise helped in the development of a tightly organized community. For many years the Shakers regarded their socialism as only incidental to the central tenets of their religious faith. But for outsiders Shakerism became the most convincing demonstration that communitarianism would work. The same lesson was drawn from the success of the Harmony Society (Rappites) in their successive communities in Pennsylvania and Indiana. From the 1820s the Shakers and Rappites were the subject of many reports, articles and visitations which cumulatively helped to promote a conscious communitive tradition in America. By 1870 John Humphrey Noyes could declare that 'the Shakers and Rappites . . . are really the pioneers of modern Socialism'.[3]

Owen was interested in the Shakers long before he came to America. In 1818 he published *A Brief Sketch of the Religious Society of People Called Shakers* by W. S. Warder, a Philadelphia Quaker, and later received accounts of the Western Shakers and the Rappites from George Courtauld of Edinburgh.[4] A few days after his first arrival in America in

[1] William Hazlitt, *Political Essays* (London, 1819), review dated 4 August 1816.

[2] The communitive sects and the evolution of a communitarian tradition in America are admirably treated in Bestor, *Backwoods Utopias*, chaps. 1–3. For the Mormons, see Hamilton Gardner, 'Communism among the Mormons', *Quarterly Journal of Economics*, XXXVII (1922), 134–74.

[3] *History of American Socialisms*, p. 669.

[4] Owen, *Life*, I, 242; IA, appendix K; and *New View of Society: Tracts Relative to the Subject* (London, 1818). Courtauld's letter to Owen dated 16 August 1819 was published in the *Glasgow Journal*, 3 November 1819, and also in *Mr Owen's Proposed Arrangements . . .* ['Letters to Ricardo'] (London, 1819), pp. 91–6.

E

November 1824 Owen visited the Shaker community at Niskeyuna, New York and was much impressed. He had known of the Rappites at least since 1815, when John Melish's account of the Harmonists appeared in William Allen's *Philanthropist*. In 1820 he corresponded with Fr. Rapp about his community experiments,[1] and in 1825 bought the settlement of Harmony, Indiana, from the Rappites for his own communitarian experiment of New Harmony. Owenism in America was thus physically and intellectually the inheritor of an established communitarian tradition, and a secular version of sectarian communism.

There was a time when American communitarianism was explained in terms of the frontier, and Owenism, with its centre in a pioneer settlement on the banks of the Wabash, fitted neatly into this pattern. The exigencies of life on the frontier, it was argued, put a premium on communitive forms of social organization; and as these needs disappeared when the settlement was firmly established so the attraction of community life waned. However, a closer analysis of the physical and intellectual record of communitarianism suggests that the frontier theory by itself is inadequate as an explanation.[2] Communitarianism did not originate on the frontier, nor were frontier conditions particularly favourable to its development. The relationship between the growth of communitarianism and the rapid advance of the frontier in the first half of the nineteenth century is to be found in the more general concept of the West as it appeared to contemporaries. Communitarianism was a method of effecting social change by means of experimental communities and as such was in harmony with certain basic assumptions which Americans made about the West. In a period of rapid growth and unbounded confidence in the future, it was possible to believe that small experiments, if successful, could vitally affect the new society which was emerging—and it was urgent to seize this opportunity before it was too late. Older and more stable societies did not present this opportunity, but the West could be shaped by the conscious efforts of the present generation. Just as in Britain there was a widespread feeling among reformers until the 1830s that the changes wrought by industrial capitalism were not permanent, and that it was therefore not too late to be able to build society on alternative principles, so in America there was an even stronger conviction that society in the West was in a state of flux, and that it was possible to fashion new institutions which would ensure a better world

[1] Flower, *op. cit.*, pp. 372–3; John Melish, *Travels in the United States of America* ... (2 vols., Philadelphia, 1812), II, 64–83.

[2] Arthur E. Bestor, Jr., 'Patent Office Models of the Good Society: Some Relationships between Social Reform and Westward Expansion', *American Historical Review*, LVIII (1953), 505–26, from which many of the ideas in this paragraph are derived.

for the future. Owenite communitarianism was acceptable because it shared these assumptions about the nature of social change. And conversely when it was clear that industrial capitalism in Britain and the institutions of individualism in America were so strongly established that they could not be radically affected by small-scale experiments, Owenism lost its rationale.

To Owenites as to other social reformers America seemed to be the ideal place for community experiments. Not only was land cheap and plentiful, but the intellectual climate was believed to be more favourable to social experiment. For British radicals the American Republic was an idea as much as a particular country, an idea to which they felt they belonged by sentiment and conviction. Things which were not possible in the Old World were not necessarily impossible in the New. Owen himself was intoxicated by the potentialities which he discovered shortly after his return to New Harmony in April 1825:

The United States but particularly the States west of the Allegheny Mountains have been prepared in the most remarkable manner for the New System. The principle of union and cooperation . . . is now universally admitted to be far superior to the individual selfish system and all seem prepared . . . to give up the latter and adopt the former. In fact the whole of this country is ready to commence a new empire upon the principle of public property and to discard private property. . . .[1]

Communitarian life in the West seemed to British Owenites an exciting but perfectly practicable adventure. As Robert Dale Owen's party approached New York they sang an ode which one of their number, the architect Stedman Whitwell, had composed:

> Land of the West! we come to thee,
> Far o'er the desert of the sea:
> Under thy white-wing'd canopy,
> Ebor Nova.

> Land of the West! we fly to thee,
> Sick of the old world's sophistry;
> Haste then along the dark blue sea,
> Ebor Nova.

> Land of the West! we rush to thee,
> Home of the brave, soil of the free!
> Huzza! she rises o'er the sea—
> Ebor Nova.[2]

[1] MS. letter, Owen to William Allen, 21 April 1825, Owen Papers, Manchester.
[2] *New Harmony Gazette*, 15 March 1826.

Such romantic enthusiasm found much to feed upon in America, and Owenites had little difficulty in discovering in the New World ideas and attitudes which were highly compatible with the new view of society. The origin of many aspects of Owenism lies in those elements of Enlightenment thought which were also influential in the early years of the Republic, so that a common base for sympathy and understanding was provided. Take for instance the case of agrarianism. In the late eighteenth and early nineteenth centuries radical movements were frequently agrarian, reflecting a concern with land and property reform in pre-industrial societies. The Spencean Philanthropists were the main exponents of this philosophy in Britain and the similarity between Spenceanism and Owenism struck contemporaries.[1] Thomas Evans, in his exposition of Spenceanism, outlined plans for an agrarian republic in which the theme of community ('agrarian fellowship') was prominent, and supported this by reference to the Harmonists.[2] Allen Davenport (1775–1846), a radical shoemaker of London, was an ardent Spencean who embraced Owenism because he regarded it as a step towards a system of community of property such as he had learned from Spence.[3] Owen himself records that in 1819 when he was travelling from London to the North two gentlemen in the coach began to discuss Owenism, and to enlighten them Owen joined in. At the end of the three-hour conversation one of the companions remarked, 'I am sure you are Spence, or else Owen'.[4] The identity of Owenism as a variety of agrarianism was confirmed by Owen's practical plans for communities. Although in theory there was to be a union of manufacturing and agriculture in the villages of cooperation, in practice the emphasis was almost exclusively upon agricultural pursuits and rural handicrafts. No attempt was made to integrate factory production on the scale of New Lanark into any Owenite community. In 1820 Owen envisaged 'a whole population engaged in agriculture, with manufactures as an appendage';[5] by 1842 he proclaimed that a communitarian Britain 'must now become essentially agricultural',[6] and said that he would 'be very sorry ever to have a cotton factory again, for the substantial wealth of the world is only obtained

[1] E.g. *Black Dwarf*, I (1817), 468; *Reformists' Register*, II (1817), 191–2. Also Olive D. Rudkin, *Thomas Spence and his Connections* (London, 1927), pp. 191–203.

[2] Thomas Evans, *Christian Policy, the Salvation of the Empire* (London, 1816), and *Christian Policy in Full Practice among the People of Harmony . . . in Pennsylvania* (London, 1818).

[3] *Cooperative Magazine*, I (1826), 329–30, 356–7. Biographical details in obituaries in the *Northern Star*, 5 December 1846, and the *Reasoner*, II (1847), 16–18.

[4] Owen, *Life*, I, 227.

[5] *Report to the County of Lanark*, in *Life*, IA, 282.

[6] *New Moral World*, 27 August 1843.

from the land'.[1] He had in fact arrived at the same conclusion as other communitarians such as Shaker Evans in America: 'Every commune, to prosper, must be founded, so far as its industry goes, on agriculture. Only the simple labours and manners of a farming people can hold a community together.'[2]

If this agrarian bias in Owenism at first seems hard to reconcile with the image of Owen as one of the great success stories of the Industrial Revolution, a clue may perhaps be found in the parallel development of agrarianism in America.[3] Jefferson's dream of America as a garden and his commitment to 'rural virtue' was the product of a pre-industrial society, but the ideal persisted long after the introduction of the factory system. In the last resort the agrarian's case for a basically agricultural economy rested not on economic considerations but on the desirability of preserving and strengthening the values of husbandry. The agrarian myth in America as elsewhere was in the eighteenth century the product of an intellectual, literary culture, but in the early nineteenth century it became popular and was accepted as part of the national ideology. As long as America was largely a republic of independent farmers agrarian ideals had some clear basis in reality, though the myth was never limited by concrete economic facts. It provided an interpretation of American experience which could take account of technical progress while rejecting industrial capitalism: machinery, for instance, could be beneficially absorbed into the agrarian ideal without any need for the factory system and its attendant urban evils. Communitarians found this ideal attractive. They already believed in the regeneration of America by means of community; now it could be by means of community in a garden.

Within Owenism there was a strong strain of pastoralism, derived largely from eighteenth-century sources, and forming a common bond with other agrarians in America and Britain. Pictorial evidence of this is provided in the illustrations of Owenite communities. A particularly fine example was published in John Minter Morgan's *Hampden in the Nineteenth Century* (1834)[4] (Plate No.17). It purported to be a design for a

---

[1] *New Moral World*, 28 May 1842.

[2] Charles Nordhoff, *Communistic Societies of the United States* (New York, 1875, repr. New York, 1960), pp. 160–1.

[3] See Leo Marx, *The Machine in the Garden* (New York, 1964); Henry Nash Smith, *Virgin Land* (Cambridge, Mass., 1950, repr. New York, 1957), bk. 3; Richard Hofstadter, *Age of Reform* (New York, 1956), chap. 1.

[4] The same illustration was later reproduced in George Fleming's journal, *The Union*, I (1842), 361, as an engraving of Harmony Hall. Other examples were printed in the *Cooperative Magazine*, III (1828), and in John Minter Morgan, *Christian Commonwealth*. See also the engraving after a drawing by R. R. Reinagle reproduced in Podmore, *Robert Owen*, I, 218.

community in Ireland by 'a young artist', but in fact was a highly romantic notion of an ideal community, far removed from the realities of Irish farming. The scene shows a classically moulded landscape, with gentle slopes, woods, rocks and a river in the background. Buildings of stately proportions, looking somewhat like an Oxford or Cambridge college, occupy the left middle distance, and sweeping lawns, dotted with a herd of deer, roll down towards the right of the picture. A building like a Greek temple is visible in the background. In the foreground groups of the happy colonists are amusing themselves in innocent diversions. A group of young females, dressed in simple flowing gowns, sits beneath the trees with their lyres: others converse on the grass or feed the deer. Children are picking flowers and looking at books, while a group of men dressed in short tunics rests upon their spades. Couples stroll beneath the huge trees in a park-like setting. The whole impression is of harmony between man and man and between man and nature, and the enjoyment of leisure and good health amidst beautiful rural surroundings. No hint of industry or the machine mars the arcadian bliss. The engraving is a crude exercise in the same style as J. M. W. Turner, whose romantic pictures were very popular.

The pastoral theme was also developed in literary form by some Owenites, the best example again being John Minter Morgan. At the back of most Owenite plans for community was a utopian vision of a propertyless, equalitarian society; of men working together in the fields, taking from the common stock according to their needs, and engaging in intellectual pursuits in their ample leisure time. In such a society there was neither luxury nor want. Work was a source of satisfaction and independence; and feelings of anger, envy and all uncharitableness were dismissed as unworthy of a rational being. It was this vision which Minter Morgan sought to capture in his Virgilian romances:

At the earliest dawn the bugle was sounded, and answered successively by each community on the borders of the lake. The birds began their songs, as if to welcome the return of light; and the lowing of the cattle and the bleating of the sheep, together with the movements of innumerable animals, appeared as if all nature was reviving. As soon as the sun had ascended the horizon, a scene of varied and wonderful beauty was unfolded. The mountains, no longer presenting an aspect of solitary grandeur, with scarcely an inhabitant in the vicinity, save here and there a lonely shepherd, now wore the appearance of presiding intelligence, and evinced that beings capable of appreciating the sublimity and loveliness of that highly favoured spot had become its fit inhabitants. Numerous flocks of sheep were browsing on the sides of the mountains, herds of deer were seen in various directions, and the cattle were grazing in the richest pastures. The meadows and fields resembled parks and gardens: care and attention had promoted the growth of trees new to the situation, and the plantations were tastefully disposed. The white stone of the buildings seen through the foliage of the trees; the various temples and colonnades, the hanging woods, the intermixture of knolls with crags of rock, and the elegant vessels and boats upon the lake, formed a picture surpassing description. At eight o'clock the bugles were again sounded, announcing the breakfast. About an hour after, the inhabitants came forth:—some repaired to the fields, others to the manufactories (which were invisible, from the buildings being surrounded by plantations, and at sufficient distance to prevent any noisy operation being heard;) while others resorted to the Athenaeums and libraries as their various pursuits directed. In some parts of the mountains, in the colonnades and groves, groups were seen conversing, and many couples in friendly communion. The females and children were engaged as well as the men in agriculture during the summer months; the fields were all cultivated in the garden style, which, together with the custom of having all the population more or less occupied in agricultural exercise, rendered the employment extremely light; nor were they engaged, unless they desired, for any longer time than was absolutely necessary to the preservation of health.[1]

This was the presentation of Owenism as community in a garden. It was an image already familiar in America, part of the myth of the experience of regeneration through the bounty of nature in the New World.[2]

Minter Morgan was aware that in his concept of community certain institutions of competitive society would have to be considerably modified. Of these institutions the most important was the family.[3] In this respect Owenism was not unique. All observers from Engels onwards have noted the preoccupation of communitarians and socialists with questions of the family, sexual relationships and the emancipation of women, and no subject was more calculated to bring down the opprobrium of society at large. The attack on the family, however unpopular it might be, could not be shirked, because it was central to the whole communitarian position. The goal of the New Harmony experiment, said Owen, was 'to change from the individual to the social system; from single families with separate interests to communities of many families with one interest'.[4] Owen saw the family as the main bastion of private property and the guardian of all those qualities of individualism and self-

---

[1] Minter Morgan, *Revolt of the Bees*, pp. 50–2.

[2] See Leo Marx, *op. cit.*, p. 228.

[3] In this discussion of the role of the family I am much indebted for ideas and suggestions to Professor William R. Taylor of the University of Wisconsin.

[4] *New Harmony Gazette*, 1 October 1825.

interest to which he was opposed: 'separate interests and individual family arrangements with private property are essential parts of the existing irrational system. They must be abandoned with the system. And instead thereof there must be scientific associations of men, women and children, in their usual proportions, from about four or five hundred to about two thousand, arranged to be as one family.'[1] The fragmentation and disharmony which Owenites deplored in competitive society they attributed largely to the institution of the private family. Owen regarded the family as a fundamentally divisive force, much more so than class. Hence he attacked the family and refused to regard class divisions as primary. Protected from the world at large by strong walls of legal and religious custom the family seemed to him an autonomous and alien element in society. It served to isolate men from each other, and to breed loneliness and self-centredness. Moreover, it was an organ of tyranny, by which the wife was subjected to, and in fact made the property of her husband. She was condemned to a life of petty domestic drudgery and endless child-bearing.

This feeling that the family was unsatisfactory in its role in the early nineteenth century was not confined to communitarians. William Cobbett lamented the change from the old farm house in which the farmer's family and his servants lived together as a unit, to the new style farm house in which middle-class notions of gentility set the farmer's family apart from their employees, thus emphasizing distinctions and differences.[2] In a quite different sphere the divisive nature of the family was the theme of many Victorian novels: with the man out at work all day in the commercial world while his wife remains at home, the couple become strangers to each other: only when he goes bankrupt does the man at last discover his home. Community was an attempt to remedy this failure of the family. To John Humphrey Noyes it was clear that 'the main idea' of Owenism (as also of Fourierism) was 'the enlargement of home—the extension of family union beyond the little man-and-wife circle to large corporations'.[3] The logic of this position was apparent to intelligent Owenite working men: believing in the paramountcy of environmental conditions they realized that their rude little homes were a restrictive and circumscribing influence, and that in community they would have a means of breaking out of this: 'we can afford to live in palaces as well as the rich . . . were we only to adopt the principle of combination, the

[1] Owen, *Book of the New Moral World*, pt. 6 (London, 1844), p. 48.
[2] William Cobbett, *Rural Rides* (London, 1830), entry for 20 October 1825.
[3] Noyes, *op. cit.*, p. 23.

patriarchal principle of large families, such families as that of Abraham which consisted of two thousand persons.'[1]

The truly radical nature of the communitarian critique of the family was well appreciated by Owen's contemporaries. Marx and Engels praised him for advocating the abolition of the family as much as they condemned him for neglecting the class struggle.[2] And the hysterical tone of the abuse which was poured out in 1840 suggests that the Owenites were attacking something held to be very fundamental and sacred.[3] Closely associated with Owenite plans for familial reform were attacks on the marriage system and the advocacy of birth control, so that the 'horrible abominations' of Owenism could easily be used to smear the concept of community. Mr Owen's community system was nothing but 'a flagrant immorality', a system for the prostitution of women, and a degradation of all the higher instincts which raise man above the brutes. Owen's denunciation of the institution of marriage followed from his views on the family: he was not, as his opponents charged, advocating sexual promiscuity but was attacking an institution which had to be broken before the New Moral World could be established. Unfortunately, his fundamentally sensible views on marriage were obscured by his desire to blame the clergy, to attribute all ills to the 'marriage of the priesthood'.[4] Christian marriage, he felt, reinforced the isolation, privateness and secrecy of the family in relation to society, and within the family it strengthened prudery and false shame and prevented a happy, frank sexual relationship between the partners. In Owen's view the basis of marriage could only be the affection of the two spouses: a marriage without love was prostitution. Celibacy he regarded as unnatural and likely to lead to disease of body and mind. The indissolubility of marriage was a prime cause of personal unhappiness and social evil, and for the New

---

[1] Speech of the Owenite lecturer, Charles Morris, in James E. Smith, *The Coming Man* (London, 1873), I, 243.

[2] *Communist Manifesto*, chap. III, pt. 3.

[3] E.g. 'Woman and the Social System', *Fraser's Magazine*, June 1840, pp. 689–702.

[4] Owen's views on marriage are set out in his *Lectures on the Marriages of the Priesthood of the Old Immoral World* (Leeds, 1835). See also 'Address of Robert Owen to the People of the United States' in the New York *Daily Tribune*, 24 September 1844. However Owenites were not always very tactful in expressing their views on marriage and sexual morality. For instance the *Crisis*, 4 January 1834, carried an advertisement by an Owenite for a wife, whose three requirements were 40 years of age, £50 per annum and womanhood. To which the editor added, 'virginity, we suppose, is not necessary—no Socialist could insist upon it'.

Marriages were sometimes performed at Owenite institutions, using the civil ceremony. A description of such a marriage at the John Street Institute, London, is given in the *New Moral World*, 29 March 1845.

61

Moral World Owen devised a system of carefully controlled divorce.[1] Owen's exact role in the birth control movement is somewhat obscure, but he was undoubtedly involved in it from 1823.[2] William Thompson advocated contraception in his treatment of population problems in communities:[3] and Robert Dale Owen's *Moral Physiology* (New York, 1830) was the pioneer tract on birth control in the United States. In contrast to the fears, frustrations and sexual tyranny characteristic of the private family system, argued Owenites, community promised an immense increase in sexual happiness. With an extended choice of partners, early (though socially regulated) marriage, removal of the fear of large numbers of children, and treatment of women as equals with men, a truly 'natural' system of personal relationships would be established.

The community element in Owenism thus had several different roots and references. Community in Britain and America was a recognizable concept, sufficiently familiar to be acceptable as a possible solution to a number of different social and economic problems—labour shortage, feelings of alienation, marriage familism. In the early decades of the nineteenth century the concept of communitarianism as a method of effecting social change appeared feasible. But in Britain after the 1840s and in America after the Civil War it ceased to be meaningful. The growth of large-scale industry as the dominant economic pattern and the hardening of the social institutions of capitalism made efforts at change through small communities seem inadequate. What had earlier been regarded as the special virtues of communitarianism—its voluntary, small-scale, self-contained nature and its non-political, anti-statist approach—became its defects. The basic characteristics of communitarianism no longer appeared relevant to the main problems of society; and the later socialist movement of the 1880s, in so far as it strove towards some of the same goals as Owenism, had to adopt quite other means. Concepts of community in Britain and America were similar in those aspects which stemmed from Enlightenment thought or from the problems of early industrialism. But there were differences when community ideas had other

---

[1] Regulations for divorce and marriage were given by Owen in an address at the Charlotte Street Institute in 1833—*Lectures on the Marriages of the Priesthood*, 4th edn. (Leeds, 1840), appendix. See also Bronterre [James Bronterre O'Brien], *Buonarroti's History of Babeuf's Conspiracy for Equality* (London, 1836), p. 441.

[2] Norman E. Himes, 'The Place of John Stuart Mill and of Robert Owen in the History of English Neo-Malthusianism', *Quarterly Journal of Economics*, XLII (1928), 627–40; *Medical History of Contraception* (Baltimore, Md., 1936). There is a useful bibliographical review by John Peel, 'Birth Control and the British Working-Class Movement', in Society for the Study of Labour History, *Bulletin*, no. 7 (Autumn, 1963), pp. 16–22.

[3] *Inquiry*, pp. 547–9; *Practical Directions for Communities*, pp. 229–48.

origins: for instance, religious sectarianism contained a much stronger bent towards community in America than in Britain, and the paternalistic community feeling of the English squirearchy was not indigenous in America. Owenism was able to draw upon these different traditions impartially—hence the heterogeneous nature of the Owenite body. As in the case of millennialism, the British and American Owenites played a mutually reinforcing role as communitarians. The Americans accepted Owen's (largely British) ideas of villages of cooperation, and the British Owenites waxed enthusiastic over American sectarian communities, especially the Shakers. Perhaps because of the greater strength of the communitarian tradition in America Owenism was faced with stronger rivalry than in Britain. Thus in the communitarian revival of the 1840s Owenism in America was eclipsed by Fourierism, whereas in Britain Owenism remained the dominant communitarian doctrine, despite the attempted introduction of Fourierism and Saint-Simonism. That Owenism should have had a similar following in two such different societies as the British and American is partly explicable by the nature of its communitarian element. Ignoring political action and minimizing economic problems, communitarians concentrated on social and psychological questions, which provided a sufficient bond between reformers who, on both sides of the Atlantic, were in revolt against the dominant orthodoxies of their respective societies. For Americans Owenism offered communitarianism without the trappings of religious sectarianism: in Britain Owenite concepts of community provided a remedy for some of the tensions, social and personal, arising from early industrialism.

2 The Economy of Cooperation

The economic doctrines of Owenism are those which have received most attention from an older generation of labour historians, whose object was usually to show some link with or forecast of the later socialist movement in Britain.[1] For such a purpose the Owenite critique of capitalism and formulation of an alternative theory to orthodox political

---

[1] Useful expositions of the economic doctrines of Owenite socialism will be found in Max Beer, *History of British Socialism*; G. D. H. Cole, *History of Socialist Thought: The Forerunners*; Esther Lowenthal, *The Ricardian Socialists* (New York, 1911); Anton Menger, *The Right to the Whole Produce of Labour*, trans. M. E. Tanner, with introduction and bibliography by H. S. Foxwell (London, 1899). An attempt at summarizing Owen's basic economic theories is made in Beatrice Webb, *The Cooperative Movement in Great Britain* (London, 1891), chap. 1.

economy were very useful, the more so as parts of them were echoed later in Marx's works. In fact, the number of Owenites who made original contributions to economic theory was very small, and the economic content of Owenism can be traced to a few key sources which were drawn upon many times over.

After Owen himself, whose main economic theories were stated in his 1820 *Report to the County of Lanark*, the chief Owenite theoreticians were William Thompson and John Gray. Thompson (1775–1833)[1] was an Irish landowner, of a strongly radical and atheistical turn of mind, whose first attempts at social amelioration among his tenants at Glandore were similar to those of Archibald James Hamilton at Dalzell. A friend and disciple of Bentham, Thompson was also indebted to Godwin, and first came into contact with Owen during the Irish tour of 1822. Thompson's *Inquiry into the Principles of the Distribution of Wealth*, published in 1824 and reprinted in 1850 and 1869, was his *magnum opus*, and together with his *Labor Rewarded* (1827) and *Practical Directions for the Establishment of Communities* (1830) made him the most influential of the Owenite socialists. Shortly after Thompson's *Inquiry*, John Gray's *Lecture on Human Happiness* (1825) supplied the need for a more concise and pungent statement of anti-capitalist economics, and the pamphlet was reprinted three times in Philadelphia. Gray (1799–1883) was in a London wholesale business but left it to join the Orbiston community.[2] However, he was so disillusioned with the Orbistonians that he did not join them but instead published *A Word of Advice to the Orbistonians*,[3] and thereafter established himself in Edinburgh as the publisher of a local newspaper. By 1831 he had dissociated himself from Owen, and later became a currency reformer.[4] A third contributor to the body of Owenite economic theory, though coming too late to influence the early Owenite movement, was the Leeds printer, John Francis Bray (1809–1897), whose *Labour's Wrongs and Labour's Remedy: or the Age of Might and the Age of Right* (Leeds, 1839) was a powerful statement of the socialist demand that every man should possess the whole produce of

[1] Richard K. P. Pankhurst, *William Thompson* (London, 1954).

[2] Janet Kimball, *The Economic Doctrines of John Gray, 1799–1883* (Washington, D.C., 1948).

[3] Reprinted in *The Social System* (Edinburgh, 1831), appendix.

[4] See the letter from John Gray, 11 April 1832, in reply to an invitation to attend the third Cooperative Congress, printed in *Proceedings of the Third Cooperative Congress . . . reported and edited by William Carpenter* (n.p., 1832), pp. 124–5; and *Proceedings of the Fourth Cooperative Congress . . . reported . . . by W. Pare* (Salford, Manchester, 1832), pp. 40–1. His theories of monetary reform are set out in *An Efficient Remedy for the Distress of all Nations* (Edinburgh and London, 1842); *The Currency Question* (Edinburgh and London, 1847); and *Lectures on the Nature and Use of Money* (Edinburgh, 1848).

his labour.[1] Chapter two of this work was reprinted as a penny pamphlet and used in the Owenite propaganda of the 1840s.[2] But Bray was disappointed that his book was not more popular, and in 1842 he returned to America, where he had originally been raised.

A second group of Owenite writers was concerned to popularize rather than make original contributions to socialist economic theory. Members of this group quoted Owen, Thompson and Gray and added their own special appeal or twist. Abram Combe, whose work and writings are described later, was of this order, and the parable of the cistern in his *Metaphorical Sketches of the Old and New Systems* (1823) was an ingenious attempt to present the question of cooperation versus competition in a lighter vein than Owen was capable of. John Minter Morgan's *Revolt of the Bees* (1826) made fanciful use of the old apiarian allegory in a tract which went through five editions. In the pages of the *Economist* (1821–22) George Mudie provided a weekly forum for the discussion of Owenite theory in terms intelligible to a London printer. Mudie was a Scots journalist and printer who came to London about 1820. He was active in promoting a working-class community at Spa Fields and later went to Orbiston.[3] Other Owenites also took upon themselves the task of putting their thoughts on paper—William Pare[4] and William Hawkes Smith[5] of Birmingham, and, a little later, James Hole of Leeds.[6]

There were also several writers who were not Owenites but whose works were influential in Owenite circles. Such was Charles Hall, the Spencean doctor whose work was discussed in the *Economist* and reprinted by Minter Morgan.[7] The pseudonymous 'Piercy Ravenstone'[8] and

---

[1] The main study of Bray's life and work is H. J. Carr, 'A Critical Exposition of the Social and Economic Ideas of John Francis Bray, and an Estimate of his Influence upon Karl Marx' (unpublished Ph.D. thesis, University of London, 1943). Carr's work largely replaces earlier work on Bray by John Edwards, Esther Lowenthal, and M. F. Joliffe. See also the introduction by M. F. Lloyd-Prichard to J. F. Bray, *A Voyage from Utopia*.

[2] *The Labourer's Library*, no. 4 (Leeds, 1842), published by the Owenite printer, Joshua Hobson.

[3] All the available biographical details have been gathered together in W. H. G. Armytage, 'George Mudie: Journalist and Utopian', *Notes and Queries*, vol. 202 (1957), 214–16.

[4] William Pare, *An Address delivered at the Opening of the Birmingham Cooperative Society, November 17, 1828* (Birmingham, 1828); and *The Claims of Capital and Labour* (London, 1854). Also the *Birmingham Cooperative Herald* (Birmingham, 1829–30), edited by Pare.

[5] See below, p. 74.

[6] James Hole, *Lectures on Social Science and the Organization of Labor* (London, 1851).

[7] See p. 33.

[8] Piercy Ravenstone, *A Few Doubts as to the Correctness of Some Opinions generally entertained on . . . Population and Political Economy* (London, 1821); and *Thoughts on the Funding System* (London, 1824).

Thomas Rowe Edmonds (1803–1889)[1] may or may not have been read by Owenites, but their anti-capitalist arguments supported much of the Owenite critique. For Thomas Hodgskin the evidence is much stronger.[2] His *Labour Defended against the Claims of Capital* (1825) prompted Thompson's *Labor Rewarded* (1827), and Hodgskin's lectures at the London Mechanics' Institute ensured that his views were widely known among that class of intelligent London artisans from which Owen drew a following in the 1820s and early 1830s.

In America the number of Owenite writers on economic subjects was small, and they drew largely upon the work of Owen, Thompson and Gray. Only two American Owenites can properly be classified as Ricardian socialists, and one of those was an immigrant from Britain. Langton Byllesby (1789–1871) was a Philadelphia printer, whose *Observations on the Sources and Effects of Unequal Wealth* (New York, 1826)[3] used the standard Owenite criteria for analysing capitalist society and relied heavily on Thompson and Owen. Robert Dale Owen's pamphlet, *Wealth and Misery* (New York, 1830),[4] was a series of six essays in which the failure of capitalism in Britain to secure an equitable distribution of wealth was used as a warning to America. Like most Owenites, Dale Owen applied his economic analysis impartially to Britain and America, since both societies were based on competition and commerce. Josiah Warren (1798–1874), an enthusiastic Owenite for two years at New Harmony, took the doctrine of unequal exchange of labour and developed it into the central principle of his *Equitable Commerce* (1846).[5] However, the result was not a variety of Owenism but the foundation of a native anarchism. As in Britain, there were other economic reformers whose work was probably read by Owenites—Thomas Skidmore, George Henry Evans, Lewis Masquerier and their agrarian and currency-reform disciples.[6] But the most completely indigenous American version

---

[1] Thomas Rowe Edmonds, *Practical, Moral and Political Economy most conducive to Individual Happiness and National Power* (London, 1828).

[2] For his life and bibliography see Elie Halévy, *Thomas Hodgskin*, ed. and trans. A. J. Taylor (London, 1956).

[3] See Joseph Dorfman, *The Economic Mind in American Civilization, 1606–1865* (London, 1947), II, 638–41; and Dorfman's Introduction to the reissue of Byllesby, *Observations* (New York, 1961). A Marxist interpretation of Blatchly, Byllesby, Maclure, Skidmore and others is given in David Harris, *Socialist Origins in the United States: American Forerunners of Marx, 1817–1832* (Assen, The Netherlands, 1966).

[4] Published originally in the *New Harmony Gazette*, 8 November–13 December 1826; and reprinted in the *Cooperative Magazine*, III (1828), 32–5, 59–63.

[5] William Bailie, *Josiah Warren* (Boston, 1906); and Lockwood, *The New Harmony Movement*, chap. 21.

[6] Dorfman, *op. cit.*, II, chap. 24.

of Owenism—that of Paul Brown—was social and educational rather than economic.[1]

The Owenite economists have usually been labelled by historians 'Ricardian socialists', on the grounds that their basic tenet of the labour theory of value was derived from Ricardo.[2] Although Owen was on friendly terms with Ricardo and probably familiar with his work, there is little evidence that either Bray or Thompson was indebted to Ricardo. The Owenites regarded the orthodox political economists as among their chief opponents, and were only too well aware of the difficulties of iconoclasm in the face of an obsessively dominant orthodoxy, from which any deviation was dismissed as mere 'vulgar error'. After Torrens's authoritative refutation of Owen in the *Edinburgh Review* of October 1819, Owenite socialism was simply ignored by orthodox political economists. As William Thompson complained, 'the leaders of the school of Competitive Political Economy' refused to discuss 'the system of Cooperative political economy'.[3] Even John Stuart Mill, who as a young man had debated with Thompson and other Owenites,[4] neglected their views in favour of Saint-Simon and Fourier when he came to examine socialism later. Nevertheless, the Owenites insisted that their system was not an offshoot from but an alternative to orthodox political economy. It was not that they had fallen into 'vulgar error', but that having seen the fruit of early competitive industrialism they violently disliked it and rejected the basic assumptions of its ideology. The significance for Owenism of the Ricardian socialists was that, much more strongly than Owen himself, they emphasized the importance of the economic element. Whereas Owen was sometimes reluctant to see social institutions as infrastructures and referred to 'social arrangements' which he considered to be the product of men's ideas, the Ricardian socialists accepted economic relationships as the basis of social institutions. From Ricardian socialism Owenites acquired tools for a deeper probing of economic and social ills than was provided by Owen's concentration on the competitive ethos as a prime cause of economic disorder, and his analysis in terms of moral evil.

---

[1] Paul Brown, *Twelve Months in New Harmony* (Cincinnati, Ohio, 1827); *A Disquisition on Faith* (Washington, D.C., 1822); *An Enquiry Concerning the Nature, End, and Practicability of a Course of Philosophical Education* (Washington, D.C., 1822); *A Dialogue on Commonwealths* (Cincinnati, Ohio, 1828); *The Radical: an Advocate of Equality* (Albany, N.Y., 1834).

[2] See Mark Blaug, *Ricardian Economics: a Historical Study* (New Haven, Conn., 1958), pp. 140–50.

[3] Thompson, *Labor Rewarded*, p. 46.

[4] John Stuart Mill, *Autobiography* (London, 1873), 2nd edn., pp. 123–5.

Owenites, even when they thought they were dealing in strictly economic categories, always had great difficulty in avoiding entanglement in moral or non-economic concepts. This was hardly surprising in that their motivation was moral indignation or a concern for justice and natural rights. A favourite starting point for Owenite discussions was the contrast between 'wealth and misery' or the paradox of 'poverty in the midst of plenty'. Owen's assertion that 'in the midst of the most ample means to create wealth, all are in poverty, or in imminent danger from the effects of poverty upon others'[1] was treated as axiomatic. And with unemployment and poor rates at the level of the years 1815–21 it was not difficult to win assent to the second half of the proposition. The extent of the new wealth was perhaps not quite so readily discerned, and it was here that Owen's calculations became impressive. He concluded that if the ratio of total productive power to the population in 1792 were taken as 1 to 1, by 1817 the ratio was over 12 to 1; in a period of only twenty-five years the productive capacity per head in Great Britain had increased twelve times.[2] Or, as Robert Dale Owen put it, Britain's scientific productive power was equal to the manual labour of 400 million working adults.[3]

The potentiality of material abundance was fundamental to the Owenite case for several reasons. In the first place it provided an answer to Malthus, for it showed that productive capacity (both industrial and agricultural) could rise faster than population. Second, it meant that Owenism, despite some elements of backward-looking agrarianism and paternalism, did not turn its back on the Industrial Revolution nor become what Marx and Engels dubbed feudal socialism, 'ludicrous in its effect through total incapacity to comprehend the march of modern history'.[4] Third, it underpinned Owen's vision of the millennium. For the first time in human history the necessary base for the good environment which would be productive of happy human beings was attainable: the possibility of happiness was for the first time within the reach of all men. The key period in this development, Owen told the workers and manufacturers, was during the French revolutionary war when 'you passed a boundary never before reached in the history of man: you passed the regions of poverty arising from necessity and entered those of permanent abundance'.[5] For Owenites the failure of classical political economy

[1] *Report to the County of Lanark*, in Owen, *Life*, IA, 286.
[2] *Two Memorials on Behalf of the Working Classes* (1818), in Owen, *Life*, IA, 214–15.
[3] Robert Dale Owen, *Wealth and Misery*, p. 4.
[4] Marx and Engels, *Communist Manifesto* (London, 1934 edn.), p. 29.
[5] 'Address of Mr Owen to the Agriculturists, Mechanics, and Manufacturers, both Masters and Operatives, of Great Britain and Ireland', *Cooperative Magazine*, II (1827), 438.

8. James E. (Shepherd) Smith

9. James Pierrepont Greaves

10. John Finch

to appreciate the revolutionary significance of this change invalidated its teachings. Adam Smith lived and wrote before this new mechanical age was perfected, argued Owen, and therefore his writings do not deal with its pressing problems. The political economists continue to deal with problems of increasing wealth, whereas the real problem is what to do with an excess of wealth which now injures all classes, producing the same effects as poverty did hitherto. Classical political economy, felt the Owenites, did not really get to grips with the contradiction between a vast increase in productive capacity and the distress of 1810, 1815–16, 1818–19 and 1825.

In contrast, Owenite economists concentrated on what Owen called 'the paralysing effects of superabundance', which they traced, in the short run, to machinery. The Owenites were not by any means unique in holding that there was substance in the complaint of labouring men that machinery put them out of work. Ricardo, in his *Principles* took it as axiomatic, and Dr Andrew Ure, the apologist of the factory system, said bluntly that 'it is the constant aim and tendency of every improvement in machinery to supersede human labour altogether, or to diminish its cost'.[1] But whereas the orthodox political economists were content to accept this as the inevitable result of the functioning of natural economic laws, Owenites protested that it was not inevitable but solely the result of the competitive system, and that given a 'rational' arrangement of society machinery could be a blessing instead of a curse. In all Owenite plans for community, machinery was posited as the basis for reduced hours of labour and the elimination of heavy or disagreeable types of work. Under the competitive system, however, machinery led to a devaluation of human labour; some men were directly displaced by labour-saving machines, and the wages of those remaining in work were forced down by the reservoir of unemployed. The market value of labour, it was argued, depends on its scarcity, and machinery diminishes that scarcity, giving almost unlimited power to the employer to cheapen production including the cost of labour.[2] This element in the Ricardian socialist analysis harmonized with the experience and reflections of people who were far from the ranks of the Owenites but who were uneasy about the nostrums of the orthodox political economists. Thus the Reverend William Edmeads, searching for an explanation of unemployment in 1818, found in the concept of the 'abridgement of labour' a countervailing principle which operated in the economy to nullify any

[1] Andrew Ure, *Philosophy of Manufactures* (London, 1835), p. 23.
[2] *Effects of Machinery on Manual Labour and on the Distribution of the Produce of Industry* (London, 1832), reprinted from *Carpenter's Political Magazine*.

F

optimistic assurances in classical economic theory.[1] Not only machinery but every scientific improvement in agriculture and industry seemed to him to contribute to the same end, namely the depression of wages to a minimum. As with other aspects of his thought, Owen's theory of the de-valuation of labour was drawn from a fairly widely acceptable set of contemporary assumptions.

Unlike the Reverend Edmeads's concept, however, the Owenite view of the effects of machinery was linked with a general labour theory of value, which was the basis of most Owenite economic thinking. The theory that labour is the source and measure of value was most commonly attributed to Ricardo, though whether the Owenites took their views from him directly is somewhat problematical. Charles Hall's *Effects of Civilisation* (1805), which contained a version of the theory, predated Ricardo's *Principles* (1817) and was read by Owenites. Even more sig-nificantly, John Locke had based his theory of the rights of property on the fruits of labour, thereby strengthening a philosophical or psycho-logical basis of the labour theory of value. Quite apart from the economic argument there was thus an argument from natural right, which could be, and was, presented by Ricardian socialists such as Hodgskin, and which was repeated in popular form in Owenite journals. If labour is the source of all wealth, and men exchange their products according to the amount of labour embodied in them, it needed little theory to con-vince working men that they had a right to the whole produce of their labour—and, as a corollary, that if they were poor it must be because they were not receiving the full value of what they produced. Col-quhoun's calculation that 'more than one fifth part of the whole com-munity are unproductive labourers, and . . . these labourers receive from the aggregate labour of the productive class about one third of the new property created annually' was widely quoted by Owenites.[2] No argu-ment in the Owenite armoury was better calculated to appeal to working men than that which told them they were unjustly exploited; none was more deceptively simple, for example, than the following specimen by Dr

[1] Rev. William Edmeads, *Thoughts on the Results of Various Inventions for the Abridge-ment of Labour* (Maidstone, 1818). Cf. also contemporary suggestions for the taxation of machine products, as in *Machinery versus Manual Labour: A Letter to the Right Hon. Lord Grey, wherein is shown the Expediency of Taxing the Produce of Machinery . . . by A Manufacturer* (Loughborough, 1830); and the formation of 'Anti-Machinery Societies' to petition Parliament, as in *Plain Sense and Reason: Letters to the Present Generation on the Unrestrained Use of Modern Machinery* (Norwich, 1831).

[2] Though omitting Colquhoun's justification of these unproductive labourers as neces-sary 'to promote, invigorate and render more productive the labour of the creating classes'. Colquhoun, *Treatise on the Wealth, Power and Resources of the British Empire* (London, 1814), p. 109.

William King (1786–1865), a Brighton physician and editor of *The Cooperator*:

The working classes have no idea of the real value of their own labour. When a man has done a week's work, and received his wages for it, he thinks he has received the whole value of his work: but this is by no means the case. He has not received above one-fourth part of the real value. He has made a bargain with his master, that he will give a week's work for a certain sum of money. Whether this be much or little, it is called, vulgarly, the value of work. But this is merely a common phrase. It is a very indefinite one, and from long habit, has become confounded in the minds of the working classes, with the whole value of the work done. If wages were the whole value of the work, how could the master take the work to market, sell it for more money than he gave for it, and grow rich upon the profit, while the workman grows poor upon the wages? This would be impossible. Therefore it is evident that the workman does not get the whole value of his work; and it is also evident that if he did he would grow rich, just as the master does.[1]

King's paragraph embodies the two main doctrines in the Owenite labour theory of value: the right to the whole produce of labour, and the theory of unequal exchanges. In some form or other these tenets are recognizable in most Owenite statements on economic questions, though there are several varieties and inconsistencies. Sophisticated economic theory was not a strong point of Owenites, and they were usually content with a labour theory of value which was vaguely felt to be derived from juridical right. Owen, in his *Report to the County of Lanark*, argued that 'manual labour, properly directed, is the source of all wealth' and 'the natural standard of value is, in principle, human labour'. He did not, however, claim for the labourer the whole produce of his labour, but only 'his fair proportion'. William Thompson agreed that labour was the sole source and measure of wealth, and ought to possess the whole product of its exertions; but this could not be effected for individual labourers, only collectively in communities.[2] George Mudie thought that in communities 'every individual will enjoy or possess the undivided fruits of his own labour', but then added 'except that portion which may be paid as rent or interest'.[3] More extreme Owenite socialists condemned all appropriation as unjust and rent as robbery.[4]

---

[1] *The Cooperator*, no. 3 (1 July 1828), reprinted in T. W. Mercer, *Cooperation's Prophet* (Manchester, 1947). See also Sidney Pollard, *Dr William King of Ipswich: A Cooperative Pioneer*, Cooperative College Papers, no. 6 (Loughborough, 1959).

[2] Thompson, *Inquiry*, pp. 6, 178; *Labor Rewarded*, pp. 13, 37, 94.

[3] *Economist*, I (1821), 305.

[4] John Watts, *Facts and Fictions of Political Economists* (Manchester, 1842). Watts was an Owenite lecturer at the Manchester Hall of Science.

The moral overtones in Owenite economic thinking come out clearly in discussion of the theory of equitable exchange. In the so-called bargain between capital and labour the injustice to the labourer cried out for redress and the capitalist appeared as an exploiter. Owenites were careful to blame the system and not individual capitalists, but the tone was moral indignation rather than dispassionate economic analysis. John Francis Bray presented the most powerful case against what he termed unequal exchanges:

The subject of exchanges is one on which too much attention cannot be bestowed by the productive classes; for it is more by the infraction of this ... condition by the capitalist, than by all other causes united, that inequality of condition is produced and maintained, and the working man offered up, bound hand and foot, a sacrifice upon the altar of Mammon.

From the very nature of labour and exchange, strict justice not only requires that all exchangers should be mutually, but that they should likewise be equally, benefited. Men have only two things which they can exchange with each other, namely, labour, and the produce of labour; therefore, let them exchange as they will, they merely give, as it were, labour for labour. If a just system of exchanges were acted upon, the value of all articles would be determined by the entire cost of production; and equal values should always exchange for equal values. ...

We have heretofore acted upon ... [a] most unjust system of exchanges—the workmen have given the capitalist the labour of a whole year, in exchange for the value of only half a year—and from this, and not from the assumed inequality of bodily and mental powers in individuals, has arisen the inequality of wealth and power which at present exists around us. It is an inevitable condition of inequality of exchanges—of buying at one price and selling at another—that capitalists shall continue to be capitalists, and working men be working men—the one a class of tyrants and the other a class of slaves—to eternity.[1]

'Labour's remedy' would be found through a system of equality of exchanges, realizable in joint-stock communities which Bray advocated as a half-way measure towards the ultimate goal of full community of possessions.

To ensure equitable exchange Owenites proposed schemes of labour notes based on labour time, thus institutionalizing Owen's demand that human labour, not money, be made the standard of value. At this point Owenism came close to being a variety of currency reform, and in fact this was the path which some Owenites eventually followed. John Gray came to believe not only that the prevailing system of exchange was

[1] John Francis Bray, *Labour's Wrongs*, pp. 48–9.

unjust but that it also limited production, and that in order to make production the cause of demand it would be necessary to abolish money and substitute labour notes. When he parted company with Owenism this aspect of his 'social system' gradually became more central, until in his later writings he espoused currency reform as the sole remedy for all national ills.[1] Similarly in America Josiah Warren, after he left New Harmony, clung to his principle of 'labor for labor' and instituted an experimental time store in Cincinnati in 1827. His *Equitable Commerce* attracted the attention of the Birmingham Owenite, William Pare,[2] who had been a chief promoter of labour exchanges in that city and an associate of the currency reformers, Thomas Attwood and George Frederick Muntz. Long after other aspects of Owenism had lost ground, a legacy of unorthodox financial theory remained.

Gray's remarks on the limitation of production indicate one further characteristic of Owenite economic thought. Like the 'Birmingham School' of Attwood and Muntz,[3] Owenism contained elements of a theory of under-consumption. 'The reason why so many are poor', argued Gray 'is that there now exists an unnatural limit to production.'[4] This limit is set by competition. In commercial society production is fettered by inadequate demand, whereas the institutions of society should be geared to making demand keep pace with production. Thompson similarly argued that the depression of wages to subsistence level destroyed incentive to higher production by labouring men, and the low level of their consumption caused by inadequate purchasing power put a ceiling on production. Trade depressions and commercial crises resulted not from over-production but from under-consumption. 'What are the multitudes of paupers but a large portion of the consumers?', asked George Mudie.[5] If the labourer were given the full product of his labour (to which he is justly entitled), argued Owenites, his purchasing power would be increased, production would boom, and crises would be avoided. But under the 'arrangements' of competitive society the vast potential of the New Industry was frustrated and the opportunity of an enormous expansion of the sum of human happiness was not taken.

It was to this point—the neglect of the goal of happiness by orthodox

[1] Karl Marx, *Poverty of Philosophy*, trans. Harry Quelch (London, 1900), appendix II, 'John Gray and his Theory of Labour Notes'.

[2] William Pare, *Equitable Commerce as Practised in the Equity Villages of the United States* (London, 1856).

[3] S. G. Checkland, 'The Birmingham Economists, 1815–1850', *Economic History Review*, 2nd series, I (1948), 1–19.

[4] Gray, *Lecture on Human Happiness*, p. 60.

[5] *Economist*, I (1821), 76.

political economists—that Owenites continually returned. They were shocked by the blunt statement of the Professor of Political Economy at Oxford, Nassau Senior, that 'It is not with happiness, but with wealth, that I am concerned as a political economist'. In his *Report to the County of Lanark* Owen assumed that the science of political economy included arrangements for the promotion of maximum happiness in society: but it soon became apparent that Owenites could not use the term political economy without risk of confusion unless they qualified it in some way, like Thompson in his *Inquiry* who referred to 'political economy, rightly understood'. The problem is neatly documented in the works of William Hawkes Smith, a Birmingham Unitarian and admirer of Owen.[1] In his 1834 pamphlet on *The Errors of the Social System* Smith made the familiar Owenite plea that political economy should be concerned with the distribution as well as the production of wealth, and used the term 'enlightened *political* economy' to designate his own views. In 1838 (*Letters on the State and Prospects of Society*) he tried using a distinction between 'aristocratic' and 'democratic' political economy. But the following year he abandoned 'political economy' altogether, and in *Letters on Social Science* (1839) used 'social science' to describe the study of the economic and social means of promoting maximum happiness.

A large part of the difficulty which Owenites had in challenging classical political economy was caused by their refusal to be limited by its declared boundaries. The economy of cooperation (probably the most useful term in the Owenite vocabulary for this purpose by the 1830s) was both more and less than a theory of economics: more in that it was an attempt to reassert the values of an older, pre-capitalist concept of 'moral economy' which was felt to be threatened: less in that it was not a coherent and complete theory of the functioning of an economy. The concerns of Owenism were not those which were primary or central in classical political economy, so that a dialogue between the champions of the two philosophies was not particularly fruitful—as John Stuart Mill discovered in his discussions with the members of the London

---

[1] Biographical detail is scarce but Hawkes Smith appears to have been a man of some means. He taught at the Birmingham Mechanics' Institute and the Unitarian Sunday School, and was also a phrenologist. He was active in the radical political reform movement and published and edited the *Birmingham Inspector* (1817); see also *A Radical Mis-represented and truly Represented* (London [1821?]). In a letter to Francis Place, dated 5 November 1835, he said that he had been acquainted with Owen for more than twenty-three years (Place Papers, B.M. Add. MSS. 35,150. f. 88–90). He died in 1840 (Obituary notice by William Pare and editorial in the *New Moral World*, 25 April 1840). Also Joseph McCabe, *Life and Letters of George Jacob Holyoake* (2 vols., London, 1908), I, 12; Owen Papers, Manchester; Eileen M. Janes, 'Quest for the New Moral World' (unpublished M.A. thesis, University of Wisconsin, 1963), pp. 57–9.

Cooperative Society in 1825. By their critique of the institutions of competitive society, their repudiation of the values of commercialism, and their rejection of Malthusianism, Owenite socialists established themselves in the anti-capitalist camp, and to this extent they grappled with the ideology, including the economic theories, of capitalism. But for many Owenites the economy of cooperation was expressed in other terms, such as security, equality and utility.

It was generally assumed by contemporaries that Owenism implied a thorough application of the principle of equality, and indeed most Owenite writers expressed equalitarian views of one sort or another. There was, however, considerable divergence over details. Although Fourier condemned Owen for advocating community of goods, in fact Owen's equalitarian views changed at different periods of his life and were never completely unambiguous on either community of property or social equality. In his 1817 plan for Villages of Unity and Mutual Cooperation Owen made provision for four classes of communitarians based upon property differences; and in a bizarre table he drew up 140 different combinations of sect and party which would enable communitarians to live in a village composed only of their own class of friends.[1] The committee which examined Owen's plans in 1819 felt it necessary to refute suspicions that the plans would have 'a tendency to the equalisation of ranks' and stated categorically that a community of goods was not contemplated.[2] Nevertheless the suspicions continued, and after his arrival in America Owen's equalitarianism became more extreme, though still ambiguous. He told the New Harmonists in April 1825 that their experiment was only a half-way house on the road to complete community, and explained and regretted differences in 'accommodations': 'I must . . . very contrary to my own feelings and inclinations admit, for a time, a certain degree of pecuniary inequality . . .; but I admit of, and submit to this evil because it cannot be avoided without sustaining a greater evil.' Even so, 'there will be no *personal* inequality, or gradations of rank or station; all will be equal in their condition, and I shall never consider myself one step higher, nor any better, than any other individual; neither is it my wish that any more deference should be paid to me than to any other individual of the same age and experience: all should be treated with equal sincerity and kindness. I mean to practice this myself towards others . . .'.[3] Notwithstanding Owen's sincere desire for social equality, community of property was not instituted even

[1] 'Fourth Letter', 6 September 1817, in Owen, *Life*, Iᴀ, 119–38.
[2] 'Address of the Committee', 23 August 1819, in Owen, *Life*, Iᴀ, 245–6.
[3] *New Harmony Gazette*, 1 October 1825.

under the revised Constitution of the New Harmony Community of Equality of 1826. There was in Owen an unresolved ambivalance—which continued throughout his career—between paternalism and equalitarianism, with the result that his views on economic and social equality were never very clearly drawn. His equalitarian inclinations were strongest in the decade after 1825: by the 1840s he had relapsed into the ambiguities of his 1817–25 period, and his Self-Supporting Home Colonies, at least in their initial stage, perpetuated existing social distinctions.

Nevertheless the contemporary notion that ideas of equality were somehow built into the foundations of Owenism was fundamentally correct. A belief in community of property distinguished Owenites from other Ricardian socialists like Hodgskin and utopian socialists such as Fourier. Owen's ambivalence was itself a cause of offence to his more thorough-going followers, of whom Paul Brown was a notable example. At New Harmony Brown was a thorn in the flesh of Owen, making constant demands for the immediate establishment of community of property and blasting any alternative arrangement as aristocratic landlordism.[1] Not many Owenites were prepared to follow Brown in his demand for immediate communism, but most were imbued with a sturdy sense of the need for a much greater degree of equality than had been practised in any civilized society hitherto. William Maclure traced the source of social conflict to inequality of 'property, knowledge and power' and he therefore advocated equal property as a basis for community.[2]

At New Harmony Owenites experienced the practical difficulties of putting their equalitarian convictions to the test. The theoretical difficulties inherent in equalitarianism were faced by William Thompson. In his *Inquiry*, originally written about 1822, Thompson concluded that complete equality in the distribution of wealth was the system 'most conducive to human happiness'. But this conflicted with what he (following Bentham) called the principle of 'security', that is the principle of securing to the labourer the entire use of his product. Only by 'voluntary' (and therefore equal) exchanges could labour receive its 'full equivalent' and thereby be stimulated to maximum production. If perfect equality were to prevail, some labourers would receive more and some less than the full products of their labours, since all would not produce alike. If perfect security prevailed, then the full enjoyment of the unequal products of their labours would deny equality of wealth. The problem was, said

[1] Paul Brown, *Twelve Months in New Harmony*: also lecture reported in the *New Harmony Gazette*, 7 June 1826. Brown also wrote an unpublished manuscript, 'The Woodcutter or a Glimpse of the 19th Century at the West'.
[2] See above, p. 38.

Thompson, 'how to reconcile equality with security; how to reconcile just distribution with continued production'.[1] The way out of the dilemma, he discovered, had been found by Mr Owen: that equality should be interpreted to mean equal distribution of wealth according to need, and that this could be reconciled with social, rather than individual security. The principle of security was to be maintained not by guaranteeing to each labourer individually the whole product of his labour, but by enabling the community as a whole to enjoy the full fruits of its collective labour; and an equality of happiness for each member of the community would be ensured by distribution of wealth according to need. In community the old, selfish and individual demand for the whole produce of labour would wither and give way to a concept of social security, based on a realization that the happiness of each was dependent on the happiness of the whole.

Thompson only arrived at this convenient solution at the end of a very long book. In its earlier parts and in his other writings the right to the whole produce of labour was still treated in an individual sense. The 'institutions of insecurity' might be undermined in various ways in the interim before the establishment of complete community. Trade unions, thought Thompson, might be useful as 'minor expedients' in this way. By setting up 'trades-manufactories' and cultivating land for their own food, trade unions could become embryonic communities of mutual cooperation: 'labourers must become capitalists, and must acquire knowledge to regulate their labour on a large united scale, before they will be able to do more than dream of enjoying the whole product of their labour'.[2] Two decades later this became the slogan of James Hole and the Redemption Society: 'not labourers and capitalists, but labouring capitalists'. The institutionalization of the right to the whole product of labour led directly to producers' cooperation, and also substituted a social for an individual interpretation of the earlier artisan ideal of securing 'an independence'.

It must be confessed that the economy of cooperation, as economic theory, was far from complete, and at certain points—such as rent, interest, investment—was quite inadequate. But Owenism was not intended as an exercise in economic theory: rather was it a response arising out of a vast discontent with early industrial capitalist society. There is a note of incredulity that anything so monstrous could ever have been deliberately devised by rational men: 'there *must* be *some* mischief in the frame of society . . . *some* fatal error which . . . prevents men from using

[1] Thompson, *Inquiry*, p. xiv.
[2] Thompson, *Labor Rewarded*, p. 73.

and enjoying the bounties of creation . . . which has turned their very blessings into curses . . . has led them into poverty while they have been creating affluence and power'.[1] It seemed impossible to believe that a society in which a subsistence theory of wages was common to political economists and socialists, and in which poverty and unemployment were the acknowledged lot of working men, could ever become the accepted norm. The collapse of the competitive system was merely a matter of time, and for prognostication the language of millennialism was felt to be more appropriate than economic theory. In the more open and less industrialized society of America there was little need for a theory of labour exploitation, and American Owenites contributed very little to the economic aspects of Owenism. British Owenites for their part refused to consider economic questions *per se*, and insisted that they be related to moral ends. Owenism was basically a philosophy of social regeneration, and happiness was the goal to which wealth was only a means. Political economy was altogether too narrowly defined to be useful to Owenites: its proper place was within the larger concept of social science.

3 A Science of Society

'I well remember', reminisced George Jacob Holyoake in the 1870s, 'when the phrase "social science" was regarded as much an indication of "something being wrong" on the part of those who used it, as mentioning Sir C. Lyell's doctrine of the Antiquity of Man, or Darwin's Theory of Evolution, afterwards became.'[2] For a period of twenty years after 1825 the 'science of society' carried Owenite implications and when the Owenites acquired buildings in which to meet they were called Halls of Science. As with their adoption of millennial language, however, Owenites used the term social science in a way peculiar to themselves. Frequently they employed it simply as a synonym for socialism. Thompson used it to mean 'the science of promoting human happiness'; and Owen at various times equated it with 'the science of surroundings', 'the laws relative to man in a social state', and 'the laws of the formation of character'. Common to all such usages was the extension to human nature and social relationships of the assumptions of physical science, and confidence in the discoverability of laws governing human action. Granted such a premise, the way was open for the reconstruction of society on a 'scientific'

[1] *Economist*, I (1821), xii.
[2] Holyoake, *History of Cooperation* (London, 1906 edn.), pp. 38–9.

basis: the immediate task of the social reformer was to establish the laws of social dynamics.

It was Owen's claim that he had done this. Beginning with the Essays on the Formation of Character in the *New View of Society* he never tired of reiterating dogmatically his psychological and sociological propositions. In their final form in the *Book of the New Moral World* (1836–44)[1] he presented them as the 'Five Fundamental Facts' and the twenty 'Fundamental Laws of Human Nature', which together comprised the 'first principles of the science of man'. 'Man', argued Owen, 'is a compound being, whose character is formed of his constitution or organisation at birth, and of the effects of external circumstances upon it from birth to death; such original organisation and external influences continually acting and reacting upon each other.' Moreover, 'man is compelled by his original constitution to receive his feelings and his convictions independently of his will', and these feelings or convictions 'create the motive to action called the will, which stimulates him to act and decides his actions'. The organization of no two human beings is ever precisely similar at birth, but all are capable of being profoundly influenced by external circumstances, and are in fact so influenced. Each individual is also responsive to the principles of utility, that is, he likes what is pleasant to him and dislikes that which is unpleasant. Because of the large number of variables involved in the combination of original constitution and external circumstances, the individual characters of men will be infinitely diverse; but their social character, which is less specific, will be determined by their basic life experiences as members of a particular group in a particular type of society. 'These', proclaimed Owen, 'are fundamental laws of nature, not of man's invention; they exist without his knowledge or consent; they change not by any effort he can make.'

In an unsophisticated form, and without the conceptual tools of later social psychology, Owen had hit upon the crucial role of character structure in the social process. Hampered as he was by moralistic terminology, and unable to refine his original 'principles', he clung firmly to his view that man's thinking, feeling and actions are determined by the culture in which he is reared. He asserted 'the innocence of man with respect to his original nature and the superstructure of character which society has raised upon it'.[2] Unfortunately Owen was led by his

---

[1] And repeated by Owenites in their propaganda pamphlets, such as Charles Southwell, *Socialism made Easy* (London, 1840); John Lowther Murphy, *Elements of Socialism* (Birmingham, 1840); and James Napier Bailey, *Objects, Pleasures and Advantages of the Science of Society* (Leeds, 1840).

[2] Owen, *Book of the New Moral World*, pt. I, p. 28.

polemicism into an overemphasis of the negative aspects of his doctrine of circumstances and character formation. 'The character of man is formed for and not by him' became a slogan to be bandied about in a crusade or proclaimed as the Great Truth of the ages. But in Owen's calmer writings and for his more thoughtful followers Owenism provided the beginnings of behavioural science. Owenite sociology and social psychology was incomplete and inconsistent, but in certain areas its conceptualizations justified its claim to be a social science in the modern sense. This was particularly so in the role of institutions, the concept of ideology, social change and the sociology of education.

In Owen's writings the formulation of these concepts is partly obscured by his terminology, particularly the use of 'circumstances' and 'arrangements'. But in Thompson the matter is put more plainly. 'Whereever we turn our eyes over the machinery of society', he observed, 'the irresistible effects of institutions . . . arrest the attention'.[1] He recognized that knowledge is conveyed and character formed 'by means of institutions alone, without any regular preceptors, without any systematic instruction'. Since the role of institutions in character formation is central, he argued, social change can be effected only by a change in institutions, political, social and religious. To Owenites it did not appear impossible that institutions could be changed: such indeed was the basic assumption of the communitarian philosophy. In the United States 'the plasticity of American institutions'[2] was taken for granted, and in Britain reformers believed that society was in such a state of flux that old institutions would before long be swept away.

The concept of ideology (in the sense of the total idea structure considered as a function of social background and life experience[3]) is implicit in much Owenite thought. Take for instance Owen's address to his workers at New Lanark in 1816:

What think you . . . , my friends, is the reason why you believe and act as you do? I will tell you. It is solely and merely because you were born, and have lived, in this period of the world,—in Europe,—in the island of Great Britain,—and more especially in this northern part of it.[4]

And he added that had they been born elsewhere or in other times they would have been quite different. Owen concluded from this that class

---

[1] Thompson, *Inquiry*, p. 300; also pp. 288–90.

[2] Arthur Eugene Bestor, Jr. 'Patent-Office Models of the Good Society: Some Relationships between Social Reform and Westward Expansion', *American Historical Review*, LVIII (1953), 523.

[3] See Karl Mannheim, *Ideology and Utopia* (London, 1936), chap. 2.

[4] *Address delivered to the Inhabitants of New Lanark, 1 January 1816*, in *Life*, I, 358.

antagonism was irrational and irrelevant, since each class was the victim of its own ideology. The lesson of this for the working classes was plain: 'you must be made to know yourselves, by which means alone you can discover what other men are. You will then distinctly perceive that no rational ground for anger exists, even against those who by the errors of the present system have been made your greatest oppressors and your most bitter enemies . . . They are no more to be blamed . . . than you are; nor you than they'.[1]

The peaceful nature of desirable social change was fundamental to all Owenite thinking. Owen went out of his way, time and time again, to emphasize that the changes he proposed could be effected without violence or upset of any kind. There was no need to destroy the existing system before building the new. Just as the old gravel roads continued to exist after the railways had largely superseded them, so the 'old system of society' would be gradually replaced by the new.[2] The problem of agency in social change exercised the Owenites continually. In his most complete analysis of the problem Owen distinguished seven 'modes' by which the change to the new moral world could be brought about.[3] These ranged from united action by the governments of Europe and America to activities by different classes within each country. After considering the potentialities of the landed aristocracy, the monied aristocracy, manufacturers, operatives and farmers, Owen concluded that the most promising agency was 'an association formed of the most rational from among all the preceding classes'. Thompson preferred to pin his hopes more unequivocally on the middle class. It seemed to him that obstacles to change arose from the effects of circumstances which conditioned individuals against it. Poverty and ignorance deprived the majority of the chance of even wishing for change, and prejudices, interests and institutional blinkers barred the aristocracy, lawyers and priests. 'There remain then to be operated upon, with some fair probability of success, the middle classes of the industrious whose pursuits do not necessarily beget peculiar interests or prejudices hostile to impartial investigation.'[4]

Consideration by contemporaries of Owenism as a non-evaluative science of society was rare because of the moralistic language in which the discussion was conducted. Emotional reactions were the usual response to Owen's moralizing. This was unfortunate because it meant that much of

[1] *Address to the Working Classes* (April 1819), in *Life*, IA, 226.
[2] *Life*, I, xxxii.
[3] *New Moral World*, 1–22 November 1834; see also the *Reasoner*, 10 June 1846.
[4] Thompson, *Inquiry*, p. 322.

the argument for and against Owenism was channelled in two grooves, neither of which was central to the main case: moral responsibility and free will versus determinism. The controversy about character formation usually fell into a chicken-and-egg type of argument as to whether good circumstances make men virtuous or virtuous men make good circumstances. Even sympathizers with Owen professed difficulty in reconciling his statement that men were products of circumstances over which they had no control, with his apparent assumption that by acting rationally they could control those very same circumstances. And Christian opponents of Owenism found it quite impossible to believe that the doctrine of circumstances could do other than undermine the concept of duty and promote moral irresponsibility.[1] Necessitarian arguments plagued all Owenite ventures, whether in Britain or America. At one of the Sunday meetings at New Harmony, for example, General Robert M. Evans asked Owen 'whether he was of opinion that man was wholly the creature of circumstances and consequently has no controlling power over any circumstances whatever; or whether he conceived that man formed one link in the chain of circumstances, and consequently possessed a controlling power to a limited extent . . .'. To which Owen replied that 'until it was fully ascertained that the character of each individual was formed for him, he believed man may be said to have been entirely under the control of circumstances;—that he is so still: but the knowledge he has acquired—that he is under the control of circumstances—forms itself a new circumstance, which will give him the power to control a large range of circumstances relative to himself'.[2] Owenites were continually pressed to declare whether or not they believed in free will, and they usually replied: 'we do not believe . . . that "men are mere passive beings", incapable of altering and improving their general character; but we do believe that man individually is subservient to circumstances, and that men collectively create most of the circumstances favorable and adverse to their own happiness'.[3]

Today it is more difficult than in the nineteenth century to appreciate what seems like the obscurantism of the champions of free will, and the fear that individual responsibility will be destroyed if it is admitted that society is subject to social laws. This was a battle which had to be fought,

[1] For typical arguments see Henry Grey Macnab, *New Views of Mr Owen of Lanark Impartially Examined* (London, 1819); *Public Discussion between Robert Owen, late of New Lanark, and the Rev. J. H. Roebuck, of Manchester* (Manchester, 1837); T. Simmons Mackintosh, *An Inquiry into the Nature of Responsibility* (Birmingham, [1840]); *Cooperative Magazine*, I (1826), 171–7, 258, II (1827), 74, 99, 118.

[2] *New Harmony Gazette*, 12 July 1826.

[3] *Ibid.*, 18 January 1826.

and later Owenites like Charles Bray and Henry Travis, put much of their energies into it. But Owen and his early followers were hardly in a position to make much headway in such a campaign; their own language and assumptions precluded any substantial detachment from the contemporary moral and intellectual milieu, which set definite limits to the type of challenge which was possible.

The frame of reference for Owenism was the complex of ideas which characterized the Enlightenment of the second half of the eighteenth century, and in their approach to the problems of man and society Owenites employed modes of thought and drew on a body of underlying assumptions which were part of the Enlightenment tradition. Most of Owen's key concepts were commonplaces of later eighteenth-century liberal thought (though he presented them as, and believed that they were, original discoveries of his own). The Owenite search for a science of society is thus to be seen as part of the emergence of the modern social sciences from the matrix of eighteenth-century social thinking. More particularly Owenism not only fell within the categories of classic Enlightenment thought, but was also closely related to Scottish moral philosophy.

It would be an easy matter, though tedious, to document the use by Owenites of the key concepts of Enlightenment rationalism. Owen's appeal to reason, consistency and the laws of nature; Thompson's contrast between natural and artificial society, and the premise of utilitarian ethics explicit in all Owenite statements represented a working out of Enlightenment ideas. For this reason the similarity between Owen's ideas and those of Helvetius, Godwin, Bentham and James Mill, which has often been noted, is hardly surprising, for they were inheritors of common experiences and traditions of thought. What is more significant is the relationship between Owenism and the 'Scottish inquiry of the eighteenth century'. The intellectual renaissance in Scotland after 1745 produced a notable school of moral philosophers and political economists who were concerned to establish 'an empirical basis for the study of man and society'.[1] In their discussions of human nature, social forces and in-

---

[1] Gladys Bryson, *Man and Society: the Scottish Inquiry of the Eighteenth Century* (Princeton, N.J., 1945). This Scottish group included David Hume, Francis Hutcheson, Adam Smith, Thomas Reid, Adam Ferguson, Dugald Stewart, Lord Kames (Henry Home), Lord Monboddo (James Burnet). See also William C. Lehmann, *John Millar of Glasgow, 1735–1801* (Cambridge, 1960), and *Adam Ferguson and the Beginnings of Modern Sociology* (New York, 1930); Ronald L. Meek, 'The Scottish Contribution to Marxist Sociology', in *Democracy and the Labour Movement*, ed. John Saville (London, 1954), pp. 84–102; and Gladys Bryson, 'Sociology considered as Moral Philosophy', in *Sociological Review*, XXIV (1932), 26–36.

stitutions, economic processes and government—all included in the omnibus category, moral philosophy—there emerged the beginnings of modern sociology and the idea of social science. At the universities of Edinburgh and Glasgow the teaching and discussion of moral philosophy nurtured a school of what a later age would label the behavioural sciences.

In this context a new perspective is given to the Owenites' search for a science of society. Their interests and procedures were close to those of the Scottish moral philosophers, especially Adam Ferguson and Dugald Stewart, and three areas may conveniently be cited as examples. First, the Owenites like the Scottish moral philosophers were concerned with no less than the nature of man and his total culture. They were interested in general social institutions, with the family as well as government, and in the agencies of social change. They sought to account for human actions and social relationships in psychological terms ('pneumatology'). Second, there was a common agreement that ethical considerations were paramount in evaluation of social organization and behaviour. The promotion of happiness through the pursuit of enlightened self-interest was the universal touchstone. Third, the procedure of investigation was held to be empirical, with Bacon and Newton quoted as the models to be followed. Communitarianism was lauded as an experimental method of social reform. But for the most part Owenites, like the Scottish moral philosophers, substituted experience for experiment. Owen appealed frequently to his experience as verification of his principles, and for most Owenites the task of the social scientist was the 'discovery' of natural laws at work in society, rather than the formulation of laws based on generalized observation of social facts.

To what extent were Owen and his followers consciously indebted to the Scottish moral philosophers? One need not doubt Owen's honesty in his claim that his views were entirely original and owed nothing to previous thinkers, but his claim cannot be taken at its face value. The origin of his ideas has perplexed most of his biographers for they could find little evidence of any formative reading, and his son had stated that his father seldom read books.[1] A possible clue has been sought in the intellectual influence which membership of the Manchester Literary and Philosophical Society in the 1790s might have had on him.[2] To a young man in his early twenties these contacts with individual members were undoubtedly stimulating, but direct links with his later ideas seem somewhat tenuous. In any case, the pedigree of ideas is not to be traced like a

[1] Robert Dale Owen, *Threading My Way* (London, 1874), p. 67.
[2] See E. M. Fraser, 'Robert Owen in Manchester, 1787–1800', *Memoirs and Proceedings of the Manchester Literary and Philosophical Society*, LXXXII (1937–38), 29–41.

11. A group of Shakers

12. Shaker village, Mount Lebanon, New York

THE CRISIS,

OR THE CHANGE FROM ERROR AND MISERY, TO TRUTH AND HAPPINESS.

1832.

IF WE CANNOT YET   RECONCILE ALL OPINIONS,

LET US ENDEAVOUR   TO UNITE ALL HEARTS.

IT IS OF ALL TRUTHS THE MOST IMPORTANT, THAT THE CHARACTER OF MAN IS FORMED FOR—NOT BY HIMSELF.

Design of a Community of 2,000 Persons, founded upon a principle, commended by Plato, Lord Bacon, Sir T. More, & R. Owen.

EDITED BY
ROBERT OWEN AND ROBERT DALE OWEN.

𝕷𝖔𝖓𝖉𝖔𝖓:
PRINTED AND PUBLISHED BY J. EAMONSON, 15, CHICHESTER PLACE, GRAY'S INN ROAD.

STRANGE, PATERNOSTER ROW. PURKISS, OLD COMPTON STREET, AND MAY BE HAD OF ALL BOOKSELLERS.

1833.

13. Title page of *The Crisis*

single line of issue in a family tree. After his marriage to Caroline Dale, Owen made his home in Scotland for a quarter of a century; at first spending the summers in New Lanark and the winters in Glasgow, and later living at Braxfield House. His fortune and his fame were made by the banks of the Clyde. He was a member of the Glasgow Literary and Commercial Society and was on friendly terms with many of the professors of the universities of Edinburgh and Glasgow.[1] Among his friends were James Mill (who corrected part of *A New View of Society* for the press), Patrick Colquhoun and Lord Kames. As Abram Combe remarked, 'the New System has had its origin in Scotland'.[2]

Though Owen seldom cited references in his writings, his followers were not so reticent. From the authors quoted in the pages of Owenite journals and the works of Minter Morgan and other popularizers the debt to the Scottish school is obvious. The most frequently used was Dugald Stewart (*Elements of the Philosophy of the Human Mind*, 1792–1827), but extracts from Adam Ferguson, Francis Hutcheson, Thomas Reid, David Hume and James Mill were also numerous. Usually the use made of these authors was superficial—eclectic extracts designed to bolster some aspect of Owenism with the weight of a learned authority, rather than genuine assimilation with the writers' basic position. The Owenites' feelings of sympathy for Scottish moral philosophy were often stronger than their understanding of it. But their terminology, assumptions and main interests reflected the more distinguished philosophers to whom they appealed.

The number of Scots among the early Owenites has already been remarked upon. When it is also remembered that a man's formative intellectual influences are those received in early manhood (so that a mature person's position may be explicable by the ideas current twenty-five years earlier) the importance of a Scottish upbringing for several prominent Owenites is further enhanced. Thus Frances Wright (1795–1852), founder of the Nashoba community and collaborator with Robert Dale Owen as a Free Enquirer and popular educator in America, was raised in a liberal Scottish environment. After her father's early death she was befriended by Robina Millar, the widowed daughter-in-law of John Millar who had published *The Origin of the Distinction of Ranks* (1771), and by James Mylne, professor of moral philosophy in the University of Glasgow and a friend of Owen's.[3] Fanny Wright attained notoriety as

[1] *Life*, I, 107; Thomas Atkinson, *Sketch of the Origin and Progress of the Literary and Commercial Society of Glasgow* (Glasgow, 1831).

[2] Abram Combe, *Metaphysical Sketches*, p. 168.

[3] William Randall Waterman, *Frances Wright* (New York, 1924), pp. 15–19; Lehmann, *Millar*, p. 412; see also A. J. G. Perkins and Theresa Wolfson, *Frances Wright, Free Enquirer* (New York, 1939).

G

the alleged champion of two of the most unpopular tenets associated with Owenism, Free Love and Free Enquiry, both of which (in their true forms of female emancipation and deism) were aspects of a basic liberalism stemming from Enlightenment ideals. At this point Owenism linked up with the 'infidel' or deist tradition of Paine, Volney and Godwin which had roots on both sides of the Atlantic.

We have it on the authority of Robert Dale Owen that his father was a deist. Owen stated his belief in an 'eternal uncaused Existence, omnipresent and possessing attributes whereby the world is governed', and that 'man . . . has been formed by a Power, in our language called God, that eternally acts throughout the universe, but which no man has yet been able to comprehend'.[1] All religions, including Christianity, he dismissed as 'so many geographical insanities'.[2] Some Owenites followed him in these views, others not; but all deplored the tactlessness of his attacks on organized religion. The concept of natural religion which was a strong element in the Scottish Enlightenment did not necessarily contradict revealed Christianity; but the general effect of the writings of David Hume and his followers was to strengthen scepticism. For most practical purposes it made little difference whether an Owenite was a deist, a freethinker or a member of some rationalist Protestant sect; the foundation of his belief was the application of the concept of natural law to religion.

The nature of the contribution of Scottish moral philosophy to Owenism can be measured by comparison with another attempt to establish a science of society in the first half of the nineteenth century. Phrenology was introduced into Britain through George Combe (brother of the Owenite, Abram Combe) and his followers in Edinburgh. Combe's chief work, *The Constitution of Man* (Edinburgh, 1828) examines the operation of natural laws on man and society. His assumptions are those of the Scottish school—utility, associationism, empirical method—and he refers to Dugald Stewart, Thomas Reid, Thomas Brown and other moral philosophers. Generally, however, he did not give the source of his ideas, but like Owen thought they were original to himself. Combe's main purpose was to show that through phrenology man would be able to know himself, and thereby attain greater happiness through obedience to the laws of nature. But as with Owen he was led into the byways of

[1] *Public Discussion between Robert Owen and the Rev. J. H. Roebuck* (2nd edn., London, 1837), pp. 7, 25, 106; and Robert Dale Owen, *Threading my Way*, pp. 166–7.

[2] Owen was not consistent. At times he appeared to condemn all religion out of hand—see his letter to the *Limerick Chronicle*, reprinted in the *Republican*, 4 November 1825; and *Life*, I, 102. At others he denied that he was 'an enemy to all religion'—Macnab, *New Views Examined*, pp. 56–7.

necessity-versus-free will and moral responsibility controversies. Combe's phrenology was but part of a broader attempt to outline a philosophy of mind and a science of society based on naturalistic, as opposed to metaphysical principles. Its appeal was basically similar to Owenism, and for some Owenites it was a milestone on the road to the new moral world.[1] 'Man, know thyself' was a slogan adopted by the phrenologists which might equally well have suited the Owenites, or indeed that even larger body of seekers for a mental and social science which would 'reveal' the laws which governed man's physical, moral and intellectual nature.

The Owenite search for a science of society was thus an outgrowth from the ideas and values of the Enlightenment. This meant that in America Owenism appeared to its respectable sympathizers to be in the great tradition of Benjamin Franklin, John Adams and Thomas Jefferson, and to others (and perhaps more accurately) in the tradition of Thomas Paine, Joel Barlow and Elihu Palmer. But however strong the appeal of this tradition until the end of the eighteenth century, by the 1820s it was distinctly *démodé*. The leading figures in American Owenism—William Maclure, Paul Brown, Fanny Wright—were typical Enlightenment characters with their devotion to deism, natural rights, environmentalism and women's rights. In so far as it was necessary to appeal to independent Jeffersonian farmers, Enlightenment ideas might be thought to have been an asset. However, such views were soon pushed into an intellectual corner under the impact of revivalism and the rapid strengthening of evangelicalism in America after 1800. When contemporaries charged Owenites with infidelity the condemnation implied that they were not only godless but also out of date. In Britain the Owenites had a different task. There the need was to comprehend and cope with the drastic changes of early industrial capitalism. In their attempt to reduce these changes to some sort of meaningful, rational order, the Owenites drew upon Enlightenment traditions to formulate a social science. By so doing they too risked imposing limitations on themselves, for by the 1820s the romantic reaction to the Enlightenment was in full swing. In Britain, as in America, this reaction was conservative in tone. It was the fate of Owenism to become one of the bearers into the nineteenth century of the liberal values of the eighteenth-century Enlightenment.

[1] For the relation between Owenism and phrenology see p. 239-40.

The Transmission
of Owenism

The Transmission of Owenism

The point has been made that the main strands of Owenism, such as philanthropy, community and Ricardian socialism, were not peculiar to the Owenites. It was the particular mixture, not the individual elements, which gave Owenism its unique characteristics. But the familiarity of these separate elements was essential for the successful propaganda of Owenite views. Every social reformer is faced with a problem of communication, how to ensure that his new views can be presented in a way that makes them acceptable to people who are still thinking along old lines. In order to communicate the reformer has to employ the language of his age. He cannot be too far in advance of it, for he will not be understood; yet at the same time he has to give a new twist of meaning to familiar concepts and phrases. This is not entirely a deliberate or even conscious process, so deeply is his thinking embedded in the mould of the age. The social reformer is therefore alike and also different from the general run of men. His problem is how to determine and establish the kind of relationship to his society necessary for him to be effective in promoting social change. Frequently he will be found using the rhetoric of the age, for only thus will he be able to gain a hearing. But within the conventional intellectual and social terminology he will seek to express new interpretations.

It is in relation to this problem that two of the most distinctive features of Owenism are to be explained. The millenarian overtones and the passion for education which characterize all except the very earliest of Owen's writings are explicable by the need to find media for the transmission of Owenism. The sect and the school were the models for effecting the new moral world.

1 Millennialism: *The Millennial Heritage*

In *A New View of Society*, which he composed in 1812–13, Owen wrote with restraint and directness. Despite reference in the Third Essay to 'the emancipation of the human mind', 'the Evil genius of the world' and 'universally revealed facts', the language was not chiliastic. In his *Address to the Inhabitants of New Lanark*, delivered at the opening of the Institution for the Formation of Character on 1 January 1816, however, he began to use biblical expressions, and declared that while he did not know 'what ideas individuals may attach to the term Millennium' he was sure that a society free from crime, poverty and misery was universally feasible. Eighteen months later, during his great propaganda campaign of the summer of 1817, he was proclaiming a 'new religion' and the commencement of the millennium:

What are the signs of the last days of misery on earth? 'And there shall be signs in the sun, and in the moon, and in the stars; and upon the earth, distress of nations, with perplexity; the seas and the waves roaring; men's hearts failing them for fear and for looking after those things which are coming on earth; for the powers of heaven shall be shaken.' 'And then shall they see the son of man (OR TRUTH) coming in a cloud with power and glory. And when these things begin to come to pass, then look up and lift up your heads, for your redemption (FROM CRIME AND MISERY) draweth nigh.' 'THIS GENERATION SHALL NOT PASS AWAY UNTIL ALL SHALL BE FULFILLED.'[1]

In October 1817 the first, short-lived Owenite journal, the *Mirror of Truth*, appeared: it was completely millennialist in tone and language, and anticipated the imminent collapse of commercial civilization. From now on the millennial note was present in most of Owen's writings and also in some of his followers'. From time to time Owen announced the commencement of the millennium, and after 1835 Owenism acquired many of the characteristics of a religious sect. Looking back on his life it seemed to Owen that 1817 marked the turning point in his career. 21 August 1817, the day when he addressed an adjourned meeting at the City of London Tavern on his community plan, he declared to be 'the most important of my life for the public; the day on which bigotry, superstition, and all false religions received their death blow'.[2] At the

---

[1] *A Further Development of the Plan for the Relief of the Poor, and the Emancipation of Mankind* (published in the London newspapers of 10 September 1817), in Owen, *Life*, IA, 134.
[2] Owen, *Life*, I, 162.

same time that he denounced all existing religions he began to use the language of millennialism.

As with other aspects of his thought, it is not possible to determine precisely the origin and development of Owen's millennialism. He was impressed at this time by the communitarian experiments of American millennialists. According to the account in his autobiography Owen had, at an early age, become convinced of the errors of all religions and in consequence rejected them all. Between 1814 and 1816, therefore, he had arrived at a position in which while disbelieving in any existing religion he was formulating his own millennialism, or 'Religion of Charity alone, unconnected with Faith'. Like his young contemporary, the Mormon leader Joseph Smith, who also, according to his autobiography, concluded in his youth that all churches and sects were in error, Owen became step by step the prophet of a new millennial sect. The rationale of this process and the use of millennial rhetoric becomes clear when the problem of communication is brought into focus. Since Owen rejected the idea of a political party, and other institutions such as a church or a business firm were inappropriate for effecting his ends, some alternative model for the dissemination of Owenism was necessary. An answer to this problem was found in a secularized version of millennial sectarianism. Just why the early socialist movement should have adopted this seemingly improbable form has not hitherto been very apparent. But an examination of evangelical religion in Britain and America suggests certain clues.

Owenism originated and flourished entirely within the grand era of evangelical ascendancy, *c.* 1800–60. The central importance of evangelicalism, especially revivalism, in shaping the American mind in the nineteenth century has frequently been noted.[1] But in Britain also, where a traditional religious establishment was more strongly entrenched, the same forces were at work for the spread of evangelical Christianity. Such central doctrines of evangelicalism as perfectionism, disinterested benevolence and millennialism, which for instance characterized the preaching of

[1] Most recently and penetratingly in Perry Miller, *The Life of the Mind in America* (New York, 1965). See also Whitney R. Cross, *The Burned-over District: the Social and Intellectual History of Enthusiastic Religion in Western New York, 1800–1850* (Ithaca, N.Y., 1950). Other useful works in this field are David M. Ludlum, *Social Ferment in Vermont, 1791–1850* (New York, 1939); Charles C. Cole, *The Social Ideas of the Northern Evangelists, 1826–1860* (New York, 1954); Timothy L. Smith, *Revivalism and Social Reform in Mid-Nineteenth-Century America* (New York and Nashville, 1957); Clara E. Sears, *Days of Delusion* (Boston, 1924); Tyler, *Freedom's Ferment*; Ira V. Brown, 'Watchers for the Second Coming: the Millenarian Tradition in America', *Mississippi Valley Historical Review*, XXXIX (December 1952), 441–58; William Miller, *Evidence from Scripture and History of the Second Coming of Christ, about the year 1843* (Troy, 1836).

the leading American revivalist, Charles Grandison Finney,[1] were also typical of the advocates of enthusiastic religion in Britain. These doctrines carried definite social implications and frequently committed their adherents to sympathy for various aspects of social reform. It was not difficult therefore for religious sectarians to espouse certain 'ultra' causes such as anti-slavery, temperance, or the emancipation of women. Indeed, at times the careers of some leaders of evangelical sects suggest a kind of spiritual entrepreneurship, with expeditions into or flirtations with communitarianism, phrenology, mesmerism or vegetarianism. One aspect of the evangelical heritage was particularly attractive to social reformers: in the biblical doctrine of the millennium they found a conceptual basis and a rhetoric for their ideas of utopia. To appreciate fully the relationship between millennialism and Owenism, however, some discussion of the nature of millennial doctrine and its place in evangelical religion is necessary.

At the start it is perhaps useful to remember the strength and persistence of millennialism in the Christian church at all times from its beginning. Millennialism is to be regarded not as an aberration but rather as an extreme form of one aspect of orthodox faith. Jesus' teachings about the Kingdom, the Last Days and the coming of the messiah in glory and majesty were taken literally by his disciples, and after His death the apostolic church continued to believe in a Second Coming which would not long be delayed. When the great promises of the Second Advent were not literally fulfilled they were subjected to interpretation, so that the Apocalyptic tradition was not discarded but adjusted to the new situation. From the early church there was handed down a body of inspired prophecy, the core of which was contained in the Books of Daniel and Revelation, the Apocrypha and the 'synoptic Apocalypse' of Jesus himself. Throughout the history of the Christian church the interpretation of this prophetic literature was the basis of innumerable theories and speculations. In particular, the symbolic prophecies of Daniel 7 and 8 and Revelation 14 fascinated generations of Christians, who exercised untold ingenuity in their exposition of the meaning of the 'Beasts' and 'Horns' and the 'Mother of the Harlots'. The object of this interpretation was to throw light on the nature of the millennium and its relation to Jesus' Second Coming, a doctrine to which all professed Christians were, in some form or other, committed.

There was general agreement in millennial theology that the world

---

[1] William G. McLoughlin, Jr., *Modern Revivalism: Charles Grandison Finney to Billy Graham* (New York, 1959), pp. 101–12; and Charles Finney, *Lectures on Revivals of Religion*, ed. William G. McLoughlin (Cambridge, Mass., 1960).

was to be transformed by the Second Coming of Christ and the establishment of the Kingdom of God on earth. This state would last for a thousand years, after which would come the Last Judgement. During the period of the millennium the Saints (that is, the Christian martyrs and all faithful Christians who have suffered) would reign with Christ. There were differences of view, however, between those Christians who believed that Christ's Second Coming would precede the millennium (premillennialists) and those who thought that the Second Advent would follow the millennium (postmillennialists). From these differences stemmed others. The premillennialists were predisposed towards the establishment of the millennium by divine, cataclysmic action, whereas the postmillennialists were prone to think that the Kingdom of God would come gradually as the result of Christian, human instrumentalities. For either of these views there was ample scriptural support, so that the choice between a revolutionary or reformist interpretation had to be made on other than theological grounds. Amongst premillennialists there was a further division between those who believed that the Second Advent had already occurred and the millennium had begun, and those who still looked for these events in the future. Again, among both pre- and postmillennialists anticipation of the millennium could provoke either pessimism or optimism, depending on whether the imminent end of the world was dreaded or welcomed.

From these differences in interpretation and emphasis a variety of types of millennial concern was possible, ranging from sophisticated study of the biblical books of prophecy to divine revelations concerning the immediate arrival of Christ on earth. In Britain and America this active millennialism between 1780 and 1860 was part of the cultural milieu with which movements such as Owenism had to come to terms. Firmly rooted in English Dissent and American Protestantism it provided a base for the development of new socio-theological ideas, which were not automatically condemned as heretical or cranky. When the limits of orthodoxy were reached the innovators found themselves out in the cold if they went any further; but until then they enjoyed the protection of respectable religion. Nevertheless, the bounds of orthodoxy were often crossed, with the result that millennialist concern became expressed in two forms: a scholarly, respectable study and interpretation of prophecy, and a popular, adventist millenarianism.

Throughout the eighteenth and first half of the nineteenth centuries the first of these forms never lacked able exponents.[1] Contemporary

[1] For a full account of the writers on prophecy see LeRoy Edwin Froom, *The Prophetic Faith of Our Fathers* (4 vols., Washington, D.C., 1946–54).

events like the Lisbon earthquake of 1755 were interpreted as evidence of the fulfilment of biblical prophecies. Above all, the French Revolution excited a spate of interpretations on both sides of the Atlantic designed to show that the world was entering upon the Last Days. There was general agreement in the late eighteenth century that the 1260 days mentioned in Revelation 12:6 were to be interpreted as 1260 years, and that this period was now ended. An alternative theory, which became increasingly popular after 1800, emphasized the importance of the 2300-year period of Daniel 8:14 and the 'cleansing of the sanctuary' which would fall due some time in the 1840s. But in either case the implications of such a theory were so compelling as to change completely the lives of those who sincerely believed in it. The fulfilment of the time prophecies meant that the believer was living in the Last Days, that the 'Midnight Cry' could already be heard, and that the coming of the messiah might be expected shortly. Such beliefs had an influence far beyond the members of explicitly adventist sects. They were part and parcel of everyday evangelical religion.

The British Evangelicals' call for a revival of 'vital religion' and earnest study of the scriptures, and the American Great Revival directed attention to the Christian's duty of striving for the realization of the prophecies in Daniel and Revelation. Thus the Society for Promoting Christianity among the Jews, founded in London in 1809, was supported by such leading Evangelicals as William Wilberforce, Sir Thomas Baring, Charles Simeon and Henry Drummond. The literal restoration of the Jews in the Last Days was widely believed to be part of the fulfilment of prophecy. In 1826 Henry Drummond, a rich banker and Member of Parliament, organized the first Albury Conference for the study of the biblical prophecies at his home in Albury Park, Surrey. This inter-denominational gathering of ministers and laymen agreed upon a premillennialist interpretation and concluded that the Second Advent was near.

Among those present at Albury was one who influenced some of Owen's followers. Edward Irving was a Scots Presbyterian minister who had recently made a name for himself as a popular preacher in London.[1] From 1825 he became increasingly interested in prophecy and published premillennial books and pamphlets.[2] He was convinced that the 1260-year period had ended in 1793, when the time of the judgement on

---

[1] On Irving and Irvingism see P. E. Shaw, *The Catholic Apostolic Church* (New York, 1946); Edward Miller, *History and Doctrines of Irvingism* (2 vols., London, 1878); Andrew L. Drummond, *Edward Irving and his Circle* (London, 1938); Margaret O. W. Oliphant, *Life of Edward Irving* (2 vols., London, 1862). An Irvingite periodical, *The Morning Watch* (London, March 1829–June 1833) was edited by John Tudor.

[2] E.g. *Babylon and Infidelity Foredoomed of God: A Discourse on the Prophecies of Daniel and the Apocalypse* (2 vols., Glasgow, 1826); Manuel Lacunza, *The Coming of the Messiah*

Babylon commenced, and the vials of the Apocalypse began to be poured out. By 1823 the first six vials of wrath had been poured out upon the Beast and the seventh was about to be poured. After this period would come the battle of Armageddon, the Second Coming of Christ, and the establishment of the millennium, some time in the late 1860s. At Irving's chapel in Regent Square, London, his discourses in 1831 were interrupted by outbursts of 'utterances' or 'speaking with tongues'. In April 1832 he was denied the use of the Regent Square chapel, and later, after an ecclesiastical trial, he was expelled from the ministry of the Church of Scotland. For a short time his followers met on Sunday mornings in the Owenite Institution in Grays Inn Road, and then formed themselves into the Catholic Apostolic Church.

The Irvingite movement shows clearly several significant features of British millennialism. First, it was not an isolated phenomenon, confined to one place. In the West of Scotland religious revivals at Roseneath and Port Glasgow in 1830, with which Irving was familiar, independently produced supernatural manifestations, prophesyings and speaking with tongues. Second, the Irvingites were impeccably respectable and middle class. Irving himself was the son of a prosperous tanner, had graduated from Edinburgh University, and was a friend of Thomas Carlyle. His congregation in London was at first highly fashionable, and when the 'apostles' of the Catholic Apostolic Church were chosen in the 1830s they were all from the middle classes and some were very wealthy. Third, Irvingism developed out of orthodox evangelical religion. Irving and his followers did not commence as premillennialists, but as Presbyterians, Anglicans and Independents.

Between orthodox evangelical concern for the prophecies and popular adventist millenarianism there was no hard and fast line. In Britain and America it was commonly observed that the seeds and sustenance for 'ultra' religious movements came from a more general evangelical revivalism. In all evangelical movements chiliasm was implicit, and sometimes temporarily gained an ascendancy. But its most challenging form was presented by sects which were numerically smaller and more uncompromising in their claims. They were the enthusiasts, the fanatics, the come-outers. Their beliefs were derived from a literal, eclectic interpretation of the prophetic scriptures, and a divine revelation vouchsafed to them directly. A simplicity, often crudity, seemed to mark their mentality, for their reliance on the supernatural enabled them to dispense

in Glory and Majesty, trans. Edward Irving (2 vols., London, 1827); *The Last Days: A Discourse on the Evil Character of these our Times* (London, 1828).

with many of the limitations imposed by logic and reason. Moderation and gradualness did not commend themselves as virtues, but rather were signs of lack of faith. The basic principles of Good and Evil in the world were crystal clear, and life was to be lived by the light of this absolute standard, with no compromises.

A feature common to many of these sects was that the Second Coming of the messiah had already taken place, and the leadership of the faithful was now in the hands of the messiah himself or one of his prophets. In some instances the messiah was a woman. Within a period of twenty years from 1772 at least four female prophets appeared, claiming to be the 'woman clothed with the sun' of the Apocalypse, or the second (female) Christ. Two of these—Jemima Wilkinson of New Jerusalem (N.Y.)[1] and Mrs (Luckie) Buchan of Ayrshire, Scotland[2]—are not directly relevant to the main theme of Owenism. But the other two—Mother Ann Lee and Joanna Southcott—appear more prominently in the Owenite story. The Shakers, who attracted a great deal of continuing interest among Owenites, were founded by Mother Ann Lee, who at the age of twenty-two joined a sect of dissenters led by Jane and James Wardley of Bolton-le-Moors in Lancashire.[3] The Wardleys had been Quakers, but separated from the Society of Friends after being influenced by the French Prophets (Camisards), a radical-Calvinist sect who had sought refuge in England after the revocation of the Edict of Nantes in 1685. At first Ann Lee did not play a dominant role in the small sect of 'Shaking Quakers', but after her marriage to Abraham Standerin, a Manchester blacksmith, in 1762, her experiences brought her to a position of leadership. She bore him four children but none of them survived, and from this misfortune she developed a strong antipathy towards sex and marriage. She declared that 'cohabitation of the sexes' was the greatest of all sins, and became more active in the sect, which, as it attracted converts in Manchester, incurred popular hostility. In 1772 Ann Lee was imprisoned in

[1] See Herbert A. Sisbey, Jr., *Pioneer Prophetess: Jemima Wilkinson, the Publick Universal Friend* (Ithaca, N.Y., 1964). Robert P. St. John, 'Jemima Wilkinson', New York State Historical Association *Proceedings*, XXVIII (April 1930), 158–75, has a useful bibliography. David Hudson, *History of Jemima Wilkinson, a Preacheress of the Eighteenth Century* (Geneva, N.Y., 1821) is a hostile account, mainly concerned to retail scandal.

[2] See Joseph Train, *The Buchanites from First to Last* (London and Edinburgh, 1846). The Doctrine of the Woman was expounded by the Rev. Hugh White in his *Divine Dictionary* (Dumfries, 1785), the chief Buchanite work.

[3] Printed literature on the Shakers runs into many hundreds of items. The best modern account is Edward Deming Andrews, *The People Called Shakers* (New York, 1953), which contains a note on sources. For an account of the French Prophets (Camisards) and their millennial influence in England, see John Symonds, *Thomas Brown and the Angels* (London, 1961).

Manchester gaol for blasphemy and on her release was recognized as the leader of the Shakers. In prison, she claimed, she had had visions and Christ had appeared to her and commanded her to preach the gospel as His Beloved. 'It is not I that speak, it is Christ who dwells in me', she proclaimed, and her followers now recognized her as the messiah. Further revelations directed her to leave the Old World and found the millennial church in America, and so in 1774 a small group of Shakers emigrated to New York, settling at Niskeyuna, near Albany. At first the 'United Society of Believers in Christ's Second Appearing' was too engrossed in the tasks of getting a living to do much proselytizing; but from 1779 the Shakers benefited from successive religious revivals to recruit new members. Mother Ann died in 1784 and the leadership passed into the hands of Joseph Meacham and Lucy Wright. By 1800 eleven Shaker communities had been organized in the north-eastern States, and thereafter they expanded into the West through successive 'in gatherings'. The climax of their growth came in the 1850s with a membership of about six thousand, organized in eighteen branches and fifty-eight families.

The Shakers attracted widespread attention from travellers and social reformers in the first half of the nineteenth century who seldom failed to admire the puritan simplicity and prosperity of their communal arrangements while ridiculing their celibacy and religious 'absurdities'. Although it was the Shakers' successful communitarianism (the 'Gospel order') which mainly interested enquirers they plainly perceived that the Shakers' premillennial faith was central to everything else. In Shaker theology the Second Coming had already taken place with the revelation to Mother Ann, in whom prophecy had been fulfilled. The millennium was begun in 1792, when the 1260-year 'reign of the Beast' was ended, the sanctuary cleansed, and the Shaker church founded.[1] Owen was sympathetic, though for his own reasons, to some of the objectives which led the Shakers to adopt community life. He too saw the need for social discipline and the breakdown of private family allegiances in favour of a larger social unit. When in addition he found that the Shakers had developed a self-sufficient economy based on agriculture and simple crafts, using hand labour skilfully, and emphasizing quality and fair dealing, he triumphantly cited them as proof that the principles of communitarianism were sound. More than that, the success of this (and other) millennial sects suggested that in them might be found a model (suitably secularized) for the Owenite movement.

The variety and wide extent of premillennial sectarianism in Britain

[1] Frederick W. Evans, *Autobiography of a Shaker, and Revelation of the Apocalypse* (New York, 1869).

and America from the late eighteenth century until the Civil War needs to be emphasized if the full strength of the millennial heritage in relation to Owenism is to be appreciated. In the German-American sects of Rappites at Harmony and Separatists at Zoar, and in the communities at Ephrata, Amana, Aurora and Bethel, millennial beliefs were maintained together with views on community property and celibacy similar to those of the Shakers. Each originated from the prophetic teachings of some inspired leader who believed that the millennium was very near. Father George Rapp from whom Owen purchased the community of Harmony, believed that he would live to see Christ's Second Coming, and even on his death bed declared to his followers: 'If I did not know that the dear Lord meant I should present you all to him, I should think my last moments come.' The Mormons and the Millerites in America numbered their adherents by the thousands, and both found followers in Britain. In the back country of America messiahs and prophets of the millennium could almost always find followers, and in Kent, England, a messiah who posed as Sir William Courtenay died with his followers in a bloody affray with the military in May 1838.[1] The Disciples of Christ (Campbellites), Swedenborgians, Plymouth Brethren and Oneida Perfectionists were but some of the better-known examples of Anglo-American millenarians.

Throughout the life of the Owenite movement there was thus what may be called a 'culture' of prophecy and eschatology. It provided a framework within which the dislocation caused by the social and political changes of early industrialism in England, the Revolution in France, and expansion in America could all be related. At the respectable level the 'Signs of the Times' were interpreted to cover whatever a particular preacher or writer wished, from Thomas Carlyle's castigation of the 'mechanical' nature of the age to John Keble's sermon on National Apostasy launching the Oxford Movement in 1833.[2] At a more popular level the Book of Revelation, with its condemnation of 'Babylon the Great, the Mother of the Harlots and of the Abominations of the Earth', provided a fascinating language of protest.[3] Given the premises of ultra-

---

[1] An Account of the Desperate Affray which took place in Blean Wood near Boughton on Thursday, the 31st of May 1838 (Canterbury, 1838); P. G. Rogers, Battle in Bossenden Wood: The Strange Story of Sir William Courtenay (London, 1961).

[2] Thomas Carlyle, 'Signs of the Times', Edinburgh Review, XCVIII (1829) referred to the contemporary 'rage of prophecy' and the millenarians. A representative sample of this 'rage' in Britain is contained in the Investigator, or Monthly Expositor and Register of Prophecy (4 vols., London, 1831–35), edited by Joshua W. Brooks (an Anglican clergyman), and his Dictionary of Writers on the Prophecies (London, 1835) listed over 2000 titles, including many published between 1790 and 1834.

[3] D. H. Lawrence, Apocalypse (New York, 1932), pp. 10–22, explained the continuing appeal of Revelation among the working-class chapelgoers whom he knew in his youth.

RATIONAL RELIGIONIST'S

ADVENT HYMN.

TO BE SUNG ON THE TWENTY-FIFTH OF DECEMBER, COMMONLY
CALLED CHRISTMAS DAY.

I.

Brothers, arise! behold the dawn appear
Of Truth's bright day, and Love's Millennial Year!
See how the Millions hail, with lifted eyes,
The glorious change that gilds their troubled skies!
Hark! hark! the Anthem, pealing from on high,—
Community, Community, draws nigh!

II.

The midnight gloom of Ignorance retires;
And fast are fading Error's fatual fires
From broken clouds effulgent Science beams,
With facts, dispelling fear and fiction's dreams.
The Social Age,—divinest birth of time!—
To being springs, in bliss and beauty's prime.

III.

The woes of war shall hence for ever cease,
And plenty bloom amid perpetual peace;
Mankind shall turn from Competition's strife,
To share the blessings of Communial life.
Justice shall triumph—leagued oppression fail—
And Universal happiness prevail.

J. Hobson, Printer, 5, Market Street, Briggate, Leeds.—PRICE ONE HALFPENNY.

14. Advent Hymn

THE
WORLD'S CONVENTION

OF

DELEGATES FROM THE HUMAN RACE

WILL BE HELD IN

ST MARTIN'S HALL,

LONG ACRE, LONDON,

ON MONDAY, MAY 14,

When will be explained the

DIVINE MELLENNIAL STATE OF
LIFE UPON THE EARTH,

And the Means of speedily attaining it peaceably in practice for the Population of the World.

WHEN ALSO WILL BE EXHIBITED A

PAINTING OF THE

DEVASTATOR

OR

NEW WAR MACHINE

Which, as it will compel War to cease, should be called

THE UNIVERSAL PEACE MAKER.

May 2nd.   **ROBERT OWEN.**

15. Handbill announcing the millennium

protestantism it was open to anyone to make his own interpretation of scriptural prophecy;[1] and once begun the process could easily be extended far beyond its original scriptural base.

The ideology of millennialism which emerged from this variety of movements on both sides of the Atlantic was marked by certain clearly defined characteristics.[2] It was first and foremost an ideology of change, and change which was sudden, total and irrevocable. In this sense millennialism was a revolutionary ideology. The change envisaged was not an improvement of the present, but an utter rejection and replacement of it by something perfect. This change was felt to be very near. Catastrophe was imminent, and the Signs of the Times confirmed the sense of expectancy and urgency. The agency of change was to be supernatural, and not therefore bounded by the limits of human possibility. Rational objections or improbabilities were simply discountenanced, and hope was boundless, for human (sinful) nature would be transformed (or, redeemed). This impending change was made known by the message of a prophet, or, in certain cases, by the messiah himself. Leadership in millennial movements tended therefore to be authoritarian or autocratic.

The millennium which would result had a recognizable pattern for most millenarians. It was to be established on earth, and enjoyed collectively by those who were saved. A privileged position for the Saints or the Chosen People was usually assumed, even if somewhat unintentionally, and their role prior to the establishment of the millennium was to proclaim the truth and prepare themselves for the Second Advent. Life during the millennium would be a state of bliss, generally thought of in the imagery of heaven described in the Book of Revelation. To the millenarian mind all issues were to be resolved in terms of absolute moral categories, a simplification which provided a powerful stimulus to action and a solution to any knotty intellectual problems which might threaten faith. Anything that hindered the speedy coming of the Kingdom was sinful. The millennial mentality reduced all complicated issues to a simple clear-cut choice between good and evil; political, economic

---

[1] The Millerite Joshua V. Himes, in his *Views of the Prophets and Prophetic Chronology* (Boston, 1842), pp. 20–32, provided a 'do-it-yourself-kit', with rules and explanations for interpreting the prophecies.

[2] Of modern writing on millennialism the following will be found most useful: Sylvia L. Thrupp, ed., *Millennial Dreams in Action* (The Hague, Netherlands, 1962); Norman Cohn, *The Pursuit of the Millennium* (London, 1957); Ernest Lee Tuveson, *Millennium and Utopia* (Berkeley and Los Angeles, Cal., 1949); D. H. Kromminga, *The Millennium in the Church* (Grand Rapids, Mich., 1945); Martin Buber, *Paths in Utopia* (London, 1949); Karl Mannheim, *Ideology and Utopia* (London, 1936); E. J. Hobsbawm, *Primitive Rebels* (Manchester, 1959); Henry De Man, *The Psychology of Socialism* (London, 1928); and Elmer T. Clark, *The Small Sects in America* (Nashville, Tenn., 1937).

and social problems were thus decided in absolute terms. However, the consciousness of living near the 'end of time,' when the whole historical process would be consummated, made such problems seem relatively minor, and involvement in political action appeared largely irrelevant. The typical millenarian mind was basically dogmatic and ahistorical. Concerned almost wholly with the future, it could find certainty for its hopes only in faith; there could not be a science of the future, only an ardent millennial hope. In premillennial adventist movements the preservation of this hope in the face of experiences of disillusion was a serious problem, and led to the elaboration of explanations of defeat and the working out of survival mechanisms.

Among millennial movements it was commonly observed that they drew their support from wider circles of religious and social concern. Revivalism was probably the most fertile seed bed for millennial prophets and their followers. The role of the frontier in America has also frequently been cited as a factor in the growth of millennialism, and it is tempting to extend the idea to a metaphorical frontier of the new industrialism in Britain—to see in Lancashire and the West Riding of Yorkshire, where so many millennial sects had their strongholds, another 'Burned-over District'. In both countries, while millennial sects were essentially popular manifestations, they were not confined to one particular class or group. Working men, farmers and (in Britain) 'the poor' probably made up a majority of the membership, but in almost all movements there was also support from substantial, and sometimes wealthy, members of the middle class. A special role was frequently played by women. Where the messiah was female, she usually attracted as her right-hand support a male disciple, frequently a clergyman; and where a male prophet appeared he was soon surrounded by the adulations of unmarried women. The unorthodox handling of sexual relationships became a marked characteristic of most continuing millennial sects, ranging from complete celibacy to free love, and in all cases justified on theological grounds.

Such, then, was the millennial matrix in which Owenism developed. Almost all the characteristics outlined in the last few paragraphs are found in Owenism. And some Owenites had close ties with the movements mentioned earlier. It has been customary to write that Owenism after 1835 'degenerated' into a 'mere' sect, the implication being presumably that in its earlier stages it might have been something different, such as a political party or a mass movement of the working class. In fact Owenism developed as a millennial sect, not through failure to achieve some other institutional form, but through the logic of its need to communicate.

Disciples and Prophets

Among the earliest of Owen's followers was Abram Combe (1785–1827).[1] He was a brother of George Combe, the phrenologist, and Andrew Combe, a well-known physiologist. Another brother, William, was associated with Abram in his Owenite community and after its collapse emigrated in 1828 to America, where he managed a brewery in Albany, New York, and later in Jersey City. Their father was a brewer in Edinburgh, and strictly instructed his children in Calvinist principles. Abram was apprenticed to a tanner, and from 1807 onwards had his own tannery business in Edinburgh. Until 1820 his interests were those of a typical Scots manufacturer and merchant. He was hard-working, just and self-centred; and 'his benevolence evaporated in a general wish for the welfare of mankind, which led to no active measures for promoting their enjoyment'.

In October 1820, however, he visited New Lanark with his brother George, and was introduced to Owen. Abram was very impressed by what he saw and by what Owen said, and after returning home began to study Owen's writings. He rapidly became an enthusiastic convert, and to his friends it appeared that the changes in his character resulting from his adoption of the New View of Society actually were akin to those usually associated with (religious) conversion. Previously he had been a severe satirist of the faults of others, and had ebulliently championed the pursuit of self-interest as man's first duty. Now he spoke of universal benevolence and justice, showed compassion for others' weaknesses, and gave up animal food, fermented liquor and the theatre. He offered to join Owen in his first proposed community, but this did not materialize.

Combe's Owenite activities began in the autumn of 1821, with the foundation of the Edinburgh Practical Society.[2] This was a club promoted by a group of Scottish followers of Owen, including Donald Macdonald, a captain in the Royal Engineers, and Archibald J. Hamilton,

---

[1] The main source for Abram Combe's life is the memoir in the *Register for the First Society of Adherents to Divine Revelation at Orbiston*, 19 September 1827, pp. 65–71. This was also reprinted in John Gray, *Social System* (Edinburgh, 1831), in Minter Morgan, *Hampden in the Nineteenth Century*, and in Alexander Campbell, ed., *Life and Dying Testimony of Abram Combe* (London, 1844). Additional material is in the Combe Papers, National Library of Scotland, and in Alastair C. Grant, 'George Combe and his Circle' (unpublished Ph.D. thesis, Edinburgh University, 1960). See also Cullen, *Adventures in Socialism*.

[2] In addition to the above references, there is an account of the Practical Society by Donald Macdonald in the *New Harmony Gazette*, 22 February 1826, pp. 173–4. See also the *Economist*, II (1821), 336, 345–52.

the laird of Dalzell. Its activities did not extend to the formation of a community, but regular social meetings, a cooperative store, and a school for 128 children were organized. Membership was over 500, 'all of them (with few exceptions) industrious and hard-working mechanics or labourers'. After about a year the Society 'languished', and Combe then tried a small-scale community experiment at his tan works. Arrangements were made for communal living and sharing of profits, but 'the individuals thus brought together . . ., like those who constituted the Cooperative Society, were unprepared in their mental habits for their new condition; and the scheme soon fell to the ground of itself'. His last and most ambitious venture was the establishment of a community at Orbiston on an estate of 290 acres lying nine miles east of Glasgow. With the support of A. J. Hamilton and several other philanthropists he began the experiment in 1825 and carried it on until his premature death in 1827, after which it was closed.

The name of the Orbiston community, 'the First Society of Adherents to Divine Revelation', puzzled and irritated both friends and enemies. Combe was at pains to explain, not very successfully, what he meant by it.[1] Divine Revelation was, essentially, 'the facts and truths which the Great Governing Power of the Universe reveals to the senses and understanding'. The voice of reason guides man in harmony with the laws of nature, and this revelation of nature and reason is sufficient to direct men into the path of duty. God has implanted in man a desire for happiness which can be fulfilled only through obedience to natural laws. Nature has been given by God as a revelation, reason as an instructor and experience as a guide. Existing religious sects and churches have disregarded this divine revelation of nature and reason and have led men astray; but obedience to the laws of nature, which are the laws of God, would avoid all theological disputation and heal sectarian differences. Although the truths in the Bible are justly termed divine revelation, strictly the written accounts in the Old and New Testaments are the history of the original divine revelation, and not that revelation itself. Not unjustly could critics at Orbiston like Captain O'Brien complain that by Divine Revelation Combe meant nothing else but natural religion.

---

[1] This he did in Abram Combe, *Address to the Conductors of the Periodical Press upon the Causes of Religious and Political Disputes* (Edinburgh, 1823); *The Religious Creed of the New System* (Edinburgh, 1824); and *The New Court No. 1* (n.p., 1825). His general exposition of Owenism was given in *Metaphorical Sketches of the Old and New Systems* (Edinburgh, 1823); and in *Observations on the Old and New Views* (Edinburgh, 1823). Plans for a community were detailed in *The Sphere for Joint-Stock Companies* (Edinburgh, 1825); and *Proposal for Commencing the Experiment of Mr. Owen's System* (n.p., 1824). In the *Register* Combe printed accounts of the community at Orbiston and also his theoretical views.

The question that arises from this is why Combe should have felt it necessary to invent and defend such a title for what was basically a typical eighteenth-century deistical position. He was certainly anxious to defend Owenism against the common charges of atheism and infidelity; and when he embraced Owen's views he may have felt a need for some token reconciliation with elements of his former religious belief. What is clear is that Owenism became for him a religion, and he accepted Owen's precepts as prophetic truths. Combe did not use the word millennium, but he began to think in millennial terms and enact the role of a minor prophet (within the Combe family he was endearingly referred to as 'the Patriarch' and regarded as a strange genius). His views were expressed in absolute categories—Truth versus Error, Good versus Evil, Knowledge and Happiness versus Ignorance, Misery and Vice. The whole of past history had been 'nothing but a catalogue of the sufferings which Ignorance entailed upon the human race', but now Truth has been proclaimed and a new era is about to begin. From Owen he took his definitions of Truth as that which is universally consistent with itself and Good as everything which promotes happiness; and then simply added that this information came from the Great Governing Power of the Universe, which was sufficient guarantee against any possibility of error.

Abram Combe exhibited many characteristics of the millennial mentality: belief in the imminence of a great and fundamental change in society, a dogmatic reduction of all issues to simple absolute alternatives, and the circumvention of logical difficulties by faith in divine certainty. Yet, in spite of its name, his goal was basically a secular millennium. There is no evidence that he was ever regarded as a religious leader, and his role at Orbiston was no more than that of any similarly placed paternal reformer. He never claimed supernatural inspiration and he did not quote scripture. Almost all his social and philosophic notions were taken from Owen, and his natural impulse was to start practical measures to put them into effect. Combe was a practical rather than a theoretical millenarian, who aimed to establish a secular utopia which he would nevertheless be prepared to designate the Kingdom of God.

Simultaneously with Abram Combe's gathering of the first Adherents to Divine Revelation in Scotland, Owen was proclaiming the millennium in America. As we have seen, for a decade prior to his arrival in New York in November 1824 Owen had been familiar with accounts of the Shakers, Rappites and Moravians in America, and within a fortnight he visited the Shaker community at Niskeyuna. Early the following January he purchased the whole Rappite village of Harmony, Indiana, and began his experiment of the new system of society on the same spot as Father Rapp had sought to prepare for the millennium. Since 1817 Owen had been presenting his ideas in millennial language and this he continued to do in America, further strengthened by association with the native millenarian tradition.

Owen's first visit to the United States, from November 1824 to July 1825, was one long triumphal tour. Everywhere he went he was honoured and listened to with respect, and in Washington he gained the ear of the President and leading members of the government. In February and March he gave two discourses on his new system of society in the Hall of Representatives in the Capitol, 'in the presence of the President of the United States, the President Elect, Heads of Departments, [and] Members of Congress'. He told his audience that he had come to America to introduce an entirely new social system, whose inauguration he announced in millennial terms: 'the time is now come, when the principle of good is about to predominate and reign triumphant over the principle of evil. ... old things shall pass away and all shall become new'.[1] Arriving back in New Harmony he made a 4th of July speech entitled 'A Declaration of Mental Independence', the full implications of which he explained at his Sunday evening lectures 'for instruction in the new system'. The measures advocated, he declared, 'may not improperly be termed the beginning of the millennium'; and three weeks later he assured the New Harmonists:

The day of your deliverance is come, and let us join heart and hand in extending that deliverance, first to those who are near, then to those who are more and more remote, until it shall pass to all people, even unto the uttermost parts of the earth. Then will be the full time of that universal sabbath, or reign of happiness, which is about to commence here, and which I trust you who are ready to put on the wedding garment, will long live to enjoy.[2]

In these Sunday evening discussions Owen was questioned closely about his views, including what he meant by the millennium. He replied:

Had I lived four thousand years ago, I could, with my present knowledge of human nature, have predicted that a millennium, or a state of universal happiness, would take place.

Question. But was not the prediction of a millennium which we find recorded in the book, revealed to those who prognosticated it?

[1] *Two Discourses on A New System of Society; as delivered in the Hall of Representatives at Washington* . . . (London, 1825), p. 14.
[2] *New Harmony Gazette*, 2 August 1826.

Answer. It was one of those perceptions of truth which the sages of former times were enabled to catch by the light of nature. The word revelation, in the sense in which it is used by sectarians, has no place in my vocabulary. You may call it revelation, if you please, but 'real knowledge' appears to me to be a less bewildering expression.[1]

This equation of the millennium with a state of successful practical Christianity, in which love towards one's neighbour would ensure complete happiness, was echoed by his followers: 'I am confident', wrote 'A Christian', in the *New Harmony Gazette* (11 January 1826), 'that King Emanuel will shortly come and reign triumphantly in N. Harmony.' To sectarians who had rejected priestcraft and who were seeking for signs of a kingdom in which the sayings of Jesus and the prophecies of Revelation could be literally realized, Owen's millennium commencing at New Harmony seemed both attractive and feasible. A significant minority of the identifiable leaders of American Owenism in the 1820s had associations with millenarian sects or professed a sectarian type of Christianity which bordered on universalism, deism and rationalism. Robert L. Jennings, who was a member of the original governing committee of New Harmony and also active in the Franklin community at Haverstraw, New York, had been a universalist preacher. William Ludlow, who experimented with communitarian projects before joining Owen at New Harmony,[2] had previously been resident at the Shaker community in New Lebanon. In his *Belief of the Rational Brethren of the West* (Cincinnati, Ohio, 1819) Ludlow presented the case for a rational Christianity which was close to the Owenite position:

Every true Rationalist, who understands the essential word of God, in the laws of nature, has seen the Christ, and for that reason knows the Father . . . [St.] John positively declares that Jesus Christ is come in the flesh; and we can with as much propriety declare that Jesus Christ is now in the flesh; and that this man Jesus Christ who was in the flesh in John's latter days, is the same that is now in the flesh, wherever men do to their fellows as they would have their fellows do to them: and that this man Jesus Christ is nothing more, nor less, than true knowledge and goodness, which forms us God-like in our dispositions, causing us to love God and man (pp. 69, 75–6).

In Cincinnati the Swedenborgian minister, Daniel Roe, and his congregation formed the Owenite Yellow Springs community, and Swedenborgians were numerous at New Harmony. At Kendal, Ohio, an Owenite

---

[1] *New Harmony Gazette*, 9 August 1826.
[2] Together with James M. Dorsey, who became a leading member of the New Harmony community, Ludlow projected a community called the Rational Brethren of Oxford (Ohio) in 1816–17, and in 1823 launched the Coal Creek Community and Church of God in Indiana.

community called the Friendly Association for Mutual Interests declared in the preamble to its constitution that since it was impossible to follow the two great principles of loving God and one's fellow creatures in the present state of society, it was necessary, in order to live a life according to Gospel precepts, to form a cooperative community.[1]

The relationship of Owenism with millennial sects was however a two-way process. On the one hand were cases like that of John Whitby, a member of the Pleasant Hill, Kentucky, Shaker community, who came to New Harmony and helped to draft the constitution: on the other, examples such as the Owenite members of the Valley Forge, Pennsylvania, community who in 1828 joined the Shakers. Probably the best known of those who made the transition from Owenism to Shakerism was Frederick W. Evans (1808–1893), an immigrant from England in 1820.[2] He was associated with his brother, George Henry Evans, a New York printer and bookseller who was a Free Enquirer and editor of the *Working Man's Advocate*. After studying Paine, Volney and Voltaire, Frederick Evans became a materialist and admirer of Owen. He walked eight hundred miles to join the Owenite community at Kendal, Ohio, but arrived only two months before its end. He had apparently had experience of other communities ('some of us had been in five or six different ones') and in 1830 was making plans for a new community in New York. While he was searching for a suitable location for it he visited the Shakers at Mount Lebanon, was impressed, and ultimately converted—not, he claimed, by reasoning 'but by spiritualism', being visited by angels in the night for three weeks continuously. He became an Elder of the society and an able propagandist for Shakerism, which he presented as including practical socialism and favourable to general social reform. At Lebanon he found another Owenite socialist—Abel Knight from Philadelphia—who had become a Shaker; and in due course they were joined by Daniel Fraser, the son of a silk weaver from Paisley, Scotland, who had emigrated in 1834, intending to found an Owenite workers' community. The cross links between Owenism and American religious sectarianism in the 1820s were strong, and this strength was drawn from two main sources, communitarianism and millenarianism, which were combined with particular success in Shakerism.

In the 1830s the identification of Owenism with millennial sectarianism was taken a stage further in Britain. The reconciliation of Divine Revelation with the laws of nature by means of a millennial synthesis, which

[1] Wendall P. Fox, 'The Kendal Community', *Ohio Archaeological and Historical Publications*, XX (1911), 178–9.
[2] Evans, *Autobiography of a Shaker*.

Abram Combe had attempted, was developed much more elaborately by a fellow Scot who had also been reared in strict Calvinist discipline. James Elishama ('Shepherd') Smith (1801–1857) was destined by his father for the Presbyterian ministry, and after obtaining his degree from Glasgow University in 1818 spent several years as a private tutor and visiting preacher.[1] His mind, however, was not satisfied by the orthodoxies of the Church of Scotland, and he began a restless search for a more acceptable faith. For a time his ideas of the millennium, or 'Messiah's Kingdom', were indefinite. Then in 1828 he first heard Edward Irving preach in Edinburgh and his millennial yearnings were strengthened. So successful was his advocacy of Irvingism that he carried his father and several members of the family into the Irvingite camp, where they remained long after Smith had moved on to fresh pastures.

For Shepherd Smith the exploration of millennial doctrine was only just beginning, and he soon made contact with the Southcottians, a sect whose history dates from 1792. In that year a Devonshire country woman heard 'Voices' which convinced her that she was a prophetess. Joanna Southcott, a middle-aged spinster employed as a domestic worker and upholstress in Exeter, began to prophesy that Christ's Second Coming was nigh, and claimed that she was the Bride of the Lamb described in Revelation 19.[2] She wrote down the messages revealed to her, many of them in doggerel, and in 1801 published her first pamphlet, *The Strange Effects of Faith*. Until this time she had failed to convince anyone of the validity of her claims, but in that year disciples began to gather. A key group of them were followers of Richard Brothers, a prophet whom the government had confined in an Islington lunatic asylum since 1795.[3]

[1] The only full-length biography of Smith is by his nephew, William Anderson Smith, *'Shepherd' Smith the Universalist: the Story of a Mind* (London, 1892), which while seriously deficient at many points has the great merit of reprinting many of Shepherd Smith's letters. There is a short account of him in R. W. Postgate, *Out of the Past* (London, 1922) and an inaccurate entry by Richard Garnett in the *D.N.B.* The most useful study of Smith as a millenarian is Donald Raymond Cook, 'Reverend James Elishama Smith: Socialist Prophet of the Millennium' (unpublished M.A. thesis, State University of Iowa, 1961), to which I am much indebted.

[2] Joanna Southcott was the author of 65 books and pamphlets, some of which were reissued by Alice Seymour in the twentieth century. The most useful modern study is G. R. Balleine, *Past Finding Out: The Tragic Story of Joanna Southcott and her Successors* (London, 1956), but lacks an adequate bibliography and notes. See also Alice Seymour, *The Express: . . . containing the Life and Divine Writings of the late Joanna Southcott* (London, 1909); and Charles Arthur Lane, *Life and Bibliography of Joanna Southcott* [Exeter, 1912]. Contemporary comment on Joanna Southcott and Richard Brothers is contained in two chapters in Robert Southey, *Letters from England: by Don Manuel Alvarez Espriella* (London, 1807).

[3] Cecil Roth, *The Nephew of the Almighty* (London, 1933) is a slight and facetious account of Brothers, though apparently based on wide reading of his writings. The British

Brothers was a young naval officer on half pay, who after studying the writings on prophecy, was convinced that the millennium was now due. Furthermore, he identified himself as King of the Hebrews and Nephew of God, and interceded with the Almighty to spare London from destruction by earthquake for its infidelity. Brothers' *Revealed Knowledge of the Prophecies and Times* (London, 1794) went through several editions and was reprinted in America. His followers included Nathaniel Brassey Halhed, an Orientalist and M.P. for Lymington, William Sharp, a noted engraver and radical reformer, three Anglican clergymen, and businessmen in Liverpool, Manchester and Leeds. These transferred their allegiance to Joanna, who began the practice of 'sealing' believers as a sign of their renunciation of Satan. By January 1804 over 8000 disciples had been sealed, and one estimate put the number of converts in London and its neighbourhood at one time at above 100,000.[1] Southcottian chapels were opened in London, Bristol, Lancashire and Yorkshire; a constant stream of publications by Joanna poured forth; and the sealing of thousands 'to inherit the Tree of Life, to be made Heirs of God and joint-heirs with Jesus Christ' went on rapidly. Joanna's doctrine of the Woman reached its tragic climax in 1814 when she announced in her *Third Book of Wonders* that her 'Voice' had told her that she would bear a son by a miraculous conception. This would be the fulfilment of an obscure passage in Genesis 49 referring to Shiloh. But although the prophetess underwent an hysterical pregnancy no child was born and Joanna died of the shock of disillusionment.

Her career brings out in several ways the complex and perhaps unexpected nature of British millennialism. Joanna was a devout member of the Church of England, and most of her efforts were directed to persuading individual clergymen and bishops to examine her prophecies. The manner in which she received these revelations was described simply and unaffectedly at the beginning of her *Second Book of Wonders* (London, 1813):

I have fresh things revealed to me every day. I am waked every morning between three and four o'clock; I sit up in my bed until the day breaks; and have communications given to me as soon as I awake. When the day breaks I rise and go down into the diningroom by myself; the moment I enter the room, I

---

[1] *Phrenological Journal*, VII (1831–32), 360–1.

Museum lists over 50 items relating to Brothers, mostly of the period 1794–96. Thompson, *The Making of the English Working Class*, pp. 117–19, 382–8, 799–801, has valuable interpretations of Brothers, Joanna Southcott, John Wroe and Zion Ward in relation to the working classes. See also Armytage, *Heavens Below*.

feel as though I was surrounded with angels; feeling a heavenly joy which I cannot describe, and which has taken from me my natural appetite.

Among her earliest and staunchest supporters were three Anglican clergymen—the Reverend Thomas Philip Foley, rector of Old Swinford, Worcestershire; the Reverend Thomas Webster, lecturer in two City of London churches; and the Reverend Stanhope Bruce, vicar of Inglesham. In Leeds her chief supporter was George Turner, a prosperous merchant. But she also attracted support in that town from poorer people, including the notorious 'wise woman', Mary Bateman, who was hanged for poisoning. Bateman posed as a follower of Joanna and collected fees for displaying millennial eggs marked 'Crist [sic] is Coming', laid by one of her hens. The attraction of Southcottianism was not confined to one specific class or group, but included scholars, businessmen and workers in different parts of the country, the main strongholds being in London, the industrial North and Midlands, and the West country. Its persistent history after the death of Joanna in 1814 suggests that it catered to religious, psychological or social needs which may have been much more widespread than the particular form of the sect itself. The ease with which an explanation of the Shiloh disappointment was found and accepted, while characteristic of millennial sects, shows the strength of the desire to retain a millennial faith.

For a time the mantle of Joanna fell on George Turner of Leeds, though many of her followers in London and the Midlands refused to acknowledge him. Turner had been a disciple of Brothers, from whom he inherited the British-Israel doctrine which henceforth was part of the Southcottian faith; and to this he added a series of prophetic forecasts of the exact date when Shiloh would appear. His proclamation of the arrival of King Shiloh and the commencement of the millennium in 1817 prompted his arrest for high treason by a nervous government; but after the jury had found him insane he was confined for three years in the Retreat, the Quaker asylum in York. Turner died in 1821 and the Southcottians remained divided into several groups. In the North the leadership was assumed by John Wroe, a hunchbacked woolcomber from Bradford, who first received visions and prophecies during an illness in 1819.[1] He had a strong following in Bradford and the West Riding of Yorkshire, and also in Ashton-under-Lyne (his headquarters) where several wealthy

[1] *An Abridgement of John Wroe's Life and Travels* (Wakefield, 1837). Another edition, in 3 vols., was published from Gravesend, 1851–55. Also *Life and Journal of John Wroe* (Gravesend, 1859). For bibliography of Wroe see *British Museum General Catalogue of Printed Books*, and Charles A. Federer (ed.), *Catalogue of Wakefield Books* (Wakefield, 1897).

manufacturers supported him. His teaching emphasized preparation for the millennium: 'God is going to establish His Kingdom and is preparing a People to partake of it.' Observance of the Mosaic law was enjoined on these 'Christian Israelites', who underwent circumcision, ate kosher meat, went unshaven and wore broad-brimmed hats and Quaker costume. An elaborate Sanctuary to hold 3000 people was built in Ashton, and missionaries were sent to all parts of the country as well as to America and Europe. Wroe ruled the sect autocratically until 1830; when finally his weakness for debauchery caught up with him, and charges of sexual indecency with three young women were laid against him. The South-cottian meetings repudiated him, but for the next thirty years he continued to win fresh adherents in Britain and Australia who built him a mansion near Wakefield. In 1853 there were over sixty Christian Israelite societies in the British Isles.

A rival prophet among the Southcottians was John (Zion) Ward, a Methodist shoemaker who was influenced by his reading of Joanna's *Fifth Book of Wonders* and Richard Carlile's freethinking works to declare in 1828 that the Last Days had begun and that he (Ward) was Shiloh, and, later, Christ.[1] He gained support in many Southcottian meetings, especially in Nottingham, and his virulent attacks on priest-craft and the Establishment introduced a new and popular note. During 1831 he drew large crowds at the Rotunda, the radical forum over Blackfriars Bridge in London; and in 1832 was gaoled for blasphemy in Derby.

Among those who made the pilgrimage to Ashton-under-Lyne was Shepherd Smith. After several visits he was convinced that the prophet John Wroe was a man of God, and in 1830 he joined the Southcottians there.[2] Smith's superior education gave him a position of influence among the Ashton Wroeites. He preached, conducted a school, and taught Hebrew. He adopted Wroe's Judaism, grew a beard, and was circum-cized. After the expulsion of Wroe by the Ashton church Smith's aspirations to the leadership were frustrated by the arrival of John Ward, the Shiloh, from London, and Smith returned to Edinburgh, where a small body of Southcottians remained loyal to him under the leadership of his

---

[1] Zion Ward's works were republished by H. B. Hollingsworth at Birmingham, 1899–1904. The British Museum lists entries under 'C. B. H.'. See Balleine, p. 105; Thompson, pp. 799–800.

[2] There is an account of Wroe and other Southcottians in Smith's *The Coming Man* (2 vols., London, 1873), parts of which are autobiographical. This work was finished in 1848 but only published posthumously. It is in the form (popular among reformers in the first half of the nineteenth century) of a novel, the characters being vehicles for the exposition of universalist doctrines and millenarian experiences.

close friend, Dr James Napier. Shortly afterwards Smith went to London, in order, as he wrote later, 'to see what Providence would do for me'.

The London in which he arrived in August 1832 was, as it happened, providential for him in several unforeseen ways. He had gone to the metropolis vaguely hoping to earn a livelihood as an artist, for which he had some talent, but rapidly discovered the possibility of supporting himself as a lecturer in Southcottian circles. John Ward's imprisonment for blasphemy had left vacant the leadership of his London chapel, and Smith stepped smartly into the breach. His followers were considerably more mixed than the ones he had known in Ashton and Edinburgh, and he soon became aware of radical social doctrines which were quite new to him. Among his hearers was Mrs Anna Wheeler, feminist and friend of William Thompson, and she introduced Smith to the ideas and followers of Owen, Saint-Simon and Fourier. This was also the period when Edward Irving, expelled from his Regent Square chapel, was using the hall of Owen's Equitable Labour Exchange in Grays Inn Road for his Sunday morning preaching; and through his acquaintance with Irving, Smith first became aware of Owen and his work. Throughout 1833 Smith's reputation as a popular lecturer on social and millennial doctrines, which he called universalism, grew steadily. He drew large audiences in the Rotunda, which established his name in radical circles, and in June he was invited to lecture to the Owenites in their Charlotte Street Institute. From then until his break with Owen in August 1834 Smith was the regular Sunday morning lecturer at Charlotte Street, and his weekly lecture appeared as the front page article in the *Crisis*. In addition, in September 1833 he took over the editorship of the *Crisis*, which had been edited earlier by Robert Dale Owen and, latterly, by Owen himself.

Smith's sudden ascendancy within the Owenite movement was, on the face of it, somewhat extraordinary. A year previously he had scarcely heard of Owen, and within a few months of coming to London he was occupying the key position of editor of the chief Owenite journal, and was the principal weekly lecturer in the Owenite headquarters institute. Yet he was not in any sense an orthodox Owenite, and inclined more to the doctrines of Saint-Simon, whose *New Christianity* he translated and published in 1834. After Robert Dale Owen returned to America in April 1833, Owen was anxious to find an editor for the *Crisis* so that he himself could be free to devote his time to other aspects of the movement, and Smith appeared sufficiently competent and unorthodox to be acceptable. From his side Smith was moving closer to a socialist position, though unwilling to commit himself to any particular doctrine:

no single individual can enlighten the world, or regenerate society. . . . We must suck honey from every flower, and collect the scattered fragments of truth together.[1]

However, he read John Minter Morgan's *Revolt of the Bees*, and by March 1834 was writing to his brother John:

Men will never be made better by preaching. It is only by improving their circumstances by an equal distribution of the produce of labour, and by setting all men to work at some useful occupation. About one-half of the present generation do nothing at all. The rich merely live on the sweat of the poor man's brow. . . . It is all vain to talk about the scriptural forms of government for the Church as long as there is such an unjust system of distribution of wealth practised.[2]

Smith's association with Owenism coincided with the trade union phase of the movement. In April 1833, when Robert Dale Owen relinquished the editorship, the subtitle of the *Crisis* was changed, significantly, from 'the change from Error and Misery to Truth and Happiness', to 'National Cooperative Trades Union and Equitable Labour Exchange Gazette'. Within a few months of becoming editor, Smith became caught up in the phenomenal rise of trade unionism which culminated in the Grand National Consolidated Trades Union, formed in February 1834. Not only did he fill the pages of the *Crisis* with trade union news, but he also contributed articles to James Morrison's *Pioneer*, the organ of the Operative Builders' Union and later of the G.N.C.T.U.[3] He was therefore in the very centre of the controversies which broke out when the G.N.C.T.U. collapsed during the summer of 1834, and had, moreover, become very critical of certain aspects of Owen's doctrines. In the struggles which developed within the council of the G.N.C.T.U. Smith sided with Morrison against Owen, and the *Crisis* became increasingly representative of Smith's views. This Owen was not prepared to tolerate, and in August he closed down the *Crisis*, leaving Smith to look elsewhere for an outlet through which to preach his doctrines.

The outcome was that Smith started a new journal, the *Shepherd*, while Owen commenced the *New Moral World* as the official organ of his movement. In the *Shepherd*, which he ran from 1834 to 1835 and again from 1837 to 1838, Smith elaborated most completely the combination of religious millennialism and social radicalism which he termed

---

[1] Rev. J. E. Smith, trans., *New Christianity*, by Henri de Saint-Simon (London, 1834), translator's preface, p. vi.

[2] Anderson Smith, pp. 95–6.

[3] See especially his 'Letters on Associated Labour' under the pseudonym 'Sennex'.

universalism. After his parting with Owen, Smith emphasized the unsatis-
factoriness of the materialist or infidel aspects of Owenism, but retained a
close interest in socialism, particularly Saint-Simonism and Fourierism.[1]
There was a suggestion that he might succeed the Owenite Lecturer,
Rowland Detrosier (1800–1834), at the Mechanics' Hall of Science in
Finsbury; but nothing came of this and Smith resumed his Sunday
lectures in the Saint-Simonian Hall in Castle Street. He also contributed
to the unstamped press, and in 1837 began the *Penny Satirist*, one of the
vigorous, racy penny serials which catered to the needs of radical working
men. Smith did not marry, and to his followers of ex-Wroeites and ultra-
progressives he appeared in the role of a millennial prophet. Among his
supporters were several wealthy females who were members of the
circle around James Pierrepont Greaves, the mystical socialist, with
whom he was on friendly terms. For a short period after 1840 his interest in Fourierism was intensified, and he wrote regularly for Hugh
Doherty's *London Phalanx* during 1841–42. But his experiences with
Fourierism and the *Phalanx* were similar to those with Owenism and the
Crisis. In neither case was he a wholly committed follower: 'I expect
nothing from Fourierism. It is one of the steps up to Universality.'[2]
However, he remained within the circle of 'ultras' who in the early 1840s
experimented with socialism, associationism and various kinds of 'physical
puritanism'.

In 1842 he commenced the *Family Herald: A Domestic Magazine of
Useful Information and Amusement*, which became widely popular among
sections of the lower middle and respectable working classes—not for
Smith's universalist doctrines (which were only occasionally in evidence) but because of his successful mixture of fiction, answers to correspondents and improving information. The *Family Herald* was much the
most successful of Smith's journalistic ventures, and provided him at last
with a regular, if modest, income. From 1848 he was attracted to occult
studies, and in the early 1850s interested himself in spiritualism along
with his former-Fourierist friends, Hugh Doherty and James J. Garth
Wilkinson. His primary interest however continued to be universalism,
and his *magnum opus*, *The Divine Drama of History and Civilization*,
published in 1854, was based on 'the science of historical analogy'. On this
work, he hoped, would rest his reputation 'for generations yet unborn'.

---

[1] Richard K. P. Pankhurst, *William Thompson* (London, 1954); *The Saint Simonians,
Mill and Carlyle* (London, 1957); and 'Anna Wheeler: A Pioneer Socialist and Feminist',
Political Quarterly, XXV (1954), 132–43.

[2] Letter to his brother, 21 December 1842. This and the following quotations from
letters are from Anderson Smith.

The Divine Drama was an interpretation of human history in terms of five great periods (or Acts), culminating in universalism, but its presentation was somewhat muted in comparison with his earlier writings and it attracted little notice. None of his earlier and more vigorous works contains a complete version of his 'dogma of universalism'. However, from his articles in the *Shepherd* and the *Crisis*, supplemented with *The Antichrist, or Christianity Reformed* (London, 1833) and *The Little Book; or Momentous Crisis of 1840* (London, 1840), it is possible to construct a fairly complete outline of his principles. Smith, like Owen, claimed that his doctrines were entirely original, but in fact they can all be found, with minor degrees of difference, in earlier millennialists, and to a considerable extent can be traced in the stages of his religious and social odyssey. At the centre of his universalism were the three ideas of polarity, analogy and the spiritual millennium.

The concept of polarity, or apparent contradictions, was based on the startling discovery that God and the Devil were one and the same. It may have been that Smith developed this view out of a need to preserve his faith at the time of John Wroe's defection; for it enabled him to recognize that Wroe was evil even though he was a genuine prophet of God. The problem of evil in a world created by a benevolent God Smith solved by declaring that what was called evil was in fact part of the divine plan for the ultimate realization of the millennium. This was the basic polarity. It was only an apparent contradiction, and likewise other contradictions were susceptible to the same interpretation. All philosophies and beliefs and movements contained some truth—and also falsehood—for all were part of God's plan, though none was final or complete in itself. This doctrine allowed Smith to choose and reject what he wanted from any system, to ally himself with any movement while not fully accepting its aims and tenets, and to make outrageous statements that seemed blasphemous. 'All doctrines I preach now,' he wrote from Ashton in 1830, '—eternal punishment and universal redemption in one and the same discourse. One Sunday I denied that Adam was made in the image of God, and perhaps I may some day deny that ever he fell.' He assured his brother in June 1831: 'I am no bigot or fanatic, . . . for I believe in all religions.' Smith's discovery of the unity of God and the Devil, good and evil, virtue and vice gave him a broad tolerance and sympathy towards any doctrine or movement in which he could find an element of truth. This was not always easy, but in his role as prophet he was certain that he had the power to extract the divine meaning from all philosophies. In the *Shepherd* his emphasis was on unity, the reconciliation of opposites, and demonstration of the need for contradictions to arrive at truth.

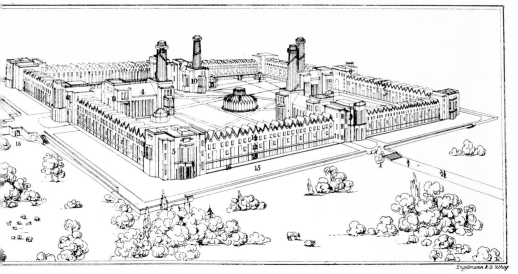

Engelmann & Co. lithog.

DESIGN

*for a Community of 2000 Persons founded upon a principle
Commended by* Plato, Lord Bacon *and* Sir Thomas More

EXPLANATION OF THE PARTS NUMBERED ON THE PLATE

1 Gymnasiums or Covered Places for Exercise, attached to the Schools and Infirmary.
2 Conservatory, in the midst of Gardens botanically arranged.
3 Baths, warm and cold, of which there are four for the Males, and four for the Females.
4 Dining Halls, with Kitchens, &c. beneath them.
5 Angle Buildings, occupied by the Schools for Infants, Children, and Youths, and the Infirmary; on the ground floors are Conversation-rooms for Adults.
6 Library, Detached Reading Rooms, Bookbindery, Printing Office, &c.
7 Ballroom and Music rooms.
8 Theatre for Lectures, Exhibitions, Discussions, &c. with Laboratory, Small Library, &c.
9 Museum, with Library of Description and Reference, Rooms for preparing Specimens, &c.
10 The Brew-houses, Bakehouses, Wash-houses, Laundries, &c. arranged round the Bases of the Towers.
11 The Refectories for the infants and children are on each side of the Vestibules of the Dining halls.
12 The Illuminators of the Establishment, Clock-towers, and Observatories, and from the elevated summits of which all the smoke and vitiated air of the buildings is discharged into the atmosphere.
13 Suites of adult sitting rooms and chambers.
14 Suites of Chambers, which may be easily and quickly made of any dimensions required; Dormitories for the Unmarried and Children.
15 Esplanade one hundred feet wide, about twelve feet above the natural surface.
16 Paved Footpath.
17 The Arcade and its Terrace, giving both a covered and an open communication with every part of the building.
18 Sub-way leading to the Kitchens, &c. and along which meat, vegetables, coals, &c. are conveyed to the Stores, and dust and refuse brought out.

16. Stedman Whitwell's design for an Owenite community

"A beam of tranquillity smild in the West."

17. Community in a garden (from John Minter Morgan,
Hampden in the Nineteenth Century, 1834)

'Nature', he wrote, 'is one splendid unity—connected in all its parts—and although apparently at times in violent opposition to itself, yet this opposition is only local and always tends to the restoration of tranquility.'[1] In Saint-Simonism, Owenism, Fourierism he found valuable elements of truth, so that he saw nothing inconsistent in working closely with these movements, even though he did not identify with them completely. He was convinced that they each contributed to the 'religion of progress, which, like the spinal marrow, has run up the backbone of Time, and is now forming the brain and intellectual system of the new world'.[2]

Closely connected with his doctrine of polarity in nature was Smith's 'science of analogy'. The eighteenth century had been fond of the analogies of scripture with nature; and somewhat in this tradition Smith argued that 'a perfect analogy subsists between the physical and the metaphysical, or moral, world. The same laws are at work in each, for both belong to the universal nature which is one grand unity throughout.'[3] The belief in progress which follows from this doctrine was as compelling for Smith as Dr Tuveson has shown it to have been for eighteenth-century millennialists such as William Worthington and Edmund Law: 'the stages of God's revelation parallel the stages of man's development; each level of history has its appropriate religion of nature'.[4] Herein lay the grounds for Smith's third dispensation—universalism or the millennium—since orthodox Christianity, which had earlier superseded Judaism, was now in its turn no longer adequate to the stage which man's development had reached.

The millennium which Smith anticipated was defined in a spiritual sense. His early belief in a personal Second Coming of Christ was superseded by

the discovery that the true Messiah was a divine principle, or in other words, the spirit of God manifested in the adoption of a beneficent ruling principle by human society; and that, whenever the fundamental character of Christianity, namely social love and equality, was received as the basis of political government, then it might be positively asserted that Christ was come, and that the Messiah had begun to reign.[5]

When the millennium was begun all men would become Christ in a spiritual sense: the messiah was the Spirit of Truth. At the same time,

---

[1] *Shepherd*, 22 August 1835.
[2] *Ibid.*, 14 March 1835.
[3] *Ibid.*, 20 September 1834.
[4] Tuveson, *Millennium and Utopia* (Harper Torchbook edn., 1964), p. 147.
[5] 'Messiah's Kingdom', *Shepherd*, 26 August 1837.

I

Smith did not rule out entirely the possibility that during the millennium or dispensation of universalism a physical messiah might reign. Like most popular millenarians Smith was tempted into predicting a precise date for the millennium. In *The Little Book; or Momentous Crisis of 1840* he juggled with numbers and prophecies and came up with 1840 as the decisive date. The millenarian's sense of crisis and longing to participate in the battle of the Last Days was strong in Smith. After the inevitable disappointment his writings lost something of their former vitality.

Other doctrines usually associated with millennialism were fitted into Smith's framework. Zion Ward had taught that the Bible was not to be taken as literal history, but as allegory. The events described as in the past were prophecies of future events. Smith accepted the Bible as historically true but was also prepared to use it allegorically. The Second Coming, for instance, while taking a spiritual form, would repeat the pattern of the first—it would be effected by a minority of reformers and iconoclasts, who would be rejected by the chosen people, persecuted, and finally triumphant. 'The Bible is written for both worlds, the old and the new; it is the tyrant's book and the people's book. . . . Like nature itself it contains good and evil, and you may take which you choose. It writes lies for the old world and truths for the new.'[1] The existing Christian churches were Antichrist, and would therefore be destroyed, so that the millennium could be begun. At the same time the restoration of the Jews would take place, in the sense that the 'truths' of Judaism would be incorporated in the third dispensation, which would thus be the new Israel, or Christ's Kingdom on earth. From the principle of analogy it was reasonable to expect that the millennium, which was 'the period of the Lord's coming in spirit', would come not to professing Christians, but to infidels. 'The Jews rejected Christ; and from analogy we may conclude that the Christians will oppose the introduction of the Millennium by the spirit of liberty.'[2] Smith's association with the Owenite infidels was thus quite logical. Owenism did not contain the whole 'truth', but its materialism was an essential element therein, and the Owenites were the heralds of the millennium.

By means of his principles of polarity and analogy Smith had little difficulty in accommodating Owen's rationalist devotion to the Laws of Nature within his universalist scheme of the millennium. Christian revelation and the laws of nature were perfectly compatible;

Mr Owen is a disciple of Nature, and only opposes Revelation so far as he thinks it disagrees with Nature; but he is perfectly willing . . . to see the two

[1] *Crisis*, 4 January 1834.
[2] *Ibid.*, 4 May 1833.

reconciled, for the leading feature of his system is 'unity'. Did Mr Owen not desire such a result, he would never have given encouragement to me. . . . If Nature and Revelation can be married together, it must be a most social union. Now they can and desire to be so united, and I now publish the banns. . . . Revelation is the bridegroom, and a stern, mystical old gentleman he is. Nature is the bride, the free woman. . . .[1]

Smith wrote this in September 1833, and at that time he evidently felt that he and Owen had arrived at similar conclusions about the millennium from different starting points.

Smith's condemnation of the churches as Antichrist paralleled Owen's long-standing rejection of all existing religions as false; and Owen from his side spoke in more generous terms of the contribution to truth made by 'Jesus of Nazareth'.[2] Smith exercised considerable ingenuity in showing a harmony between Christian and Owenite doctrines. On the problem of non-responsibility which followed from Owen's environmentalist theories, Smith argued:

the doctrine of non-responsibility is the doctrine of Scripture. . . . Thus, for instance, the beautiful doctrine of the atonement is nothing but the doctrine of non-responsibility, clothed in the outer garment of an historical fact. . . . Jesus Christ . . . is called God, or the Son of God. Then he is said to bear our sins—to stand in the room of sinners—to be their sponsor—that is, to take the blame of all our sins upon himself. This is the same as saying, in plain English, that God becomes responsible for all the sins of mankind, that they did not form themselves, that their natures were formed for, and not by them; that, therefore, not the individual man, but nature or God is accountable for all that is done by the individual whom He has brought into being.[3]

The most complete identification of Owenism with millennialism was in Smith's *Lecture on a Christian Community* (London, 1833),[4] delivered at the Surrey Institution early in 1833 and repeated in the Rotunda in April and May. It was this lecture which first attracted the attention of the Owenites to Smith and led to the invitation to lecture at the Charlotte Street Institute. The *Lecture* was written before Smith was actively working in the Owenite camp and it established his credentials, as a millenarian, among the Owenites. The burden of his discourse was that 'the establishment of the social system is nothing but the Christian millennium'. True Christianity, he argued, had never yet been established

---

[1] *Crisis*, 14 September 1833.
[2] E.g. letter read by Owen at a Sunday evening meeting at the Owenite institute, *Ibid.*, 7 September 1833.
[3] *Ibid.*, 10 August 1833.
[4] From which the quotations in this and the next paragraph are taken.

in the world, and could exist only in a 'system of society where equality of rank and privileges, as well as a community of goods, is acknowledged'. The Apostles had understood Christianity in terms of a community, and Jesus' teaching denounced the rich and respectable and elevated the poor and humble. That the existing Christianity of the rich should in fact be Antichrist was to be expected, for Christ forewarned against the coming of wolves in sheep's clothing:

If Christianity were truly established as it falsely pretends to be, it would . . . put an end to private capital, to private monopolies, to private ambition, to distinctions of rank, to unequal distribution of wealth, to ruinous competitions amongst manufacturers, to swindling, to adulteration of goods, to quackery and imposition of every description; . . . But in this present state of false Christianity, all these evils are daily increasing.

Nevertheless, the advance to true Christianity, or community, is inexorable, for it is a law of nature that evil always precedes good, and the experience man acquires in evil is the means by which he introduces the good. It is quite natural therefore that Christianity should prove a curse before it is a blessing, that it should first be Antichrist before it be Christ. The Christians of the present day will do nothing to further the true Christian community, which they regard as a fanatical vision. Instead, the infidels will be its promoters. 'The millennium must be introduced by infidels, even to preserve the analogy of the scriptural doctrine; "He came to his own, and his own received him not". . . . Thus the infidels, by denying Christianity, fulfil it.'

The millennium which Smith envisaged was in its practical aspects Owenite, 'the social system of communities'. It would begin in England (as 'the reign of righteousness') and would convert 'by its moral power, every nation of the world'. The wealth already produced in Britain would be sufficient to ensure an ample living for all if properly distributed, and every year it was growing greater. A liberal education would be available to all men and women, and every trade and profession would be equally respected. Leisure for the cultivation of the arts and sciences, and the refinement of mind and manners which comes therefrom, would be procured by the use of labour-saving machines. Lastly, women would be emancipated from their dependence on men, and the present enslaving marriage system would be replaced by the 'marriage of nature'.

Smith did not develop these ideas on women and marriage in the *Lecture*, but elsewhere he elaborated his 'Doctrine of the Woman' in detail.[1] From his principles of analogy and polarity he deduced the

---

[1] Notably in a series of ten articles in vol. I (1834–35) of the *Shepherd*.

equality of male and female, since each was essential to the whole. God, or the positive principle he assigned as male; Nature, or the negative principle, female. Spiritual power is male, and its reign is now coming to an end, to be superseded by materialism, or the visible world, which is feminine. The new world will be the offspring of both the spiritual and the material, male and female. Smith noted the number of female messiahs in recent times, so numerous that the present might be called the 'Age of the Bride'. As the first messiah had been male, so would the second be female. In origin this doctrine owed most to Southcottianism, but Smith was also influenced by the Saint-Simonians in their search for 'La Femme'. The practical result of the doctrine was to lead Smith into sympathy with Owen's views on marriage and with the feminist position of Anna Wheeler and William Thompson.[1]

On such issues as the emancipation of women Smith and Owen found a broad measure of agreement, and where they did not wholly agree each was sufficiently tolerant to accept the other's sincerity. When they parted company in August 1834 it was over practical issues of trade union tactics and policy, rather than irreconcilable doctrinal differences. Smith had been working in the Owenite movement for only fifteen months, and thereafter he was often critical of Owen. Nevertheless, his universalism still contained much that was acceptable to Owenites, and his lectures in London and articles in the *Shepherd* were important auxiliaries to Owenism. In spite of attacks by Smith on Owen's doctrines from time to time it seemed to some universalists that the communitarian and millenarian principles which they had in common with the Owenites made possible a fruitful interchange of ideas between the two groups.[2] From 1835 Owen's increasingly deistic millennialism was seen by Smith as a rival to universalism; and when the Owenites were attacked by the Bishop of Exeter in 1840 Smith took the opportunity in the *Little Book* to castigate both parties and proclaim his 'new Revelation of Demonstrated Truth'. The differences between various brands of millennialism and socialism in the early 1840s seemed vitally significant to the participants, but in effect they operated as mutually reinforcing agencies. Their millennial goals and modes of thought distinguished them clearly from other groups, and directed them in similar ways in any given decade.

[1] A sexual element in Smith's doctrines is apparent, though its exact role is difficult to determine. See the remarkable series of letters which he wrote to Lady Bulwer Lytton (daughter of Anna Wheeler) in Anderson Smith, chap. XXI.

[2] E.g. exchange of letters between William Ward and William Evans in the *Star in the East*, 5, 19 January 1839. The *Star* later published a series of articles on 'The Bible Scrutinized; or Christianity Reformed' purporting to be by Shepherd Smith; but he denied that he had written them and suggested that they were pirated extracts from some of his writings.

The meteoric career of Smith within the Owenite movement and his subsequent fringe association with it demonstrated the ease with which a certain type of millenarian could become at home in the environment of Owenism. While retaining his religious millennialism he acquired a new social radicalism and involvement in trade union struggles. The destructive criticisms of church and society which he had learned from Zion Ward were transformed into a more comprehensive and theoretical critique of industrial capitalism, and his millennium became, in its practical aspects, socialist communitarianism. Smith's career suggests that to some extent Owenism, despite its strong secularist elements, was sufficiently millenarian to be acceptable as a parallel or alternative to religious sects of the Southcottian type.

For those who could not accept the intricacies of Shepherd Smith's position a less sophisticated and more 'orthodox' doctrine of Owenite millenarianism was provided by a Liverpool iron merchant, John Finch (1784–1857).[1] Born in Dudley, the son of a poor mechanic, he attended a local Unitarian charity school, and at fourteen was apprenticed as a clerk in a nail warehouse. He remained there for twenty years, and became a partner in the firm. During this period of his life in the Black Country Finch was an active Unitarian preacher. From the age of seventeen he taught a boys' Sunday school at the chapel, and in 1814 founded his own Sunday school at Walsall Wood. In 1818 he joined a firm of iron merchants in Liverpool, and from 1827 ran his own business in partnership with his son. He continued to be an active Unitarian in Liverpool, and was a member of the Renshaw Street chapel which, under the pastorship of the Rev. John Hamilton Thom, and with the support of the Rathbones and other leading Unitarian families, became one of the greatest centres for middle-class philanthropy in Britain. Finch's already keenly developed sense of benevolence was thus further strengthened by membership of this group of Liverpool Unitarian merchants who combined business success with firm adherence to principles of moral and social obligation.

His philanthropic impulses were at first directed mainly into the temperance movement, and in 1830 he helped to found the first Liverpool Temperance Society. From his concern for the dock workers came his Dock Labourers' Society, and he planned a cooperative hostel for

[1] Biographical details from *New Moral World*, 15 February 1840. Also references in Peter T. Winskill, *The Temperance Movement and its Workers* (4 vols., London, 1891–92), I, 75–7; and *Temperance Standard Bearers of the Nineteenth Century* (2 vols., Liverpool, 1897–98), I, 376–7. Two recent articles are R. B. Rose, 'John Finch, 1784–1857: a Liverpool Disciple of Robert Owen', *Transactions, Historic Society of Lancashire and Cheshire*, CIX (1958); and James Murphy, 'Robert Owen in Liverpool', *ibid.*, CXII (1961).

seamen complete with savings bank, library, school and lecture rooms. After he had successfully reclaimed his partner, Thomas Swindlehurst, from drunkenness Finch became a firm believer in total abstinence, and as he travelled the country for his business took the opportunity to preach teetotalism. In this way he is credited with having founded some seventy teetotal societies. Until 1837 he was an untiring missionary and pamphleteer for teetotalism, but in that year the Liverpool Total Abstinence Society expelled him because of his Owenite convictions, and he then concentrated his missionary zeal on socialism.

Finch had become interested in cooperation as a means of working-class self-help as early as 1829 and he helped to found the first Liverpool Cooperative Society. He soon became an admirer of Owen (whom he may possibly have first met through the Rathbones) and attended the Cooperative Congresses at Birmingham in 1831 and at London and Liverpool in 1832. A small Owenite society which he organized in Liverpool in 1832—the 'Institution of the Intelligent and Well-Disposed of the Industrious Classes for the Removal of Ignorance and Poverty by Means of Education and Employment; and for Promoting Union and Kindly Feelings Among all Ranks, Sects and Parties'—did not last long. Its title and philanthropic-type objectives (evening lectures, with differential fees for workmen, gentlemen and 'ladies coming alone') indicated Finch's approach to social problems at this time. He started a short-lived Owenite journal in Liverpool, *The Bee* (1832), edited jointly with M. V. Falvey, a Roman Catholic socialist. They agreed to accept denominational differences about the Bible and work together on a basis of essential Christianity, defined as belief in one God, the divinity of Christ and practical Christian morality. During the next five years Finch made a reputation for himself as an enthusiastic defender of Owen against religious attacks, and increasingly he came to feel the limitations of temperance reform and the sectarian narrowness of many of its societies. By 1836 he declared that in his recent lectures on 'Teetotal Temperance' he had preached temperance 'as the forerunner of an improved Social System'.[1]

From 1837 Finch became one of the most devoted of all Owen's followers and an untiring worker for the Owenite cause. He was secretary of the Liverpool branch of the Association of All Classes of All Nations, which in 1839 built one of the largest and most expensive of the Halls of Science, and was also President of the Liverpool Rational School Society. When Harmony Hall was acquired in October 1839 Finch was

[1] MS. letter, Finch to Owen, 12 October 1836. Owen Papers, Manchester.

one of the trustees and was appointed Acting Governor. He resigned in May 1840, returned as Governor in August 1842 after Owen's management of it, and finally in 1846 saw to its winding up. His residence at Harmony Hall was not continuous, however, for in April 1843 he left for a visit to America, accompanied by his daughter. In a tour of nearly eight thousand miles he visited Shaker, Rappite and Zoar communities, as well as Brook Farm and the Northampton Association of Education and Industry. The resulting 'Notes of Travel in the United States' constituted the first comprehensive survey of American communities.[1] Finch remained a perennially hopeful Owenite until his death, and his last practical venture in socialism was a scheme for the transfer of his Windsor foundry in Liverpool to the Amalgamated Society of Engineers to be run as a cooperative workshop. But the negotiations were frustrated by the engineers' lock-out of 1852.

Finch conceived of his relationship with Owen as that of a disciple to his master, and Owenism as a new religion. When he was first drawn towards the Social System he cautioned Owen against involvement in religious arguments: 'Christianity really has nothing to do with your social arrangements. . . . I believe that your principles would have been adopted to a great extent long ago if you had been silent upon Religion.'[2] A few years later he had come to regard Owenism as true Christianity and suggested that the Owenite organization should adopt the title of Millennial Christian Church, founded on the Rock of Truth, the doctrine of circumstances.[3] Furthermore, he asked Owen to make him a bishop:

Dear Father,
      'He that desireth the Office of a Bishop desireth a good thing.' I know that I was orally ordained *first Bishop* of the New Moral World by you at the Meeting of Congress, *I now wish to be 'Confirmed' in that office by a writing given by your own hand*, and may I request that you will give it.—You are aware that I take the place of St. Peter, and therefore it is necessary that you should deliver up to me the 'Keys' with your blessing and solemn charge as was done on a similar occasion. . . .[4]

He customarily addressed Owen as 'Father' (even 'your Most Sacred Highness') and signed himself 'Your dutiful son in the Truth'.

These extravagances—which annoyed more rationalistic Owenites and provoked charges of blasphemy from opponents—stemmed from

[1] Twenty-two letters in the *New Moral World*, 13 January–6 July 1844.
[2] MS. letter, Finch to Owen, 16 February 1831. Owen Papers, Manchester.
[3] Letter, 27 February 1838, *New Moral World*, 17 March 1838.
[4] MS. letter, Finch to Owen, 6 August 1838. Owen Papers, Manchester.

Finch's interpretation of Owenism as practical millennial Christianity. His progress to this position from his earlier Unitarianism was outlined in *The Millennium: The Wisdom of Jesus, and the Foolery of Sectarianism, in Twelve Letters* (Liverpool, 1837). Originally published in the Liverpool *Albion*, the letters were reprinted in the *New Moral World* (1837), and a second part appeared in that journal in 1838. The whole was incorporated in his *Seven Seals Broke Open; or, The Bible of the Reformation Reformed* (London, 1853), in which he rearranged the chapters and books of the Old and New Testaments and added explanatory introductions.[1] The foolery of sectarianism which Finch castigated was the conflict of doctrine and practice among the various Christian churches, from which he concluded that none of them was wholly in accord with Christ's own teaching. The corruption, ineffectiveness, and selfishness of these 'sects' had led to a debasement of Christianity, which could only be remedied by a second reformation, based on a return to Christ's original precepts:

Jesus, the author and finisher of his religion, dictated no creed, enjoined no sabbath, gave no encouragement to public worship, instituted no outward forms and ceremonies of religion, appointed no priesthood, gave no authority to his disciples or his followers to earn their living by teaching his doctrines, whether paid by voluntary contributions or taxation by the state; allowed no artificial distinctions of higher and lower classes, nor gave any pre-eminence of the one sex of the human race over another. All this has been abundantly proved from the sayings of Christ and from the writings of his apostles.[2]

Having defined true Christianity as the pursuit of benevolence and universal charity, and adopting a by-their-fruits-ye-shall-know-them test, Finch had little difficulty in demonstrating to his own satisfaction that Owenism was synonymous with the spirit of Christ's Gospel. He then embroidered this with language of the millennium.

First, he argued, the doctrines of Owenism are in perfect accord with Scripture. The doctrine of character formation, for example, is implicit in the parable of the sower. The non-responsibility of man and consequent irrelevance of praise and blame was proclaimed by Christ when he prayed for forgiveness of his murderers and enjoined his followers to judge not and forgive their enemies. Happiness, which can only be attained in society, was recognized as the true end of man's being when God said that it was not good for man to be alone. Above all, Owenism

---

[1] Finch also edited *The Book of the Inspired British Prophet of the Seventeenth Century, containing the Religion of the Millennium, New Law of Righteousness, and most Remarkable Prophecies* ... (Liverpool, 1842). The book was first published in 1649, and reprinted in the *New Moral World*, 8 December 1838–6 April 1839.

[2] *Bible of the Reformation Reformed*, I, xliv–xlv.

is the religion of love, thereby fulfilling the greatest of Christ's com-
mandments. Second, since the principles of socialism are more fully
scriptural than those of any Christian sect, the millennial prophecies of
the Bible are to be interpreted by reference to Owenism. Sectarianism is
Antichrist, and its approaching destruction is heralded by the Second
Coming of the messiah in the person of Robert Owen. (For Finch,
through his temperance work, was reserved the role of John the Baptist:
'for the purpose of making him manifest was I sent baptizing with water;
no drunkard shall enter the kingdom of heaven hereafter, and no drunkard is fit for the millennium here. Repent therefore drunkards, hypocrites,
tyrants, sinners . . . .'[1]) The New Moral World is no other than the
promised Christian millennium: 'the fulness of time is come. Mankind
are now able to bear the Truth. The Messiah has appeared.'[2]

The crudities of Finch's millennialism did not make it the less appealing
to many readers of the *New Moral World*. His lack of logic and plentiful
use of unrelated texts as 'proof' of his assertions probably did not greatly
trouble reformers whose ideas of Christianity were largely favourable
to a non-credal, sectarian type of Protestantism. The idea that Owenism
was practical Christianity, as opposed to the superstition and falsity
taught by the so-called Christian churches, was fairly widely echoed in
the movement.[3] The millennium which Finch built on this foundation
was essentially earthly and secular, and capable of early realization. It
required no special agency beyond that already provided by the Owenite
organization. The problem of social change was solved by simply declaring that the change was already taking place. All that was necessary
was to declare it—which is what Owen did at periodic intervals.[4] With
true millennial faith Finch continued to believe that ultimate triumph was
inevitable, and in the year before his death he assured Owen that the end
of the Crimean War marked the beginning of the millennium: 'My dear
husband says your Millennium has begun', wrote Mrs Finch to Owen,
'and that you have lived to see the close of the last great War which will
ever agitate mankind.'[5]

By the 1840s the structure of the Owenite movement could be

---

[1] *The Millennium*, p. 17.

[2] *Ibid.*, p. 24.

[3] E.g. letter from 'A Rational Religionist', *New Moral World*, 11 April 1840. William
Hawkes Smith, the Birmingham Owenite and fellow Unitarian, made similar remarks when
he lectured with Finch at the Manchester Social Institution—*New Moral World*, 30 September 1837.

[4] In 1844 Finch proposed that the Queen be called upon to issue a proclamation announcing the beginning of the millennium. *New Moral World*, 31 August 1844.

[5] MS. letter, Mrs Finch to Owen, 12 May 1856. Owen Papers, Manchester.

described as a central core of dedicated members surrounded by a series of concentric circles composed of followers whose commitment decreased in intensity the further they were from the centre. Some of the followers in these circles accepted the greater part, but not all, of Owen's new view of society; others were primarily interested in some parallel 'ism' and accepted only those parts of Owenism which touched their main enthusiasm. Even members of the central core were seldom exclusive in their allegiances, and were quite likely to be also involved in fringe activities. Owen was from time to time faced by the challenge of rival prophets, whose teachings could be either alternative or supplementary to his own. Such a one was James Pierrepont Greaves, the 'Sacred Socialist' (1777–1842). He was not an Owenite but he attracted some of Owen's followers, along with Fourierists, millennialists and transcendentalists.

Greaves was a prosperous London merchant whose business was ruined by the Berlin and Milan decrees of 1806.[1] After being declared bankrupt he rebuilt his business, but then left it when he became interested in educational reform after reading of Pestalozzi's work in Switzerland. In 1817 he went to live with Pestalozzi at Yverdun, and for four years served as an assistant teacher and disciple. He spent another four years as a tutor in the Universities of Basel and Tübingen and in 1825 returned to England, where he founded the London Infant School Society and promoted Pestalozzian educational principles. His ideas of practical social reform were those of enlightened middle-class philanthropy and within those limits not far removed from Owen's,[2] but in addition he had for some time been an enthusiast for Physical Puritanism[3] and had absorbed a fair amount of transcendentalism. In the 1830s his reputation as a sage and a mystic grew, and he attracted support from the same clique of wealthy women as did Shepherd Smith. For some months in 1834 Greaves travelled round with Zion Ward (lately released from gaol), whose claim to be Christ he mistook for an expression of mystical deification. In the later years of his life Greaves presided over a salon at

---

[1] The main source of biographical details is the 'Memoir of J. P. Greaves' by Alexander Campbell in *Letters and Extracts from the MS. Writings of James Pierrepont Greaves*, ed. Alexander Campbell (2 vols., Ham Common, Surrey, 1843, and London, 1845).

[2] In 1832 he devised a plan to relieve distress among unemployed labourers at Randwick, Gloucestershire, payment being by tokens exchanged for food, clothing and tools. He first met Owen at Pestalozzi's in Switzerland through their common interest in infant education.

[3] The name given by the writer of an article in the *Westminster Review*, CXII (April 1842) to include all such reforms as vegetarianism, temperance, homeopathy, hydropathy, mesmerism, animal-magnetism and hypnotism.

his home in Burton Street, London, and finally established himself at Alcott House, Ham Common, Surrey—a community and boarding school run by his followers, William Oldham, Henry Gardiner Wright and Charles Lane. After Greaves's death, and following a visit of the eponymous Bronson Alcott, Wright and Lane returned with Alcott to America where they started the Fruitlands community near Harvard. Alcott House was then reorganized as the First Concordium, a community based on Greaves's transcendental, vegetarian and ascetic principles.[1]

Owenite interest in Greaves had begun with notices of his Pestalozzian infant schools in the *Cooperative Magazine* in 1828 (III, 31) and John Minter Morgan published Pestalozzi's letters to Greaves. The social missionary and ex-Orbistonian, Alexander Campbell, fell strongly under Greaves's influence after 1838, and Samuel Bower, the Bradford Owenite, was also attracted and later joined Alcott and Lane at Fruitlands. Lane's second wife, Hannah Bond, had been a member of the Harmony Hall community. Other Owenites from Harmony Hall likewise joined the Concordium: Frederick Bate, the wealthy treasurer, and William Galpin, formerly a banker and general secretary of the Rational Society. Owen visited the Concordium in 1843, and it held a fascination for Owenites even when, like George Jacob Holyoake, they were sceptical and later made fun of its eccentric inhabitants.

The impact of Greaves's philosophy upon a convinced Owenite was seen most clearly in the case of Alexander Campbell (1796–1870).[2] He was a Glasgow joiner by trade and a member of the Orbiston community, for which he suffered by being gaoled for debt when it collapsed. In the 1830s he was an active Owenite cooperator and trade unionist in Glasgow, and was imprisoned for publishing an unstamped newspaper. His activities as a social missionary in 1838 first brought him into contact with Greaves, whom he met in Cheltenham. There ensued a long exchange of letters between the two men, Greaves's contributions being published after his death by Campbell as *Letters and Extracts from the MS. Writings of*

[1] Contemporary accounts of Alcott House and the Concordium are given in 'C. L.' [Charles Lane?], 'Social Experiments', *Star in the East*, 22 February 1840; and in the pages of the *New Age, Concordium Gazette and Temperance Advocate*, 1843–44. See also Thomas Frost, *Forty Years Recollections, Literary and Political* (London, 1880); and Holyoake, *History of Cooperation in England*. Useful detail is given in Armytage, *op. cit.*; Frank B. Sanborn, *Bronson Alcott at Alcott House, England, and Fruitlands, New England, 1842–1844* (Cedar Rapids, Iowa, 1908); and Odell Shepard, *Pedlar's Progress: the Life of Bronson Alcott* (Boston, Mass., 1937).

[2] Most of the scattered biographical data on Campbell is collected in W. H. Marwick, *Life of Alexander Campbell* (Glasgow, 1964).

James Pierrepont Greaves.[1] In these letters Greaves expounded his theo-sophic doctrines for the benefit of an enquiring and admiring Owenite, who was thus led for a time into the paths of 'sacred socialism'. That such doctrines should have been attractive to the middle-class clientele who frequented Greaves's salon is not surprising. Their appeal to a veteran Owenite like Campbell, who remained a lifelong radical, trade unionist and cooperator, was of a somewhat different order, and was similar in some respects to Shepherd Smith's relations with the trade unionists in 1833–34.

From his writings it seems unlikely that Greaves was the towering genius that Alcott and Lane imagined him to be (Carlyle regarded him as an old humbug), but his presence and powers as a conversationalist appear to have been sufficient to convince those already sympathetically inclined that he was a profound mystic. Something of his appeal lay in his obscurity and the unfamiliarity of his hearers with mysticism. Campbell, for instance, records that at his first meeting with Greaves there was a mutual 'affectionate attachment for each other, even though I could not then fully comprehend the peculiar language in which his ideas were spoken'.[2] Greaves taught that there were three aspects of man's existence —the external (or physical), the inward (or intellectual) and the spiritual (or moral)—and that it was necessary to strive continually to live on the third, or spiritual plane. To this end he advocated (and practised) vege-tarianism, cold-water therapy and celibacy. Owenism fitted into this pattern at the first, inferior level: it was physical, as opposed to sacred socialism—useful as a starting point but incapable of reaching spiritual ends. The sacred socialist would be guided always by the need to be filled with the Love Spirit. Owen had failed because he had been unable to change public opinion: 'If Mr. Owen had appealed to Love, Love would have worked the wonder required. We must now do what Mr. Owen did not.' Owenite social missionaries like Campbell were mostly on the wrong track, and Greaves wrote him that 'if you would come to London, and spend a week with me in Love and on vegetable diet, you would be the better for it all the remainder of your days on the earth'.

Greaves made no secret of his disagreement with Owen, but since by 1840 many Owenites also doubted parts of Owen's doctrines and were curious about alternative theories, this created little difficulty. The issues which concerned the Sacred Socialist throughout most of his philan-thropic life—infant education, the marriage system, the role of social

[1] A further selection of Greaves's writings was published as *New Theosophic Revelations* (London, 1847).

[2] This and the following quotations are from the *Letters and Extracts*, I, iii, 85, 87–8, 155.

institutions—were those which interested Owenites. Latterly he claimed that it was through his earlier educational experiences that he had been led to see that the root of all social ills lay in man's disobedience to the Love Law. Certain basic Owenite doctrines could be given a sacred twist: 'sacred circumstances are needed for the sacred character'. Others had to be reinterpreted or regarded in the light of the higher life of the spirit. No specifically millennial doctrines appeared in Greaves's writings, but it was not difficult for sacred socialists to retain millennial elements in their thinking while exploring the paths of mysticism. Thus Bronson Alcott believed that although Owen's reforms were but 'partial and secondary', Owen came to many 'as a saviour from want and dependence, and . . . the harbinger of the spiritual Messias whose advent is near'.[1]

A stronger millenarian note was struck by William Galpin. He had been a banker in Salisbury, became an admirer of Owen, and was a large contributor to the funds of the Harmony Hall community. In 1842 he was general secretary of the Rational Society, but resigned in 1843 and went to live at the Concordium. His Owenism then became tempered by sacred socialism, and when Harmony Hall was dissolved in 1845 he became the 'Patriarch' of a group of Harmony colonists who moved from the Hall to Little Bentley, an adjoining farm which Galpin leased jointly with Isaac Ironside, the leader of the Sheffield Owenites. In this little community Galpin lived by a spartan, vegetarian regimen, wearing his long black beard to his waist and going barefoot. 'I am missioned', he announced, 'to make a general and particular call to the Faithful in Christ, for the gathering of the nucleus of a Universal Church, preparatory to His second appearance.'[2] He appealed to all members of the Rational Society to participate, and emphasized that the call must be individual and would include the giving up of all earthly ties: 'the standard of the Cross is to be erected on the grave of socialism'.

George Jacob Holyoake was scornful of Galpinism, as he called it, but his comment in the *Reasoner* (21 October 1846) was not unjust:

J. Pierrepont Greaves enjoyed the distinction, while living, of being the Prince of Mystics among small philosophers. His mantle fell on Ham Common, where it was taken up and tried on by various persons. William Oldham, Alexander Campbell, William Galpin and Samuel Bower have worn it at different times, and in their turns have carried obscurity all over the country.

[1] Letter from Alcott, while staying at Alcott House, to his cousin, 30 June 1842. Sanborn, p. 18.
[2] *Reasoner*, 16 September 1846. There is an account of the Patriarch and the Little Bentley community in the *Moral World*, 13 September 1845.

What Holyoake did not explain, either in 1846 or in his later histories of cooperation, was why the mantle should have seemed desirable to some Owenites. It was, of course, not desired by many of Owen's followers. But to those susceptible to a millenarian or sectarian appeal the Sacred Socialist could, in certain contexts, exert the same kind of attraction as the Social Father himself.

Contemporary with Greaves and his circle in England was a revival of American Owenism in which the millennial element was still strong. Owen himself continued to announce the beginning of the millennium on his visits to the States.[1] His disciples concluded their letters and addresses with millennial perorations.[2] But more significant was the appearance of the *Herald of the New Moral World and Millennial Harbinger*, published in New York from January 1841 to August 1842. It was edited by the Rev. J. M. Horner, formerly minister of Jamesville Congregational Church and one time agent of the American Society for Promoting the Principles of the Reformation. By 1841 his followers were organized in a Society for the Promotion of Human Happiness which met in New York for regular Sunday addresses.[3] The programme was orthodox Owenism, which the *Herald* reprinted largely from its British contemporary, the *New Moral World*. Rejecting the 'notions of theologians and divines relative to the Millennium' as 'spurious and absurd, tending to mystery, darkness and doubt', the *Herald* (18 March 1841) asserted: 'We believe that the only Millennium spoken of in the Sacred Scriptures is that which shall grow out of a scientific and general knowledge of man.' This could only be realized through the creation of favourable circumstances, which was impossible under 'the present individual, competitive and demoralizing arrangements of society'. Past prophecies of the exact date of the commencement of the millennium failed because knowledge of Hebrew alphabetical calculations was lost:

Let us, therefore, do away with the idea of any Millennium, save that which shall be brought about by the adoption of such arrangements and institutions as shall give a predominancy to the moral and intellectual faculties of man,

[1] E.g. *New Moral World*, 18 January, 28 June 1845.

[2] E.g. Lewis Masquerier, writing a 'Letter to Mr. Owen' from New York City, 6 February 1836, concludes: 'Ignorance . . . is what prevents millions from finding the true saviour, from becoming thoroughly regenerated, and from reaching the only possible heaven in their power, the New Moral World.' *New Moral World*. 9 April 1836.

[3] This was in addition to the New York branch of the Universal Community Society of Rational Religionists, which had been formed in 1840 by Benjamin Timms and a group of immigrant British Owenites. See *New Moral World*, 12, 19 September, 7 November, 12 December 1840; *Herald of the New Moral World*, 21 January, 8 July 1841.

which alone will lead him to change the lion-like voraciousness of his animal propensities into the calmness and docility of the lamb—change his selfishness into benevolence—his viciousness into calmness—his sectional love of country into a universal love of the world—his family love into a love of community—his implements of death and destruction into the instruments of education—his artificial character into the dignity of the man—when the soldier will become a teacher—the Jesuit will throw off his cloak of covering—and the idle will become industrious.[1]

In August 1842 the *Herald* came to an end, and Horner and his associates organized an Owenite sect of One Mentians, probably so named from St Peter's injunction, 'Be ye of one mind'.[2]

Nevertheless, by the 1840s the attractiveness of Owenism to millenarians in America was considerably weaker than it had been in the 1820s. Owen himself was largely disregarded, even by professed Owenites, who found his name an embarrassment rather than a help. The charges of infidelity and memories of the failure at New Harmony were encumbrances from the past. The main millennial emphasis lay elsewhere, among the Millerites, Perfectionists and Fourierists. In the communitarian field the Owenite cooperative village was supplanted by the Fourierist phalanx; and the crude and largely semantic Owenite millennialism failed to satisfy the intellectual demands of Brook Farmers or Oneida Perfectionists. The Swedenborgians, who earlier had been drawn towards Owenite community experiments, in the 1840s became Fourierists. In comparison with their British counterparts, the American Owenites were faced with much stronger sectarian and communitarian rivals and at the same time their institutional strength was much less. To those in search of the millennium in the 'forties there seemed more suitable, less discredited philosophies than Owenism.

It will by now have become apparent that the millennial element in Owenism was not limited to a particular place or period. It was continuous throughout the history of the movement and closely associated with Owen himself. From the time when he decided that his *Plan for the Relief of the Poor* (1817) was synonymous with the 'Emancipation of Mankind', he never tired of reiterating his belief that the redemption of man was at hand. For forty years he announced each new venture, whether it was the community at New Harmony, the National Equitable Labour Exchange or Harmony Hall, as the commencement of the millennium. It would be tedious to catalogue these successive announcements. His editorial in the first number of the *New Moral World* (1 November

[1] *Herald of the New Moral World*, 21 October 1841.
[2] Details of their community are given on p. 174 below.

18. New Harmony, Indiana

19. New Harmony. Community House No. 2

20. New Harmony. The church

1834) was representative of innumerable statements both before and later:

The rubicon between the Old Immoral and the New Moral World is finally passed: ... This ... is the great Advent of the world, the second coming of Christ,—for Truth and Christ are one and the same. The first coming of Christ was a partial development of Truth to the few. ... The second coming of Christ will make Truth known to the many. ... The time is therefore arrived when the foretold millennium is about to commence. ...

Enthusiastic followers at New Harmony and similarly later at Harmony Hall adopted a new chronology, dating their letters from the beginning of the new dispensation. At Queenwood the letters 'C.M.' (Commencement of the Millennium) were carved on the outside of the building. The social missionaries frequently played upon the millennial theme. James Rigby described the effects of his lecturing on the Owenites in the Bradford branch:

while painting the horror of the old system ... each seemed to feel his own case; the tears stole down many a cheek, and all appeared to feel that this old world must pass away, and that a new one must arise, fulfilling ... the Scripture. ... I endeavoured to take them up to the pinnacle of the temple, and show them the glories of the world to come. ...[1]

In the *New Moral World* and other Owenite journals many aspects of the culture of millennialism appeared. Contributors discussed biblical prophecy, the restoration of the Jews in relation to socialism, and animal magnetism as a herald of the millennium. Versifiers sent in millennial poems. Owenite converts wrote letters saying how much they longed for the day of salvation.

In extent and variety these millennial elements in Owenism conformed to certain recognizable variants within the general pattern of eighteenth- and nineteenth-century millennialism. Generally Owenites were inclined to be post rather than premillennialists, though at times their precise position was confused. Owen was basically a typical eighteenth-century postmillennialist, believing that the millennium was simply a more perfect state of society, which could with equal propriety be called 'the Rational State of Human Existence', or 'the Union of Humanity for the Happiness of All' or 'The Brotherhood of the Human Race'.[2] But at times he spoke of a Second Advent and sudden cataclysm which implied a premillennialist position at variance with his previous meliorist statements. The interpretation of the millennium which was most favoured by Owenites, including Owen himself, was inherited from

[1] *New Moral World*, 28 July 1838.
[2] Owen, *Life*, I, 210.

K

those eighteenth-century millennialists who had secularized the idea of the millennium into a theory of evolutionary progress, by disguising Providence as natural law, and making reason and revelation embrace each other. The New Jerusalem became a state of universal happiness, the millennium a gradual progress towards human betterment. Such millennialists formed 'a bridge between the chiliasm of the seventeenth century and the liberal political progressivism of the nineteenth'.[1] The Owenites helped to extend this bridge, and to carry further, in popular (often crude) form, the secularization of the millennium. While using the language of prophecy, revelation and scripture, the Owenites emptied the concept of the millennium of all theological content, leaving it simply and essentially a description of a state of society in which the new system prevailed. No longer was the millennium the end of human history, but rather the latest and highest stage in historical evolution.

Not all Owenites were prepared to secularize the millennium to this extent, and for them liberal Christianity provided a path which led to practically the same destination. The unshakable optimism and belief in unlimited progress which characterized Owenism was shared by most Protestant postmillennialists in Britain and America, and was in tune with the general ideology of the age. If necessary the millennium could be spiritualized or allegorized in some way, and thus accommodated to specific ultra causes or social reform programmes. By redefining as true Christianity certain selected moral and ethical principles which harmonized with Owenism, the new system of society could be identified as the millennium. Even the pursuit of happiness which the Owenites premised as basic to all human motivation presented no real problem to universalists and Christians inclined towards a 'religion of healthy-mindedness'. By one or other route the universalists, Unitarians, Swedenborgians, deists and mystics who found their way to Owenism formulated their notions of the millennium.

As it gathered support Owenism increasingly manifested the secondary characteristics of a millenarian movement. There is little evidence that Owen ever regarded himself as a charismatic leader, despite the adulation of his more extravagant disciples such as Finch. He insisted on the complete originality of his views, but claimed no personal merit for them. Nevertheless, in the year before his death he concluded:

In taking a calm retrospect of my life from the earliest remembered period of it . . . there appears to me to have been a succession of extraordinary or out-of-the-usual-way events, forming connected links of a chain, to compel me to

---

[1] Tuveson, p. 140; *passim* for general development of this theme.

proceed onward to complete a mission, of which I have been an impelled agent.[1]

At times his paternalism assumed a patriarchal quality: describing the disciplinary system of the silent monitor in the New Lanark mills, he mused: 'The act of setting down the number in the book of character, never to be blotted out, might be likened to the supposed recording angel marking the good and bad deeds of poor human nature.'[2] Owen frequently stated that the millennium would come suddenly and unexpectedly, 'like a thief in the night', but unlike other millennialists who used this text to caution against the attempt at exact prognostication, he repeatedly announced that the millennium had begun; nor was he embarrassed to find an explanation mechanism to account for successive failures. Again, like other millenarians, Owen and his disciples were much concerned with marriage and the sexual relationship, which in the New Moral World were to be considerably changed.

The millennial strand in Owenism was reinforced by the values and attitudes of sectarianism. Except for a brief period of a few months in 1833–34 when Owen put himself at the head of the mass trade union movement in Britain, the Owenites were a millenarian sect,[3] using the term in its general sense of a small religious group, in which membership is voluntary and limited to persons having certain special convictions or experiences in common. A rejection of the values of society, and withdrawal or separateness from the world, together with an expectation of some form of adventism further typify the sect. A mission to preach the kingdom, an emphasis on fellowship (brotherly love), and allegiance understood as 'belief in the truth' are also commonly found.[4] By these criteria the Owenites were a sect, although a somewhat loosely organized one. Their communitarianism implied some degree of separation from the world, but since most Owenites were not living in communities their separateness took the form of opposition rather than withdrawal. They were indifferent to the normal political processes and hostile to the basic institutions of society such as the family, private property and the churches. Most sects exercise a considerable degree of dominance over their members' lives. In an Owenite community social dominance was

[1] Owen, *Life*, I, xliii.

[2] *Ibid.*, I, 81.

[3] In the *Cyclopedia of Religious Denominations* (London and Glasgow, 1853), the chapter 'Socialism, by Robert Owen' is sandwiched between chapters on the Shakers and the Mormons.

[4] See Bryan R. Wilson, 'An Analysis of Sect Development', *American Sociological Review*, XXIV, no. 1 (February 1959), 3–15; and *Sects and Society* (London, 1961), to which I am indebted.

inevitable, even though complete religious freedom was permitted as at New Lanark or New Harmony. For the majority of non-community settled Owenites sect dominance could be no more than ideological.

The circumstances of sect emergence further clarify the nature of Owenism as a millennial sect. Owen did not like the terms Owenian or Owenism, and many of his followers in the 1840s preferred not to acknowledge his name; nevertheless Owenism was essentially a sect which emerged round a leader whose teaching was accepted by followers, and which did not institutionally survive his death. It has often been noted that conditions of rapid social change encourage the formation of sects. Problems of readjustment for individuals and groups, and the fears, insecurity and general upset that accompany the interruption of normal economic and social relations probably account for the pro-liferation of sects at such times. In America westward expansion and frontier conditions, and in England the combined effects of demographic, agrarian and industrial revolutions, produced conditions in which sects might emerge and flourish. That Owenism was but one among many millennial sects at the time has already become clear, and with them it shared a common role. To this extent adherence to Owenism can be explained in the same terms as support for any other contemporary religious sect, or in fact for religious belief in general.

In Britain after 1835 and in America to a lesser extent in the 1840s Owenites adopted many of the forms of a religious organization. Meet-ings were patterned on church services, with the *Book of the New Moral World* used in place of the Bible. A small book of *Social Hymns* went through several editions, and the main tenets of Owenism were laid down in a Creed, Catechism and Articles. Owenite lecturers were desig-nated social missionaries and delivered homilies. Owen himself was re-ferred to as the Social Father, and performed baptisms (or 'namings') and delivered funeral orations.[1] The reaction to the Bishop of Exeter's attack on Owenism in 1840 was to intensify the religious protestations of Owenites who claimed the protection of the law as 'a congregation of Protestants called Rational Religionists'. Two of the social missionaries, Robert Buchanan and Lloyd Jones, were prepared to make the necessary declaration on oath required by the Act of 19 George III for 'the relief of Protestant Dissenting Ministers and Schoolmasters'. A writer in the *New Moral World* (11 April 1840) claimed that the Owenite Halls of Science

---

[1] *Crisis*, 6, 13 July 1833; *New Moral World*, 26 October 1844; *Reasoner*, XXIV (1859), 3. Charles Bray had a story that he was present at Owen's christening of the first child born at Harmony Hall, who was called Primo Communis Flitcroft. Charles Bray, *Phases of Opinion and Experience during a Long Life* (London, 1879), p. 63.

were the new churches of the people and suggested that Congress elect
Owen 'First Patriarch of Socialism' and nominate sixty-two 'Bishops of
Socialism'.

The function of Owenism as a sect in relation to the needs of individuals was not markedly different from similar millenarian groups. As the
settler at New Harmony imbibed from Owen the vision of a New Moral
World he was not far removed in basic aspiration from the Mormon
convert who listened to the promises of an early millennium in the City
of Zion from Joseph Smith. The Owenite working man who sang his
social hymns in the Manchester Hall of Science was striving for much the
same goals as his neighbour who sang Wesley's hymns in the Primitive
Methodist chapel or listened to the prophet in the Southcottians' meeting
place at Ashton. Within the sect he found a congenial home, where the
values and goals were different from those of the wider society which he
had rejected. The injustices and enormities which outraged him in early
capitalist society were replaced by the dream of an earthly millennium as
he sang:

> Community! the joyful sound
> That cheers the social band,
> And spreads a holy zeal around
> To dwell upon the land.
>
> Community is labour bless'd,
> Redemption from the fall;
> The good of all by each possess'd,
> The good of each by all.
>
> Community is friendship's throne,
> With kindred minds around:
> 'Tis in community alone
> That friendship can abound.
>
> Community doth wealth increase,
> Extends the years of life,
> Begins on earth the reign of peace,
> And ends the reign of strife.
>
> Community does all possess
> That can to man be given;
> Community is happiness,
> Community is heaven.[1]

[1] *Social Hymns*, no. 129.

The cohesive strength of the ideology of a sect provided an emotional stability and intellectual certainty: the Owenite knew that he possessed the Truth, and all else was Error. In sects where the experience of religious conversion was conditional for membership a further bond of exclusiveness, certainty and security was created. Owenism did not require more than acceptance of the new view of society, but some converts testified that this knowledge came to them with the full force of revelation.

The existence of so many millennial sects contemporary with Owenism, their recruitment from among different classes, and in two such different societies as the American and British, suggests that either the role of the sect was very fundamental or it played several different roles. Presentations of millennialism as the 'religion of the oppressed' or the 'chiliasm of despair' are adequate only for certain groups of millenarians: but Owenites were drawn from wealthy philanthropists, farmers, lower middle-class tradesmen, and working men. Correlation between periods of depression and the strength of millennial sentiment is at best inconclusive. In America religious revivalism, from which millennialism usually emerged, was fostered more by moderate economic recession than by an extreme depression of the 1837 order. However, a severe economic depression could persuade men that only millenarianism was a sufficiently radical remedy for present ills.[1] For Britain the correspondence between the growth of millennial sects and the cycle of booms and slumps is similarly ambivalent. The total impact of economic change and the consequent upheaval in social relationships is the only context in which all the manifestations of millennialism can be understood. Both Britain and America between 1790 and 1850 were societies undergoing unprecedented changes, the one being transformed into the world's first industrial civilization, the other expanding to conquer a fabulous continent of unbelievably rich resources.

The millennialist sectarian was one who rejected what was being done in this process, rejected the values, goals, institutions of society—all that for the Owenite was meant by the 'old immoral world'. Early industrial society in Britain and the young expansionist republic in America created social realities which were divorced from the social and religious values which they professed. The millenarian refused to accept the incompatibility, as he saw it, between Christian professions and *laissez-faire* capitalist society, either industrial or agrarian. Owenism was an expression of this conflict and an attempt to resolve it through the creation of a

[1] Whitney Cross, pp. 269–70, 317.

socio-religious ideology which was compatible with industrial-scientific civilization while rejecting competition and commercialism. In the development of this role Owenism became the millennial sect of Rational Religionists.

2 Education

The central role of education in Owenite thought and activity has been noted by most of Owen's biographers and elaborated in recent text books and educational dissertations.[1] The spectacular nature of the experiment at New Lanark, the advocacy of a non-violent and widely acceptable method of social change, and Owen's repeated emphasis on the importance of education in character formation, all contributed to a focusing of attention on this aspect of his achievement. Owenism became practically synonymous with education. 'The basis of Owenism', wrote G. D. H. Cole, 'was his [Owen's] theory of education.'[2] Evidence for this came from Owen's statements on the relation between education and social reform, and from descriptions of the detailed workings of his infant school. His first and most important work, *A New View of Society*, was in one sense a general treatise on education.

It has been customary to consider Owenite education as a more or less self-contained element in Owenism; sometimes to present it as the central core around which other aspects were wrapped. At times Owen himself spoke in terms suggestive of these interpretations, and in most places the school remained the most enduring part of the local institutions of Owenism. Nevertheless, Owenism was not primarily a movement to found schools and literary institutes; it was a new view of society whose adherents wanted a radical transformation of the economic and social structure which they believed could be effected in accordance with the laws of social science. Why then did Owen and his followers come to be so concerned with education, and what did they mean by that term? The answer lies beyond the familiar account of Owen's views on infant schools and character formation (important though these are) and is to be found in the totality of Owenite thought. In the preceding chapters Owenism has been approached as a body of social thought which was rooted in the late eighteenth and early nineteenth centuries and which can be broken

---

[1] For a recent example see Harold Silver, *The Concept of Popular Education* (London, 1965), which is largely a study of Owenite education.
[2] *Robert Owen*, p. 96.

down into its constituent parts for analysis. Each of these parts—millennialism, philanthropy, socialism, communitarianism—had some educational content; and when the interlocking and reinforcing nature of the parts is demonstrated the strength of the educational element in Owenism becomes explicable. What emerges is the working out of Owenism in educational terms. The complex of separate ideas drawn from various sources reached a synthesis in education, which became central to the transmission of Owenism. A common resort of reformers, when other methods of achieving social or political change appear to have failed, has been education. But for Owen education was more fundamental; he did not adopt it only when other methods had failed. As with its millenarian characteristics, Owenism was from the beginning an educational movement through its need to communicate.

Few social reformers have openly accorded education such a central place in their philosophy as the Owenites. They spoke in lyrical terms of what could be achieved by it, and attributed vast power to its influence. Speaking at a dinner in Glasgow in 1812 in honour of the educationist, Joseph Lancaster, Owen declared:

By education... I now mean the instruction of all kinds which we receive from our earliest infancy until our characters are generally fixed and established. . . . Much has been said and written in relation to education, but few persons are yet aware of its real importance in society, and certainly it has not yet acquired that prominent rank in our estimation which it deserves; for, when duly investigated, it will be found to be, so far at least as it depends on our operations, the primary source of all good and evil, misery and happiness which exist in the world. . . .[1]

The school and the lecture hall were prominent in all Owenite institutional arrangements. At New Lanark the infant schools and the Institution for the Formation of Character attracted the most enthusiastic encomiums from the scores of visitors. The Edinburgh Practical Society, the Orbiston community, and New Harmony conducted schools on advanced (usually Pestalozzian) lines. At New Harmony William Maclure's efforts made the settlement a cultural and scientific centre in the West which continued long after the communitarian efforts were ended. The various endeavours of the Cooperative and Economical Society of London, and later of the British Association for Promoting Cooperative Knowledge included lectures and discussions for the members and schools for their children. In all later Owenite ventures the same pattern of educational provision and priority was evident. Other

---

[1] *Glasgow Herald*, 20 April 1812, in Owen, *Life*, I, 249.

contemporary bodies of reformers in Britain and America—the Working Men's Parties, the phrenologists, the Fourierists, the Chartists—had educational goals and used educational methods. But none was so continuously saturated with education as the Owenites. Their concern was not that of radical reformers who turned to 'moral force' when 'physical force' methods proved impracticable or inexpedient. They were committed to educational solutions from the very nature of their approach to problems of man and society. At times education (in Owen's sense of producing 'the whole man') became for the Owenites not a means but the end itself.

As with all Owenite argument, the starting point for the discussion of education was happiness.[1] The individual's happiness is dependent on that of the community. Moreover, every action will be followed by its natural reward or punishment, that is, 'the necessary consequences, immediate and remote, which result from any action'. Education is concerned to bring knowledge and distinct conviction of the necessary consequences of conduct. This will be sufficient to direct the child; all rewards and punishments, except those of nature, are to be excluded. For nature has provided her own sanctions, and the child will therefore learn that nature's rewards will bring pleasure and her punishments pain. The child's notion of right and wrong will be derived from the natural consequences of his conduct, not from artificial rewards and punishments; and the teacher will also strive to show him the intimate connection between his own happiness and that of others.

Although this argument was philosophically incomplete (for as we have seen it suffered from the difficulties inherent in all theories of hedonism or utilitarianism), it produced in the New Lanark and other Owenite schools a type of education greatly superior to the mechanical instruction of the age. A fundamental rule of kindness, not severity, to children was observed, and all harshness, anger and violence was eschewed. A child who did wrong was to be pitied, not blamed, since he had not yet learned his own best self-interest. The material of instruction was chosen for its ability to hold the child's interest and adapted to his capacities. Visual aids, play methods, dancing and singing were introduced; and the general emphasis was placed on child-activity and participation. In the new schools the children were not to be taught by 'the present defective and tiresome system of book learning' but by new methods of instruction 'founded in nature'.[2]

[1] E.g. Robert Dale Owen, *Outline of the System of Education at New Lanark* (1824).
[2] *Report to the County of Lanark*, in *Life*, IA, 297. See also the rules for an infant school laid down in ten points by Owen, *Life*, I, 232–3.

Most writers on Owen have remarked how the crucial role of education in his thought follows from his doctrine of character formation; and
his stress on the importance of environment has prompted speculative
comparisons with Locke and Helvetius. At the Lancaster dinner in 1812
Owen made his first public statement that '. . . we can materially command those circumstances which influence character'[1] and it is clear
from the context that he was thinking of the effects of education on a
community. Likewise the famous passage in the first essay of *A New
View of Society* referred to the influence of environment on a community:

> Any general character, from the best to the worst, from the most ignorant
> to the most enlightened, may be given to any community, even to the world at
> large, by the application of proper means; which means are to a great extent at
> the command and under the control of those who have influence in the affairs
> of men.

Many contemporary liberal reformers and educationists were in broad
agreement with this. The roots of their social psychology were in the
moral philosophy of the Scottish Enlightenment, and can be traced
similarly in James Mill[2] and Dugald Stewart. Owen did not accept fully
the doctrine of associationism. But Paul Brown made it the basis of his
philosophy of education,[3] and other Owenites quoted Dugald Stewart
in support of their argument. In any case, belief in the effects of environment led to much the same position, especially in regard to the role of
education. Owenites were in full agreement with Dugald Stewart when
he wrote:

> I am well aware of the tendency, which speculative men sometimes have, to
> magnify the effects of education, as well as to entertain too sanguine views of
> the improvement of the world; and I am ready to acknowledge that there are
> instances of individuals whose vigour of mind is sufficient to overcome every-
> thing that is pernicious in their early habits; but I am fully persuaded that
> these instances are rare, and that by far the greater part of mankind continue
> through life to pursue the same track into which they have been thrown by
> the accidental circumstances of situation, instruction and example.[4]

---

[1] Owen, *Life*, I, 250.

[2] E.g. James Mill, *The Article 'Education' reprinted from the Supplement to the Encyclopedia Britannica* (London, 1824).

[3] Paul Brown, *An Enquiry Concerning the Nature, End, and Practicability of a Course of
Philosophical Education* (Washington, D.C., 1822).

[4] Dugald Stewart, *Elements of the Philosophy of the Human Mind* (1792–1827), in
Collected Works, ed. Sir William Hamilton (11 vols., Edinburgh, 1854–60), II, 76.

The powerful effect of tradition and public opinion in shaping men's ideas attests the strength of education, and shows its role when once the correct principles of human nature are acknowledged and acted upon:

The long reign of error in the world and the influence it maintains, even in an age of liberal inquiry, far from being favourable to the supposition that human reason is destined to be for ever the sport of prejudice and absurdity, demonstrates the tendency which there is to permanence in established opinions, and in established institutions, and promises an eternal stability to true philosophy, when it shall once have acquired the ascendant and when proper means shall be employed to support it by a more perfect system of education.[1]

Basically the Owenites were concerned with education as an instrument for the formation of social character. The role of education, they argued, is to mould the character of the individual to resemble an ideal social character, to inculcate in the child those desires which are necessary for him to be able to identify his own happiness with the happiness of society. The importance of educational techniques and training methods in early childhood was emphasized by Owen and Paul Brown, for they recognized them as mechanisms for the formation of character.[2]

From the premise of happiness and through the doctrine of circumstances the Owenites were led into educational paths, and other constituents of Owenism strengthened the trend in this direction. The Poor Law context of much early Owenite thought united ideas of unemployment relief, communitarianism and philanthropy with education. 'It is obvious', wrote Owen, 'that training and education must be viewed as intimately connected with the employments of the association [i.e. community or "village of cooperation"]. The latter, indeed, will form an essential part of education under these arrangements. Each association, generally speaking, should create for itself a full supply of the usual necessaries, conveniences, and comforts of life.'[3] One of the fundamentals of Owenite social reform was that it provided radical change without violence or upheaval. Education was to be the lever, first for dealing with the problem of the poor, but soon for effecting change throughout the whole of society.

It was of the essence of Owen's plan that the villages of cooperation should be self-supporting; and to link this principle with education was in harmony with strong contemporary predilections. The school of

[1] Dugald Stewart, *Elements of the Philosophy of the Human Mind* (1792–1827), in *Collected Works*, ed. Sir William Hamilton, (11 vols., Edinburgh, 1854–60), II, 73.

[2] In his *Book of the New Moral World*, pt. II, p. 33, Owen also noted that Oxford and Cambridge were primarily institutions 'for forming the character of the upper classes'.

[3] *Report to the County of Lanark*, in Owen, *Life*, IA, 297.

143

industry was the institutional result of this linkage and found much favour with Owenites. They were impressed with Fellenberg's school of industry at Hofwyl in Switzerland, and George Mudie typically devoted one issue of his paper, the *Economist* (24 March 1821), to descriptions of Hofwyl and New Lanark. He quoted the object of Fellenberg in his school of industry as being

to make the very employment of children, which is so essential to their sub-sistence, the means of their education, and thus to afford a solution of that most interesting problem, which seeks how to develop the moral and intellectual faculties, upon the most useful system, without taking one day from necessary manual labour.

William Maclure likewise favoured industrial schools, partly because they were self-supporting, but also because they gave a 'utilitarian' rather than an 'ornamental' education. He admired Fellenberg's project of com-bining teaching on Pestalozzian principles with manual labour, which he considered especially suitable in America, where land was cheap and labour dear. The Americans ought to have been 'the first people to put in practice so useful and necessary a procedure for the success, security and durability of our free and independent political association, that can only have a solid foundation on the knowledge of the great mass of pro-ductive labourers, who have the control of our government by universal suffrage'. This was written in 1828; and in 1835 plans for a Manual Labour College at New Harmony were developed in detail.[1] The idea of the school of industry had travelled far; first from its charity school origins in the seventeenth and early eighteenth centuries to the Society for Bettering the Conditions of the Poor in the 1790s; and thence to Owenite community education and the education for democracy in the New World. In Owen and Maclure an original philanthropic impulse, com-bined with radical social reform sentiments, led into educational channels.

In their utopian communities the Owenites found yet further con-firmation of the primary role of education. This process was two-sided; from the one side progressive educationists had arrived at a concept of community as integral to the educative process; and from the other communitarians had come to regard education as their indispensable

---

[1] *New Moral World*, 5 December 1835. Cf. also the following from Karl Marx, *Capital*, trans. Samuel Moore and Edward Aveling, and ed. Frederick Engels (London, 1886), p. 489: 'From the Factory system budded, as Robert Owen has shown us in detail, the germ of the education of the future, an education that will, in the case of every child over a given age, combine productive labour with instruction and gymnastics, not only as one of the methods of adding to the efficiency of production, but as the only method of producing fully developed human beings.'

ally in building a successful community. In an overall sense the experiment of community living was educational, in that it aimed at rapidly diffusing 'the dispositions, manners and mind' necessary for the success of the 'new system'. By this means, Owen told the communitarians at New Harmony, 'a whole community can become a new people, have their minds born again, and be regenerated from the errors and corruptions which . . . have hitherto everywhere prevailed'.[1] More specifically, he planned lectures three times a week for adult members of the community, convinced that if they were 'well informed' they would not fail to be better (happier) communitarians. He was concerned to promote happy personal living among them, and was upset by their quarrels and grumblings and dishonesties. Only when they were brought to realize that anger and irritation were irrational, and that other men were not blameworthy because their opinions were formed for them by environment, would the members of the community act and think charitably. At times the Owenites virtually despaired of the present generation, whose pernicious, anti-social habits had been formed so deeply by the old immoral system of society, and pinned all their hopes on the children. As a writer in the *New Harmony Gazette* (29 October 1825) put it, 'It is on the education of youth, the projector of the new social system relies for ultimate success.'

There were other reasons too for the reinforcing relationship between communitarianism and education. William Thompson pointed out that it would be vain to teach children to love and respect one another if they were 'surrounded by the hourly example of all the bad passions that afflict humanity and give the lie to the good principles inculcated at school'.[2] The community was regarded by Owenites as a social experiment, in which everything would be on record. There was here a great field of opportunity for the 'enlightened moralist' to try out his social schemes, including educational plans. William Maclure was an admirer of Owen before coming to New Harmony and sensed correctly that the atmosphere there would be congenial for the development of his educational interests; accordingly he persuaded the Pestalozzian teachers, Mme Fretageot, William Phiquepal and Joseph Neef to join the community. Maclure's scientific interests and his concern for the education of adults were similarly able to flourish in the New Harmony setting, despite his subsequent disillusionment with Owen.

For the Owenite who had not yet joined a community there was still a premium on education: this time it was as a preparation for community

[1] *New Harmony Gazette*, 23 August 1826.
[2] Letter in *Cooperative Magazine*, III (1828), 43.

life. William Pare, addressing the members of the Birmingham Co-operative Society in 1828, warned his hearers that they should not think they understood the cooperative system perfectly; he therefore urged them to attend weekly meetings to hear lectures and discussions about it.[1]

Lastly, there was a deep Owenite faith in the pleasures of education.[2] Into the utopian vision of a happy, equalitarian community fitted the concept of life-long education. Schools, colleges, libraries, museums, scientific apparatus, lectures for adults—all appeared in profusion against a setting of arcadian bliss. It was easy to dismiss this vision as mere utopianism, but it had the practical function of sustaining the workers for the cause amidst the disappointments and indifference of the old immoral world.

Thus from different angles the various aspects of Owenism came together, reaching a synthesis in educational terms. Education was a key for the Owenites because of their conviction that man's 'ideas and habits . . . are the powers that govern and direct his conduct'. And it followed that by education they meant not the 'arts of reading and writing' but 'the acquisition of ideas'. 'Education', wrote Abram Combe 'means the ideas which are impressed on the mind of the individual, by which his judgement is formed, and by which the bent is given, in a great measure, to his inclinations. The desire of respect or approbation appears to be the mainspring; and this spring, it will be found, may be made to pull in any direction.'[3] There was a breadth in the Owenite conception of education which was frightening to orthodox religious and social opinion of the early nineteenth century; and the reaction to it was therefore hostile and scornful. Perhaps Owen was correct when he diagnosed: 'I am termed a visionary only because my principles have originated in experiences too comprehensive for the limited locality in which people have hitherto been interested.'[4]

Despite the differences between American and British society in the 1820s the Owenites tended to think of a common educational pattern for both countries. A school run on the principles of Pestalozzi, Fellenberg or Owen was sufficiently unusual to be detached from its contemporary surroundings, whether in America or Britain. And the importance which Owenites attributed to the informal educational influences of the social

[1] William Pare, *Address Delivered at the Opening of the Birmingham Cooperative Society* (Birmingham, 1828), pp. 22–3.
[2] See William Thompson, *Practical Directions for the . . . Establishment of Communities* (1830), pp. 205–25 ('Education and Mental Pleasures').
[3] Abram Combe, *Metaphorical Sketches*, p. 99.
[4] See also Owen, *Life*, IA, 102, 218.

environment was equally applicable in either country. Indeed, the principles of Owenism were considered as universally valid, irrespective of time and place; and the educational process was held to be fundamentally similar in all societies. The primary role of education for the Owenite was to produce men and women suitable for a new moral world, which was not yet in existence; and to this extent at least the differences between early industrial Britain and rural America were irrelevant. Everywhere Owenites manifested an enthusiasm for education, for they believed with George Mudie that the school was 'the steam engine of the moral world'.[1]

[1] *Economist*, I (1826), 96.

Building the
New Moral World

L

Building the New Moral World

Owen and his followers insisted that their schemes were eminently practical, based on the experience of men who had run successful businesses (Owen, Maclure, Abram Combe, Finch) or who had managed landed estates (Hamilton, Thompson, Vandeleur). They envisaged a literal building of the new moral world in bricks and mortar, a translation of Owenite philosophy into actual communities of land and buildings. Like other millennial sects, the Owenites needed a partial withdrawal from the world in order to live according to their principles and precepts. Only in a community could alternatives to the evils of the old immoral world be worked out. The main efforts of Owenites in Britain and America therefore went into founding communities and wrestling with the problems which community life produced. Shakers, Rappites and Mormons were faced by similar problems, and the model of the millenarian sect was adopted by the Owenites. But at first Owenism was identified with the model not of a sect but of a business firm, and it was only gradually that Owen came to see that the New Lanark Twist Company was unsuitable for his larger purposes.

1 Foundations: New Lanark

The mother church of Owenism, as New Lanark has always been regarded from Owen's times to the present, remains its most lasting physical monument in Britain. To this day the village of New Lanark remains virtually as it was in 1825, a cluster of tall gaunt mills and rows of grey stone houses huddled on the right bank of the river, below the

Falls of Clyde.[1] The steep banks of the river are wooded, and the village is built on a shelf of land between the stream and the rising ground. A road runs along the side of the valley to the old town of Lanark, about a mile away. The mills are built nearest the water's edge, and the houses—four storeys high in granite stone—behind them in long blocks. From the long tunnel cut through the solid rock of a hillside roars the water providing motive power for the mills. Owen's Institution for the Formation of Character still serves as the social centre of the village. Still too comes a steady procession of visitors from all parts of the world, attracted by its fame as a home of pioneer social experiments.

During Owen's residence at New Lanark the number of visitors was phenomenal, sometimes as many as thirty per day for months at a time. Between 1815 and 1825 the number of names recorded in the visitors' book was nearly twenty thousand, including the Grand Duke Nicholas of Russia. The village became one of the most visited places in Europe, and for ever after the name of Robert Owen was associated with New Lanark. Many of the visitors recorded their impressions and these accounts were reprinted widely in Owenite and other journals.[2] Few social experiments in the nineteenth century received wider publicity than Owen's work at New Lanark.

Owen's special identification of himself with New Lanark and his insistence on its direct relevance to the formulation of his social theories is attributable in a large measure to his previous experience in Manchester. He had gone to that city about 1788, when he was only seventeen, at the crucial time of great expansion. Before 1773 there was not one spinning mill in the town; by 1800, when Owen left, there were about fifty, many

[1] In 1963 the New Lanark Association Limited was formed as a housing association for the preservation and restoration of the village.

[2] Owen's main accounts of his work at New Lanark are in his *Statement regarding the New Lanark Establishment* (Edinburgh, 1812); *A New View of Society*; *Life*, I; *The Revolution in the Mind and Practice of the Human Race* (London, 1849); *Robert Owen's Journal*, I–IV (1850–52); and *New Existence of Man upon the Earth* (1854–55). Robert Dale Owen's *Threading My Way* is also informative. Accounts by outside observers are Macnab, *The New Views of Mr Owen of Lanark Impartially Examined*; *Report of a Deputation from Leeds* (1819), in Owen, *Life*, IA; *Report of the Proceedings in Dublin* (Dublin, 1823); James Smith, 'Notes taken during an Excursion in Scotland in the Year 1820', *New Moral World*, 30 April, 7–21 May 1836; Griscom, *A Year in Europe*, II; One Formerly a Teacher at New Lanark, *Robert Owen at New Lanark* (Manchester, 1839); Byllesby, *Observations* (from the *National Gazette*, by 'A Friend to the Plan'); *New Harmony Gazette*, 28 June 1826 (from the *New York Statesman*, 20 May 1826); 'A Day at New Lanark and a Sketch of its Present Condition', *New Moral World*, 13 April 1839. Most of the contemporary descriptions show considerable similarity, suggesting that after 1817 an approved stereotype was produced for the benefit of enquirers on their conducted tour round the village and the mills.

of them powered by steam. The population had increased from 27,000 in 1773 to 95,000 in 1801, and the town had developed separate living areas for workers and employers. Manchester had become the first modern city. It was this rapid development of Manchester, both physically and socially, that probably provided the data for Owen's characterization of industrial society as confused and artificial. The extremes of wealth and poverty, the breakdown of communication between classes, and the lack of unity and order everywhere formed a pattern of an 'irrational' society. On his removal to New Lanark Owen found himself in a very different world. In sharp contrast with Manchester, New Lanark was isolated and rural, with no streets or alleys or steam engines or middle classes or villas. It belonged to the first (water-power) stage of the Industrial Revolution, and Owen saw that because it was not so 'advanced' as Manchester it might be possible to preserve something of the spirit of community and close industrial relationships that had been lost in the larger city. New Lanark offered an alternative to chaotic Manchester as a model of industrial and social organization, which was paternal, community-oriented and only semi-urban. Essentially New Lanark was a repudiation of the city; it was industry in a rural setting; and it provided what was to become the prototype of the villages of cooperation in the new moral world.

In later life Owen claimed that he had always regarded New Lanark as the 'great experiment which was to prove to me, by practice, the truth or error of the principles which had been forced on my convictions', and when asked how he would change society at large he replied, 'in the same manner that I commenced the change in New Lanark'.[1] As always he set a very high value on his efforts: in fact they were no less than 'the most important experiment for the happiness of the human race that had yet been instituted at any time in any part of the world'. Nevertheless the regime at New Lanark was not his new system of society, but only the best that could be done in an existing factory village: 'I could do no more for a mere manufacturing population; for manufactures are not the true foundation of society.'[2] But if the improvements at New Lanark had even so been sufficiently remarkable to earn for it the title of 'the Happy Valley', how much more, argued Owen and his followers, could be expected from a community experiment unhampered by previous commitments. Curiously, neither of Owen's main ventures—New Lanark

[1] Owen, *Life*, I, 59, 78. The contrast between New Lanark in Dale's time and after Owen's improvements is brought out in an article, 'Facts about New Lanark, Motherwell and Orbiston', *New Moral World*, 4 January 1840.

[2] Owen, *Revolution in the Mind*, p. 21. Also Owen, *Life*, I, 79, 80.

and New Harmony—was started from scratch. In each case he bought from a pioneer founder a going concern and adapted it to his own ends. Neither village was more than an approximation to his stated plans, and afterwards he was able to claim that his new system of society had never been properly tried out. Like other millenarians the Owenites provided themselves with a mechanism to explain apparent failures. The pilgrimage to New Lanark, then, did not reveal to the hordes of visitors a model of the new moral world. But it did demonstrate three aspects of Owen's achievement which in themselves were sufficiently remarkable to attract attention, and which in combination accounted for the uniqueness of New Lanark. These three aspects of the great experiment were a model factory, an attempt at community organization, and an educational institution.

New Lanark attracted attention in the first instance as an outstanding symbol of the new industrial order. In 1816 it was the largest cotton undertaking, measured by numbers employed, in Britain, possibly equalled only by Strutt's factories at Belper and Milford in Derbyshire. It was exclusively a cotton spinning mill, producing up to 7000 lb. of yarn daily, and dependent on water power to drive the machinery, which was made and repaired on the premises. The total labour force fluctuated around 1400–1500, of whom about two-thirds were female.[1] Children were employed from the age of ten, though Owen would have preferred not to take them below twelve. He refused to continue the system of pauper apprentices inherited from Dale's regime. Until 1816 the hours of labour were thirteen per day (6 a.m. to 7 p.m.), and sometimes even fourteen, with half an hour allowed for breakfast and three-quarters of an hour for dinner; but thereafter they were reduced to twelve, with ten and a half hours of actual labour per day. Wages were low in comparison with other mills,[2] but were apparently acceptable because of the superior social welfare benefits. Owen also maintained full employment and during the four months of the American cotton embargo in 1806 when the machines were idle, he paid wages in full, at a total cost of £7000. Profits were sufficiently high to absorb this and later expenditures on education; and Owen calculated that during his thirty years of association with New Lanark (1799–1829) more than £300,000 in profit was

---

[1] MS. Notebook, New Lanark Mills, gives a breakdown of numbers employed in the three mill units and machine shops in 1810 and 1815.

[2] Average weekly wages for youths under eighteen were 4s. 3d., and for girls under eighteen, 3s. 5d. Adults on day rates averaged 9s. 11d. for men and 6s. for women. Adult piece workers averaged 14s. 10d. (men) and 8s. (women) weekly. *Report of a Deputation from Leeds*, in Owen, *Life*, IA, 256.

divided among the partners over and above the 5 per cent per annum paid on the capital invested and the cost of all his social experiments.[1]

Tied in with these arrangements was a much-lauded scheme of social security and welfare. Housing—improved and extended since Dale's day—was provided at a moderate rent. A contributory sickness and superannuation fund was maintained, and free medical services were available. All children were encouraged to attend the village schools, for which a nominal charge of 3d. per month was made. A large store enabled the employees and their families to buy food, clothing and household goods at cost price, purchases being recorded in a passbook and debited from wages. A savings bank took care of workers' deposits to the extent of £3000 per annum. Social and recreational facilities were provided in the New Institution, gardens and allotments laid out.

These measures were usually praised as a fine example of enlightened philanthropy and occasionally also as enlightened management. They were in no sense charity, but were grounded on hard actuarial and financial principles.[2] The whole operation could never be mistaken for anything other than what it was: a profit-making cotton mill. It was life in a factory colony which the Quaker visitor, James Smith of Liverpool, described in 1820:

[1] Owen, *Revolution in the Mind*, p. 30. Since few of the early business records of New Lanark have survived it is impossible to make an accurate assessment of the profitability of the mills in Owen's time. The best that can be done is to compare the various statements that Owen himself made from time to time in his different writings. A rough index of the growth in capital value is afforded by the purchase price of the mills when they changed hands. In 1799 Owen and his partners purchased them from David Dale for £60,000: when a new partnership was formed in 1809 the mills changed hands at £84,000: by the time of the third partnership in 1813 the price had risen to £114,000, and Owen considered that the true value was about £130,000. A visitor's account in 1825 stated that 'a capital of £200,000 is embarked, divided into thirteen shares of which seven belong to Mr Owen. The annual profits are about 10 per cent' (*New Harmony Gazette*, 28 June 1826). Other estimates mentioned 12½ per cent annually on the original stock (Griscom, II, 385; Byllesby, p. 165). Owen calculated that during the four years of his second partnership (1809–13) a net profit of £160,000 was made after allowing 5 per cent for the capital employed (Owen, *Life*, I, 98); and in a letter to Bentham dated 21 February 1821 Owen explained that the profits on the last year's business to be divided amounted to £15,000, in addition to 5 per cent interest on the capital of each parner (B.M. Add. MSS. 33545. f. 392).

[2] For example, contributions to the sickness and superannuation fund were deducted from employees' wages at the rate of one-sixtieth part, i.e. 1d. in 5s. For nearly twenty years these payments, with the addition of 50 gns. per annum from the company, were adequate. But in 1823, as a result of the prevalence of typhus fever and an increase in the number of aged, the fund was no longer sufficient to meet the claims made upon it. Owen therefore proposed to increase the workers' contributions, which became the occasion of a public controversy. *Glasgow Chronicle*, 17 January 1824, cutting in Jane Dale Owen, Scrapbook. Also Rev. John Aiton, *Mr Owen's Objections to Christianity* (Edinburgh, 1824), p. 37.

At half past one o'clock the dinner bell was rung. We were then near the lodge at which the people go out, and in the course of a few minutes they had all passed through the gate. .... At twenty minutes past two o'clock the return bell was rung and the gates were re-opened. .... As soon as the last person had passed through, the time was ... two minutes [before] the expiration of the hour allowed for dinner.[1]

Smith might equally well have been describing the very similar establishment of Jedediah Strutt and his sons in Derbyshire.[2] Physically the factory villages at Belper and Milford resembled New Lanark: tall mills, workshops and rows of workers' houses set by the banks of the Derwent river, which provided motive power. The same patriarchal regime, with housing, schools, sick club and cooperative store prevailed; the same daily work routine was observed. The Strutts were family friends of Owen: they were also Unitarians and liberal Whigs, supporters of Lancasterian schools, mechanics' institutes and 'improvement'. They were interested in Owen's schemes and were prepared to support his British and Foreign Philanthropic Society with a subscription of £5000. Yet visitors did not flock to see their villages at the rate of 2000 per year, nor did the Strutts consider their paternalistic efforts the germ of a new system of society. Clearly it was not the model factory which Owen had in mind when he described New Lanark as 'a model and example to the manufacturing community',[3] but rather other aspects of his great experiment.

Mill life at New Lanark was very far removed from the pastoral idylls portrayed in Owenite romances. Very few of the inhabitants were in any sense Owenites, and very few understood, probably, the wider implications of Owen's views. Yet both they and the visitors were aware that New Lanark was more than just an efficiently run and humanely managed factory. It was also a genuine attempt, even though rudimentary and clumsily paternal, at community organization. Owen had a deep compassion for the poor and a shining sincerity which transformed his efforts into something beyond what most philanthropic mill owners could achieve. Only after repeated conflicts with his partners was he able even to begin the more important parts of his social experiment. In 1809 his original partnership was dissolved because of opposition to his plans for the 'farther improvement of the community', and he chose new partners

---

[1] *New Moral World*, 30 April 1836.

[2] Details in Fitton and Wadsworth, *The Strutts and the Arkwrights, 1758–1830*. See also the valuable article by Sidney Pollard, 'The Factory Village in the Industrial Revolution', *English Historical Review*, LXXIX (1964), 513–31.

[3] Owen, *Statement*, p. 4.

whom he thought would be more sympathetic. But in 1812–13 the search for amenable partners began again, and a new partnership which included Jeremy Bentham, four Quakers and an Anglican was formed. The significance of the change was not lost upon the inhabitants of New Lanark, who upon Owen's next return to the village unharnessed the horses from his carriage and drew him in triumph through the streets.

Imperfect as the community organization at New Lanark was, it nevertheless suggested lines of development for the new moral world of the future. Features which later became characteristic of Owenite communities and ideas which Owen later repeated in new contexts appeared first in the great experiment. Thus what Harriet Martineau called Owen's 'remarkable ability in the . . . conduct of the machinery of living'[1] was first demonstrated at New Lanark. The detailed and comprehensive arrangements for the work, health, education and leisure of a village of more than 2000 people provided him with practical hints for his community plans. His concern for the emancipation of women from the tyranny of household drudgery (which became a notable feature of all Owenite schemes) led him to devise communal dining-rooms and kitchens:[2] similarly the schools, which admitted children from the age of two, lightened the burden of child rearing for women in the home. By 1812 Owen was already convinced of the need for communal alternatives to the individual family system if his new view of society was to make any headway. To a friendly visitor it seemed that it was in 'the practical application of philosophy to the purposes of domestic life that the institution at New Lanark differs so essentially from others'.[3] Owen was not able to do very much while at New Lanark to weaken the family system, mainly because of the opposition of his partners and possibly the womenfolk of the village. But the measures which he instituted to secure social control at New Lanark were mainly such as to strengthen community relationships at the expense of the individual family.

The most important factor of social cohesion and social discipline was of course Owen himself. In his New Lanark days he was not yet referred to as the Social Father, but his patriarchal position was very obvious. James Smith suggested that the effect of Owen's 'indisputable power of

---

[1] Obituary notice, *Daily News*, 19 November 1858, reprinted in Harriet Martineau, *Biographical Sketches* (4th edn., London, 1876), p. 309.

[2] It is doubtful whether these public dining-rooms and kitchens were actually used. As early as 1812 Owen announced plans to build them (*Statement*, p. 14); but visitors in 1819 and 1820 reported them as 'nearly completed' (Griscom, II, 384; *New Moral World*, 7 May 1836); and they were apparently still in this state when Owen left for America in 1824. Cf. also the account by a visitor in 1839 (*New Moral World*, 13 April 1839).

[3] Report from the *National Gazette*, in Byllesby, *Observations*, p. 165.

control' was insufficiently realized by him—that the fear of dismissal, for instance, vitiated some of Owen's sanguine claims for the acceptability of his innovations. But in fact Owen was well aware of his position—and later realized only too clearly the limitations which it imposed.[1] The furthest that he was able to go in the matter of self-government was the establishment of an elected board of twelve jurymen to see that his code of regulations for the health, cleanliness and good order of the village was enforced.[2]

The positive measures of social control at New Lanark were often imaginative, not to say ingenious. Owen placed his greatest hopes in the schools, for the younger generation was more likely to successfully internalize the values and attitudes to which they had been exposed. But the store, the dancing and lectures in the evenings, and the public inspection of homes were also powerful social instruments—though the women at first resented the intrusions of the 'Bug Hunters' who had been deputed to inspect their houses. In the mills Owen's device of the 'silent monitor' added a bizarre touch to the problem of discipline. Near the workplace of each operative was suspended a small wooden block, each side of which was painted a different colour—black, blue, yellow or white. The colour showing at the front denoted the conduct of the worker during the previous day. A record of this was kept in a 'book of character' provided for each department and maintained by the superintendent: 'by which arrangement', commented Owen, 'I had the conduct of each registered to four degrees of comparison during every day of the week, Sundays excepted, for every year they remained in my employment'.[3] Acceptable social behaviour was enforced negatively by prohibition and fines. No public house was permitted in the village, and fines were imposed for drunkenness. Illegitimacy was also penalized by fining, and the mother and father were required to make weekly payments to a poor fund.[4]

There was widespread agreement that these measures were effective in producing a very respectable and orderly body of inhabitants. Visitors

[1] 'The people were slaves at my mercy; liable at any time to be dismissed; and knowing that, in that case, they must go into misery, compared with such limited happiness as they now enjoyed'. Owen, *Revolution in the Mind*, p. 21.

[2] Owen, *New Existence*, pt. V (1854), appendix. Owen claimed that before he left New Lanark he proposed to transfer the establishment to the workers, for their own profit, after paying 5 per cent for the capital; and that he offered to manage it for them until they could conduct it themselves through directors of their own choosing. But his partners would not agree. Owen, *Revolution in the Mind*, p. 31.

[3] Owen, *Life*, I, 81.

[4] The Leeds deputation in 1819 stated that 'the moral habits of the people are . . . very exemplary', and supported this by the figure of only 28 illegitimate births among a total of

repeatedly commented on the 'order, neatness and regularity' which they observed, and on the healthy, cheerful appearance of the work people. The contrast with conditions in Dale's time was often used by Owen to show that an idle, dirty, dissolute and drunken population could be transformed by the 'application of proper means'. Contemporaries were impressed that Owen seemed to have found a solution to the problem of what James Smith called the 'moral government of a manufacturing population'. The question which they had doubts about, and which later communitarian experience tended to confirm, was how relevant New Lanark would be to other types of community organization.

Experience at New Harmony, Orbiston and later Owenite communities repeated the difficulties of patriarchalism, from which it was difficult to escape when one individual provided most of the capital and alternative types of social control were ruled out. In other respects New Lanark was a less than perfect model for Owenite communitarians. First, it was a single-industry village, and even though mechanics, blacksmiths and foundry workers were employed in the machine shops, it lacked the diversification of agriculture and manufacturing that Owen postulated for his villages of cooperation. Second, the population was unbalanced, in that cotton spinning employed a majority of women and children, and there was no employment for many of the men in the village.[1] Also, the inhabitants were almost entirely working people, the only white-collar element being about twenty managers, clerks and teachers, so that middle-class influence was virtually non-existent. Lastly, the inhabitants were not Owenites or utopians but ordinary Scots folk among whom the traditional sanctions of puritanism were probably still strong.[2] As an experience from which to generalize about building the new moral world New Lanark was seriously deficient in these respects.

One institution, however, was considered by Owenites to eclipse all others as a vindication of Owen's theories and to be a practical model for

[1] In 1811 when the total population of New Lanark was 2206 some 1360 were employed at the mills, and 846 elsewhere (probably in Old Lanark). MS. Notebook, New Lanark Mills.

[2] Cf. Griscom, II, 387. 'Here the moral influence of the Gospel is in active operation. The inhabitants of the village are attentive to their religious observances.'

1380 females during the preceding 9½ years. The MS. Register of Births, Marriages and Deaths (1818–53) at the New Lanark Mills gives the following summary figures:

Year	Births legitimate	Births illegitimate	Marriages	Deaths
1818	48		29	53
1820	57	7	16	41
1821	49	10	14	30
1822	49	9	27	46

future communities. The schools at New Lanark drew more encomiums from reformers than any other aspect of the great experiment.[1] Owen had a great love of children, and his infinite patience and good temper made him a beloved figure to them everywhere. Opposition from his partners prevented him from extending and remodelling the schools which Dale had established until 1809, but by 1812 the New Institution was built, and in 1816 he opened the more ambitious Institution for the Formation of Character. This last served a threefold purpose, as an infant school, a day school and a centre for adult education and recreation. The pedagogical techniques and assumptions in the schools were quite revolutionary and, apparently, original to Owen himself. Although the building was constructed according to the fashionable Lancasterian plan, with large numbers of children in one room, the monitorial system was not used, and Robert Dale Owen later thought that smaller rooms, each for twenty or thirty children, would have been preferable. In fact, the schools were far removed, both in purpose and method, from the contemporary instruction-factories of Bell and Lancaster. Owen decided that small children should not 'be annoyed with books', but were to be taught by 'sensible signs' and 'familiar conversation'. The interests of child-nature were utilized in teaching basic subjects, and play (and the playground) was treated as an educative agency. Dancing, singing and 'military exercises' were part of the daily curriculum, and the need for variety and flexibility in teaching methods was enjoined on all teachers. No 'artificial' rewards or punishments were permitted, and kindness was observed in precept and practice. So original were these educational views that Owen had difficulty in finding teachers whom he could trust to carry them out.[2]

[1] The only original record of the New Lanark schools is the MS. Cash Book of the New Lanark Institution, 1816–25, in Edinburgh University Library, which gives details of the teachers' pay and expenditures on equipment and children's clothing. All of the works listed in n. 2, p. 152 above contain references to the schools. In addition, Robert Dale Owen, *Outline of the System of Education at New Lanark* is an indispensable source. See also Owen's evidence in *Report of the Select Committee on the Education of the Lower Orders in the Metropolis* (1816), pp. 238–42; and *Report of the Select Committee on the State of Children employed in the Manufactories of the United Kingdom* (1816), pp. 20–8, 36–40, 85–95; 'Account of the New Lanark Schools' (Rathbone Family Papers), reprinted in James Murphy, 'Robert Owen in Liverpool', *Transactions, Historic Society of Lancashire and Cheshire*, CXII (1961), 100–1. Useful summaries of the schools are given in Podmore, chap. VII, and in Silver, pp. 117–26. For comparison with contemporary educational reformers see Hugh M. Pollard, *Pioneers of Popular Education, 1760–1850* (Cambridge, Mass., 1957).

[2] Owen's selection of James Buchanan ('a poor simple hearted weaver . . . who had been previously trained by his wife to perfect submission to her will') and the seventeen-year-old Molly Young as his first infant school teachers is recounted in his *Life*, I, 139.

It has been usual to see the significance of the New Lanark schools in their pioneering role of predecessors to modern infant and junior schools, and to link the name of Owen with Froebel and Pestalozzi. But it is possible that the happy children dancing in their kilts and tunics, singing Scots airs to the amusement of visitors, and learning geography by means of a parlour game were indicative of much wider implications in Owen's thought. His enthusiasm for admitting children into the school from as early as the age of one was clearly connected with his desire to diminish parental influence and maximize the exposure to a beneficent environment. Owen's attitude towards the child, as towards the family, was part of his new view of society; and just as the private family had to be abolished in the new moral world, so a new and more appropriate concept of childhood was required. Ideas of childhood derived from apprenticeship (which so easily degenerated into the 'factory slavery' of pauper children which Owen found on his arrival at New Lanark) were replaced by attitudes which could only view the employment of children under the age of twelve with abhorrence. One of the first measures Owen had taken after coming to the village was to refuse to employ any more pauper labour or any child under ten. Until 1816 his general reputation as a social reformer rested mainly on his efforts to secure legislative restriction of child labour in the mills.[1] In this struggle for the first factory act the gap between Owen's views of childhood and those of other manufacturers was apparent. Unlike his fellow cotton spinners Owen did not see a child of seven as virtually a little adult and therefore, like other labour, as a suitable 'instrument of gain'; but as a human being in a distinct phase of life, which like young manhood or old age had its special needs and problems.[2] Such criticism of the New Lanark schools as there was usually centred on an alleged neglect of bible study or a

[1] See his *Observations on the Effect of the Manufacturing System* (1815), *Letter to the Earl of Liverpool on the Employment of Children in Manufactories* (1818), and *Letter to the British Master Manufacturers* (1818), in Owen, *Life*, IA, appendices H, M, N.

[2] On the general theme of changing concepts of childhood, see Philippe Ariès, *Centuries of Childhood*, trans. Robert Baldick (New York, 1965).

Robert Dale Owen gave the total number of children in the schools as 600, of whom half were day scholars (under ten) and half attended in the evenings (being over ten and therefore working in the mills). The MS. Cash Book, covering the period 1816–25, shows a steady turn-over in teachers, but usually there were 13–16 on the books each month. Some of these were part-time, and some possibly were for evening classes. Additional staff were hired for painting and music. Only three teachers remained at New Lanark throughout the whole period 1816–25; the others stayed about six years on an average. Maximum rates of teachers' pay were 21s. per week for men, and 9s. for women, but most earned less than this. The annual expenditure on the schools fluctuated from a low of £479 in 1817 to a maximum of £1345 in 1822. Teachers' wages accounted for a little over half of the total.

puritanical objection to dancing.[1] But it may be that the doubts which some visitors expressed stemmed from a more basic unease about the assumptions on which the educational experiment rested. (Conversely enthusiastic Owenites explained the practical success of the schools as due to the radical nature of the 'principles' upon which they were based.) After all, if Mr Owen's views on such important institutions as religion and marriage were said to be unsound might not his views on education and childhood also be suspect?

A deep interest in advanced views of childhood and education was a characteristic of all subsequent Owenite ventures—witness the Pestalozzian schools at New Harmony or the work of James Pierrepont Greaves and the Concordium. From a communitarian point of view the schools were the most exportable of the institutions at New Lanark. They were also among the most enduring: a visitor in 1839 found that the schools were still much the same as in Owen's time, and that some of the old teachers were there.[2] Granted the crucial role of education in Owenite thought, the New Lanark schools were inevitably regarded as prototypes for the new moral world.

With other institutions the transition from New Lanark to communities of cooperation was not so obvious. Owen blithely imagined that his successes at New Lanark had equipped him to deal with the problems of a fully fledged communitarian experiment, but New Harmony soon showed that this was not so. Similarly at Orbiston, Abram Combe and Archibald Hamilton rapidly discovered that Owen's experiences and plans did not provide them with solutions to many of the practical questions which necessitated immediate answers. Owen and his apologists were correct, strictly speaking, when they said that the new system had not been tried out at New Lanark. Nevertheless they generalized from this local and partial example to prove the validity of universal

---

[1] Owen's dispute with the Rev. Mr Menzies and the Presbytery of Lanark in 1822–23 was over the teaching of scriptures in the schools, and there had been constant friction between Owen and his Quaker partners, especially William Allen, on the same point for some years. Allen further objected to the children's dancing and the wearing of the kilt, as also did William Cobbett later. Press cuttings from Glasgow newspapers in Jane Dale Owen, Scrapbook; William Pare, Scrapbook (F.W.A.); William Cobbett, *Tour in Scotland* (London, 1833), p. 209; Aiton, *op. cit.*

[2] *New Moral World*, 13 April 1839. There is an almost complete dearth of information about New Lanark from 1825 until 1881, when it was acquired by Henry Birkmyre from Charles Walker. A critical account by W. Davidson, *History of Lanark and Guide to the Scenery* (Lanark, 1828) admitted that Owen's absence was deeply regretted and that it was felt that the prosperous days of New Lanark were over and that it would soon be degraded to the level of other establishments. Although dancing was still taught, the schools had reverted to 'the British and Foreign system'.

communitarianism. By 1824 Owen had come to the conclusion that a cotton mill and its attendant factory village was an inadequate base from which to usher in the millennium: New Lanark had at most indicated possibilities for the future building of the new moral world. A more total commitment to practical communitarianism was now required, and was moreover being urged on Owen by his more enthusiastic followers. Increasing opposition from his partners probably further strengthened his resolve to leave New Lanark, and in October 1824 he sailed for America to establish the first Owenite community. From that date he was absent from the establishment which he had managed for twenty-five years, and in 1829 he relinquished his connections altogether. While he was engaged with the problems of New Harmony his Scottish followers founded the first British community at Orbiston. With these two ventures the Owenite movement entered upon a new phase.

2 The Lost Communities

The largest practical commitment of the Owenite movement, measured by the amount of time, effort and capital involved, was to community building. The community, or Village of Cooperation, was the central institution of Owenism. In America at least sixteen communities, either avowedly Owenite or influenced considerably by Owenite ideas, were founded. In Britain there were seven Owenite communities, and another three experiments in which Owenites participated. Further, there were in both countries several projected communities which never materialized. For the three largest communities (New Harmony, Orbiston and Queenwood) useful secondary studies exist, but material on the smaller communities is scanty and scattered. It is possible nevertheless to build a simple typology of Owenite communities and identify certain recurring problems and themes. First, however, a brief outline of the chronology of what George Jacob Holyoake called the lost communities is necessary.

New Harmony was the earliest and the most ambitious Owenite community.[1] To this day the little Indiana town on the banks of the Wabash river remains basically unchanged from the day in December 1824 when Owen first saw it and made up his mind to buy it from the Rappites.

---

[1] There is a considerable literature on New Harmony. But the definitive work is Bestor, *Backwoods Utopias*, which has a complete bibliography. Older accounts are Lockwood, *New Harmony Movement*, and Podmore, *Robert Owen*, chaps. 13 and 14. There is useful detail on Owen's relations with the Rappites in Karl J. R. Arndt, *George Rapp's Harmony Society, 1785–1847* (Philadelphia, Penn., 1965). In addition to the MS. sources listed in

Although the two original churches have disappeared, many brick and frame houses built by the Rappites survive along the streets laid out on a grid plan. The population is scarcely larger than in Owen's time, and no industrial or suburban developments have subsequently altered the physical appearance of the town. Like New Lanark, it remains a monument to the Owenite past, a quiet backwater,which time has passed by.

Owen's investment in New Harmony was very considerable. The purchase price of the town was $125,000 and his additional expenditures brought the total to about $200,000, which accounted for the bulk of his $250,000 fortune. For the sum paid he acquired 20,000 acres of land and a complete village with houses, churches, dormitories, four mills, a textile factory, distilleries and brewery, a tan yard and mechanics' shops. Two thousand acres of the land were under cultivation and there were vineyards and extensive orchards. All was ready for immediate occupation as a community, and so as the Rappites moved out some nine hundred new-comers moved in, answering Owen's public invitation to 'the industrious and well disposed of all nations'.

Community life was begun in May 1825 with the adoption of the constitution for a Preliminary Society. During the early months of its existence Owen was away from New Harmony most of the time, and his second son William was left in charge. Great expectations were set upon Owen's return in January 1826, when he arrived with William Maclure and the famous 'Boatload of Knowledge'. Early confusions, frustrations and hardships, it was felt, would disappear once Owen himself was on

---

Bestor the following contemporary accounts are indispensable for a picture of the community: William Owen, *Diary . . . from November 10, 1824 to April 20, 1825*, ed. Joel W. Hiatt, Indiana Historical Society, *Publications* (Indianapolis, Ind., 1906), vol. IV, no. 1; Donald Macdonald, *Diaries . . . 1824–1826*, ed. with introd. by Caroline Dale Snedeker, Indiana Historical Society, *Publications* (Indianapolis, Ind., 1942), vol. XIV, no. 2; *New Harmony, An Adventure in Happiness: Papers of Thomas and Sarah Pears*, ed. Thomas Clinton Pears, Jr. (Indianapolis, Ind., 1933); 'Letters of William Pelham, Written in 1825 and 1826', ed. Caroline Creese Pelham, in Harlow Lindley, ed., *Indiana as seen by Early Travelers*, Indiana Historical Collections (Indianapolis, Ind., 1916); Paul Brown, *Twelve Months in New Harmony*; Bestor, ed. *Education and Reform at New Harmony*. The *New Harmony Gazette* provides a weekly commentary on life at New Harmony and also contains reports from other communities. In addition to the articles and monographs listed for each community, Noyes, *History of American Socialisms* is still most useful for Owenite experiments in America. Noyes based his work on the papers of A. J. Macdonald, a Scots printer and Owenite, who came to the United States about 1842 and who collected materials for a history of communities in the U.S. which he did not live to write. Macdonald's 'Manuscripts and Collections', now in Yale University Library, is a main source for the history of Owenite communities in America. A useful secondary source is Ralph Albertson, 'A Survey of Mutualistic Communities in America', *Iowa Journal of History and Politics*, XXXIV (1936), 375–440.

SOUTH ELEVATION

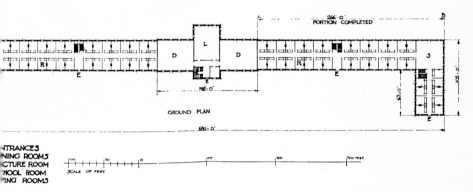

266·0"
PORTION COMPLETED

L

D   D

R   R

E   E

148·0"

GROUND PLAN

680·0"

NTRANCES
NING ROOMS
CTURE ROOM
HOOL ROOM
/ING ROOMS

SCALE OF FEET

21. Orbiston community

22. Harmony Hall, Queenwood

23. Equality: the end of a dream. Thomas Steel's drawing of his cabin on the Wisconsin frontier, 1844

the spot; and indeed his infectious optimism did for a time carry the Harmonists along after he had convinced them that they were sufficiently advanced to form themselves into a permanent Community of Equality. But practical difficulties soon led to separatist tendencies and in February–March 1826 New Harmony began to divide up into several communities: Macluria was formed out of settlers who disliked Owen's religious views, while the English farmers (who had come from Birkbeck's settlement across the river in Illinois) organized themselves under the strange name of Feiba-Peveli.[1] These were followed by three more independent communities—a School Society, an Agricultural and Pastoral Society and a Mechanic and Manufacturing Society. Continual reorganizations preoccupied the colonists throughout the year 1826, and Owen and Maclure drifted apart. Owen made a final unsuccessful attempt to reorganize the whole community in the spring of 1827 and then left New Harmony for a year. He returned briefly in April–June 1828, and thereafter New Harmony lapsed into individualism, with such property as they did not lease or sell remaining in the hands of Owen and Maclure. As an experiment in Owenite communitarianism New Harmony virtually came to an end with Owen's departure in June 1827.

In relation to the lesser Owenite communities of the 1820s New Harmony was as a sun to its planets. At Wanborough, Illinois, a Joint Stock Society was begun in July 1825.[2] Its leader was William Hall, a member of Birkbeck's English Settlement in Edwards County, Illinois, and it was directly inspired by Owen's visit to Albion and the experiment across the river at New Harmony. A constitution was drawn up and a dozen members joined, but it is doubtful whether community life was actually started.

More substantial was the Blue Spring Community, near Bloomington, Indiana.[3] Here in January 1826 a tract of eighty acres of government land was purchased and additional land held by individual members gave them control of some 325 acres in all. Twenty-seven members and their families joined the community. Log houses were built in the form of a square, together with stores, granary and school. Manufactures were planned, but during its short existence the community did not get beyond the farming stage. The precise reasons for the dissolution of the community

---

[1] Stedman Whitwell, the architect who accompanied Owen to New Harmony, invented a system of nomenclature in which the name of a place was formed by translating its latitude and longitude into letters. Thus Feiba-Peveli represented 38.11 N., 87.53 W. *New Harmony Gazette*, 12 April 1826.

[2] See Walter B. Hendrickson, 'An Owenite Society in Illinois', *Indiana Magazine of History*, XLV (1949), 175–82.

[3] Richard Simons, 'A Utopian Failure', *Indiana History Bulletin*, XVII (1941), 98–113.

are not known, though it has been suggested that the introduction of a system of communal property in the spring of 1827 may have caused dissension. By the end of the year the experiment was finished.

Farther afield, but still in the Ohio Valley, were other Owenite communities. The Friendly Association for Mutual Interests at Kendal (now Massillon), Ohio, was formed in the spring of 1826.[1] An estate of over 2000 acres was purchased for $20,000 and 150 members were settled on it. The backbone of the community was made up of substantial farmers from the neighbourhood, but there were also mechanics and workers in a woollen mill. Unlike New Harmony and some other communities the Kendal Community was not torn by dissensions but carried on its operations amicably for nearly three years. By the autumn of 1828, however, members began to withdraw, and in January 1829 the community was wound up. There was no dramatic crisis to account for this: apparently the members came to the conclusion that communitarian life did not benefit them substantially more than individual society, and so when seven heads of families died of summer-fever and creditors pressed for payment of the mortgage, the experiment was quietly abandoned.

At Cincinnati Owenism was the beneficiary of an earlier sectarian and communitarian tradition, and the local minister of the Swedenborgian Church of the New Jerusalem, Daniel Roe, was an enthusiastic follower of Owen. In July 1825 a community was begun at Yellow Springs, Greene County, Ohio, on a domain of 720 acres (now Antioch College).[2] Between seventy-five and a hundred families were involved, and included professional and business men as well as farmers and labourers. The community was modelled closely on New Harmony and soon ran into the same kind of problems. Despite attempts by Paul Brown and William Maclure successively to straighten out difficulties between factions the community fell apart, and at the end of 1826 the property was given up. Another contemporary Owenite community, the Friendly Association for Mutual Interests at historic Valley Forge, Pennsylvania, had an even shorter life. Formed by a group of Philadelphia and Wilmington Owenites in January 1826 it lasted only until September of that year, and upon its demise a number of the members joined the Shakers.

Migration from one community to another was by no means uncommon, and the Kendal Community received members who had already been in two earlier Owenite ventures. The first of these was the

---

[1] Noyes, 78–80; Bestor, *Backwoods Utopias*, 205–6. The record book and constitution of the Kendal Community are printed in full in Wendall P. Fox, 'The Kendal Community', *Ohio Archaeological and Historical Quarterly*, XX (1911), 176–219.

[2] Noyes, 59–65; Bestor, *Backwoods Utopias*, 210–13.

Franklin Community at Haverstraw, Rockland County, New York, which began operations on a 120-acre farm two miles from the Hudson river in May 1826.[1] Eighty persons were located there, being a mixed body of artisans, farmers and intellectuals. The leaders were free-thinkers and deists: George Houston (who had been jailed in England for publishing blasphemy), Abner Kneeland (who was to be tried and imprisoned for blasphemy in the 1830s) and Henry A. Fay (a lawyer of similar sympathies)—shortly to be joined by Robert L. Jennings from New Harmony. The community lasted only five months, and was ended amidst charges of dishonesty against the managers. Some of the members then joined the second Owenite community, Forestville, which had been organized in December 1825 near Coxsackie in Greene County, New York. A tract of 325 acres was entered upon in 1826, and some sixty colonists engaged in farming and handicrafts. Suggestions for a merger with the Kendal community were made, but in October 1827 the Forestville community came to an end and its property was sold.

One community within the New Harmony orbit differed considerably from the pattern hitherto described. Frances Wright, a young Scottish radical and admirer of Owen, visited New Harmony in 1825 and soon formulated a plan for a community of negro slaves.[2] Her object was to buy or persuade benevolent masters to donate slaves who would be able to earn enough to purchase their emancipation and at the same time prepare themselves for freedom by education. Assisted by George Flower, the communitarian and anti-slavery enthusiast from Albion, Illinois, she purchased Nashoba, a 2000-acre plantation about fourteen miles from Memphis, Tennessee, in November 1825. Several negro families were acquired by gift and purchase, and Frances Wright, her sister Camilla, James Richardson and George Flower and his family went to live on the estate. After another visit to New Harmony and discussions with Owen and Maclure, Frances Wright became convinced of the necessity of religious and sexual no less than slave emancipation. Nashoba then became an experimental, racially integrated community based on Owenite doctrines. As such it was well calculated to incur local displeasure, and after

[1] James M'Knight, *A Discourse Exposing Robert Owen's System, as Practised by the Franklin Community, at Haverstraw* (New York, 1826); Noyes, 74–7.

[2] For Frances Wright see Waterman, *Frances Wright*; and Perkins and Wolfson, *Frances Wright, Free Enquirer*. Four articles deal with Nashoba: Anna B. A. Brown, 'A Dream of Emancipation', *New England Magazine*, n.s., XXX (1904), 494–9; Edd Winfield Parks, 'Dreamer's Vision: Frances Wright at Nashoba (1825–30)', *Tennessee Historical Magazine*, 2nd series, II (1932), 75–86; O. B. Emerson, 'Frances Wright and Her Nashoba Experiment', *Tennessee Historical Quarterly*, VI (1947), 291–314; Helen Elliott, 'Frances Wright's Experiment with Negro Emancipation', *Indiana Magazine of History*, XXXVI (1939), 141–57. See also Robert Dale Owen, *Threading My Way*.

Richardson's tactless disclosures of his relations with one of the slave wo-men Nashoba was denounced as a brothel. Because of ill-health Frances Wright was not able to remain in Nashoba continuously. In February 1828 she and Robert Dale Owen, who had spent some time in the community, admitted that modification of the original plan was necessary and that only a 'preliminary social community' was feasible. Nashoba continued for another year, under the leadership of Camilla Wright and her husband, Richeson Whitby, whose experience had included residence in a Shaker community as well as at New Harmony. In January 1830 the experiment came to an end when Frances Wright arranged for the trans-portation of the slaves to Haiti and accompanied them on this last stage of their emancipation.

No other specifically Owenite communities were founded in the United States in the 1820s. In Fountain County, Indiana, William Ludlow started his Coal Creek Community and Church of God along the lines he had suggested earlier in his *Belief of the Rational Brethren of the West* (Cincinnati, 1819).[1] Over a thousand acres of government land were purchased, to be held in common ownership, and the community lasted from 1824 until 1832. Ludlow lived for a time at New Harmony and was an admirer of Owen, but the Coal Creek community was not strictly an Owenite experiment. Following the disagreements at New Harmony in 1826–27 a group of eighty dissidents planned a community at Nevilsville, about thirty miles from Cincinnati, Ohio, but there is no evidence that it ever got started. Similarly Owen's own plan for the acquisition from the Mexican government of the provinces of Coahuila and Texas, which he put forward after the collapse at New Harmony, came to naught.[2] He visited Mexico in 1829 and for a time apparently believed that his gran-diose scheme for a huge social experiment would be seriously entertained by the Mexican Republic.

In Britain Owenite community building in the 1820s followed a parallel though not so extensive course. As early as 1821 a Cooperative and Economical Society was formed by George Mudie and a group of London printers whose object was to establish an Owenite community.[3]

---

[1] See p. 107 above. Also Bestor, *Backwoods Utopias*, pp. 207–9.

[2] Robert Owen, *Memorial of Robert Owen to the Mexican Republic and to the Govern-ment of the State of Coahuila and Texas* (Philadelphia, Penn., 1828). Also Wilbert H. Timmons, 'Robert Owen's Texas Project', *Southwestern Historical Quarterly*, LII (1949), 286–93.

[3] The main source is the *Economist* (1821–22); also [George Mudie] *Report of the Com-mittee Appointed at a Meeting of Journeymen . . .* (London, 1829); and Robert Southey, *Sir Thomas More* (London, 1829), pp. 134–9. Secondary accounts are given in Podmore, *Owen*, pp. 349–55; and Armytage, *Heavens Below*, pp. 92–5, which also has sections on some of the other British communities which follow.

They got as far as setting up an interim system of 'family union' at Spa Fields, under which they shared living costs while continuing to work at their normal jobs in the outside world. Twenty-one families were 'congregated' and enjoyed the benefits of cooperative dining, housekeeping and a school; but by 1823 the project was dead. A more ambitious plan for a complete Owenite community at Motherwell in Lanarkshire was nurtured by Archibald James Hamilton from 1820 and in 1822 was adopted by the British and Foreign Philanthropic Society. But this body, as we have seen, failed to raise the necessary capital, and when Owen turned his attention to the New World as a more likely prospect, the Motherwell scheme had to be abandoned. In its place Hamilton and Abram Combe devised the Orbiston community.

Orbiston in Lanarkshire was an estate of 290 acres belonging to the Hamilton family.[1] The purchase price was met by subscribers who had previously promised to support the Motherwell scheme, but by far the largest share of the financial burden was assumed by Hamilton and Combe. In March 1825 a stone building large enough to accommodate a thousand persons was begun, and a year later one wing was sufficiently completed for the first settlers to move in. Community life was begun in April 1826 and continued until December 1827, and at one time over three hundred persons were in residence. The community was basically agricultural, but a flourishing iron foundry encouraged the development of other trades such as printing and weaving. Abram Combe was at first the directing spirit in the whole enterprise, but soon fell ill and had to leave Orbiston. His death in August 1827 was the severest, though not the only blow that the young community had to suffer. As at New Harmony, fundamental differences on issues of organization and community of property created factions and led to constant feuding and changes of policy. When the mortgagees began to press for payment in the autumn of 1827 William Combe, who had assumed the management of the community after his brother's death, ordered the members to quit, and the first British Owenite community thus came to an end.

Collapse of a particular Owenite community did not necessarily mean collapse of faith in Owenism or in community. As in America, where communitarians migrated from one Owenite venture to the next or from

---

[1] The Orbiston *Register* (1825–27) provides a weekly chronicle of the affairs of the community; and a full account is given in Cullen, *Adventures in Socialism*. For material on Hamilton and Abram Combe pp. 26-32, 103-5 above. The largest subscribers to the Orbiston Community, after Hamilton and Abram Combe, were Henry Jones, Mrs Rathbone, James Morrison (of London), William Combe, Robert Foster, John Minter Morgan and William Brown (of Manchester). MS. 'List of Subscribers', dated 27 May 1827. Hamilton Papers.

Shakerism to Owenism, so in Britain the leading Orbistonians turned up in later Owenite experiments. Some, indeed, extended the links with Orbiston even farther afield. Joseph Applegarth, a shareholder and manager of the schools at Orbiston, went to New Harmony. Henry Jones, a retired naval officer from Exeter, Devon, was an early supporter of Owen's plans, including the Motherwell scheme. At Orbiston he was one of the leading proprietors and played some part in directing affairs during Abram Combe's absence. In 1827 he apparently concluded, like Owen, that the New World offered better prospects for community than the Old, and went to Canada to look for a suitable site. He obtained ten thousand acres of land on Lake Huron in Lambton County, Ontario. Here he brought a party of Scots immigrants and in 1828–29 began the community of Maxwell, investing in it his fortune of £10,000.[1] Little is known of its history, but it seems that a fire destroyed the community house and possibly discouraged the members from continuing with the experiment. Whether Jones was associated in any way with another Owenite community in his native Devon is impossible to determine. In the spring of 1826 well-attended meetings in Exeter and neighbouring towns aroused local interest in Owenism, and a Mr Vesey appeared as the sponsor of the Devon (or Exeter) Community.[2] A small estate of 37 acres located six and a half miles from Exeter was purchased and thirteen colonists set to work on it. By August twelve cottages were available and plans for a community of 400 families were aired. However, in the autumn of 1826 'domestic circumstances' compelled Vesey, the chief financial supporter, to withdraw. The communitarians then took another farm between Honiton and Exeter and formed themselves into the Dowlands Devon Community. Its progress can be traced fitfully in the Owenite press throughout 1827 but thereafter nothing more is heard.

The next Owenite community was in Ireland. John Scott Vandeleur, a young squire of County Clare, had been impressed by Owen's public meetings in Dublin in 1823, and after an outbreak of peasant violence on his estate in 1830 turned to Owenism as a solution to Irish agrarian problems. Seeking someone to manage a cooperative experiment, he was put in touch (probably through John Finch) with Edward Thomas Craig

[1] See Rev. John Morrison, ' "The Toon o' Maxwell"—an Owen Settlement in Lambton County, Ontario', Ontario Historical Society, Papers and Records, XII (1914), 5–12. There is a MS. letter of Jones to Hamilton, dated 23 March 1827, in the Hamilton Papers. Jones demanded payment of the money owed him, and accused Hamilton of 'an aristocracy of decision' respecting 'the New Views' to which he (Jones) was not disposed to submit.

[2] The sole source for this community is the Cooperative Magazine and Monthly Herald (1826–27).

(1804–1894) a young Manchester Owenite who edited the *Lancashire and Yorkshire Cooperator*. Craig took over the 618-acre estate and in November 1831 outlined to the peasantry his plans for a community to be known as the Ralahine Agricultural and Manufacturing Cooperative Association.[1] The community agreed to lease the land from Vandeleur for a fixed rent to be paid in kind, and to work the estate cooperatively under the direction of an elected committee. A system of labour notes, social security benefits and a school were instituted. By the second year eighty-two persons were in residence, and until 1833 all went well. Then suddenly it all collapsed. Vandeleur, who had a fatal addiction to gambling, wagered away his estate and fled the country. Ralahine was sold for the benefit of his creditors, the members of the community received no compensation, and Craig sold all he had to redeem for cash the labour notes of the members.

With the unquenchable optimism of the true Owenite, Craig appeared again in another community five years later. At Christmas 1838 William Hodson founded a community on his 200 acres of land at Manea Fen, Cambridgeshire.[2] Hodson was a farmer and had formerly been a seaman and Methodist lay preacher before being attracted to Owenism. He invested about £6000 in the community which soon had living cottages, communal dining-room and kitchen, workshops, a brick kiln and a windmill. Between 35 and 50 members formed the little colony, including Craig as schoolmaster. The agricultural operations at Manea Fen prospered but there were complaints that the craftsmen such as the stockingers had difficulty in finding a market. In February 1841, after Hodson had decided that he could no longer continue his financial support, factions within the community came to blows; and shortly afterwards a majority of the members left. Before this demise another

---

[1] Three Owenites left first-hand accounts of the Ralahine Community, which for the rest of the century was accorded an honoured place in the cooperative tradition: E. T. Craig, *The Irish Land and Labour Question, Illustrated in the History of Ralahine and Co-operative Farming* (London, 1882) [see bibliography for subsequent editions]; William Pare, *Cooperative Agriculture: A Solution of the Land Question as Exemplified in the History of the Ralahine Cooperative Association . . .* (London, 1870); and John Finch, 'Ralahine; or Human Improvement and Human Happiness', *New Moral World*, 31 March–29 September 1838 (a series of 15 letters originally published in the *Liverpool Chronicle*). See also Alfred R. Wallace, *Studies Scientific and Social* (London, 1900), II, 455–77. Most of the available material on Craig is gathered together in R. G. Garnett, 'E. T. Craig: Communitarian, Educator, Phrenologist', *The Vocational Aspect* (Summer, 1963), pp. 135–50.

[2] The detailed history of Manea Fen can be traced in its journal, the *Working Bee* (1839–41), edited first by Thomas Green and later by W. H. Bellatti. There are useful accounts of Manea Fen and Pant Glas in Armytage, *op. cit.*; and Robert Daniel Storch, 'Owenite Communitarianism in Britain' (unpublished M.A. thesis, University of Wisconsin, 1964).

Owenite community, this time in Wales, had also enjoyed a brief existence. It was formed by the Society of United Friends, a splinter group from the main Liverpool branch of the Owenites, and was led by John Moncas and James Spurr. They secured a thousand acres of land at Pant Glas (Green Vale), Merionethshire, about eight miles from Dolgelly, in January 1840, at an annual rent of £140. Capital was to be raised by the weekly subscriptions of the members of the Society, plus entrance fees of £12 for a man and £8 for a woman. The first colonists soon discovered that the estate was so rocky and mountainous as to be virtually useless and before the end of the year the community was abandoned.

Both Pant Glas and Manea Fen were 'unorthodox' Owenite communities and suffered some dissipation of their energies in quarrels with other sections of the movement whose interests were differently placed. From October 1839 the main body of British Owenites focused their attention on a grand new communitarian venture which was to begin the millennium. After a false start in 1838, when negotiations were begun for the purchase of an estate at Wretton in Norfolk from James Hill (an educational reformer and Owenite sympathizer), land was leased from Sir Isaac Lyon Goldsmid, a London banker who had been joint treasurer of the British and Foreign Philanthropic Society and a subscriber to the Motherwell project. The property of 533 acres was at East Tytherly, Hampshire, and was named Queenwood after the principal farm on the estate.[1] The community was given the title of Harmony Hall. In addition Owen leased three adjoining farms, thus making the community's total holdings more than 1000 acres. A capital of at least £30,000 was raised, partly by small subscriptions from the Owenite body in all parts of the country and partly by large sums from wealthy backers such as Frederick Bate. The largest number of members resident at one time was 57; there were also hired day labourers, and the boarding school had 90 children. A large building, 'in the baronial style', was designed by Joseph Hansom, the Owenite architect from Birmingham, and fitted out with every comfort and labour-saving device. This was partly completed in 1842. Apart from the school, the activities of the members were largely agricultural, and the work of the blacksmith, carpenters and bricklayers was entirely absorbed by the community itself. Some discontinuity was suffered through the successive changes in the governorship of the community.

---

[1] See *New Moral World* for weekly reports on the progress of Queenwood from 1839 to 1845. Also details in Minute Books, Central Board, Universal Community Society of Rational Religionists. A visit by Alexander Somerville in 1842 is described in his *Whistler at the Plough* (Manchester, 1852), pp. 105–17. The best secondary accounts are in Podmore, *Owen*, chap. 22; and Storch.

But the fatal weakness was the failure to produce as much as was consumed, with the result that the community got deeper into debt each year. In 1844 there was a revolt within the Owenite body directed against Owen's extravagant policies, and a group of working-class Owenites took over control of Harmony Hall. They were unable to extricate the community from its financial plight, and in the summer of 1845 most of the residents left. John Buxton, the last Governor, remained with his family until June 1846 when he was forcibly evicted, and the premises were let as a college.

Within a year another Owenite community—the last in Britain—was begun. In 1845 a group of Yorkshire Owenites led by David Green and James Hole had established the Leeds Redemption Society, and in 1847 they were offered an estate in South Wales by a Mr George Williams who had recently returned from America enthusiastically in support of communitarianism.[1] The land was at Garnlwyd, Carmarthenshire, and consisted of 220 acres, ninety of which were ready for immediate occupation. The Redemptionists settled fourteen of their members on the little Welsh farm, where they managed to support themselves and also to produce dairy products and boots and shoes for sale to the members of the Society back in Leeds. But they were crippled by lack of capital and by the marginal nature of the land, and in 1855 the community came to an end. All its debts were paid in full and a surplus was divided among 'some Leeds public institutions'.

For nearly thirty years a steady succession of Owenite communities had followed one another, spread widely over England, Scotland, Ireland and Wales. In America the chronology and distribution were more concentrated. After the burst of community building between 1825 and 1829, mainly in the Ohio Valley and New York, Owenism was dormant if not dead. Only Josiah Warren's community of Equity in Tuscarawas County, Ohio, in 1835–37 showed signs of life; and although Warren had been at New Harmony and was influenced by Owen, Equity was not basically an Owenite community.[2] The great revival of communitarianism in America came in the early 1840s and was mainly Fourierist. However, in 1843 amidst the general communitarian boom and climax of millenarian hopes four new Owenite colonies were founded.

---

[1] Information is from the organ of the Redemption Society, the *Herald of Redemption* [continued as the *Herald of Cooperation*], 1847–48. A full account of the community and its leaders is given in J. F. C. Harrison, *Social Reform in Victorian Leeds: the Work of James Hole, 1820–1895* (Leeds, 1954).

[2] Material on Equity is scanty. See Bailie, *Josiah Warren*; and Eunice M. Schuster, 'Native American Anarchism', *Smith College Studies in History*, XVII, nos. 1–4 (1931–32).

First, the Society of One-Mentians organized the Promisewell Community in Monroe County, Pennsylvania, under the leadership of the Rev. J. M. Horner and a Dr Humbert, and supported by branches in New York, Philadelphia and New Jersey.[1] Seven hundred acres of woodland were bought cheaply and 30 to 40 persons began working together. Before the community had existed for more than a few months disagreements with the branches caused friction, and a Mr Hudson seceded to form a second community at Goose Pond on the site of an earlier Fourierist phalanx (the Social Reform Unity) in Pike County, Pennsylvania. About 60 people were engaged in it. But by 1844 both communities were dead. A third experiment, the Skaneateles Community at Mottville, Onondaga County, New York, flourished somewhat longer (1843–46).[2] John A. Collins, formerly a Massachusetts anti-slavery agent, invested $5000 in a $15,000 farm of 350 acres, and 150 people responded to his invitation to join. Collins was agnostic, vegetarian and a believer in community of property, and although he sought to distinguish his views from Owen's, the community was generally Owenite in character. Ideological dissensions and a struggle for leadership reduced the number of residents to 26, who then operated a successful saw-mill and turning shop. The community ended in May 1846, not through any financial embarrassment apparently, but because Collins came to the conclusion that human nature was not yet ready to accept the full implications of the community ideal.

The fourth community—the Anglo-American venture of Equality, Wisconsin—followed a different pattern.[3] Thomas Hunt, a prominent London Owenite, became disappointed and critical of the management of Manea Fen and Queenwood and announced his intention of leading a group of emigrant Owenites to America to found a 'colony of united interests'. The party of 21 persons arrived in Milwaukee in July 1843 and

---

[1] See Noyes, pp. 252–9 for the One-Mentian and Goose Pond Communities. Also pp. 131-2 above. There are reports in the *New Moral World*, 26 October 1844, 19 April 1845.

[2] The chief source is the *Communitist* (1844–46), edited by Collins; and there are also reports in the *Harbinger* (1845–46), and in the *New Moral World*, 30 September, 4 November 1843, 6, 27 April 1844, and in the *Moral World*, 4 October, 1 November 1845. Also Noyes, pp. 161–80.

[3] Hunt's original scheme for a cooperative colony is set out in his *Report to a Meeting of Intending Emigrants* (London, 1843); and his account of the progress at Equality can be followed in his letters to the *New Moral World*, 9 March–13 September 1844, 2 August 1845. See also the *Herald of Progress*, 14 February 1846. Two MS. collections in the Wisconsin State Historical Society throw light on the early days of the colony: the Thomas Steel Papers, and the Thomas C. Tinker MSS. There is a short account also in Montgomery Eduard McIntosh, 'Cooperative Communities in Wisconsin', Wisconsin State Historical Society, *Proceedings*, LI (1903), 113–16.

purchased 263 acres of land at Spring Lake, Waukesha County, Wisconsin. The resources of the colony were entirely absorbed in clearing the land, erecting buildings and trying to raise crops. The difficulties of pioneer farming discouraged several families who soon left the community, but the remainder struggled on, and in 1845 a second party of sixteen persons arrived from London and settled on land south of the first colony. By the summer of 1846 the community came to an end, and early in the following year the land was sold up for the benefit of the shareholders.

In the preceding chronology only Owenite communities have been mentioned, but it must be remembered that many more communitarian experiments, secular and religious, were tried, and an even larger number was projected. Professor Bestor has identified 130 communities in America before the Civil War. In many of these, Owenite influences or personnel can be traced. Thus Josiah Warren, after his New Harmony days, went on to found Utopia, in Clermont County, Ohio, in 1847 and Modern Times on Long Island, New York, in 1851. In London the Concordium (Alcott House) at Ham Common (1838–48) attracted Owenites, and John Goodwyn Barmby's Communitorium at Hanwell (1843) was in the same tradition.[1] Owenites recognized their affinity with other communitarians such as the Shakers or Fourierists, and conversely men like Shaker Evans or John Humphrey Noyes regarded the Owenite communities as part of a larger movement.

The record of the lost communities outlined above seems at first to be a dismal one. Few of them lasted more than two or three years, most of them were plagued by internal strife, and their impact upon society at large appears to have been negligible. It is hardly surprising that the general verdict has been that they were a failure, particularly when contrasted with other methods of social reform which are judged to have been

---

[1] John Goodwyn Barmby (1820–1881) claimed that he was the first person to call himself a communist in England. Born at Yoxford, the son of an attorney, he became a leading Chartist in Suffolk. He visited Paris in 1840 and was influenced by Cabet and the French socialists. In 1841 he founded the Communist Propaganda Society, later renamed the Universal Communitarian Association and afterwards the Communist Church. He published the *Promethean or Communitarian Apostle* (1842) and the *Communist Chronicle* (1843). His community was established in a house at Hanwell, Middlesex in 1843. He was a point of contact between the British communitarians and their opposite numbers in France, Germany and America. Catherine Barmby (*née* Reynolds), his wife, was also a socialist and contributed to liberal journals under the pseudonym of 'Kate'. In later life Goodwyn Barmby became a Unitarian minister, probably through the influence of his friend, W. J. Fox, and remained active in liberal causes. See *D.N.B.*; Thomas Frost, *Forty Years' Recollections* (London, 1880); A. L. Morton, *The English Utopia* (London, 1952); Armytage, *Heavens Below*.

successful. Most discussion of Owenite communities has been cast in this mould. The success–failure dichotomy, however, is not adequate for analytical purposes, nor does it altogether square with the views of the communitarians themselves. Owenites always had explanations for the collapse of a particular community, and reaffirmed that their faith in the soundness of the 'social principles' was unshaken. An experimental approach implied that there would be trial and error, not necessarily success. Moreover, a variety of factors could be adduced for the relative success or failure of an experiment. Despite Owenite blueprints no two communities were identical. Each one was a special blend of characteristics within a general Owenite communitarian framework. A judgement of failure in any absolute sense is not therefore very useful. The meaning of failure (or success) has first to be examined, and this can be done only in relation to the goals which communities set themselves. When these have been analysed, the pattern of institutions and the endemic problems of Owenite communities fall into place.

The aims and objectives of the experiments were of two kinds. First, there were the declared aims of the community, usually embodied formally in a constitution or declaration. 'For the promotion of science and industry,' declared the Blue Spring communitarians, 'we, the undersigned, believing that the numerous ills which are inflicted on mankind ... may be avoided ... by adopting the social system of society recommended to the world by Robert Owen, do mutually agree hereby to enter into an association of union and cooperation. ...'[1] Second, underlying this, and not always revealed in the clauses of the constitution, were more general objectives. These were in the nature of assumptions about the role of the community in society at large. The goals of the community were interpreted as encouragement of certain processes or solution of various problems. By the time the first communities were founded Owen's original idea of community as a solution to Poor Law problems had receded, though it is probable that some of the philanthropists who subscribed to the Orbiston Community still thought along these lines. Certainly Ralahine was regarded by its founder, and later by its apologists, as a method of dealing with the 'Irish problem'. The Owenite community under E. T. Craig replaced a regime of agrarian outrage during which the steward had been murdered and Vandeleur had fled for his life.

But it was in the American communities that the larger purposes showed through most clearly. Although the ideology of Owenism was

[1] Simons, p. 99.

not the product of frontier conditions the communities themselves were in part a response to problems of life on the frontier. The success of New Harmony in attracting so many settlers in such a short time was partly due to the reputation which the Rappite community had gained as pioneers. George Flower of the English Settlement in Illinois observed:

All who went to Harmony, with surprise observed with what facility the necessaries of life were acquired and enjoyed by every member of Rapp's community. When compared with the privations and discomforts to which individual settlers were exposed in their backwoods experience, the contrast is very striking. The poor hunter that brought a bushel of corn to be ground, perhaps from a distance of ten miles, saw with wonder people as poor as himself inhabiting good houses, surrounded by pleasant gardens, completely clothed with garments of the best quality, supplied regularly with meal, meat, and fuel, without any apparent individual exertion, and he could not fail to contrast the comforts and conveniences surrounding the dwellings of the Harmonist with the dirt and discomfort of his own log hut, and it opened to his mind a new train of thought.[1]

The Owenite community became in practice, if not always in original intent, a means of coping with such difficulties of pioneer settlement as shortage of capital, technical knowledge and social institutions. Even New Harmony, the most highly developed of all the Owenite communities, had many frontier characteristics: houses were over-crowded, living conditions were rough, and 'a new book', as Thomas Pears's wife complained, 'is indeed a rarity and a very great treat'.[2]

At Equality in Wisconsin the issues can be seen much more starkly, and the question of success or failure is posed clearly in contemporary terms. Thomas Steel, a Scottish doctor, emigrated with Hunt's party, and in a series of letters to his father and sister in London has left a vivid case-history of an Owenite communitarian.[3] Details of his early life are scanty but sufficient to suggest conformity to elements in a recognizable Owenite biographical pattern. He was a firm believer in the 'social principles', and continued to be so much later in life. Some frustration, difficulty or restlessness in existing society may have been at the root of his radicalism. After qualifying as an M.D. from the University of Glasgow in 1833 he could not get started as a doctor and roamed around for ten years. He served as a ship's doctor and lived for six months in China. He came to Wisconsin as the community's doctor but within a

[1] Lockwood, *New Harmony Movement*, pp. 18–19. Also Arndt, pp. 328–9.
[2] *Pears Papers*, p. 66.
[3] This account is based on letters written between 1843 and 1847 in the Thomas Steel Papers.

few weeks had decided to leave because he was convinced that none of the members was 'prepared for any other state of society than the one they have left'. He purchased 40 acres of land for himself in the neighbourhood, to which he later added the land of the community when it dissolved in 1846. Other members of Equality also left, and either bought their own farms nearby or migrated to Milwaukee to follow their original trades. Steel attributed the break-up of the community to lack of harmony among the individuals concerned, not to the 'principles'. But it is clear that he, like several others, soon discovered that he could do better for himself outside the community. The Society of Equality was useful in securing a foothold in the new surroundings, but once these were familiar the community was no longer necessary to him. He felt that he was more competent than Hunt and some of his fellow-communitarians and that to remain with them was to limit himself unnecessarily. Steel did not regret the ending of the community: he thought that it had served a valuable function as an introduction to settlement in America for him and the other members. In this sense it was not a failure; it had simply made itself unnecessary.

Contemporary reports from Equality by Hunt and Steel deal almost exclusively with the daily problems of frontier settlement—housebuilding, clearing the land, fencing and getting a crop of some sort. The colonists were so overwhelmed by these necessities that they had little time or inclination to debate the relation of their activities to communitarian theories. It was on this score that Steel complained about Hunt who, he said, did not explain the 'social principles' to the members. The Society never met to discuss Owenism nor indeed to engage in any intellectual activities. The Owenite community had become primarily an instrument for tackling collectively the harsh realities of frontier life. When the initial hardships of the first two or three years had been softened the advantages of cooperation seemed less compelling and the independence of the 'individual system' more attractive. This was also the experience of the Fourierist phalanxes in Wisconsin—Ceresco, Spring Farm Association and the Pigeon River Fourier Colony—formed in 1844–46.

'Much surprise will doubtless be felt by those who have witnessed my zeal and anxiety in the cause of Socialism when they shall hear that I have become an advocate of emigration', wrote Hunt.[1] Like Owen himself, most Owenites were ambiguous in their attitude to emigration. On the one hand they denied that emigration could solve any of the

[1] Hunt, *Report to . . . Intending Emigrants*, p. 2.

important problems of capitalism;[1] on the other they were attracted by the more favourable opportunities for establishing communities which America offered. 'Emigration upon Cooperative Principles', as Hunt called it, appeared to be a practicable method of achieving sound Owenite objectives when it was mooted in London and discussed by enthusiastic artisans. But in its practical working out in Wisconsin the project became transformed. The colonist at Equality found himself in virtually the same position as his non-Owenite compatriots who had emigrated to Wisconsin under the British Temperance Emigration Society or the Potters' Emigration Society.[2] The ideology wore thin, and the Owenite experiment became a lost community—lost amidst the general settlement of the Western lands.

Among the incidental purposes of the communities was the accommodation of persons who were in some way social misfits. Community was a solution to problems of personal deficiency or social maladjustment, and had an obvious appeal to those who sought security or escape from the world. An English admirer of Owen who visited Harmony in 1823 observed that communities were particularly suited to 'the relief of those who are unable to withstand the excessive competition, the redundancy of talent, or the pressure of the times singly; and to those who prefer tranquillity and security to turmoil and uncertainty'.[3] The larger communities such as New Harmony and Orbiston collected their share of such types, as well as some flotsam and jetsam from frontier speculation or industrial depression. The intellectual's desire to reform mankind is also observable in many of the leading colonists, both British and American. All the communities had their vegetarians, teetotallers, non-smokers and fresh-air-and-cold-water faddists. One of the more general purposes of an Owenite community was to enable a certain type of social reformer to try out his theories in practice.

As opposed to these general purposes, the formal objectives of the

---

[1] In a letter to Sir Robert Wilmot Horton, the emigration advocate, dated 24 January 1831, Owen argued that emigration would afford only temporary relief, and would ultimately make things worse, because (1) it would reduce the number of consumers (even the unemployed consume some commodities), and (2) it would increase the supply of goods because the emigrants would establish competing industries in the colonies. MS. copy of letter, William Pare, Scrapbook, f. 35–8.

[2] Vivian Vale, 'English Settlers in Early Wisconsin: the British Temperance Emigration Society'. *Bulletin of the British Association for American Studies*, n.s. no. 9 (December 1964), 24–31, lists the main sources for the B.T.E.S., including the papers in the Wisconsin State Historical Society. Also, Wilbur S. Shepperson, *British Emigration to North America: Projects and Opinions in the Early Victorian Period* (Minneapolis, Minn., 1957).

[3] William Hebert, *A Visit to the Colony of Harmony in Indiana* (London, 1825), reprinted in Lindley, ed. *Indiana as Seen by Early Travelers*, pp. 343–4.

communities were limited and explicit. In all the communities the drawing up and adoption of a constitution loomed large in the early days, and subsequent revisions and debates took up a great deal of time at New Harmony, Orbiston, Queenwood and Skaneateles. Constitution-making could become a favourite Owenite pastime: at New Harmony the constitutional arrangements were changed six times in two and a half years, and at Queenwood the Governorship was changed eight times between 1839 and 1844. In the formative stages of a community immediate decisions had to be made on issues which had not been adequately considered (or even considered at all) in advance. The translation of Owen's theories or Thompson's advice into practice produced shocks and confusion. After the initial decisions as to the site, number of settlers and type of occupation, three big constitutional problems remained, involving capital, property relationships and democratic control. The constant reorganizations which the communities suffered were attempts to grapple with these problems.

The raising of capital to commence a community was perhaps the crucial issue. It was primary in point of time, and also in its effects. It determined where the legal ownership lay, and ultimately he who paid the piper called the tune. In his *Report to the County of Lanark* Owen considered four possible sources of capital: landed proprietors or large capitalists, 'established companies having large funds to expend for benevolent and public objects', parish and county authorities and associations of farmers, mechanics and tradesmen. All the Owenite communities which were founded in fact fell into the first or last categories. Nine communities were financed by a single person (as at Maxwell, Ralahine and Manea Fen) or by a small group of proprietors (New Harmony, Orbiston and Queenwood). The remainder relied upon the subscriptions or shares of the settlers themselves, as at Blue Spring, Kendal and Equality. At Queenwood, Pant Glas and Garnlwyd attempts were also made to raise funds by subscriptions from an outside body of supporters located in the branches of the Rational Society or the Redemption Society. Each constitution reflected the particular community's financial basis. In the case of proprietorial communities the main problem was the relationship of the settler-colonists, who contributed only their labour, to the gentlemen owners of the property, who might or might not be actually resident. The usual solution was an agreement whereby the settlers became lessees of the proprietor, paying him interest on the capital and sometimes also a fixed rent. In most cases it was envisaged that the members would ultimately pay off the whole of the capital, which would thus be treated like a mortgage or loan. At New Harmony

24. The school at New Lanark

25. National Equitable Labour Exchange, Grays Inn Road, London

26. Labour note

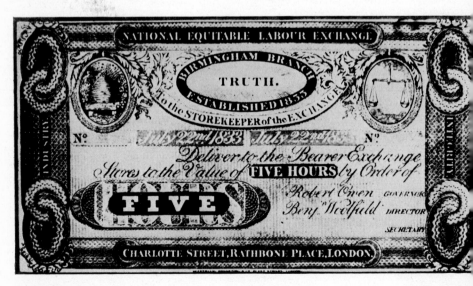

the arrangements were never drawn up very clearly; at Orbiston the proprietors formed a joint stock company which let the land and buildings to the settlers as tenants. At Ralahine the tenants, organized collectively in the society, paid Vandeleur, the sole owner of the estate, a fixed rent in kind and shared the remainder among themselves in wages and accumulated profits. At Queenwood the situation was more complicated. The land was leased from Sir Isaac Goldsmid for £350 per annum, with an initial premium of £750; and the capital was supplied mainly by Owen, Galpin and Bate through the Home Colonization Society which lent the money to the Central Board for the use of the community. Funds were also raised by the Owenite branches, and the members in residence were those who had either subscribed £50 themselves or who had been nominated by branches which had subscribed £50 on their behalf. They were provided with food and accommodation but did not apparently receive wages. The relationship of the settled members was in the first instance to the Governor and the Central Board. In the shareholder type of community these problems of relationships with a proprietor of course did not arise. At Equality each member of the community had subscribed his share of the capital before leaving England. The Blue Spring Community had only the capital brought by the local citizens who formed it. Kendal raised the necessary $20,000 for the purchase of the land by the members selling their individual farms. In each case the constitution had to be drafted to take account of the realities of legal ownership and liability.

Unfortunately these realities did not always harmonize with communitarian aspirations. Property relationships, and especially the degree of communism to be expected, were a fruitful cause of constitutional argument. Owen was in theory an advocate of community of property and equality of remuneration, but was by no means consistent in his statements at various times. Certainly he had no intention of handing over immediately his property at New Harmony to the members, even after the reorganization into the Community of Equality. Yet this was the demand of a group of thorough-going communists led by Paul Brown. Similarly at Orbiston the editor of the *Register*, Henry Kirkpatrick, agitated for absolute equality among the members and community of property. At Queenwood in 1844 the working-class communitarians under John Buxton's leadership stood for immediate equality of status and community of goods, even though their total investment was less than £200, compared with the £13,000 contributed by Owen and Bate. Attempts to effect community of property in all cases produced prolonged wrangles about constitutional changes. In no Owenite

N

community was complete communism attained. The nearest to it was communal ownership of all the land under some form of trusteeship and individual ownership of personal property. Nor was complete equality of remuneration practised, but rather credit was given according to the number of hours worked or the value of goods produced.

Intertwined with the constitutional arguments about property were issues of democratic control. In all communities careful provision was made for weekly or monthly meetings of all the members to discuss business and elect officers, and no aspect of community life seems to have flourished more strongly. Preliminary arrangements were necessarily in the hands of the initiators of a community, but all Owenites agreed that when once established some degree of control by the working members was desirable. Difficulties arose in deciding the exact amount of power which they should have in relation to the subscribers. Generally the resident members were able to assert their control over social matters and day-to-day life in the community, but were frustrated when they tried to question its basic economic and property structure. This is the impression derived from, say, Thomas Pears's account of New Harmony and his wife's complaints of the 'aristocracy' or 'despotism' of its government. At Queenwood the Governor was appointed by the Central Board, not elected by the community; and charges were made at the Owenite Congress in 1843 that the residents were not allowed to make decisions affecting their own affairs.[1] A committee of nine was elected by the members at Ralahine, but Vandeleur, as president, retained a right of veto. In contrast the reports of the Kendal Community, which was of the non-proprietorial type, seem to be free from these problems.

Discussion of self-government inevitably raised questions about leadership. Who were the leaders in Owenite communities, and how was the role of leadership conceived? Here again each community was different from others, but certain broad generalizations can be made. Owenites were in theory committed to full democratic participation and the constitutions of their communities provided for election of the leadership. Where the initiators or chief proprietors were resident they usually occupied the top positions of leadership as directors, committee members or governor. Despite the millenarian aspect of Owenism there was little that could be described as charismatic leadership. Owen's position was unique in that he was accorded a certain pre-eminence, and some communitarians regarded him almost as a prophet: 'he is an extraordinary man—a wonderful man—such a one indeed as the world has never

[1] *New Moral World*, 27 May 1843.

before seen', wrote William Pelham from New Harmony.[1] When disillusionment with Owen crept in, his power as the greatest proprietor
at New Harmony nevertheless remained. Even at Queenwood, where
his investment was more modest, it was considered natural that he should
be the first Governor, and even when he resigned the office his recom-
mendation for a successor (John Finch) was followed. But what in Owen
was acceptable as a patriarchal quality, in other proprietors smacked too
strongly of despotism and was ultimately resented. It is curious that the
top leaders were frequently absent from the community. Owen was
resident at New Harmony for only short periods, Abram Combe's
illness forced him to retire from Orbiston, Frances Wright had to leave
Nashoba for the same reason, and Vandeleur did not live at Ralahine. In
each case the direction of the community devolved upon a deputy or
group of top residents. E. T. Craig at Ralahine was a bailiff or manager
appointed by Vandeleur, but the more general pattern was for affairs
to fall into the hands of a small group of business men, philanthropists
and intellectuals. Below them, though frequently overlapping, was another level of leadership—the heads of departments who were responsible
for agricultural operations, manufactures and the schools. On their skill
depended the practical success of the daily work of the members. William
Sheddon's foundry at Orbiston, Heaton Aldam's farming at Queenwood
and Madame Fretageot and William Phiquepal's schools at New Harmony
were among the more solid achievements of the Owenite communities.
The leadership at all levels seldom went unchallenged, usually on ideological grounds but also at the level of material grievances. Paul Brown
led the dissidents at New Harmony, basing his opposition on communistic doctrine. The Skaneateles Community was torn by the opposition of Quincy A. Johnston to John A. Collins's freethinking principles.
At Queenwood the division followed class lines, culminating in the
election of John Buxton, a self-educated calico printer from Manchester,
as the last Governor.

Corresponding to the different types of leadership were various categories of members. No questions are of greater significance for an understanding of the Owenite movement than those which concern the sort
of people who joined the communities. It is possible, for instance, to
construct biographical patterns of Owenite communitarians, and do we
have sufficient evidence to generalize about their motives? For the larger
communities such as New Harmony and Orbiston there is no complete
and detailed breakdown of the whole membership. But for some of the

---

[1] 'Pelham Letters', Lindley, p. 409.

smaller communities, including Queenwood, it is possible to account for almost all of the residents. As with most social movements it is easier to document the background and ideas of the leaders than of the rank and file. Except for a very small percentage of the membership only the name and perhaps occupation can be traced. Further details have to be deduced obliquely from the evidence of the articulate minority.

If the communities are surveyed as a whole the total membership embraces a wide range of social status and occupation. Retired philanthropists, business men, professionals, intellectuals, farmers, skilled artisans, labourers—together with their wives and children—can be found. Only members of the aristocracy were conspicuously lacking. Somewhat more useful than this overall classification, however, is a division into communities with a relatively homogeneous membership and those which were heterogeneous. To the former belong Blue Spring, Ralahine and Queenwood: to the latter New Harmony, Yellow Springs and Orbiston. Contemporaries were very ready to correlate the amount of confusion and disagreement in a community with the degree of heterogeneity. Thompson and Gray thought this way, and Hamilton later regretted that selection by phrenological principles had not been applied at Orbiston. The problem of selection of the membership was crucial but in many cases was given little attention. Owen's open invitation to New Harmony attracted some drifters and freeloaders, though exactly how many is impossible to determine. His son William wrote in October 1825: 'We have been much puzzled to know what to do with those who profess to do anything and everything: they are perfect drones, and can never be satisfied here.'[1] Similar complaints were made from Orbiston. More serious was the lack of balance between different occupational skills, and, in some cases, the absence of any technical knowledge of the jobs which had to be undertaken. All of the communities founded were basically agricultural, but this was not always evident from the type of person recruited. The Queenwood residents were mostly artisans from northern industrial towns, and local farm labourers had to be hired to do the agricultural work. At Equality there was only one farmer in the party and no one who had any knowledge of prairie farming; with the result that they completely failed to raise any crop the first year and had to rent already cultivated land in order to subsist.

When the mistakes of heterogeneity were recognized various remedies were suggested. After a year the Orbiston members were required to vote for each others' re-admission, but the ballot did not (as was intended)

---

[1] Quoted in Podmore, *Robert Owen*, p. 292.

exclude the 'undesirable' persons. At Ralahine Craig and Vandeleur carefully screened all applicants to eliminate any possible 'Terry Alts' or terrorists. But in a majority of the communities the membership was mixed, both in terms of class and occupational background and in degree of ideological commitment. Such differences need not necessarily have caused dissension, though the way they were handled did not always promote harmony. In the communal dining-room at Orbiston class distinctions were maintained by the richer members eating superior food at a table separate from the majority. 'Oh, if you could see some of the rough uncouth creatures here, I think you would find it rather hard to look upon them exactly in the light of brothers and sisters', wrote Sarah Pears from New Harmony.[1] Clearly the middle-class communitarians experienced some discomfort in having to live so closely with members of the working classes. Owenite theorists felt that such unworthy irritations would not even be noticed if members were truly convinced of the correctness of the social principles; and it was certainly true that many middle-class Owenites were prepared to put up with hardship and unpleasantness in the belief that this was but a small price to pay for the realization of their higher ideals. In most of the communities there was at least a core of devoted (sometimes fanatical) Owenites, whose intellectual convictions accounted for their being there. At New Harmony they were the educated members whose letters and diaries provide the record of the experiment. At Queenwood they were working-class cooperators from the industrial North whose views are heard through the reports of their spokesmen in the *New Moral World*. But it is very unlikely that the Irish peasants at Ralahine knew anything of Owenism beyond what they learned practically from Craig. And some of the smaller American communities seem to have had only one or two members who were thoroughly conversant with Owenite theories.

Lack of direct evidence makes it difficult to generalize about the motivations of many members of the lost communities, but something can be gleaned indirectly from negative or oblique references. For instance, the following analysis of the Orbistonians was by J. Lambe, a superintendent of one of the departments. He regretted the divisions among the members and categorized them by aims and motives into

(1) Those who wish to adopt and follow mutual co-operation and equal distribution wherever it may lead.

(2) Those who began the journey, but find that the route proceeds in a direction of which they were not aware, and consequently wish to turn back.

---

[1] Sarah Pears to Benjamin Bakewell, 28 January 1826. *Pears Papers*, p. 60.

(3) Those who are determined to oppose their individual interests to that of the community.

(4) Those who have only one idea, viz., self; and, unable to form an opinion, have adopted that of another; have joined because their leader, Abram Combe, did so, yet are too blind to follow him in the splendid cause he has marked out.[1]

Sometimes an analysis of those who left a community can suggest possible motivation, or lack of it. Here is William Pelham's account of the types of members who withdrew from New Harmony. First were 'scheming speculators' who 'come here with the view of staying a few months, [and] accumulating property at the expense of the industrious'. Such cases have gone away 'highly displeased' and disappointed. 'Others have withdrawn because their sectarian notions in religion were not prevalent here—others again, because their ambition and self-importance were not estimated according to their own ideas—others again to look after their private affairs which they had hastily abandoned.'[2] A division into worthy and unworthy motives was frequently made by Owenites in their accounts of communities, and provided a simple typology of membership.

Problems of membership were frequently aspects of the larger problem of social control. In all types of community social discipline had to be maintained in some way, and a variety of means was used to enforce it. Some of these means were available to Owenites but others were not. John O'Driscol, an Irish landowner, saw the matter clearly when considering the merits of Owen's plan for communities. Only 'despotic power' or 'religious zeal', he argued, would be sufficient to hold a community together, and how does Mr Owen propose to supply either of these?[3] It was obvious to other contemporaries that the autocracy of a Fr. Rapp or the religious discipline of the Shakers would not be feasible in an Owenite community. Nor was there the internal pressure of cohesion which was produced by the isolation of non-English-speaking communities. Theoretically, devotion to the social principles was a sufficiently strong bond, but in practice it proved to be considerably less compelling than a religious faith. Later in the century John Humphrey Noyes concluded, on the basis of his extensive research and experience, that 'the two most essential requisites for the formation of successful communities are religious principle and previous acquaintance of the

---

[1] Orbiston *Register*, 27 December 1826.
[2] 'Pelham Letters', Lindley, p. 397.
[3] John O'Driscol, *Views of Ireland*, 2 vols. (London, 1823), I, 216–17.

members'.[1] Failure to exercise an adequate degree of social control over their members was probably the greatest weakness of the larger Owenite communities. But in the smaller ones the situation was easier, and in all the communities some favourable factors existed.

In the first place, all the Owenite communities were, by definition, at least partially withdrawn from society at large. Some of them were also physically isolated—on the American frontier, in the Welsh mountains or even in remote rural parts of England. They frequently encountered hostility or suspicion from their nearest neighbours. The Orbiston Community was derisively known as Babylon, and the alleged infidel and immoral goings-on of the socialists at New Harmony and Queenwood was a by-word to respectable citizens. There was thus some external pressure favourable to social cohesion. The introduction of a distinctive dress may also be interpreted in this way. Karl Bernhard, Duke of Saxe-Weimar-Eisenach described the New Harmony costume: 'that for the men consists of wide pantaloons buttoned over a boy's jacket, made of light material, without a collar; that of the women of a coat reaching to the knee and pantaloons, such as little girls wear among us'.[2] (Sarah Pears, somewhat less reverently, said that a fat man in this garb looked like a feather bed tied in the middle, and that when she first saw the men with their bare necks she was struck how very suitably they were attired for the executioner.) More positive controls included the banning of liquor, and also (at Ralahine and Orbiston) the disapproval of tobacco. Arrangements for communal dining-rooms, kitchens and wash-houses, which were part of a general policy to promote cooperation and labour-saving efforts, were not usually welcomed by the women, and were not therefore as effective instruments for control as other communal institutions such as the schools.

There is evidence that life in an Owenite community could be quite regimented. James Atkinson, secretary of the Queenwood Community, reported that in order to extend the gardening operations all male members, whether horticulturists or not, were required to do two hours digging every afternoon. 'At a quarter past five . . . the bell rung for leaving work, when, at the word of command, each, after cleaning his spade, pick or fork . . . shouldered it and marched to the tool house, and from whence all marched to the hall in strict military order, led by the governor.'[3] This of course is a rather superficial sort of discipline, and

[1] Noyes, p. 57.
[2] Karl Bernhard, Duke of Saxe-Weimar-Eisenach, *Travels Through North America During the Years 1825–1826* (Philadelphia, Penn., 1828), reprinted in Lindley, ed., *op. cit.*, p. 424.
[3] *New Moral World*, 4 March 1843.

smacks of that humourless, mechanical aspect of Owenism that emerges from time to time. The Shakers, who were extremely successful gardeners, needed no such external aid.

On the surface Owenite communities seemed to be very tolerant. Although no official church was allowed at New Harmony visiting preachers of all denominations were permitted to use the pulpit on Sundays. Owenite belief in democratic procedures encouraged a plethora of meetings at which all aspects of community life were debated. Visitors remarked on the state of near-anarchy and confusion which seemed to exist as a result of extreme permissiveness and tenderness to individual demands. Yet underneath there was often a rigidity in Owenism which contradicted this and which seemed to be an attempt to contain community decisions within certain limits. When Owen visited Queenwood in April 1842 he was upset by the quarrels and differences between the residents, as he had been earlier at New Harmony. He advised them that when they found themselves engaged in disputes they should remember his eternal principles, and then they would immediately become rational and would cease to feel, speak or act unkindly towards anyone. This was essentially a simplified version of the Enlightenment view that through reason men would become more uniform. Men and their beliefs would become simplified and standardized by the application of rational principles, and diversity—far from being a mark of excellence—would be greatly reduced. With such views it was hard for Owenites to get at the heart of many of their problems in communities. At New Harmony or at the British Owenite Congresses alternative views or plans of action were opposed by Owen and the central leadership. The idea that Owenites might legitimately differ in their interpretations of basic principles was inconceivable, since it would contradict the attainment of 'perfectly consistent behaviour'. Hence there was little appreciation of the possible benefits of diversity and no resources within a community for dealing with fundamental disagreements when they arose.

The problems of community life had to be handled in the light of Owenite ideology and within the boundaries of communitarian institutions. Knowledge of, or commitment to Owenite theory was in some cases not very deep, but the institutional pattern of Owenite communities was well enough established to suggest certain generalizations. In all communities, except those which had only a handful of members, the general body was subdivided into separate departments under the direction of a superintendent. Commonly these departments were each responsible for agriculture, manufactures and the schools, with sometimes additional sections for printing and domestic economy. At Blue

Spring the eight departments also included police and health. The system was usually successful in organizing the practical affairs of a community, but was inclined to be somewhat divisive. The success of the foundry department at Orbiston occasioned envy and strife, and at New Harmony the Community of Equality dissolved into separate communities partly based on departmental divisions. A centralizing institution in the community was the store, around which a large part of the domestic and economic life revolved. It was non-profit making, and in the early days of the community, especially at New Harmony and Orbiston, was a great drain on the capital of the proprietor, for it was the sole source of the members' food, clothing and supplies, which they obtained on credit. Closely tied in with the store was a system of time credit or labour notes. Each member was credited with the value of his services daily and allowed to draw upon the store up to a fixed amount. The costs of housing, fuel, washing, medical attendance and schooling were debited to each member's account. Sometimes labour notes were issued, in other cases a book-keeping entry was made. Trading between departments was conducted in the same way.

Institutions for communal living were attempted in all the larger communities. Dining-rooms, kitchens and laundries were usually provided, though as already noted, they were not over-popular with the women-folk. Living quarters, whether in apartment blocks or separate houses, were separate for each family. However, in most communities accommodation was chronically short, so that overcrowding and making-do with temporary arrangements was common. Also the children were some-times accommodated in dormitories when the school was organized for boarders. Generally the schools were among the more successful institutions of the communities, and were always accorded a high priority by all sections of the membership. At their best they were pioneer Pestalozzian academies and the centre of a vigorous intellectual life, as at New Harmony. Even in the Blue Spring Community, which had none of the brilliant intellectual leadership of New Harmony, and where the school house was a simple log cabin, educational provisions were written into the constitution. Every child was to learn the three Rs, some science, geography, and natural history, as well as a practical course in agriculture and one useful trade, 'so that his employment be varied for the improvement of his physical and mental powers; and lastly a knowledge of himself and of human nature to form him into a rational being'.[1] At Orbiston the children were said to be undisciplined until Alexander

---

[1] Simons, p. 101.

Campbell came to the assistance of the school teacher, a Miss Whitwell who had previously taught at New Lanark. The boarding school at Queenwood was a superior educational institution, and after the collapse of the community was continued as a private college by George Edmondson, a Quaker educationist. The Owenite ideal of the community as a cultural centre was strongly rooted. Printing and publishing, including a journal, were undertaken at New Harmony, Orbiston, Manea Fen and Queenwood. Theatrical and musical productions were highly regarded—Orbiston even had a theatre for three hundred people fitted up on one of the upper floors of the building. And of course no Owenite gathering was complete without dancing: in the granite stone schools of New Lanark, in the community house by the Wabash, in the John Street Institute in London, the Owenites amused themselves with their cotillions, reels and waltzes. The new moral world was to be no place for puritans.

As the institutions of the Owenite communities conformed to a recognizable pattern, so did their economic life. Basically all the communities were agricultural colonies, in which the farming was carried on collectively. In most cases it was subsistence farming and in no community was large-scale commercial farming undertaken. The first responsibility was to produce food for the members, and this primary task became also a social function. Karl Bernhard recorded an amusing incident at New Harmony:

Virginia, from Philadelphia, is very young and pretty, was delicately brought up, and appears to have taken refuge here on account of an unhappy attachment. While she was singing and playing very well on the pianoforte, she was told that the milking of the cows was her duty, and that they were waiting unmilked. Almost in tears, she betook herself to this servile employment, deprecating the new social system and its so much prized equality; ... the cows were milked, in doing which the poor girl was trod on by one and daubed by another.[1]

In some communities there was talk of selling the surplus, but in most cases the experiment did not last long enough for the crop to be expanded sufficiently for this. Similarly the small industries, which were glowingly described as the germ of large manufacturing establishments, seldom did more than meet the requirements of the community itself. Craftsmen such as carpenters, bricklayers, shoemakers and bakers had no shortage of work, but they did not produce marketable exports. Most communities had, or planned to have, a sawmill, gristmill, machine shop and textile

[1] Karl Bernhard, in Lindley, p. 431.

factory. There was no intrinsic reason why Owenite industries should not have flourished: the garden seeds of the Shakers, the woollen cloth from Amana and the silverware from Oneida showed that communitarians could succeed in this direction. The Owenite communities had great hopes for their potential industrial production: the list of goods advertised by the Orbiston Community included 'steam engines on the newest and most improved principles'. In fact they usually had very little to sell, and even then had some difficulty in finding markets. As a minimum it would be true to say that cooperative agriculture in most of the communities was adequate to feed the members, and that the manufactures were of good quality.

The main economic weaknesses of the communities were due not so much to the system of cooperative production as to other factors. The problem of raising capital has already been mentioned. Some communities complained of a shortage of capital, while at the same time they tried to undertake over-ambitious projects; other experiments were handicapped by inadequate resources to tide them over the early years when little return could be expected. It was common for communities to acquire far more land than they could possibly cultivate, in the belief that this was prudent and far-sighted policy. Similarly they sometimes commenced elaborate and costly buildings far beyond what could be justified by the immediate prospects of the community. At Orbiston a massive stone building, 330 feet long, 40 feet broad, and four storeys high was completed—and this was but one wing of the projected plan. Harmony Hall at Queenwood was a most handsome building in which no expense was spared in the materials and fittings. George Jacob Holyoake recalled:

No cathedral was ever built so reverently as was Queenwood Hall. Hand-made nails, not machine-made, were used in the work out of sight. . . . The great kitchen was wainscoted with mahogany half-way up the walls.[1]

---

[1] Holyoake, *History of Cooperation* (1908 edn.), pp. 640–1. The original plans for Queenwood are outlined in the Minutes, National Community Friendly Society, 21 February 1841. There were to be 14 houses in the main line of buildings and 7 houses in each of the two wings, each house being '30 feet in the clear'. Each house was to have 8 rooms and a dormitory on the third storey. There was to be one W.C. for every four rooms and a dressing closet for each bedroom. A married pair or two single adults would have a sitting and bedroom to themselves. Children would sleep in the dormitories. The whole would provide accommodation for 224 adults and 448 children.

Nothing now remains of Queenwood or Orbiston. When the Orbiston estate was put up for sale to pay for the debts of the community in 1830 it was bought by the owner of an adjoining estate and she had the buildings razed to the ground and sold as stone. Queenwood lasted until 1901 when it burned down.

As a fitting building for the Commencement of the Millennium Queen-wood Hall made some sense. But as a wise use of the capital available it was exceedingly questionable. Owen was never a man to think small. Everything he undertook was on a grand scale, and Queenwood was his last practical effort to translate his vision of the new moral world into reality.

The gap between ideals and reality is perhaps the most poignant impression left by the records of the lost communities. From the detailed plans drawn up by Owen, Thompson and Minter Morgan, Owenite communitarians had a clear idea of what they were trying to achieve.[1] But in no case did they manage to create a community which conformed to the specifications laid down for optimum numbers, size of land holding, types of members and architectural design. No community had anywhere near the two thousand members regarded by Owen and Thompson as necessary for a viable experiment. The only community which was built on the famous parallelogram plan seems to have been Blue Spring, where the double log cabins were arranged to form a square. Admonitions about the need for careful selection of applicants were largely ignored and no community had a membership that was properly balanced in skills and backgrounds. The contrast between the vision of arcadian bliss portrayed in pictures of Owenite communities and the rough realities of Equality or Nashoba could hardly have been greater. When Thomas Steel first saw the site of Equality on the Wisconsin prairie he wrote home describing it as like English park land. Two months later, living with twenty-one people in a cabin 17 feet by 12 feet amidst the rigours of a Wisconsin winter, he decided that the community could not succeed. Owen was later able to argue that none of the communities had been a fair trial of his system, since nowhere had conditions been as he required. In fact Owenites had had to adapt their ideas as best they could to what was available, braced by that optimism which they had learned from their leader. 'Let the business be at once set about in good earnest,' wrote Owen, 'and the obstacles which now seem so formidable will speedily disappear.'[2] Alas, the experience of community building in Britain and America proved otherwise.

[1] See particularly Robert Owen, *Report to the County of Lanark* (1821) and William Thompson, *Practical Directions for the Speedy and Economical Establishment of Communities* . . . (London, 1830).

[2] Owen, *Report to the County of Lanark*, in *Life*, IA, 300.

Anatomy of a Movement

Anatomy of a Movement

The year 1829 marked a turning point in the history of the Owenite move-ment. All the American communities of the 1820s had come to an end and a similar fate had befallen the British communitarian experiments. Owen him-self, after his widely publicized debate on religion with the Rev. Alexander Campbell in Cincinnati, returned to England, and did not visit the United States again until 1844; though his sons remained at New Harmony. The Owenites at this stage did not abandon their communitarian goals, but there was, not surprisingly, some disillusionment with the methods which had been employed to realize the new moral world. A fresh approach, using new in-stitutions and agencies, seemed to be called for, and the initiative did not need to be confined to the benevolent Mr Owen—whose fortune was in any case no longer available for philanthropic enterprises after the investment in New Harmony. Until 1829 Owen had largely dominated the movement on both sides of the Atlantic, but thereafter his pecuniary influence was reduced and orthodox Owenism had to meet the challenge of alternative interpretations of doctrine and practice. Owen was by no means insensitive to these changes, and for the next five years (1829–34) his thinking was more radical than either before or later.[1]

The change in tack after 1829 was not due solely to the failure of the com-munities and Owen's straightened financial situation. Even more was it due to changes in the balance of social forces, particularly the emergence in Britain and the eastern United States of working men's organizations. Hitherto Owen had not seriously considered the working classes as a possible

---

[1] Contrary to the opinion of most of Owen's biographers that his views, once formulated, remained unchanged from about 1820 for the rest of his life.

instrument of social change. His hopes had been centred on 'the most experienced and intelligent' men of the age and 'the leading governments of the civilised world', and he had 'studiously avoided connecting myself with any sect or class or party'.[1] *But the enthusiastic reception of his views in working-class circles and the rapid growth of working-class institutions opened up new possibilities, and suggested that perhaps here was the agency by which the change to the new moral world might be effected. In its attempt to capture the working-class movement Owenism developed along new lines, adapting itself to the demands and interests of artisan leaders.*

In America this process did not get very far. Robert Dale Owen, Frances Wright and Robert L. Jennings transferred their Free Enquirer *from New Harmony to New York, and in 1829 purchased an old church near the Bowery which they converted into a Hall of Science. They launched a campaign for the promotion of secularism, women's rights and, especially, 'national, rational, republican education; free for all . . . under the guardianship of the state'. An Association for the Protection of Industry and for the Promotion of National Education was organised, and the Owenites aligned themselves with the newly formed New York Working Men's Party led by Thomas Skidmore and George Henry Evans.*[2] *The resulting mixture of agrarianism, the ten hours question, secularism and education, however, proved unstable, and the party soon split into three factions. Although the Owenites were successful in capturing sections of the Working Men's Party for their scheme of state guardianship education, the victory was pyrrhic, for after the election of 1830 this first working-class political movement dissolved. The attempt to achieve Owenite goals by winning working men's political support for a system of state boarding schools was thus frustrated, and it was not followed by a more broadly based organisation. The American Owenites were left without any effective institutions or means of leverage until the general communitarian revival in 1843.*

In Britain, by contrast, the flirtation with the working-class movement was more sustained and its impact was deeper. Here the approach was not through working-class political power, since the British workers (unlike their American contemporaries) did not have the vote, but through consumers' cooperation and trade unionism. For five years the British working-class movement was saturated with Owenism. When this phase came to an end

[1] Letter to the editor of the *Glasgow Chronicle*, 23 October 1823, reprinted in Abram Combe, *Metaphorical Sketches*, p. 175.

[2] See John R. Commons, *et al.*, *History of Labour in the United States* (New York, 1936), vol. 1, pt. II; and Waterman, *Frances Wright*. The chief contemporary sources are the *Free Enquirer*; and George Henry Evans's *Working Man's Advocate* (New York, 1829–30).

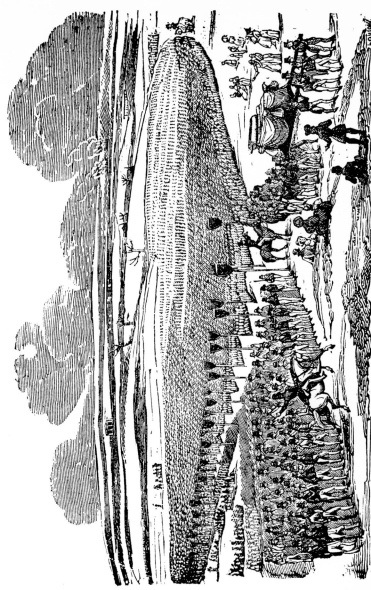

GREAT PUBLIC MEETING OF THE LONDON MEMBERS OF THE GRAND NATIONAL TRADES' UNION, ON MONDAY, APRIL 21, 1834.

27. Demonstration in Copenhagen Fields, London, 1834

The above view was taken by a Member of the Miscellaneous Lodge, from the upper part of Copenhagen-fields. The Procession consisted of from forty to fifty thousand Unionists, was between six and seven miles in length; and it is estimated that no less than four hundred thousand persons were assembled on the occasion.

28. Hall of Science, Manchester

in the summer of 1834 the Owenites reverted to their earlier classless ap-
proach, but they had learned the value of popular organization at the national
and local levels. Until 1829 Owenism in Britain, as in America, was sus-
tained by small groups of disciples, more or less isolated, and dependent on
personal relationships or a few periodicals for news of how the new view of
society was progressing. But for the next decade and a half British Owenism
was a visible social movement with its distinctive institutions, known leaders
and widespread publications. To the anatomy of this movement in Britain
we must now turn.

1 Working-men Cooperators

Working-class interest in Owenism had of course existed long before
1829. Although Owen had appealed to philanthropists to initiate his
plans, the chief beneficiaries were to be working people. When his
denunciations of the factory system, competitive economy and the
churches began to alienate the wealthy and respectable, his *bona fides* with
working-class leaders were correspondingly strengthened. By 1820 a
group of London printers, including George Mudie and Henry Hetherington, was prepared to embrace Owenism. Their only difficulty was how
to apply the new doctrines. In the pages of their journal, the *Economist*
(1821–22), correspondents were continually searching for an answer to
the question of what they could do to implement Owen's ideas. They
were convinced intellectually but could not see the possibility of any
practical activity. The formation of a community required too much
capital to be immediately practicable; hence the search for some quicker,
cheaper way of realizing Owenite principles. Failure of the Spa Fields
venture only reinforced the lesson that something simpler and more
completely within the reach of labouring men was required. Within a
short time an answer was found in the cooperative trading store.

Cooperation, both of consumers and producers, antedated Owenism.
In the second half of the eighteenth century the dockyard workers of
Woolwich and Chatham founded cooperative corn mills and there were
similar ventures in Yorkshire. Cooperative store-keeping was pioneered
in Scotland and the North of England from 1769 onwards. But these
early cooperatives were isolated affairs and not part of any identifiable
movement. They serve only to suggest that in this as in other fields
Owenism was able to draw upon ideas and institutions that were not
entirely unfamiliar. For Owenite purposes the cooperative store might

o

be valuable as 'the ante-chamber to the new moral world'. The accumulated trading profits could become the capital required to start a community and the experience of cooperating to run the store would be useful training for communitarian life. Cooperative institutions also had an appeal as devices for challenging or at least by-passing competitive capitalism. Various arrangements too could be made for handling the profits: for instance, the profit margin could be reduced and prices consequently lowered; or prices could be maintained at the market level and the profits distributed as dividend on purchases. With such flexibility possible the idea of an Owenite cooperative was interpreted in several ways. Arguments about the viability of isolated cooperative experiments in an unfriendly competitive environment, and doubts as to whether communitarian goals could ever be achieved through cooperative stores were voiced in the Owenite press. Owen himself was at first not interested in 'mere trading associations', and to many Owenites there was something distasteful in the notion that the new moral world could be built out of trading profits. But to working men the small cooperative store or cooperative workshop was an institution within their grasp, already familiar or easily assimilable to the indigenous friendly or trade society.[1] If Owenism were to be successfully presented in such a garb it would have a popular appeal far beyond the narrow circle of philanthropists. It might even become a mass movement. Such was the vision that tantalized its leaders for a brief spell culminating in 1833–34.

Institutionally the period of working-class Owenism which began in 1829 had roots stretching back for almost a decade. In the London area the Cooperative and Economical Society and its journal the *Economist* were followed in the winter of 1824 by the London Cooperative Society, which issued the *Cooperative Magazine and Monthly Herald* (1826–30). A trading store was established, with James Watson and later William Lovett as storekeepers, and supported by the leaders of the working-class radicals. Contemporary with this Union Exchange Society (as the store was called) was Dr William King's Brighton Cooperative Benevolent Fund Association, whose object was to raise capital for a community by means of cooperative trading. King was not an Owenite, but his journal, the *Cooperator* (1828–30), achieved a wide circulation and served as a handbook for cooperators in many parts of the country.[2] The Brighton

---

[1] As a background to the working-class Owenism of the 1820s cf. Andrew Larcher, *A Remedy for Establishing Universal Peace* (n.p., 1795?) in which he outlines a plan for a cooperative community and a comprehensive trade society among the Spitalfields silk weavers.

[2] See Pollard, *Dr. William King of Ipswich*; and T. W. Mercer, *Cooperation's Prophet; the Life and Letters of Dr. William King of Brighton* (Manchester, 1947).

Society had a largely working-class membership and survived until 1832.

The increasing ferment of Owenism among working men from 1829 can be documented in several ways. In the early numbers of the *Co-operator* in 1828 only four cooperative societies are mentioned: in the final number (August 1830) it is stated that over 300 are in existence. A spate of new cooperative journals appeared;[1] and in London the British Association for Promoting Cooperative Knowledge was founded in May 1829.[2] This last society was intended to be a clearing house and propaganda centre for cooperation through the provision of pamphlets, lectures and missionaries, and it also succeeded the London Cooperative Society in some of its functions. It united under the Owenite banner a notable collection of metropolitan working-class radicals: William Lovett, a cabinet maker who was later active in the free press and Chartist movements; James Watson, previously one of Richard Carlile's shopmen and a well-known radical and secularist bookseller; John Cleave, a bookseller and publisher who was an admirer of Cobbett and later a Chartist; Henry Hetherington, printer and publisher of unstamped papers and active in the reform and Chartist movements; George Foskett, a founder of the Metropolitan Trades' Union; Benjamin Warden, a Marylebone saddler and leading trade unionist; William Carpenter, who published reform and unstamped papers and pamphlets; John Gast, originally a Deptford shipwright, and a pioneer trade unionist and friend of Francis Place; George Petrie, an old mechanic who aspired to write verse; as well as James Tucker, Robert Wigg, William Millard and Thomas Powell—working men whose names recur frequently in Owenite and working-class journals but about whom little is now known. They were joined by middle-class sympathizers such as Julian Hibbert, a Shelleyan figure who had supported Richard Carlile; and Philip Orkney Skene, an ex-army officer and educationist, and his brother

---

[1] *The Associate* (London, 1829–30); *The Belfast Cooperative Advocate* (Belfast, Ireland, 1830); *The Birmingham Cooperative Herald* (Birmingham, 1829–30); *The British Co-operator* (London, 1830); *Chester Cooperative Chronicle* (Chester, 1830); *Herald to the Trades Advocate and Cooperative Journal* (Glasgow, 1830–31); *The Lancashire and Yorkshire Cooperator* (Manchester, 1831–32); *The Magazine of Useful Knowledge and Cooperative Miscellany* (London, 1830); *The Union Pilot and Cooperative Intelligencer* (Manchester, 1832); *The United Trades Cooperative Journal* (Manchester, 1830). The *Weekly Free Press* (formerly the *Trades Newspaper*, London, 1825–28) became a cooperative paper from mid-1829 until the end of 1830.

[2] Information about the B.A.P.C.K. is to be found in reports of the quarterly meetings, some of which were published separately and others in the cooperative press. Also William Lovett, *Life and Struggles* (London, 1876), chap. 2; and Place MSS., 27,822. f. 17 (account of the B.A.P.C.K. by Lovett to Place), reprinted in G. D. H. Cole and A. W. Filson, *British Working Class Movements: Select Documents, 1789–1875* (London, 1951), pp. 212–13.

George Skene. In this gallery of London artisans were the future leaders of the National Union of the Working Classes, the champions of the unstamped press, and the Chartist movement. They had read Owen, Thompson, Minter Morgan and Gray, and were prepared to try to put the principles of cooperation into practice. Some of them had reservations about Owen himself; all of them translated Owenism in terms of their own institutional experience.

The terminology used by working-men cooperators suggests a central concept of 'union'. Working-class institutions for various purposes were described as union societies, trade unions, National Union of the Working Classes. The idea of a cooperative store was not clearly de-marcated from a trade union or a friendly benefit society. Nor were the processes of production, consumption and exchange necessarily to be isolated in separate institutions. The great Reform Bill struggles of 1831–32 did not divert working-class energies away from cooperation but were carried on in addition to it. Proletarian endeavour in the period 1829–34 was not so much a collection of separate movements, some of which waxed as others waned, as one massive, complex response to problems facing the working classes. When a working man declared himself a cooperator he did not necessarily cease to be a trade unionist nor give up the struggle for the vote. His hopes of economic and social betterment were embodied in the various 'union' institutions which we read about in the pages of the *Crisis* or the *Poor Man's Guardian*. Working-class Owenite institutions did not differ markedly from other contemporary popular institutions and frequently were multi-purposive. Nevertheless, for purposes of analysis three main types of union may be distinguished; the cooperative store, the labour exchange and the trade union.

The early (i.e. pre-1844) cooperative stores in what George Jacob Holyoake called the 'enthusiastic period' have been allotted an honoured place in histories of the British cooperative movement.[1] Unfortunately

---

[1] The main source for the early history of cooperative societies is the periodical press listed in n. 1, p. 199 above, together with the *Cooperator, Crisis*, and *Poor Man's Guardian*. The standard history is G. D. H. Cole, *A Century of Cooperation* (Manchester, [1944]); but older accounts are still useful, e.g. Beatrice Potter [Webb], *The Cooperative Movement in Great Britain* (London, 1891); Catherine Webb, *Industrial Cooperation: the Story of a Peaceful Revolution* (Manchester, 1904); William Maxwell, *The History of Cooperation in Scotland: Its Inception and its Leaders* (Glasgow, 1910); and Holyoake, *History of Co-operation in England*. There is also a large number of jubilee and centenary histories of individual cooperative societies, the best of which are listed in the bibliography. A valuable recent study is Sidney Pollard, 'Nineteenth Century Cooperation: from Community Building to Shopkeeping', in Asa Briggs and John Saville, eds., *Essays in Labour History* (London, 1960).

almost nothing is known about them except their names and approximate total number. In April 1829 the *Weekly Free Press* reported 68 cooperative societies in existence; by August 1830 there were more than 300; and in 1832 there were perhaps 500. But they left no records and in the vast majority of cases the only clues to their existence are the brief reports in the cooperative journals. They seem to have extended over all parts of Britain with the exception of Wales, and were especially numerous in London and the industrial North and Midlands. No very clear picture of their activities has ever been drawn, nor any adequate explanation given of their remarkable flowering in such a brief space of time. For a handful of the more famous societies such as Brighton or London a few more details can be filled in—the names of the secretary and leading personalities, the amount of cash transactions each month, and the type of trading carried on. But for a majority of the societies there is no such information. Probably the activity of most stores was on a very small scale, restricted to trading in a few basic commodities, with little capital and dependent on the support of a few families. How many societies progressed beyond the simple retailing of a bag of flour, how many paid dividend on purchases, and how many sought to accumulate funds for a community it is impossible to estimate. The life of most of the societies was short—usually two or three years— and the continuous history of the modern cooperative movement is usually traced not from this period but from the Rochdale pioneers of 1844.

The more vigorous cooperative societies, however, were something more than grocery stores. Some of them had been founded to help unemployed artisans by providing capital for the purchase of materials and a market for the finished product. In due course this might be extended to all the members, and the society become in effect a marketing cooperative. By still further extension of the idea a wider market could be obtained through an exchange bazaar (so called) to which each cooperative trading society could send its surplus products. In London and in the North-West such institutions were opened, supported in each case by some 30 to 40 societies. Another stage was reached when a labour currency was substituted for cash transactions in the exchange bazaars, and there then emerged the second main type of institution of the working-class Owenites—the labour exchange bazaar or, as it was later designated, the equitable labour exchange.

Just as the cooperative store was an attempt to circumvent the principles of capitalist trading, so the labour exchange was an institutionalization of the labour theory of value and the right to the whole produce of labour.[1] As finally worked out after some experimenting, the Owenite labour exchange was essentially a depot where individual cooperators or trade unions exchanged their products without the use of money. A currency of labour notes was used, representing hours of labour time. Goods brought in were valued by a committee according to the number of labour hours judged to be necessary for their making (the 'socially necessary labour time' of Marx) plus the cost of raw materials. The standard of valuation was taken to be 6d. per hour, based on an average worker's wage of 5s. for a ten-hour day. Benjamin Warden described the working of the system thus:

A tailor will bring—say, a waistcoat, or topcoat, say it cost four shillings for the cloth, etc. and six hours' labour; we give him a note to this amount; he turns round and sees a pair of shoes; they cost four shillings and six hours' labour; he gives his labour note the same as we give a shilling over the counter; the shoes are taken away, and the note destroyed, because it ceases to represent real wealth.[2]

A small commission was charged on each article deposited, and an entrance fee on joining the exchange.

Owen had suggested in 1820 that labour be made the standard of value, and, as described previously, his followers had elaborated the doctrine of 'labour for labour'. Labour notes were introduced at New Harmony in 1826 for trading between the three communities into which the settlement had been reorganized; and in other Owenite communities plans for a labour currency were made. Josiah Warren, after he left New Harmony, opened a time store in Cincinnati in 1827, and later experimented with labour notes in New Harmony when he returned there in 1842. In Britain a Union Exchange Society was started by William King (not to be confused with Dr William King of Brighton) at the headquarters of the London Cooperative Society in Red Lion Square in the summer of 1827. The members met weekly to exchange goods, on which a general percentage was levied, but they do not appear to have used labour notes. King was not satisfied with this short-lived experiment

---

[1] The fullest reports of Owenite labour exchanges are in the *Crisis*. See also the *Birmingham Labour Exchange Gazette* (1833); the *Lancashire and Yorkshire Cooperator* (1831–32); *Reports of Cooperative Congresses* (1831–32); Benjamin Warden, *Rewards of Industry* (London, [1832?]); William King, *Gothic Hall Labour Bank* [n.p., n.d.]; *Rules and Regulations of the Equitable Labour Exchange* (London, 1832). There are also relevant letters in the Robert Owen Papers, Manchester. Recent studies are W. H. Oliver, 'The Labour Exchange Phase of the Cooperative Movement', *Oxford Economic Papers*, n.s. X (1958), 355–67; and John Richard Knipe, 'Owenite Ideas and Institutions, 1828–1834' (unpublished M.A. thesis, University of Wisconsin, 1967).

[2] *Lancashire and Yorkshire Cooperator*, March 1832.

and in 1830 suggested that labour exchanges, using labour notes, should be established by the British Association for Promoting Cooperative Knowledge as part of their bazaar.[1] The idea was favourably received in the B.A.P.C.K., but a system of exchangeable receipts for goods deposited was preferred to facing the practical difficulties of operating with labour notes. In February 1832 Benjamin Warden opened the First Western Union Exchange Bank, and in April William King began his Gothic Hall Labour Bank in Marylebone. Both of these drew heavily on Owen's ideas and apparently used labour notes. Throughout 1832 the cooperative press was full of suggestions and reports about opening new labour exchanges.

The undoubted initial success of these ventures and the obvious appeal which they had to many working men aroused Owen's interest in a way that the cooperative trading stores had never done. On his return to England in 1829 Owen found himself without any organization for promoting his new view of society and bereft of the bulk of his fortune. Early in 1830 he took the Burton Street chapel, London, and delivered a series of Sunday morning lectures, published as *Lectures on an Entire New State of Society* (London, 1830). These showed a marked radical progression in his social thinking, for he now came out quite unequivocally against private property, commercialism and inequality in general. His solution to social problems was still basically communitarian, but during the next few months his approach was modified by the efforts of working-men cooperators who professed to be following his lead. William Lovett, at this time an enthusiastic communitarian, recorded:

When Mr Owen first came over from America he looked somewhat coolly on ... Trading Associations, and very candidly declared that their mere buying and selling formed no part of his grand cooperative scheme; but when he found that great numbers among them were disposed to entertain many of his views, he took them more into favour, and ultimately took an active part among them.[2]

In fact, it was not the humble trading store, but the potentialities of the equitable labour exchange that attracted Owen, and which for a short time even eclipsed his communitarian vision.

Owen was later to declare that he had been reluctant to start a labour exchange as early as 1832: he wanted the working classes to wait until

---

[1] *Weekly Free Press*, 20 March, 7 August 1830. There are also letters from William Pare and James Tucker supporting the idea of labour exchanges and labour notes (21, 28 August 1830).

[2] Lovett, *Life*, p. 43.

they had adequate capital and had devoted at least two years to its planning.[1] But the exchange banks opened by Warden and King forced his hand, and he determined to do the best he could in the circumstances. Such was Owen's story in 1835, but there was no hint of any such doubts when the great National Equitable Labour Exchange was launched in September 1832. However, the pattern of his efforts up to this time was in accordance with his earlier principles and did not as yet reflect any new-found confidence in the working classes as an independent force for social change. His Institution of the Industrious Classes for Removing Ignorance and Poverty by Education and Beneficial Employment, founded in December 1831, was no different in tone from the British and Foreign Philanthropic Society of a decade earlier. The same collection of wealthy philanthropists, bankers and M.P.s graced the committee of directors, and it was resolved to ask members of the royal family to be patrons and vice-patrons. A working committee, however, did include Warden, King, Corss and other working men alongside middle-class sympathizers. This Institution, thanks to an enthusiastic disciple of Owen's named William Bromley, was splendidly housed in a building in Grays Inn Road, London, and it was here that the labour exchange was located after it had been decided to graft it on to the Institution of the Industrious Classes. The original objects of the Institution also included weekly lectures, a school, and the purchase of land for growing vegetables and teaching horticulture, but these faded into the background once the labour exchange and bank were launched.

As with all Owen's ventures, the National Equitable Labour Exchange was on a grandiose scale. The premises had been a horse and carriage repository and the buildings were arranged round a central courtyard, with an open gallery on the first storey.[2] There was a large assembly room in the classical style, with an embossed ceiling and gold ornamentation. Owen added a platform and organ to complete the arrangements for festival nights, when five or six hundred people attended for a lecture and ball. The property was valued by Bromley at no less than £17,000 and he asked Owen for a rent of £1400 exclusive of ground rent of £320.

---

[1] 'Memoranda Relative to Robert Owen', *New Moral World*, 10 October 1835. These memoranda were clearly written from information supplied by Owen. Samuel Austin, secretary of the National Equitable Labour Exchange, confirms Owen's view in an article in the *Crisis*, 21 September 1833. Owen was under pressure from his friends to start a labour exchange—see MS. letter from William Watkins to Owen, 23 January 1832. Robert Owen Papers, Manchester.

[2] A description by a participant is given in the *Life of Allen Davenport*, quoted in the *National Cooperative Leader*, 22 November 1861; and a woodcut of the building appeared on the title page of each number of the *Crisis* from 14 April 1832 until 26 January 1833.

From the first the Exchange attracted a great deal of attention. Deposits flowed in and crowds thronged the halls. For a time the handsomely produced labour notes were accepted as currency by local tradesmen, and Owen triumphantly announced that equitable labour exchanges were the bridge over which society would pass to a new and better world.[1] Reports in the *Crisis* suggest that during the autumn of 1832 business at Grays Inn Road was brisk,[2] and in December a branch exchange was started at the Rotunda in Blackfriars Road. In January 1833 the Grays Inn Road premises had to be given up, as Owen refused to pay the rent demanded by Bromley, and operations were transferred to the Blackfriars Road branch. This resulted in some falling off in the amount of business and in May 1833 Owen found a new home for the parent exchange in Charlotte Street, Fitzroy Square.

It was intended that labour exchanges should be opened in all the main towns of Britain, and that through a national system of exchange the excess stock of cooperative societies would be disposed of. Only in Birmingham, however, did these plans materialize. There the local Owenites—William Pare, William Hawkes Smith, John Rabone—succeeded in interesting Attwood of the Birmingham Political Union and Muntz, the currency reformer, in the idea of labour exchanges and they welcomed Owen on his missionary visit in November 1832. Pare had prepared the ground by distributing ten thousand copies of a leaflet on exchanges. It was resolved to open a labour exchange in Birmingham; a short-lived journal, the *Birmingham Labour Exchange Gazette*, appeared in January 1833; but not until July did the exchange begin to operate in Coach Yard, Bull Street. Business was on a more modest scale than in London, and an attempt was made to develop inter-city exchange. Reports from the secretary, Charles West, appeared in the *Crisis* until December 1833 and at the end of the year there was a profit of £200.

Both the Birmingham and the London labour exchanges were wound up in the early summer of 1834. As with the lost communities it is not possible to isolate one factor to which their lack of continuing success

---

[1] *Crisis*, 29 September 1832. The *Crisis* was started by Owen in April 1832 and is the main source of information on the National Equitable Labour Exchange. The paper was edited first by Owen, then by his son, Robert Dale Owen, and finally by J. E. (Shepherd) Smith.

[2] Total deposits from 3 September to 29 December 1832 were 445,501 hours (over £11,000) and exchanges (i.e. withdrawals) 376,166 hours (£9400). For the week ending 15 December deposits reached a record 38,772 hours (nearly £1000). At the Blackfriars Road branch, from 8 December 1832 to 5 January 1833, deposits were 32,759 hours and exchanges 16,621 hours. After the move of the parent exchange to Blackfriars Road the weekly deposits fell to 9500 hours and exchanges to around 12,000 hours. *Crisis*, 12 January, 23 February, 9 March 1833.

can be attributed. A typical Owenite verdict was that of William Pare, who considered that the equitable labour exchange did not come to an end through 'any inherent defect in the principle' but because 'those who availed themselves of it were too ignorant, too selfish, too dishonest; added to which the whole forces of a vast erroneous system were against us'.[1] Specific weaknesses and frustrations can nevertheless be discerned, though these need not necessarily have been fatal. In the first place, the movement was limited to handicraftsmen who produced their goods in small workshops without any large amount of capital and equipment. As such, it found a natural home in two areas where such craftsmen preponderated—north London and Birmingham. Tailors, shoemakers, carpenters, cabinet-makers, chairmakers, hatters, brushmakers and glaziers there were in plenty. But their capacity to supply each others' needs was very limited. Without textiles from the factories and food from the farms the labour exchanges could not become self-sufficient, and despite efforts to obtain supplies of bread, meat, provisions and coals, food and raw materials remained largely outside the system. Again, talk of exchanges between towns did not materialize to any considerable extent, and the movement therefore remained local in scale.

A second, and more fundamental problem, was that the labour notes in fact remained tied to current market values. The system of valuing goods deposited in the exchanges caused a good deal of discussion and some dissatisfaction. Theoretically the labour note was a device for exchanging goods with reference to the amount of labour in each, expressed in labour hours. But the definition of a labour hour was taken to be an hour's work at the standard rate of sixpence an hour, and adjustment was made for workers whose standard rate was higher. This in effect meant that the labour notes were not an independent currency but only a translation into labour time of values determined by that competitive economy which the Owenites rejected. Difficulties in assessing the value of the raw materials also arose, and the practice of exchanging cash for notes (instead of issuing notes only on deposits) made it impossible for the system to become insulated from the pressures of the commercial world outside.

The statistics of deposits and exchanges suggest a third area of difficulty. Since the total of deposits exceeded the exchanges or withdrawals there must have been a stock of goods left in the labour exchange. Whether or not this was a permanent residue is impossible to determine from the figures alone, but Lovett and Holyoake asserted later that the

[1] The *Cooperator*, 15 August 1865.

exchange became a dumping ground for unsaleable items. It was also claimed that the members' wives objected to shopping at only one store. In general the parallel between the pattern of development of the Owenite labour exchanges and the Owenite communities is close. There was Owen's insistence at the beginning on the need for a large and generously capitalized experiment; then an enthusiastic and apparently successful launching, followed by increasing disillusionment after six months or a year, to the accompaniment of extended theoretical discussions at meetings and in the press; and finally the wistful conclusion of the faithful disciples that the principles were sound but ordinary human beings were not yet worthy to receive them. In both the exchanges and communities there was the same mixture of idealistic Owenites and freeloaders who hoped to benefit from Owen's generosity. The same ambivalent attitude of respect and gratitude to Owen as initiator and benefactor coupled with exasperation at his apparent remoteness from the practical needs of the institution is found among the members. And the baffling problem of how to operate socialist institutions in the midst of a still competitive society remained as insoluble as ever.

Before the demise of the equitable labour exchanges in 1834 they had become closely associated with a third and more strongly indigenous institution of the working classes, the trade union. The National Equitable Labour Exchange had at first been run by philanthropists and lower middle-class Owenites, but its success attracted increasing numbers of handicraftsmen and in July 1833 they took over control of the institution. This was effected through the United Trades Association which had been established in March 1833 to coordinate the efforts of working men who wished to use the exchange. The Association was composed of a number of trade societies (or unions) which had already embarked upon schemes of cooperative production for their unemployed members. At first they sent their goods to the exchange bazaar run by the British Association for Promoting Cooperative Knowledge but after the opening of the National Equitable Labour Exchange they soon became its chief users, and expanded their projects for the self-employment of craftsmen. The Association assisted members of the trades societies, especially unemployed members, to purchase raw materials for their crafts and then used the labour exchange to market the product. Via cooperative self-employment and the equitable labour exchange the trade societies were thus drawn into the Owenite camp. Owen for his part suddenly became aware of the potentialities of his new audience, and for a brief spell put himself at the head of the whole working-class movement.

The complex story of the development of British trade unionism in the years 1831–34 has never been satisfactorily unravelled.[1] Union records are extremely sparse and reports in journals are tantalizingly incomplete at crucial points. Above all the hostility of government and employers forced union men to keep information about their organizations and their intentions secret or deliberately misleading; they became part of what E. P. Thompson has described as 'the opaque society'.[2] The relations of Owen and his followers with such a movement are very difficult to decipher, even though the Owenite journals provide almost the only consecutive account of union history at this time. Some aspects of the story, however, are reasonably clear and from these it is possible to comment on the geography, institutions, personalities and policies of Owenite trade unionism.

Geographically support was concentrated in four main areas: London, Birmingham, Yorkshire and Lancashire, and the Staffordshire Potteries; although when once the mushroom growth began late in 1833 unions were reported from many other counties too. Each of the four main centres had its distinctive organization and leadership which remained largely autonomous. Trade unionism was still essentially local in its institutions and aspirations, and the sudden transcendence of these bounds was perhaps the most remarkable achievement of the brief period of Owenite enthusiasm. Owen emerged as a national leader, cooperation provided a common programme and ideology, and at last a national organization was found in the shadowy Grand National Consolidated Trades Union.

In London the United Trades Association, with its headquarters at the Equitable Labour Exchange, was firmly based on the craftsmen's unions and led by a junta of able Owenite cooperators. The *Crisis* provided an organ for them, and from September 1833 the editor was James E. (Shepherd) Smith, whose millenarian career has been traced earlier. At Birmingham the pattern was similar, though here the key group was the Builders' Union, which since 1831 had grown rapidly in the direction of a national organization.[3] Through two local architects, Joseph Hansom[4] and Edward Welch, who were enthusiastic cooperators, the

---

[1] Without new evidence it does not seem possible to get much further than did G. D. H. Cole in his *Attempts at General Union* (London, 1953); and Sidney and Beatrice Webb in chapter 3 of their *History of Trade Unionism* (London, 1894). The main contemporary sources are the *Crisis*, the *Pioneer* and the *Poor Man's Guardian*.

[2] Thompson, *Making of the English Working Class*, p. 484.

[3] See R. W. Postgate, *The Builders' History* (London, 1923), chaps. 3 and 4.

[4] Joseph Aloysius Hansom (1803–1882) was born in York, the son of a joiner. After serving an apprenticeship to a local architect he practised in Yorkshire, and in 1828 entered

Builders' Union was persuaded to listen to Owen and give consideration to his plans. As a result, in September 1833 the Grand Lodge (or 'Builders' Parliament') formed a Grand National Guild of Builders, intended to erect buildings directly, without reliance upon the masters. Strikes and lock-outs strengthened the determination of the builders to try to devise means of cooperative self-employment, and work was begun on a guildhall for the union in Birmingham. James Morrison, a painter by trade and a faithful devotee of Owen, greatly aided the Owenite cause with his *Pioneer*, which became the semi-official journal of the Builders' Union and, later, of the Grand National Consolidated Trades Union.[1]

Throughout 1833 reports of the favourable reception of Owenism by unions in all parts of the country grew more and more numerous. Owen toured the country, lecturing and attending union meetings at which he tirelessly repeated his prophetic plans for fundamental social change, and by the summer of 1833 he was the acknowledged national leader of the trade union movement. No small part of his efforts was directed towards the industrial North, where he succeeded in gaining the support of prominent Lancashire and Yorkshire trade unionists. John Doherty, leader of the Lancashire cotton spinners and an advocate of general

---

[1] James Morrison (1802–1835) concluded a letter to Owen: 'I shall look upon you as a Father and try to become a faithful Son. May circumstances be auspicious to my Baptism and make me worthy . . .' (MS. letter, Morrison to Owen, 23 July 1833, Robert Owen Papers, Manchester). Morrison was born in Newcastle and apprenticed as a painter and grainer, but always had literary yearnings. By 1831 he was married and living in Birmingham, where he became active in workers' education, the cooperative movement and the unstamped press agitation. He was a member of the Painters' Union (one of the constituents of the Builders' Union), and worked actively to swing the Builders' Union towards Owenism. Early in 1834 he moved to London, where he continued to edit his journal, the *Pioneer*, begun in Birmingham in September 1833. With the collapse of the G.N.C.T.U. his journal came to an end in July 1834, and he died suddenly of brain fever in August 1835, leaving a widow and five young children, for whom a charitable subscription was raised. His wife, Frances Morrison, was also an Owenite and in 1838–39 lectured in Owenite institutions in Lancashire and the North (see Frances Morrison, *The Influence of the Present Marriage System*, Manchester, 1838). The available biographical material on Morrison is collected in John Sever, 'James Morrison of "The Pioneer": Notes on His Life and Background' (unpublished typograph, 1963. Copies in British Museum, Bodleian, Cambridge University Libraries, etc.).

---

into a partnership with Edward Welch, in Birmingham. He designed Birmingham town hall (1831) and is perhaps best known as the patentor of the hansom (safety) cab (1834). In 1842 he founded and edited the *Builder*. He was a Roman Catholic, designed many churches and ecclesiastical buildings, and for a short period (1862–63) worked with E. W. Pugin. His interest in Owenism continued after the collapse of the Builders' Union, and he designed Harmony Hall at Queenwood.

union, was enthusiastic for the Owenite cause.[1] His National Association for the Protection of Labour (1830–32) and succession of trade union journals provided a foundation for agitation and organization which could later be directed to Owenite goals. The movement in Yorkshire remains more obscure, for there the shadow of secrecy lay darker and was not chronicled in local union journals comparable to Doherty's *Voice of the People* and *Poor Man's Advocate*. But from scattered and fearful references in the local press it is clear that the 'Trades Union' was an acknowledged force in the Yorkshire textile industry. From 1829 the northern trade unionists had been actively engaged in the struggle for factory reform, supported by middle-class help from Sadler, Oastler and Bull, and this aspect of the working-class movement the Owenites were also able to exploit. In November 1833 the National Regeneration Society was founded in Manchester by Owen, Doherty and John Fielden, the radical mill-owner and M.P. for Todmorden.[2] Its demands were for an eight-hour day in the factories, as a prelude to the extinction of competitive society. Branches were started in most of the northern towns and a journal, the *Herald of the Rights of Industry*, flourished for a few months in 1834. Finally, in this brief survey of the areas of Owenite strength there must be included the potters of Staffordshire. A Potters' Union had been established by Doherty in 1830, and from the first had been susceptible to Owenite influences. Owen's visits to the Potteries in

[1] John Doherty (1789–?), described by Francis Place as a hot-headed Roman Catholic, was born in Buncrana, Co. Donegal, Ireland, and worked in an Ulster cotton mill at the age of ten. In 1816 he went to Manchester where he soon became secretary of the local Cotton Spinners' Union. He may have been concerned in the struggles for a general union in 1818 and 1826, and certainly was active in the agitation against a re-enactment of the Combination Laws in 1825. In 1829 he led the Hyde spinners in their fight against wage reductions, and became general secretary of the Federation of Spinners Societies and of the N.A.P.L. He served two years in gaol—for misconduct according to his enemies, for his share in the general turn-out according to himself. He was secretary of the Manchester Short Time Committee. In 1838 he retired from union work and set up as a printer and bookseller in Manchester. He edited and wrote for the *Conciliator* (1828); the *United Trades Cooperative Journal* (1830); the *Voice of the People* (1831); the *Poor Man's Advocate* (1832–33); and the *Herald of the Rights of Industry* (1834). See *Manchester Notes and Queries*, VII (1887–88); A. E. Musson, 'The Ideology of Early Cooperation in Lancashire and Cheshire', Lancashire and Cheshire Antiquarian Society, *Transactions*, LXVIII (1958); and D. C. Morris, 'The History of the Labour Movement in England, 1825–1852: The Problem of Leadership and the Articulation of Demands' (unpublished Ph.D. thesis, University of London, 1952).

[2] Society for Promoting National Regeneration, *Rights of Industry: Catechism of the Society* (Manchester, 1833); and reports of activities in the *Crisis*; *Herald of the Rights of Industry*; and *Voice of the West Riding* (Huddersfield, 1833–34). For the factory reform movement and its connections with the Owenites see Cecil Driver, *Tory Radical: the Life of Richard Oastler* (New York, 1946); and J. T. Ward, *The Factory Movement, 1830–1855* (London, 1962).

the fall of 1833 swept them into the socialist maelstrom, and in June 1834 they entered the field of cooperative production with a separate pottery factory which continued until the end of the year.

Owen, as we have seen, was unresponsive to the growth of cooperative stores, but enthusiastic for equitable labour exchanges. After he had grasped the dimensions of the trade union movement he declared that in comparison the labour exchanges were 'but a mere drop in the bucket'. His contact with the unprecedented development of trade unionism in 1832–33 confirmed his millenarian convictions that the crisis was at hand and the old immoral world was about to be swept away. In October 1833 he outlined his new conception of future developments:

I now give you a short outline of the great changes which are in contemplation, and which shall come suddenly upon society, like a thief in the night. . . . This change is to be accomplished not by violence, bloodshed, or any species of injustice. . . . It is intended that national arrangements shall be formed to in-clude all the working classes in the great organisation, and that each depart-ment shall become acquainted with what is going on in other departments; that all individual competition is to cease; that all manufactures are to be carried on by national companies. . . . All trades shall first form associations of lodges to consist of a convenient number for carrying on the business; . . . all indi-viduals of the specific craft shall become members.[1]

This syndicalist plan was adopted by the delegates to the Owenite con-gress held in London a few days later, and a Grand National Moral Union of the Productive and Useful Classes was projected. All trade unions, cooperative societies, benefit societies 'and all other associations intended for the improvement of the working classes' were advised to form lodges, 'for the purpose of emancipating the industrious and useful classes from the difficulties which overwhelm them'.[2] Early in 1834 this body emerged as the Grand National Consolidated Trades Union.

The meteoric rise and fall of the G.N.C.T.U. is one of the most colourful episodes in the early history of British trade unionism. It has been chronicled in many places, and only such details as are relevant to the Owenite story need be repeated here. Within a few weeks the Union was reported to have a million members, and the alarm which it aroused among the government and employers soon provoked con-flict. From the very beginning it was faced with strikes and lock-outs in many parts of the country. In fact, the Union even inherited one of its most protracted conflicts, the great Derby turn-out, which had begun in

[1] *Crisis*, 12 October 1833.
[2] Minutes of a meeting held at Huddersfield, 1 November 1833. Robert Owen Papers, Manchester. Cole, *Robert Owen*, p. 278.

November 1833. Then came the sudden set-back of the Tolpuddle Martyrs when, in March 1834, six agricultural labourers from Dorset were sentenced to seven years' transportation for administering an illegal oath in their newly formed trade union lodge.[1] The main efforts of the G.N.C.T.U. were thenceforward directed to protesting against the sentence on the Dorchester labourers and trying to raise funds for the support of members on strike or locked out. This proved to be far beyond the Union's means, and as the employers vigorously pursued their union-breaking tactic of requiring all workers to sign 'the document' (renouncing the union) the individual unions collapsed or left the G.N.C.T.U. By the summer of 1834 discord arose within the top councils of the Union, and Owen parted company with his two lieutenants, James Morrison and J. E. (Shepherd) Smith. Morrison's *Pioneer*, which had been adopted as the official organ of the G.N.C.T.U., was displaced, and came to an end in July. The *Crisis*, which Smith edited, was closed down by Owen the following month. Both editors resented the intrusion of Owen's religious views, and even more his dominance of the executive committee of the Union. Owen on his side accused them of stirring up class hatred and objected to their subordination of his grand notions to bread-and-butter trade union issues. By August the G.N.C.T.U. was clearly breaking up, and at this point Owen called a meeting of delegates in London which resolved that the Union should be renamed the British and Foreign Consolidated Association of Industry, Humanity and Knowledge. It was agreed that 'effective measures be adopted . . . to reconcile the masters and operatives', and Owen was elected Grand Master.[2] The trade union phase of Owenism was over.

For labour historians the significance of the G.N.C.T.U. has been that it was the most impressive of the early attempts to form a national organization of all trade unions, and at the same time an example of how labour's true interests can be diverted by entanglement with socialist theories. From an Owenite position the perspective looks somewhat different. Perhaps the first thing to be noted is that the G.N.C.T.U. was a loose federation of various types of 'union' and cooperative organizations, resembling (as the Webbs remarked) the later Knights of Labor in America rather than the British Trades Union Congress. The typical Owenite organization was never narrow and exclusive like a craft union, but quite the reverse; it was concerned with the general 'rights of industry' rather than job control and wage bargaining. Owenite ideals and

[1] The fullest treatment of this case is in the Trades Union Congress centenary volume, *The Martyrs of Tolpuddle* (London, 1934).
[2] *Crisis*, 23 August 1834.

29. Robert Owen (by Matilda Heming: published 1823)

30. Robert Owen (by J. Comerford)

31. Robert Owen (sketched as he was standing at the door of a newspaper shop in Manchester, c. 1838)

objectives went far beyond the horizons of the trade societies and made an appeal outside the ranks of craftsmen and operatives. Nothing was more remarkable than the numbers of farm labourers and women workers who responded to the missionaries from the G.N.C.T.U. The fever of unionism which gripped the country in the first months of 1834 was quite different from earlier recruitments, and should perhaps be related to the millenarian hopes described in an earlier section. Owen's style was very prophetic during 1833–34 and he was clearly carried away by the size of the unions' response and the vast possibilities for immediate change which he thought were opening up.

The second comment to be made on the union phase is the extent to which it modified the views of Owen and orthodox Owenism. When Owen spoke of the great changes which would come suddenly upon society 'like a thief in the night' he may have just been indulging in millennial rhetoric; but it is possible that he was thinking of a general strike. The tactics of the executive of the G.N.C.T.U. were to conserve their forces until they were ready to call a national strike for the eight-hour day and the emancipation of the working classes, but in fact this was frustrated by the sectional strikes in which the unions got involved. Owen favoured the official Union policy, though he emphasized that the general strike must be conducted without any class hatred or unchari-tableness. Indeed, since he expected that 'all the intelligent, well disposed, and superior minds among all classes of society, male and female, will now rally round the Consolidated Union, and become members of it', it was logical to expect that the revolution would be 'without bloodshed, violence, or evil of any kind'.[1] After the general strike the workers, organized in their unions, would take over the control of industry. Pro-ducers' cooperation was recommended by the G.N.C.T.U. as a prepara-tion for the take-over, and also as an immediate form of relief for mem-bers on strike, as in the case of the Derby turn-outs. The new moral world was to be ushered in through cooperative workshops and labour exchanges, after 'a strong strike and a strike all together'. For the time being Owenism appeared as a variety of syndicalism.

The third aspect of Owenite trade unionism which is significant is that it was a mass movement. Neither before nor afterwards, in Britain or America, did Owenism assume this form. Owen himself became for a few months a popular leader. The picture of him marching at the head of a monster procession of London trade unionists to present a petition against the sentences of the Dorchester labourers in April 1834 is in the

[1] 'The Legacy of Robert Owen, to the Population of the World', *Pioneer*, 29 March 1834.

P

style of William Cobbett or Henry Hunt.[1] Exactly why should Owenism have become a mass movement in 1833–34? The usual, and in a limited sense correct explanation is that the Owenites captured the trade union movement and subverted it for their own purpose. Yet it is clear that they could only do this because Owenism appeared to offer a solution to problems which had hitherto proved intractable. What those problems were is apparent from the radical reform journals: universal suffrage, the taxes on knowledge, factory reform, inadequate wages, unemployment—and above all a vast resentment against that combination of wealth, power and privilege which Cobbett had dubbed 'the Thing'. Various roads out of this impasse had been tried, but all were found to be blocked. The latest disillusionment was the Reform Bill of 1832. The idea of 'union' suggested yet another road for working-class self-help, and when the Owenites interpreted this in terms of a complete transformation of the whole of society they found a large, receptive audience. Owen's actual participation in routine trade union affairs was minimal, but the influence of Owenite socialism on a whole generation of trade union leaders went much deeper—while beyond them Owen's effect on general working-class opinion was, as Frances Place said, enormous.

The three institutions of working-class Owenism—the cooperative store, the labour exchange and the trade union—have so far been treated separately but in fact they overlapped and supplemented each other. The focus of their interaction was in the cooperative congress.[2] Beginning in May 1831 a series of eight congresses was held up to April 1835. They were composed of delegates from cooperative societies, labour exchanges and trade unions in all parts of the country, and were held in a different town each time. The resolutions of congress provided guide lines for future policy and there was usually a thorough discussion and clashing of views. Plans for work were aired, and the institution became the nerve centre of the Owenite movement.

As the doctrines of cooperative socialism spread rapidly among working men it was not long before the Owenites had to define their relationship to other reform movements, especially political reform. For Owen himself the problem scarcely existed, since he had never recognized that parliamentary reform was at all relevant to bettering the condition

[1] An account and woodcut illustration of the great Copenhagen Fields demonstration in London is in the *Pioneer*, 26 April 1834.

[2] No formal report of the first Congress, held in Manchester, was published, but there are relevant documents in a volume titled *Cooperative Congresses: Reports and Papers, 1831–32* in the Goldsmiths' Library, University of London. *Proceedings* for the second, third and fourth Congresses were published; and the later Congresses were reported in the *Crisis*.

of the people. What practical good could extension of the franchise effect, 'in the present state of ignorance in which the mass of the British population has been hitherto allowed to be trained'?[1] The Owenite journals largely ignored the issue and from them one would never suspect that from 1830 to 1832 the whole country was seething with excitement over the question of the Reform Bill. But working-class Owenites had a very different attitude. They formed the National Union of the Working Classes and threw their weight behind the political unions in the provinces. This fusion of political radicalism with cooperative socialism is seen most clearly in the pages of Henry Hetherington's *Poor Man's Guardian*, edited from 1832 by James Bronterre O'Brien. Both Hetherington and O'Brien were cooperators, but this in no way conflicted with their belief in the necessity of political struggle: 'let the Radical take the Owenite by the hand, and the Owenite do the same by the Radical, for both parties are the *real*, and only *friends* of the working people'. The Owenites differed from the political radicals only in their methods, but both had the same goal, namely 'to establish for the workman dominion over the fruits of his own industry. . . . The Owenite thinks that without property the working classes can never get represented in Parliament, and therefore he sets to work with his "Equitable Labour Exchange" to get property; while the Radical thinks that without representation they will never be able to acquire property at all, and accordingly he begins at the other end, and goes to work for Universal Suffrage.'[2] Owen was not persuaded by these arguments to change his attitude, and so the advocates of independent political action went their own way, taking with them such parts of Owenism as suited their purposes. It was thus that the Lovetts, Hetheringtons and O'Briens could claim to be cooperative socialists while criticizing Owen and the orthodox Owenites. This was a repetition of what had happened in the case of the cooperative store and certain aspects of communitarianism: Owenism provided a kind of reservoir from which different groups and individuals drew ideas and inspiration which they then applied as they chose. The working men, building on popular traditions of community, anti-capitalism and millenarianism, found a badly needed social theory in cooperative socialism; and when they subsequently needed a democratic political philosophy

[1] Macnab, *New Views of Mr Owen Examined*, p. 93, quoting from Owen's account of his work in the *British Statesman*, 9 August 1819. Owen was referring to the great reform agitation which culminated in Peterloo, August 1819, but his views were substantially unchanged at the time of the 1830–32 demonstrations.

[2] *Poor Man's Guardian*, 22 September 1832. The *P.M.G.* reported debates in the National Union of the Working Classes on this issue, and from September to November 1832 conducted a thorough discussion of the problem.

they added that too. In the period 1829–34 this process was greatly intensified, reaching a series of climaxes in the founding of hundreds of cooperative stores, the Great Reform Bill struggle, and the Grand National Consolidated Trades Union.

It is possible to see the whole five-year Owenite involvement with the working-class movement as an aberration, or an interruption in 'normal' development. Owen's social thinking in the fall of 1834 reverted to the positions he had held in 1829. The new institutions of Owenism—stores, exchanges and national union—all disappeared by 1835. The leading Owenite journals, the *Crisis* and the *Pioneer* came to an end. Yet the events of 1829–34 were in fact a logical working out of certain Owenite attitudes and positions. Just as the gentlemanly philanthropists had earlier welcomed Owenism as a solution to the problems of poor relief and rural distress and the Owenite communitarians had hoped to find an answer to difficulties encountered in America, so the working men sought in Owenite cooperation a remedy for the ills of competitive society. None of these was more typically Owenite than the others. All were legitimate expressions of that cluster of concepts, attitudes and theories which was Owenism. Nor was its evolution by any means yet finished. From 1835 the Owenite movement in Britain gave a new twist to certain doctrines and built a new organization.

2 All Classes of All Nations

Late in January 1840 the Bishop of Exeter, Henry Phillpotts, attacked the Owenites in a speech in the House of Lords.[1] He saw in socialism a grave national menace and outlined the Owenite organization, which he claimed was illegal. This dangerous body had an annual congress, composed of delegates from sixty-one chartered branches. There were fourteen main districts in the kingdom, in each of which was a social missionary appointed by a Central Board and paid a weekly wage of thirty shillings. The missionaries visited regularly no fewer than 350

[1] Reported in the *New Moral World*, 1, 8, 15 February 1840, including special supplements. Also Hansard, *Parliamentary Debates*, 3rd series, LI (1840), col. 530, 1187. The Bishop's speeches encouraged a spate of attacks on Owenism by various shades of clerical opponents. These ranged from scurrilous and personal abuse of Owen by John Brindley to reasoned theological debates on the evidences of Christianity. See bibliography for debates of Alexander Campbell, Lloyd Jones, Frederick Hollick, Robert Buchanan, John Hanson and C. J. Haslam, and the anti-Owenism of the Reverends Grant, Bedford, Kidd, Giles, Roebuck and of F. R. Lees.

towns. In a further speech the Bishop elaborated new details. He mentioned a tract committee, meeting halls in many large towns, and an extensive estate which had been acquired for a socialist community in Hampshire. A journal, the *New Moral World*, had a circulation of 2000 and each copy was read by perhaps 200 people. The *Weekly Dispatch*, which also advocated socialism, sold 40,000 copies weekly. Half a million copies of publications were issued in the past year, 360,000 of which were published by the Central Board and the London Tract Committee. The names of leading socialists—Fleming, Hawkes Smith, Finch and Pare— were mentioned by the Bishop, as well as cases where misguided mayors had let guildhalls for socialist lectures. William Pare, in his capacity as Superintendent Registrar of Births, Deaths and Marriages at Birmingham, was singled out for special condemnation, since he was also Vice President of the Central Board.

Although the Bishop's attempt to alarm the Lords was largely vitiated by his obvious Tory partisanship and desire to use the issue as a stick with which to beat the Whig government, the speeches are an interesting comment on Owenism in several ways. They provide an outsider's view (albeit hostile) of how the Owenite movement looked in 1839–40—and, as often with radical movements, while the members were aware mainly of their internal divisions and weaknesses, the outsiders were impressed with their apparent solidity and strength. The statistics which the Bishop used were derived partly from Owenite publications and partly from the reports of clerical anti-Owenites, and gave a very favourable, if not exaggerated idea of the amount of activity in the movement. Probably a peak in membership, branches and publications was reached in 1840–41. The Bishop's concern, however, was almost exclusively with a single aspect of Owenism—infidelity. It was not the Owenites' communitarianism nor their other plans for social change which were considered dangerous, but their attack on organized religion. The impressive organization which had been described was thought to be geared primarily to the subversion of Christianity; the other Owenite goals were overlooked. Now this was a very different image of Owenism from that current only five or six years earlier. In 1833–34 socialism was associated with turn-outs, mass demonstrations and hostility to competitive economy: by 1840 it was referred to as a rapidly growing sect which challenged established re-religion and encouraged immoral practices. The change in popular estimation of Owenism was shown in the attitude of the government. Whereas in 1834 Lord Melbourne had acted with alacrity and severity in supporting the sentences on the Dorchester labourers, the Home Secretary, Lord Normanby, refused to be in the least alarmed by the Bishop's hair-raising allegations, and Melbourne had considered Owen sufficiently respectable to be presented at court in the summer of 1839.[1] While the Bishop and the Home Secretary differed in their evaluation of the Owenite organization they agreed that, in its present form, it was something new. Owen's doctrines had long been familiar and his philanthropic endeavours recognized: but the activities, institutions and personalities which now comprised the Owenite movement made it recognizably different from its earlier phases. The period 1834-45 was a decade in which the British Owenites developed an elaborate national organization as well as a network of local institutions, and it was this growth which by 1840 had so alarmed the Bishop.

The central Owenite body changed its name several times.[2] After Owen left the Grand National Consolidated Trades Union, he founded a new body in the autumn of 1834 which he called the British and Foreign Consolidated Association of Industry, Humanity and Knowledge. This was reorganized in May 1835 as the Association of All Classes of All Nations. At the Manchester Congress in May 1837 a Missionary and Tract Society was set up and also the National Community Friendly Society, to promote the foundation of communities. In May 1839 the A.A.C.A.N. and the N.C.F.S. were amalgamated to form the Universal Community Society of Rational Religionists, which from May 1842 was known simply as the Rational Society. A Home Colonization Society was established in 1841 to raise funds for communities, and a Central Board served as the executive committee of the U.C.S.R.R. Annual congresses were held, continuing the tradition established by the series of Co-operative Congresses of 1831-35. There is more than antiquarian significance in this catalogue of names and dates. The grandiose titles (characteristic also of other contemporary popular institutions such as millennial sects, trade unions and friendly societies) indicate objectives and assumptions. Through the successive reorganizations can be charted the changing emphases on different parts of Owenism—education, community, secularism. In the creation of new sub-bodies is seen the

[1] Nevertheless the government was stimulated by the publicity of the proceedings to investigate possible cases of blasphemous publications and blasphemy at meetings. See correspondence and reports between the Home Office and local magistrates in 1840. P.R.O. HO/41/30 and HO/44/38.

[2] The MS. minutes of the central organization are complete from 26 May 1838 to 5 March 1845, bound in 3 volumes, in the International Institute of Social History, Amsterdam, Netherlands. Apparently the minutes before May 1838 were included in the minute book of London Branch A.1. but this has not been traced. The Central Board met weekly or fortnightly, usually attended by half a dozen members. Robert Owen, if present, was chairman. A paid secretary was employed to conduct the routine business.

method of tackling organizational problems. Equally expressive was the title of the new journal which Owen started in November 1834 to replace the *Crisis*. For over a decade the *New Moral World*, edited by George Alexander Fleming, provided a weekly record of striving towards the overall Owenite goal.

It is a truism that the vitality of popular movements depends ultimately not on an elaborate central organization but on the strength of local branches. This was one of the things that some Owenites learned from their experiences with working men in 1829–34, and it reinforced the communitarian and sectarian notions of the primacy of local institutions. To stimulate and nourish grass-roots activity, and at the same time keep such activity in line with central policy is the task of the regional organizer or agent, and most voluntary bodies in England have relied on such men to provide a cadre or skeleton. The Owenites called their organizers Social Missionaries. At the Second and Third Cooperative Congresses (1831–32) the idea of missionaries had been broached, but nothing was done because of lack of funds. In May 1838, however, the Manchester Congress appointed six missionaries, and in 1839 the number was raised to ten, with several assistants. Financial difficulties in 1842 led to the discharge of all missionaries, but in the following years several were re-engaged. The men who accepted these full-time, paid positions became as it were professional Owenites.[1] Their number was not large, though a fairly rapid turn-over meant that there were perhaps as many as thirty men (and women) who had had experience at some time as social missionaries. They were the best-known people in the movement: they lectured and debated publicly, they organized branch activities, they spoke at annual congresses, and their reports and articles were prominent in the *New Moral World*. Each social missionary was stationed in a large town and had a responsibility for the surrounding region. From time to time they were moved around by the Central Board. Their job was not always very enviable and at times required more than a little faith to make it bearable. The following report from George Connard is a wry comment on the other side of the medal which the Bishop of Exeter described. Connard was the newly appointed social missionary for the Wigan district and after two months' labour in the Lancashire towns found them indifferent to his message. He reported:

[1] Some idea of the qualifications expected of a social missionary is given by the entry in the Minute Book, Central Board, A.A.C.A.N., 10 January 1839. On his appointment as S.M. for Hull, James Napier Bailey was examined by the Central Board, with Pare in the chair. He was given a study list which included all the major works of Owen and Thompson, as well as titles by Locke, Adam Smith, McCulloch, Malthus, Godwin, Helvetius, Mirabeau, Volney and Minter Morgan.

In consequence of there being but one room, namely, at Wigan, and no district funds, I have been obliged to go round the districts on foot, and at my own expense, which, but for the cause I am engaged in, would be very unpalatable; for I have several times returned with aching bones, disappointed hopes, and skeleton pockets. My initiation into 'Holy Orders' has hitherto not been of the most agreeable kind. I like to be busily engaged; but at the same time I want my labours to be productive of benefit to society: as it is, Wigan alone can avail themselves of my services; and I shall hail with joy the announcement of our other friends that they are prepared for me.[1]

Recruitment of the social missionaries was mainly from the ranks of those who had already proved their capabilities as voluntary workers in the Owenite cause. They were mostly intelligent working men who had educated themselves, served an apprenticeship in the Short Time Committees, unstamped press agitation or cooperative movement, and then moved on to become teachers or radical journalists. The first six missionaries appointed in 1838 may be taken as typical. Lloyd Jones was a Manchester fustian cutter of Irish origin and had been an active cooperator and radical reformer.[2] He was appointed to the London district. James Rigby had worked in a Manchester cotton mill and had later become a teacher.[3] He had opened a pioneer cooperative store in Salford and was a Short Timer and member of the National Regeneration Society before going as social missionary to Birmingham. From the same stable as Jones and Rigby came Robert Buchanan, a Scots weaver-schoolmaster who was appointed to Manchester.[4] The Glasgow joiner and ex-Orbistonian, Alexander Campbell, went to Liverpool.[5] Frederick Hollick, a self-

---

[1] *New Moral World*, 22 August 1840. Connard had attained modest notoriety the previous year when as an insolvent debtor he had refused to take what he considered was a religious oath and had been remanded in Lancaster gaol by the Chief Commissioner of the insolvent debtors court. See *New Moral World*, 14 September, 5, 19 October 1839.

[2] Lloyd Jones (1811–1886) was born at Bandon in Ireland and came to Manchester in 1827, where he followed his father's trade of fustian cutting. He helped to found and run a cooperative store in Salford, 1829–31, and after his tours of duty as a social missionary in London, Yorkshire and Lancashire became a master tailor in Oxford Street, London. He was later associated with the Christian Socialists and the Cooperative movement and became a successful journalist. For further references see Harrison, *Social Reform in Victorian Leeds*, p. 57.

[3] James Rigby (1802–?) was later Deputy Governor of Queenwood and from about 1853 acted as Owen's personal secretary and attendant. *Northern Star*, 1 January 1842 (memoir, quoting largely from the *Social Reformers' Almanac for 1842*, Leeds, 1842); *Reasoner*, XXIII (1858), 178.

[4] Robert Buchanan (1813–1866) later returned to Glasgow where he edited a local paper and worked with Alexander Campbell. He was the author of several Owenite works (see bibliography).

[5] For Alexander Campbell (1796–1870) see p. 128.

educated mechanic from Birmingham was sent to Glasgow.[1] And at Leeds, John Green, a working man from Manchester, was appointed.[2] Subsequent appointments confirmed the general pattern.[3] In addition to the social missionaries, whose job was mainly organizing in their districts, there were also for a time 'stationed lecturers'. The two categories totalled sixteen persons in 1840.

It was the ambition of every social missionary to see established in the main town of his district a stable organization and permanent base from which to conduct his operations. There are of course various ways in which a voluntary body can accomplish this end, and an investment in bricks and mortar is a well-tried device. As every parish priest knows, there is nothing like a large debt and an ambitious building programme for holding a congregation together. On the other hand, if the faithful are poor in pocket and few in number the burden of real estate is probably best avoided. Most voluntary movements in England, except the churches, have been very shy of investing their resources in buildings and even large trade unions have contented themselves with extremely modest, not to say shabby, offices. The policy of the Owenites in building large meeting halls was therefore unusual, and their experiences may well have strengthened the caution which other voluntary movements displayed. To some extent the Owenites were pushed into this policy by the difficulty of securing places for their meetings. Church and municipal officers became increasingly reluctant to let their halls to a body which had a reputation for advocating blasphemy and immorality. But too much weight should not be placed on this negative argument from necessity. As the Owenite movement from 1835 shifted its emphasis back to its sectarian position, so the need for institutions appropriate to a sect was felt. A permanent, visible home, in which at least a glimpse of the virtues of the new moral world might be caught, would strengthen and encourage the members. Here, if only for an afternoon or evening, there could be a withdrawal from the corrupting pressures of an immoral society. Owenites, as communitarians, were used to thinking in terms of land and buildings and were familiar with the problems of raising capital. In

[1] Frederick Hollick (1813–?) was a fellow student with Holyoake at the Birmingham Mechanics' Institute, whence he graduated to Owenism. He later emigrated to the United States, where he made a name for himself as a lecturer on neuropathy (a system of cure by means of electricity, galvanism, etc.) and writer of popular medical works.
[2] Information on Green is sparse. According to Holyoake he emigrated to America, where he worked for a railway company and was killed by a train.
[3] E.g. John Watts (1818–1887); Robert Cooper (1819–1868); George Jacob Holyoake (1817–1906); George Alexander Fleming; Thomas Simmons Mackintosh (?–1850?); Charles Southwell (1814–1860); John Colier Farn (1815?–?); John Ellis; and Joseph Smith.

comparison with a community a meeting hall was small beer, but it was attractive precisely because it seemed so much more manageable.

The new buildings were named Halls of Science (replacing the earlier designation of Social Institution), for they were to be centres for the dissemination of the new science of society.[1] A fever of building enthusiasm gripped the U.C.S.R.R. for three years, 1839–41, and then quickly subsided. At the Sixth Annual Congress in 1841 it was estimated that £32,000 had been invested in halls of science capable of holding 22,000 people. Sheffield, Huddersfield, Glasgow and Radcliffe Bridge led the way in 1839, and smaller halls of science were opened in Worcester, Yarmouth and Macclesfield. Manchester Hall of Science replaced the earlier Social Institution. It held 3000 people and cost £6000, which was to be raised by selling shares in a building association. The Liverpool Hall cost £5000 and held 1500 people. At Birmingham the Owenites bought a chapel from the Southcottians for £800 and converted it in 1841. Halifax, Stockport and Bristol also built new Halls of Science during 1841, raising the capital by share clubs. These buildings were in addition to premises which were leased elsewhere as in Leeds and London and used as Owenite social institutes. The Halls of Science were planned for a full range of socialist activities, both convivial and educational. Sunday schools, adult evening classes, day schools for children, as well as the large lectures were catered for. Sometimes a small library was provided, and always kitchens for the ubiquitous refreshments. The model for an Owenite Hall of Science was a cross between a mechanics' institute and a Methodist chapel, but unfortunately the Owenites were not able also to adopt the means of survival which these two institutions possessed. Like the Owenite communities of the 1820s, very few of the Halls of Science survived more than two or three years in their original condition. Some had simply to be sold and used for whatever purposes their purchasers wanted. Others were able to continue a transformed existence as a public library (Manchester) or a secular hall (Leicester). Probably the financial burden was too great, especially since it coincided with two other expensive projects—the social missionaries and the Queenwood community. There was something of a conflict of interest between the Central Board, which wanted all the energies of the movement channelled towards a large national community, and the local branches who preferred

---

[1] Full reports of the Halls of Science appeared weekly in the *New Moral World*. See also A. Black, 'Owenite Education, 1839–1857, with Particular Reference to the Manchester Hall of Science' (unpublished Dip. Ed. dissertation, University of Manchester, 1953); and 'Education Before Rochdale (2); the Owenites and the Halls of Science', *Cooperative Review*, XXIX, no. 2 (February, 1955).

to spend their funds on something nearer home. The Owenite Hall of Science may also have suffered from being too ideological in its appearance. The earnest working man or lower middle-class clerk who wanted educational self-improvement or rational amusement could get it at the mechanics' institute without the taint of infidelity; and the political radical would find himself in more congenial company at the Chartist rooms or the Rotunda. Only those who required secular sectarianism would attend regularly at the Owenite Hall.

Branch life, whether based on a brand new Hall of Science or rented rooms, flourished according to a fairly standard pattern. From the weekly or monthly reports which the local secretaries wrote for the *New Moral World* emerges a picture of Sunday schools, adult classes and tea parties with a lecture by the district missionary as the chief event of the week. Excitement rises high when a clerical opponent agrees to enter into public debate; indignation boils up when a member refuses to take a religious oath and is imprisoned, or a local bookseller is charged with selling blasphemous pamphlets. The weekend was the time for social functions, especially dancing for which Owenites became quite notorious. John Finch, reporting the 'first public social festival and ball' of the Liverpool branch of the A.A.C.A.N. conveys faithfully the tone of the occasion:

About two hundred well-dressed males and females, principally of the working classes, sat down to an abundant supply of excellent bun-loaf, bread and butter, tea and coffee. A band of good musicians was in attendance, and the evening's amusements, consisting of dances, marches, songs, duets, recitations, etc, commenced at about eight, and were kept up with great spirit and mirth until twelve o'clock. . . . Lemonade, gingeretta, peppermint, etc, were provided . . . but not a drop of intoxicating drink was used.[1]

Before the dancing began Finch gave a short address in which he admonished his hearers not to be critical of any member's dress or language or manners, but to be charitable towards all. He reminded them 'that all mankind are by nature equal', and hence he hoped that 'there will be no aristocracy of feeling manifested among you this evening, but that you will treat each other with the greatest kindness, like children of one family'. In his report Finch commented that such an evening of rational entertainment gave the members 'a foretaste of the pleasures that will be within the reach of every member of a community, male and female, every evening of their lives. "The kingdom of heaven is like unto a certain king that made a marriage for his son."'

[1] *New Moral World*, 1 December 1838.

Finch's account brings out two fundamental aspects of the Owenite movement at this time. First is the continuing sectarianism which is very similar in its values and attitudes to the Owenite communitarianism of the 1820s in America. The local branch, as Finch said, was a first instalment of community. The activities in the Hall of Science were a part-time version of the New Harmony ideal, or perhaps a preparation for the contemporary community at Queenwood. Second is the handling of social class. Although the existence and in fact the problems of class differences are recognized, they are to be played down rather than exploited. A majority of the branch members was from the working class but the Association was intended to unite All Classes of All Nations. Again, the situation was similar to the earlier communities. Given the great economic and cultural gulf between classes and the strength of class consciousness in early Victorian England, the Owenites could not ignore the matter entirely. But they tried to disregard class as an activating force, to set it aside as irrelevant to the main task of changing society through moral suasion and environmental improvement. If members would charitably ignore shabby clothes and a working-class accent the bogey of class would be exorcized: treat all men as if they were equal and they will in fact become equal.

The social missionaries, halls of science and branches of the A.A.C.A.N. which have so far been mentioned were all associated with London and the industrial parts of the country. Reports in the *New Moral World* confirm this impression of the geography of British Owenism. Like Chartism and other popular movements of the time, the strongholds of Owenism were in the North and Midlands, with relatively little impact in the South and South-West. London held a special position in the movement. It was the scene of many of Owen's personal labours, from the time when he first launched his community plans at the City of London Tavern in 1817 to his last enfeebled proclamations of the millennium in the 1850s. The population of the metropolis was much larger than any other single city and it was possible to maintain Owenite activities in several different centres: the West End, Finsbury, Lambeth, Tower Hamlets, Hackney. North London was an area of skilled craftsmen and lower middle-class tradesmen—the groups from which Owenism derived its strongest support. Beginning with Mudie's Economical Society in 1821, London had a continuous Owenite organization for nearly thirty years. For ten years after Owen's return from America the Owenite headquarters was established in a succession of institutes in Grays Inn Road, Charlotte Street and Burton Street. Finally in 1840 Branch A.1. of the U.C.S.R.R. opened a new Social Institution in John Street, off

Tottenham Court Road, and this became the best-known centre of London Owenism. Alfred Russel Wallace, the Darwinist, remembered attending the John Street Institute with his brother, who was then a journeyman carpenter:

It was really a kind of club or mechanics' institute for advanced thinkers among workmen, and especially for the followers of Robert Owen. . . . Here we sometimes heard lectures on Owen's doctrines, or on the principles of secularism or agnosticism, as it is now called; at other times we read papers or books, or played draughts, dominoes, or bagatelle, and coffee was also supplied to any who wished for it. It was here that I first made acquaintance with Owen's writings. . . . I also received my first knowledge of the arguments of sceptics, and read . . . Paine's 'Age of Reason'.[1]

The leaders and most of the members of the London Owenite movement were from the skilled working and lower middle classes, with some support from professional and business men. After the cooperative and labour exchange period the leaders of metropolitan working-class radicalism withdrew from active leadership in the organization, being mainly concerned with political agitation.[2] But they continued to look more or less benevolently on the work of the Institute and more than one could have echoed Henry Hetherington's *Last Will and Testament* that he remained an Owenite socialist at heart. A similar rationalist faith coupled with a taste for radical causes was characteristic of the middle-class Owenites—William Devonshire Saull, a wine merchant and keen amateur geologist; William Henry Ashurst, a solicitor whose home was a salon for the friends of all liberal causes; and Thomas Allsop, a member of the stock exchange, who refused to serve on a jury at the Old Bailey because he believed that the accused should not be held responsible for their actions as they were the victims of bad institutions.[3]

Outside London the strongest Owenite centre was Manchester. The early cooperative societies had flourished strongly in the area from 1828 to 1832, and in Salford especially Owenism struck deep roots. A very able

[1] Alfred Russel Wallace, *My Life* (2 vols., London, 1905), I, 87. There is another description, recalling a little later period at the Institute, in W. E. Adams, *Memoirs of a Social Atom* (2 vols., London, 1903), II, 313–14. The Institute continued until shortly after Owen's death in 1858, though from 1846 its name was changed to the Literary and Scientific Institution.

[2] Francis Place, describing Sunday morning lectures on political economy and similar topics at the London Working Men's Association in 1836–37, stated: 'Nearly all the men who attended these discussions had been Owenites, but had abandoned it in consequence of their being unable to foresee any practical result'. B.M. Add. MSS. 27,835, f. 132.

[3] There are entries for Saull (1784–1855), Ashurst (1792–1855) and Allsop (1795–1880) in the *D.N.B.*, but details of their Owenite interests have to be gleaned from references in the Owenite press.

group of young leaders emerged: E. T. Craig, James Rigby, James Hole, Lloyd Jones, Robert Cooper—men who later became social missionaries and communitarians. They sat at the feet of Rowland Detrosier, a self-educated deist and radical, who lectured at the breakaway New Mechanics' Institution.[1] The trade unions under the leadership of John Doherty went Owenite, and institutions such as the Manchester and Salford Association for the Promotion of Cooperative Knowledge spread socialist doctrines. The first Cooperative Congress met in Manchester in May 1831. Five years of intensive organization and propaganda came to an end in 1834, but sufficient remained to provide a base for a branch of the A.A.C.A.N. in 1835. The early success with day and Sunday schools continued, and the opening of the great Hall of Science in Campfield in 1839 reasserted Manchester's pre-eminence in the movement. In the same year the Salford branch of the U.C.S.R.R., with 440 members, was the largest in the country. In the surrounding towns of Lancashire and Cheshire was the greatest concentration of Owenite branches in any county.

No other single town in the North quite equalled Manchester's record as an Owenite centre. But in Yorkshire several places were distinguished by notable leaders and a continuing organization. Leeds, perhaps by virtue of its size and location, was most in the news. Joshua Hobson,[2] after his move there from Huddersfield, published both the *New Moral World* and the Chartist *Northern Star*, and with John Francis Bray and later James Hole in the town it was an area in which socialist ideas could be aired. Huddersfield was another Owenite stronghold, under the leadership of Thomas Hirst, Christopher Tinker and Lawrence

---

[1] A valuable monograph which gathers together the available primary and secondary material is Gwyn A. Williams, *Rowland Detrosier: A Working Class Infidel, 1800–34*, Borthwick Papers, no. 28 (York, 1965). See also E. T. Craig's 'Socialism in England: Historical Reminiscences', *American Socialist*, 13 December 1877, 3, 10, 17, 24 January 1878.

[2] Joshua Hobson (1810–1876), a joiner by trade, was a leading Huddersfield radical. He was active in the Short Time movement and was imprisoned for publishing his un-stamped paper, the *Voice of the West Riding*, in 1833. He moved to Leeds in the autumn of 1834 and set up as a printer and bookseller in partnership with Alice Mann, the widow of a Leeds radical bookseller. In 1836 he was again imprisoned for selling unstamped papers; on his release he continued as a printer and publisher of radical journals. He was elected Chartist councillor for Holbeck ward on the Leeds Town Council in 1843. In 1846 he returned to Huddersfield and was appointed Surveyor of Highways for Fartown and worked under the Huddersfield Improvement Commission until 1854, when he became editor of the *Huddersfield Chronicle* (until 1871) and of the *Huddersfield Weekly News* (1871–76). See obituary in *Huddersfield Weekly News*, 13 May 1876; *Northern Star*, 9 December 1843 (details of his early life given by Hobson in a speech welcoming the release of Oastler from gaol); D. F. E. Sykes, *History of Huddersfield and Its Vicinity* (Huddersfield, 1898), pp. 301–2.

Pitkethly.[1] By contrast in Halifax, which had an early cooperative society, Owenism was weaker and the Chartist movement stronger. Bradford had a notable republican tradition and the Owenites there regularly celebrated Paine's birthday.[2] In Sheffield Owenism was mainly promoted by Isaac Ironside, a radical tradesman whose flamboyant personality took him in and out of most of the reform movements of the 1830s to the 1850s.[3] Elsewhere the local variations continue. Birmingham, the main centre of Owenism in the Midlands, was led by William Pare,[4] William Hawkes Smith and John Rabone, and the Mechanics' Institute was an important recruiting agency. Other Midland towns with a continuous Owenite organization were Leicester and Coventry; but reports in the *New Moral World* suggest that given a local leader with sufficient time and enthusiasm it was possible to start an Owenite branch in 1839–41 in a great many places.

[1] Thomas Hirst (?–1833) lectured and toured for the cooperative cause in 1831–33. He was an active member of the Huddersfield Cooperative Trading and Manufacturing Association, 1829; and played an active part in the third and fourth Cooperative Congresses.

Christopher Tinker (?–1844) was a radical printer and bookseller in Huddersfield who was imprisoned for selling unstamped papers. In 1842 he emigrated to America, intending to select a site for the Owenite community of Equality in Wisconsin, but died in Milwaukee without being able to take part in the venture. See his son's letters in the Thomas C. Tinker MSS., Wisconsin State Historical Society.

Lawrence Pitkethly (?–1858) was active in local reform causes, including Chartism, in the 1830s. He had plans for a community of West Riding Owenites in 1837 and was interested in emigration. In the summer of 1842 he visited the United States and on his return founded the British Emigrants' Mutual Aid Society, to acquire land for a colony in the West. His valuable letters on his American tour appeared in the *Northern Star*, 1 April–29 July 1843. See also Dr John Smyles, *Emigration to the United States: A Letter Addressed to Mr Pitkethly of Huddersfield* (London, 1842); obituary in *Huddersfield Chronicle*, 5 June 1858. Useful recent studies are Michael Brook, 'Lawrence Pitkethly, Dr Smyles, and Canadian Revolutionaries in the United States, 1842', *Ontario History*, LVII, no. 2 (June 1965), 79–84; J. T. Ward, 'Centenary of Lawrence Pitkethley's Death', *Huddersfield Daily Examiner*, 2 June 1958; and 'Some Industrial Reformers', *Bradford Textile Society Journal* (1962–63), pp. 125–6.

[2] The veteran Paineite was Squire Farrar, and the chief Owenite in Bradford was Samuel Bower, who was attracted to the mystical socialism of J. P. Greaves, and who later emigrated to America.

[3] Isaac Ironside (1808–1870) finally ended up as a Russophobe and follower of David Urquhart. The fullest treatment of him is in John Salt, 'Isaac Ironside and Education in the Sheffield Region in the First Half of the Nineteenth Century' (unpublished M.A. thesis, Sheffield University, 1960). Also by the same author, 'Isaac Ironside and the Hollow Meadows Farm Experiment', *Yorkshire Bulletin of Economic and Social Research*, XII, no. 1 (March 1960), 45–51.

[4] A summary of William Pare's career (1805–1873) is given in R. G. Garnett, *The Ideology of the Early Cooperative Movement*, First Kent Cooperative Endowment Lecture, University of Kent (Canterbury, 1966).

In one area Owenism developed along very different lines. The largely self-contained industrial region of the North Staffordshire Potteries followed a special interpretation of Owenite doctrine which did not produce the familiar sectarian institutions of orthodox Owenism in its 1835–45 phase. A strong Owenite movement in the Five Towns dated from 1833, rooted in the potters' trade union, and this influence reasserted itself ten years later. Here working-class Owenism was channelled into a scheme of emigration through the enthusiasm of William Evans who edited the *Potters' Examiner*.[1] So successful was Evans that for some time the Potters' Union became virtually nothing but an emigration society. The Potters' Joint Stock Emigration Society, formed in May 1844, was not an Owenite institution: it was not proposed to form a community on the land bought in Wisconsin nor to set up cooperative industry. Nor was emigration as a remedy for social ills unusual in the 1840s: similar schemes were afoot in the West Riding. What distinguished the potters was their complete adoption of Owenite arguments, though for non-Owenite ends.

The *Potters' Examiner* documents the paradox of a wide diffusion of Owenite ideals among the working class and an abandonment of Owen and Owenite institutions. The language and assumptions of Ricardian socialism, the ideals of community and the millennium, the merits of spade husbandry and the right of labourers to the land, are reiterated in letters and editorials. But with the acceptance of Owenite anti-capitalist analysis and Owenite ideals there came a search for some practical way out, some institutional alternative. The problems pressing on the potters were precisely those which had obsessed Owen and his followers in 1817—unemployment and machinery—which was why the potters felt that Owenism spoke to their condition. But the institutional pattern of halls of science, social missionaries and popular lectures did not seem relevant. Owenism in the Potteries was entirely a working-class movement, without any influence from wealthy philanthropists or middle-class tradesmen. Its categories of thought were trade unionist: it eschewed politics (including Chartism, towards which it was nevertheless friendly and tolerant) as irrelevant to labour problems. Evans argued that instead of spending £70 a week to support unemployed union members, or

---

[1] The *Potters' Examiner* ran from 1843 to 1848, but only odd numbers are available after 1845. It is the main source for Owenism in the Potteries and for the Potters' Emigration Society. Useful secondary sources are Harold Owen, *The Staffordshire Potter* (London, 1901); and W. H. Warburton, *The History of Trade Union Organisation in the North Staffordshire Potteries* (London, 1931). The Pottersville, Wisconsin end of the story is outlined in Grant Foreman, 'Settlement of English Potters in Wisconsin', *Wisconsin Magazine of History*, XXI, no. 4 (June 1938), 375–96.

32. Robert Owen (silhouette by Auguste Edouart, 1838)

33. Robert Dale Owen

striking against the introduction of machinery, it would be wiser to re-move the cause of distress, which he said was a surplus of labour: 'make labour scarce and you make it valuable—make it valuable and you make the working man respectable'.[1] And this was to be done by settling some hundreds of families on 20-acre plots of land in Pottersville, Wisconsin. There is no evidence that these North Staffordshire Owenites were conscious of any inconsistencies in their social theories. Owenism for them, as for other groups, was a body of social thought from which they took what they wanted. Of what consequence to them was it if their socialist arguments led to individualist farming in Wisconsin? As one prosperous immigrant farmer echoing his Owenite past put it, he was now 'enjoying the fruits of his own labor'.[2]

The Owenite movement of the 1840s in the Potteries was in a sense a throw-back to the 1820s. But another, and less institutional, way of looking at it is to see in it the extent of Owenite penetration of working-class social consciousness. It was probably some such awareness that led a writer in the *Westminster Review* to remark that Owenism 'is at present, in one form or another, the actual creed of a great proportion of the working classes'.[3] For this reason it is very difficult in some cases to say whether a working-class leader was an Owenite or not. Many men absorbed Owenite views on social and economic questions, some had a definite Owenite phase in their career, most rejected the personal leader-ship of Owen himself. Owenism was never intended as a gospel for the working class, nor for any class, but rather for all men everywhere. The reconstruction of anything like a composite biography of a typical Owenite is therefore more than usually difficult. From the whole history of the movement it is possible to identify about 150 known Owenites, that is people who at some time were associated with an Owenite insti-tution or whose speeches and writings show unmistakable Owenite in-fluence. The actual number about whom more than their name, dates and place of residence are known is smaller still, say about half. This is only a fraction of the membership of the A.A.C.A.N., which was claimed to be 70,000–100,000. But small as the sample is it includes the active leadership of the Owenite movement, and from it certain significant points can be gleaned.

As with the Owenite communities, the leadership of the A.A.C.A.N. was at several levels. Owen, as the Social Father, occupied a special,

[1] *Potters' Examiner*, 15 June 1844.
[2] *Manchester Examiner and Times*, 26 April 1851, Supplement, quoted in Grant Fore-man, p. 393.
[3] *Westminster Review*, April 1839.

patriarchal position, which was both an asset and an embarrassment to the movement. His stature as a national figure with an established reputation was useful for publicity and for ensuring attention from important people; but his desire to direct activities in the direction of his personal whims was resented.[1] Nevertheless, he outlived all Owenite organizations and his presence could never be ignored. Standing close to Owen was a small group of trusted disciples, men like Pare, Finch and Henry Travis, whose business or profession enabled them to give time and money to the cause. They were active at both the national and local levels. The social missionaries formed another layer of leadership, full-time and dedicated organizers, having regional responsibilities. Below them in the branches were voluntary officers—presidents, treasurers, secretaries, trustees, tract distributors—whose only record is the weekly report or occasional letter in the *New Moral World*. This type of organization has a familiar air: it is in fact a prototype for many voluntary bodies in the nineteenth and twentieth centuries.

Take for example the role of the local bookshop. Even today the quickest way of contacting the radical and reform groups in any town is to enquire for the socialist or progressive bookshop. Such stores serve as a focus for local reform agitation and the proprietor is usually a radical himself. In the first half of the nineteenth century radical booksellers were key figures in local movements and their shops were meeting places and centres for the distribution of propaganda. Owenism was essentially a movement of ideas, heavily dependent on the printed word, and a chain of sympathetic radical booksellers across the industrial parts of England was a vital part of the Owenite organization.[2] These booksellers were often also printers, and usually autodidacts. They were subject to frequent government harassment for selling unstamped, blasphemous or seditious publications, and they were handicapped by lack of capital. But their little shops continued year after year, sometimes changing hands, and always able to draw on a fresh supply of young apprentices and shopmen. None of the bookshops was exclusively

---

[1] Owen was always an extremely hard worker in any cause to which he was attached. Robert Dale Owen described his father's work habits in 1832 when Owen was 61: 'He generally rises at 5 or half past five, goes immediately to his institution, takes his meals there and returns about 9 o'clock at night. Yet his health is very good and he does not seem unduly fatigued. I think I can undergo a good deal, but I do not think I could stand what he does.' MS. letter, Robert Dale Owen to James M. Dorsey at New Harmony, 20 October 1832. Dorsey Papers, Indiana Historical Society.

[2] Among the better known were Carpenter, Cleave, Hetherington and Watson in London; Heywood in Manchester; Tinker in Huddersfield; Nicholson in Halifax; Hobson and Mann in Leeds; Ibbotson in Bradford; Guest in Birmingham.

Owenite. Deist, republican, Chartist and trade union papers and pamphlets were printed and sold, emphasizing once again the interconnection between all radical social reform movements in early Victorian England.

Comparison with other movements is helpful in bringing out the effectiveness and limitations of Owenism. As a propaganda machine the Owenite organization was not to be equalled. In the peak years 1839–41 two and a half million tracts were distributed: 1450 lectures were delivered in a year, and Sunday lectures were attended by up to 50,000 weekly. But Owenite rallies never resembled the vast open-air demonstrations of the Chartists, and the A.A.C.A.N. was never a mass movement in the way that Chartism was. To compare an account of a Chartist meeting on the moors at midnight addressed by J. R. Stephens or a Whitsuntide rally in the West Riding under Feargus O'Connor, with the annual celebration of Robert Owen's birthday or a Sunday lecture by the Social Father in the John Street Institute, is to realize the great difference between Chartism and Owenism. Not only is the whole tone of the gatherings different, but so also is their basic purpose. For the Chartists their meeting was an instrument for action; the Owenite meeting was for education, proclamation or even rational amusement. Chartist leaders expected their followers to take industrial or political mass action to get the Six Points of the Charter. The Owenites believed that if Truth were proclaimed loudly and insistently enough people would accept it and the millennium would begin. Mass action in the Chartist sense was not the goal of the A.A.C.A.N., but rather the sectarian values of withdrawal and redemption.

Before the sectarian nature of Owenism is condemned as impractical and visionary it is perhaps salutary to remember that some sects, such as the Primitive Methodists, the Shakers or the Mormons, achieved a high degree of effectiveness. A sect, *per se*, is not necessarily impractical. In fact, for its specific purposes, it is usually quite practical. If sectarian goals are desired then a sect is a logical and practical type of institution, and such was the case with Owenism. The A.A.C.A.N. did not set out to be another Chartist movement or Anti-Corn Law League, but which failed and became a sect by default. Owenism, except in its short trade union phase of 1833–34, was always a sect, and the sectarianism of the A.A.C.A.N. was a logical continuation of those same qualities which were present in the earlier communities. The significance of religious and secular sectarianism in Britain in the nineteenth century has not been explored by historians, and as a consequence a vital dimension is missing in most accounts of the Owenite movement. Instead of trying to force

Owenism into some procrustean bed called the history of the working-class movement it might be more fruitful to examine the history and sociology of sectarianism. It was after all as a dangerous sect that the Bishop of Exeter condemned Owenism; and only a millennial sect could have inspired the boundless hope implied in the title, the Association of All Classes of All Nations.

The Owenite Legacy

1 The Fading of the Communitarian Vision

2 The Literature of Owenism

The Owenite Legacy

In the previous chapters Owenism has been presented as a practical and theoretical response to various personal and social needs. After 1846 the organized Owenite movement disintegrated and it would be tempting to conclude that this was because Owenism was no longer felt to be adequate for its tasks and was accordingly discarded. In Britain the ending of Queenwood and the central Owenite organization was soon followed by the severe economic crisis of 1846–47; in America the second period of communitarian enthusiasm, Fourierist and Owenite, was over by the same date; and it would be convenient for historians if they could assume that the whole business was tidily finished by 1848. In fact, Owenism did not die out, any more than Chartism suddenly disappeared after 10 April 1848. Old Owenite works were republished[1] *and new ones written in the 1850s and later. The vision of the new moral world continued to inspire men, though fresh ideas on how to bring it about had to be found. A transformed Owenism, or perhaps more accurately a legacy of Owenism, is a recognizable element in the philosophy of liberal reform in the 1860s and 1870s.*

If this at first seems surprising it is only because of the fixed categories into which the social history of the nineteenth century has been forced. It has already been shown that Owenism was not the ideology of a particular class, either rising or falling economically in the Marxist sense, but rather a generalized response to the experience of social change. And the problems

---

[1] Minter Morgan reprinted a series of earlier pamphlets in his Phoenix Library, 1849–50. Pare brought out a new edition of Thompson's *Inquiry* (1824) in 1850 and there was a 3rd edition in 1869. Owen's *Life*, 1857–58, reprinted his early pamphlets; and Charles Bray's *Philosophy of Necessity*, 1841, appeared in a 2nd edition in 1863 and a 3rd edition in 1889.

with which Owenites were preoccupied did not come to an end in 1848. Again, the segments of history into which historians chop their periods (such as 1837–48) do not coincide with the physical or intellectual lives of their characters. Men who were in their forties in the 1850s had acquired their Owenism twenty years earlier, and a few who were older had been followers since the 1820s. The mental climate of an age has to be analysed in terms of generations, since men carry forward into their maturity the ideas which they acquired in their formative years. There is a generational lag between the founder of a movement and many of his disciples. The gap is greatest after his death, but it is no less real and hard to bridge during his lifetime, especially if, like Owen, he lives to a great age. Such was the experience of the later Owenites in the 1850s and 1860s.

1 The Fading of the Communitarian Vision

The absence of effective institutions after 1846 faced the Owenites with their biggest problem. In America they were reduced after the ending of the Skaneateles community and the One-Mentians to occasional gatherings in New York for the celebration of Mr Owen's birthday or lectures on social regeneration. In Britain Owen continued to publish a succession of journals, expressive of his personal views. The John Street Institute in London was a forum for lectures and the exchange of Owenite news; and the Redemption Society in Leeds struggled to collect funds for a final attempt at community building. Elsewhere the Social Body was isolated and impotent. The question which haunted Owenites was why, if the principles of Owenism were basically correct (as they believed), the practical results should be so inadequate. Various answers were propounded. First was the argument of Henry Travis that Owen's theories, though sound fundamentally, were vitiated by certain errors which prevented them from being widely accepted; correct these and all would be well. Less sanguine and more widely adopted by Owenites was Charles Bray's conclusion that the majority of men were not yet ready to receive Owenite doctrines: the thraldom of the old immoral world was as yet too strong for the higher ideals of cooperation to gain a hold upon the mass of mankind. A third view regarded the practical, communitarian side of Owenism as sound but condemned Owen's theories as unnecessary or erroneous: thus James Hole and the members of the Redemption Societies. Others felt the need to supplement Owenism by allying it with phrenology (E. T. Craig), or democratic politics (Bronterre

O'Brien). Finally there were those like George Jacob Holyoake who thought the practical efforts of Owenites had been a mistake, and who argued that the spirit of Owenism would be realized through other movements or channels such as consumers' cooperation and secularism.

Common to all members of this diverse group of advanced liberals (as they called themselves from the mid-1850s) was a reluctance to give up their Owenite nostrums and ideas. With some of them this may have been no more than an inability to think beyond the bounds of their intellectual youth; with others it was probably that pride which is found in many old reformers—the dislike of admitting that they may have been mistaken in their judgements. But in the best of them there was something more. They were reluctant to admit the necessity of accepting industrial-capitalist civilization, even though some of them as individuals had done quite well out of it financially. Throughout the late 1840s and the 1850s Owenites continued to discuss the principles upon which societies should be based, the nature of man and his role in society. They were no more ready to accept society in its post-1848 style than they had been earlier. What they desired above all was that man should be able to control his destiny and shape the new society which was emerging, and they felt that all too little progress had been made towards this goal; man was still the victim of circumstances. In their discussions they groped towards a new psychology and a new sociology within the terminology, common also to their non-Owenite contemporaries, of moral, mental and social science. For most of them Owen's theories alone were unsatisfactory, and so vestigial Owenism was supplemented, developed and transformed in a variety of ways. From these changes a pattern of later Owenism appears.

Among the older generation of Owenites Henry Travis and William Pare were content with the smallest modification of traditional Owenism. Both were very close to Owen and were his joint literary executors. Travis (1807–1884) is the stranger of the two and indeed something of an enigma. Like his father and grandfather he was a physician from Scarborough, though he appears to have lived in London a good deal. He was chairman of the Central Board of the U.C.S.R.R. in 1839–40, went to Queenwood for a time, and helped Owen with editorial work in the 1850s. After Owen's death Travis became a self-appointed champion of the master's doctrines, which he preached with increasing dogmatism as late as 1880. In articles and pamphlets throughout the 1860s and 1870s he continued to propound the original Owenite theories of character formation and communitarianism in terms of truth and error with truly

Owen-like repetition.[1] On only one point did he consider Owen to have been wrong, namely his denial of free will and human responsibility. But this defect, argued Travis, was sufficient to account for Owen's failure to get his views accepted, and so Travis laboured obsessively to correct this fatal flaw.

Travis's analysis was to say the least confused. In the first place it is by no means clear that Owen held the strictly determinist views ascribed to him. Second, Travis used his terms so loosely that it is difficult to be sure that he understood the real nature of his subject. In *Moral Freedom Reconciled with Causation* (London, 1865) he drew a convenient line between libertarians and necessitarians, equating the latter with determinists. Yet contemporary necessitarians like Charles Bray took the same position as Travis and distinguished the philosophy of Necessity from the philosophy of Determinism. The significance of Travis's free-will-versus-necessity campaign lies not so much in his precise position as in his concern to establish an accurate view of human nature. The failure of Queenwood, he thought, was caused by Owen's faulty psychology, not by any weakness in the communitarian idea. At Queenwood the children and settlers were in the same position as the lady Owenite's servant who when she was caught robbing her mistress pleaded that she was the creature of circumstances over which she had no control. There was something a little quixotic about Travis's attempt to rehabilitate communitarianism in the eyes of cooperators and trade unionists by the 1870s.[2] Almost the only change from the original Owenite plans for villages of cooperation which he allowed was to rename the system 'Effectualism'. For the rest, enlightened benevolence and education, propagated by an élite band of effectualists would be sufficient to begin the new system. As he blandly remarked: 'The only reason why it has not been done has been that men and women have not had the requisite knowledge, and therefore have not had, and could not have, the requisite enlightened goodness.'[3]

As for Travis so for William Pare (1805–1873) cooperative stores and

---

[1] In addition to the works listed in the bibliography Travis also wrote articles in the *Cooperator* (1866–70), the *Bee Hive* (1876), and the *American Socialist* (1877–78). Biographical details are sparse but see E. T. Craig, *Memoir and In Memoriam of Henry Travis, M.D., English Socialist* (Manchester, 1884).

[2] Travis referred to 'my good friend Mr George Potter' and distributed 200 free copies of *Effectual Reform in Man and Society* to the delegates to the Trades Union Congress at Newcastle in 1876. Travis, *A Manual of Social Science* (London, 1877), p. 7. His last work, *English Socialism* (London, Manchester, 1880) was a series of tracts designed to present Owenism (or 'Advanced Cooperation' as he called it) to the working classes.

[3] Travis, *Effectual Reform in Man and Society* (London, 1875), p. 67.

manufactures were only a limited and rudimentary form of cooperation. 'We must not be content to remain a nation of mere shopkeepers,' urged Pare in 1868, 'cooperation must result in an entire reorganization of society.'[1] Although he organized the first modern Cooperative Congress in 1869 and was first secretary of the Central Cooperative Board, Pare retained his earlier communitarian vision. Ralahine was for him still relevant, though it was thirty-seven years since he had briefly visited the short-lived community.[2] His prosperity in the iron business did not blunt that condemnation of capitalist society which he had first learned from William Thompson and whose memory he cherished.[3] Pare, the son of a Birmingham cabinet maker, had a broad experience as a radical in the 1820s and 1830s,[4] but it was his Owenism which remained the dominant element in his philosophy of social reform and which, through his reputation as a statistician, he was able to present at gatherings of social scientists.[5] Two years before his death he presided over the festival commemorating the centenary of Owen's birth. For Pare, Owen remained a hero always and Owenism the only valid social truth.

Few of the later Owenites subscribed to so pure a version of the master's teachings as did Pare and Travis. The need to supplement Owenism with other social and psychological theories had of course been felt much earlier, and no philosophy had been more attractive for this purpose than phrenology.[6] Originating in Vienna with Franz Joseph Gall, an anatomist, and his collaborator, Johann Gaspar Spurzheim,

---

[1] *Cooperator*, 11 April 1868.

[2] Pare, *Cooperative Agriculture* (London, 1870), in which he suggested that the Ralahine community experiment offered a solution to the Irish land problem, then much in the news.

[3] See Pare's preface to his edition of Thompson's *Inquiry* (1850). Pare was one of the trustees of Thompson's estate, left for the purpose of founding communities, and from 1833 waged a long but finally unsuccessful legal struggle with relatives who contested the bequest.

[4] In addition to his work as an Owenite cooperator Pare was a leading member of the Birmingham Political Union, and was elected to the first Birmingham Town Council in 1836. He was active in the struggle against Church rates and was a Poor Law Guardian. He was the first Superintendant Registrar of Births, Deaths and Marriages in Birmingham but resigned in 1840 after the Bishop of Exeter's charges of the impropriety of such an office being held by a socialist.

[5] *Claims of Capital and Labour* (London, 1854); *Equitable Commerce* (London, 1856); *Plan for the Suppression of the Predatory Classes* (London, 1862). Pare was said to be writing a biography of Owen at one time but this was never published. *Report of . . . the Festival in Commemoration of the Centenary Birthday of Robert Owen* (London, 1871), p. 4.

[6] There is at present no satisfactory study of phrenology in Britain, but J. C. Flugel, *A Hundred Years of Psychology, 1833–1933* (London, 1933), chap. 3, is useful. For America see John D. Davies, *Phrenology; Fad and Science* (New Haven, Conn., 1955).

phrenology was popularized in Britain by George Combe, who maintained a prolific output of phrenological publications from 1819 onwards. In America Combe's influence was reinforced by Orson S. Fowler's works and there rapidly developed a vigorous propaganda for the new 'science', which by the 1830s boasted societies and journals on both sides of the Atlantic. The claim of phrenology was to have established the localization in the brain of various mental traits which could be diagnosed by an examination of the skull. A person's intellectual and moral character could thus be ascertained with scientific accuracy by reading the bumps on his head. To liberals of all shades this suggested interesting possibilities. It offered an alternative to metaphysical explanations of human behaviour. It was eminently democratic, since particular bumps were not the monopoly of any one section of society. And it seemed to point the way to a truly rational organization of society. For the first time it appeared possible to 'put the right man in the right place',[1] to regulate education and legislation upon rational principles, and check vice and encourage virtue at their source. Formally Owenism and phrenology were opposing social philosophies, for it was difficult to reconcile Owen's categorical insistence that man's character is fashioned almost exclusively by his social environment with the phrenological claim to discover innate mental characteristics.[2] But since the function of both systems was to provide an analysis of human nature and a critique of existing society based on very similar assumptions and attitudes, in practice a reconciliation of the two was by no means impossible. For Archibald James Hamilton and George Jacob Holyoake phrenology was only a step on the road to Owenism; Hawkes Smith subscribed to both philosophies simultaneously; and for two later Owenites—E. T. Craig and Charles Bray—phrenology provided a vital element in their reconstruction of a viable social theory.

Edward Thomas Craig has been introduced earlier as a pioneer Manchester cooperator and organizer of Ralahine. After the sudden collapse of that community he made a living as a teacher and lecturer, and

[1] Gall the Younger, *Practical Uses of Phrenology* (Glasgow, 1856), inscription on title page.

[2] There were two main periods of dispute between the Owenites and phrenologists. The first was started in 1824 when Combe published an article entitled 'Phrenological Analysis of Mr Owen's New Views of Society' in his *Phrenological Journal*, I (1823–24), 218–37. Owen repudiated this as a travesty of his views and demanded a published correction (MS. letters, Owen to Combe, 30 January, 26 February, 4 March 1824, in Combe Papers, Edinburgh, 7213/154–9, and replies by Combe in letter books, 1822–24, 1824–28). The *Cooperative Magazine* (1826–28) continued the discussion. The second series of arguments began in 1835. See *New Moral World*, 3, 11, 18, 25 April, 2 May 1835; and *Phrenological Journal*, IX (1834–36), 489–94.

later as a journalist. His long life stretched from memories of the Luddites and Peterloo to the new socialism of H. M. Hyndman and William Morris. Phrenology he thought was the missing element which would have made Owen's plans practicable. In the 1890s Craig would sit in the garden of Kelmscott House, telling stories of his early cooperative days and reading the bumps of irreverent young socialists like George Bernard Shaw. The interesting jumble of reminiscences which appeared in 1877–78 as 'Socialism in England'[1] showed Craig to be an unrepentant communitarian and a defender of Owen's views. But it was Owenism combined with much else—everything in fact from progressive education to fresh-air faddism and dietary reform. He was still searching for a new moral world but in the process had become almost a pathological collector of reform causes.

The same was true in a more sophisticated way of Charles Bray (1811–1884), a ribbon manufacturer who became the leader of the Coventry intelligentsia.[2] On the famous bear-skin beneath the acacia tree in his garden at Rosehill, George Eliot, George Combe, Ralph Waldo Emerson and other liberal luminaries argued their philosophical differences. Under the impact of Bray's agnosticism George Eliot lost her religious faith, and even consented to have her head shaved in order that her bumps might be studied. Bray had come to Owenism in the 1830s, having shed his earlier Evangelicalism and developed an admiration for Abram Combe and the Orbiston experiment. His experiences as a manufacturer and social investigator in Coventry convinced him that subsistence wages were all that the labourer could ever achieve under capitalism. Since he had come to believe that the labourer was entitled to the full product of his labour, Bray attacked competitive society and argued the Owenite case for communitarianism. He attended the opening of Queenwood and for a time entertained great hopes for it. In the first edition of his *Philosophy of Necessity* (London, 1841) the social and economic analysis was Owenite, and a long appendix by his sister-in-law, Mary Hennell, surveyed the various communities which had been attempted up to that time. By way of practical effort he helped to found the Coventry Labourers' and Artisans' Cooperative Society, which first provided gardens for working men and then developed cooperative trading. To provide a mouthpiece for his liberal views he bought a local newspaper, the *Coventry Herald*, in 1846 and ran it for over twenty years.

---

[1] *American Socialist*, II (1877)–III (1878).

[2] The main source for Bray's life is his autobiography, *Phases of Opinion and Experience During a Long Life* (London, 1879). There are also useful letters from Bray to George Combe in the Combe Papers.

Bray's development forward from Owenism was the result of several different experiences and provides a case-history of an Owenite intellectual. The ending of Queenwood necessitated a rethinking of his communitarian convictions, and in particular an alternative answer to the problem of how to effect 'the re-union of capital and labour—by the labourer himself becoming a capitalist, and the owner of the machinery with which he produces'.[1] From the late 1840s he began to use the term 'Organization of Industry'. Unlike some other Owenites he was able to give an exact meaning to this phrase by virtue of his position as a manufacturer. The Coventry ribbon industry was in a transitional stage between the domestic and factory systems, and in the 1850s the curious anomaly of the cottage factory developed.[2] This was the adoption of steam power in the weaver's home by means of a steam engine placed at the end of a row of weavers' cottages and connected to each separate workshop by a shafting which ran the length of the row through the partition walls of the houses. The object of this arrangement was to enable the domestic weavers to compete with the steam-powered factories, but for Bray it offered exciting cooperative or even communitarian possibilities. He had always sided with the domestic weavers in their struggle to maintain the traditional agreed list of prices, preferring the old-style master's paternalism and sense of obligation towards his workers to the under-cutting and competition of the new masters. Now he saw in the cottage factory a new way to community. Bray's plan was for squares of three or four hundred houses, with a steam engine to provide power, and as much land attached to each house as a man could cultivate.[3] In this version of the Owenite parallelogram individual homes and interests were preserved, but it was hoped that in time they would weaken and be replaced by communal facilities. No such squares were ever built and the cottage factories were abandoned after the great strike of 1860.

Long before this Bray had realized that his earlier expectation of the speed of communitarian advance would have to be revised. With the help of phrenology he worked out a philosophy which he thought was

[1] Bray, *Philosophy of Necessity* (London, 1841), II, 407. In the second edition of this work (1863) Bray substituted a chapter entitled 'The Socialist Utopia' for the earlier chapter on 'Social Reform'.

[2] For this and several of the ideas in the following two paragraphs see the excellent monograph by John Prest, *The Industrial Revolution in Coventry* (London, 1960). Also useful for the Coventry background is Peter Searby, *Coventry Politics in the Age of the Chartists, 1836–1848*, Coventry and North Warwickshire History Pamphlets, no. 1 (Coventry, 1964).

[3] Bray, *Philosophy of Necessity* (1863 edn.), p. 410. Also Bray, *An Essay Upon the Union of Agriculture and Manufactures* (London, 1844).

more in keeping with social reality than Owenism. He called it the philosophy of Necessity, or Causation. 'All Science', he explained, can 'be resolved into the knowledge of antecedence and consequence—of cause and effect.'[1] Man can know 'neither the beginning nor the end of things . . . but only the order in which one event follows another, or in which one sensation follows another'. If we know the motives of an individual and also his character and disposition we can infer unerringly the manner in which he will act. Anticipating the usual objection that this would do away with free will Bray denied that the free agency of man was annihilated: 'true necessity is not opposed to that which is voluntary, but to that which is contingent. It is undoubtedly true . . . that man can always do as he pleases; but what he pleases to do will ever depend upon his mental constitution (which is only another word for himself) and the circumstances in which he is placed.' This was the view of Owen in the 1820s, but subsequently he emphasized the role of circumstances almost to the exclusion of 'original constitution'. To redress the balance Bray brought in phrenology with its limits set by the bumps on the head. The result was a philosophy of social reform which promised that 'our educational and political systems can be properly based, in accordance with the nature of the being to be educated and governed'. Bray was more successful than Travis in constructing a neo-Owenite philosophy, though much of it was unoriginal and heavily dependent on Bentham and J. S. Mill. Today the paradox of free will and determinism with which Bray and Travis wrestled seems sterile and remote. Only in the novels of Bray's brilliant pupil, George Eliot, do the implications of the doctrine of consequences come alive through the actions of the men and women she described.

The fashionable slogan in vogue with social reformers of the Bray stamp after 1848 was the Organization of Industry, or the Organization of Labour. Inspired by Louis Blanc and the national workshops in Paris, the phrase was used to denote any scheme of cooperative production or profit-sharing. The basic idea was that the antagonism of capital and labour would be eliminated once the worker had a share in the capital or prosperity of an undertaking. From there it would be possible to develop higher forms of communitarian life. An even more popular label was Association, which also had strong French (Fourierist) overtones. It was used to cover almost any social activity from cooperative communities to free public libraries and civic wash-houses. The germ of association could be discovered in the most unlikely corners of society, and it encouraged

[1] The quotations in this paragraph are from Bray, *Philosophy of Necessity* (1863 edn.), pp. 2, 7, 21.

the belief that social action was making headway despite the collapse of communitarian plans. The 'associative principle' was at work in society at large and its ultimate triumph was only a matter of time.[1] For Owenites this was a very comforting doctrine indeed. As James Hole put it, almost everyone is now a socialist without knowing it.[2]

At the same time that he was engaged in the affairs of the communitarian Redemption Society, James Hole (1820–1895) was publishing a series of *Lectures on Social Science and the Organization of Labor* (London, 1851). His early Owenism which he had acquired as a youth in Manchester seemed to him unsatisfactory because it circumscribed practical operations too narrowly. He still retained his Owenite critique of *laissez-faire* society, but suggested that the socialist no longer had 'to cut up mankind to pattern, and initiate society into some Owenian parallelogram'. The precise form of socialism could be left to the future, so long as the doctrine was established. 'In what forms the Associative power of society will finally manifest itself,' he wrote, 'it is neither possible nor necessary to predict. We need not lose ourselves in speculating for the future. In social as in individual progress it is ever the wisest to do efficiently the duty that lies nearest. Effort and experience will alone accomplish true social reform.' Twenty years later Hole was still advocating association, and in the meantime this philosophy had taken him into the mechanics' institute movement, working-class housing and consumers' cooperation in Leeds.[3] Later in London he supported similar social reform movements, and his final effort was on behalf of nationalization of the railways.[4]

The use of the term association is at first somewhat misleading, as it suggests that Owenism was largely supplanted by Fourierism. In Britain this was not so. Although Fourierist ideas were circulating in the 1820s,[5] it was not until 1840 that a Fourierist journal and organization were established, and even then the movement gained little support. A few Owenites, notably Hugh Doherty, were attracted to Fourierism, but for

---

[1] Discussion of association is found in such journals as the *Leader, Howitts' Journal, Cooper's Journal, Spirit of the Age, Christian Socialist*. The old Owenite, George Mudie, in his *Solution of the Portentious Enigma of Modern Civilisation* (London, 1849) argued that successful Organization of Labour could only be effected in self-sufficient communities.

[2] James Hole, *Lectures on Social Science* (London, 1851), p. v. These lectures had appeared previously in the *Truth Seeker and Present Age* (1849–50). Quotations in the following paragraph are from *Lectures*, pp. vii, xi.

[3] Details are in Harrison, *Social Reform in Victorian Leeds*.

[4] James Hole, *National Railways: An Argument for State Purchase* (London, 1893).

[5] The London Cooperative Society published a translation of Fourier's *Political Economy Made Easy* in 1828. For a general account see Richard K. P. Pankhurst, 'Fourierism in Britain', *International Review of Social History*, I (1956), 398–432.

34. E. T. Craig

35. George Jacob Holyoake

36. James Bronterre O'Brien
(from *The Penny Satirist*, 1840)

the most part Fourierism was just one more store-house from which social ideas could be appropriated as necessary. Theoretically Owenites and Fourierists differed in their approach to the essence of human nature, religion and property, but in practice the two main branches of utopian socialism were often not far apart.[1] Few of the reformers who called themselves associationists were Fourierists, in the sense that they were either disciples of Fourier or advocates of phalansteries. But they used a vocabulary of associationism as an alternative to Owenite terminology which had become an embarrassment. In America Fourierism was much more formidable. Under the leadership first of Albert Brisbane[2] and then of the transcendentalists of Brook Farm it became the dominant form of socialism in the 1840s. Yet here too it developed into something very different from Fourier's original plans, and for Horace Greeley and the contributors to his New York *Tribune* it was a banner under which to unite a wide variety of social reformers. What was left of Owenism was swept into this general reform front. Fourierism was the last widespread attempt at a communitarian solution to social problems before the institutions of individualism had become so firmly based as to make efforts at challenging them appear quite impracticable.

All the later Owenites considered so far retained a belief in communitarianism, variously interpreted. But there were others who abandoned it and looked elsewhere for the realization of their earlier vision of a new moral world. George Jacob Holyoake (1817–1906) worked in a Birmingham iron foundry before becoming a social missionary.[3] He came to Owenism via phrenology, Unitarianism and the local mechanics' institute, and was at first an enthusiastic communitarian—even to the extent of forming a little community in a house with three fellow students from the mechanics' institute. But he soon became more interested in rational religion than in communitarianism and his anti-clerical activities were not favoured by the Central Board. By the time that Queenwood was struggling through its last months he was openly critical of community building, and had come to regard socialism as primarily a movement for

---

[1] On his visit to the United States in 1844 Owen noted the spread of Fourierism and welcomed it as an intermediate stage on the road to the Rational System. He urged his followers to be friendly with the Fourierists. *New Moral World*, 6, 13 December 1844, 11 January 1845.

[2] Albert Brisbane's *Social Destiny of Man* (Philadelphia, Penn., 1840) became the main work on Fourierism in America and Britain. On American Fourierism see A. E. Bestor, 'Albert Brisbane—Propagandist for Socialism in the 1840s', *New York History*, XXVIII (1947), 128–58.

[3] In addition to Holyoake's autobiographies and his voluminous output of books and pamphlets listed in the bibliography, see McCabe, *Life and Letters of George Jacob Holyoake*.

R

freethought. After the collapse of the central Owenite organization he began the *Reasoner* in 1846 to continue the rationalist traditions of Owenism. In addition the paper was to be communistic [meaning co-operative] in social matters, utilitarian in morality, and republican in politics.

Holyoake called his new philosophy secularism. In 1841 he was still a theist, but the trial and imprisonment for blasphemy of his fellow Owenite, Charles Southwell, was, as he said, 'the cradle of my doubts and the grave of my religion'.[1] Holyoake was himself imprisoned for blasphemy in 1842–43 and suffered considerable hardship, becoming thereby a martyr. At that time he described his beliefs as atheism, but later realized that this was unnecessarily provocative. He experimented with a re-definition of rationalism,[2] but finally adopted the term secularism, which was calculated to be more respectable and expressive of a distinctive position. Secularism was basically the religion of doubt. It aimed to provide a system of ethics and morality which was independent of revealed religion, amenable to rational discussion and progressively discoverable by scientific advance. Holyoake worked for the creation of a central Secular Society from 1851, and in the 1850s about thirty-five provincial Secular Societies were founded. They resembled in many respects the branches of the U.C.S.R.R. and were the most direct descendants in personnel and organization of the old Owenite body. However, Holyoake's concern for respectability led to opposition within the Secular Society, and in 1860 he was replaced as leader by the more militant Bradlaugh. Holyoake's agnosticism was shared by many old Owenites[3] and it was not difficult to organize them in a new anti-religious sect. But a more promising future for the realization of Owenite principles seemed to lie in Holyoake's second enthusiasm (which he often interspersed with his secularism), namely, consumers' cooperation.

At the end of his life Holyoake declared that of all the causes in which

---

[1] Holyoake, *Spirit of Bonner in the Disciples of Jesus* (London, 1842), p. 4. Holyoake's imprisonment was for blasphemous statements made at a meeting in Cheltenham where he was lecturing as a social missionary. He published an account of his trial as the *History of the Last Trial by Jury for Atheism in England* (London, 1850). Charles Southwell (1814–1860) was imprisoned for publishing a blasphemous article on 'The Jew Book' in his journal, the *Oracle of Reason*. He was supported by William Chilton, a Bristol printer, and Malthus Questell Ryall, a London engraver. When Southwell went to gaol Holyoake took over the editorship of the paper. Southwell had been a soldier and an actor, and was a vigorous, melodramatic lecturer. He became a social missionary and in 1856 emigrated to Auckland, New Zealand, where he died.

[2] Holyoake, *Rationalism: A Treatise for the Times* (London, 1845).

[3] Charles Bray's agnosticism has already been mentioned. James Hole was the (anonymous) translator of Ernest Renan's *Life of Jesus* (London, 1864).

he had worked the cooperative movement stood highest in his esteem. Yet consumers' cooperation in the 1850s was very different from the thriving cooperative movement at the end of the century. A majority of the early cooperative stores did not survive beyond 1834–35 and consumers' co-operation had to be reborn in the 1840s. Holyoake later romanticized the Owenite Rochdale Pioneers who started their famous Toad Lane store in 1844. For a decade cooperation grew but slowly and only in the 1860s was there anything that could legitimately be called a 'cooperative advance'. Nevertheless, the founding of cooperative societies and the enthusiasm manifested for them in various quarters faced Owenite intellectuals with a dilemma. On the one hand the lead in most of these ventures was taken by working-class Owenites, and at a time when Owenism was hard pressed to show any practical results from its principles. Owenite ideals of community, education and the redemption of labour were frequently written into the rules of the societies. On the other hand it was by no means clear that store-keeping was the way to the new moral world: in fact the qualities encouraged by trading could be diametrically opposed to those required for life in a community. Consumers' coopera-tion could be a means of reconciling rather than rejecting the old im-moral world. Owenites therefore had to decide where they stood in relation to the new developments. Bray and Travis classified them as a lower or rudimentary form of cooperation, in contrast with the higher (communitarian) forms, which alas the working classes were not yet ready for. Holyoake embraced the idea of the cooperative store whole-heartedly and abandoned communitarianism completely. He described the Rochdale society as a venture in Self Help by the People.[1] Yet even among those who had moved furthest from their original communi-tarian beliefs there was always a desire to see in the cooperative movement something nobler than a trading concern. The pages of the *Cooperator* in the 1860s are full of such idealistic discussions as 'Coopera-tion: the Social and Moral Regenerator of Society'.[2] It is almost as if the stronger and narrower the practices of the societies became the wider

---

[1] Holyoake, *Self Help by the People: History of Cooperation in Rochdale. Part I, 1844–1857* (London, 1858); *Part II, 1857–1877* (London, 1878). Holyoake's role was similar to that of Dr William King in 1828–30, in that the origin of several new societies was said to be due to a reading of his work.

[2] A prize lecture by J. C. Farn, in the *Cooperator*, 15 June 1867. John Colier Farn was a Coventry Owenite and social missionary. A self-educated working man from a radical home background, he was active in the unstamped press, trade union and Chartist move-ments. He was an associate of Charles Bray and became a leading figure in the cooperative movement of the 1860s. See 'The Autobiography of a Living Publicist', *Reasoner*, XXII (1857), XXIII (1858).

grew the claims of cooperation as an ideal. There is probably a gap here between the rank and file members of the societies and the national leadership which, heavily weighted with Owenites, wanted a philosophy of social reform. Holyoake became the chief publicist for the new ideology of cooperation, with its emphasis on the cooperative store and the Rochdale model; and the publication of his two-volume study of the *History of Cooperation* (London, 1875–79) fastened this version as an orthodoxy on the later cooperative movement. Ironically this was the type of cooperation least likely to effect radical social change but it triumphed mightily to the virtual exclusion of other forms like cooperative workshops which were more attractive to intellectuals.[1]

One more name must be added to complete this representative selection of attempts at major adaptation or reconstruction of Owenism. James Bronterre O'Brien (1805–1864)[2] had rejected the communitarian aspects of Owenism while retaining its economic and anti-capitalist analysis, which he vigorously propounded in the *Poor Man's Guardian*. An admirer of the French Jacobins and a believer in political action, he was mainly preoccupied with Chartism and radical reform until the later 1840s. 'While I admire both Babeuf and Robert Owen,' he wrote, 'and agree generally with both as to the end sought, I am obliged to dissent from both as regards means.'[3] By 1847 he thought that Chartism as a means was inadequate, but he still had no use for 'Redemption Societies and Land Lotteries, and Cooperative Leagues and Harmony Halls, and all that sort of thing'.[4] They were mere bubble schemes. Instead he proposed a union of Owenism and Chartism which he called State Socialism.[5] Together with elements of his earlier taste for agrarianism and currency reform he presented his programme as the basis for a National Reform

---

[1] The ideal of producers' cooperatives has a continuous history in the nineteenth century. It received a strong fillip from the 1848 Revolution in France and was taken up by the Christian Socialists in their 'working associations' of handicraftsmen. Lloyd Jones and some other Owenites were attracted to these schemes in the 1850–54 period, and supported the (Christian Socialist) Cooperative League.

[2] O'Brien, the son of an Irish merchant, was educated at Trinity College, Dublin, and read for the Bar. He came to London in 1830, abandoned his law studies, and took to journalism and radical reform. He edited a series of radical papers, of which the best was the *Poor Man's Guardian*, and was active in the unstamped press agitation. He was a leading Chartist and was imprisoned for seditious speaking in 1840.

[3] O'Brien, *Buonarroti's History of Babeuf's Conspiracy for Equality* (London, 1836), p. 214 n.

[4] *National Reformer*, 24 April 1847.

[5] The idea of a union of socialism and Chartism under the title of Republican Socialism had been put forward in 1843 by James Napier Bailey. *The Model Republic*, January–March 1843.

League in 1850.[1] There is no evidence that the League ever gained much support, but O'Brien's views may possibly be one of the very few direct links between early English socialism and the modern socialist movement of the 1880s. His works were reprinted posthumously[2] and in America he inspired admirers.[3]

Although the communitarian vision faded in the late 1840s and 1850s the desire for some personal and social equivalent of the new moral world remained. The most enduring aspects of a social movement are not always its institutions, but the mental attitudes which inspire it and which are in turn generated by it. Habits of thought may long outlive the institutions of the movement in the minds of the men and women who participated in it as much as a quarter of a century earlier. In many cases this is the real area in which change has been effected, rather than in legislation or the outward arrangements of society. The physical and intellectual experience which participation brings makes a lasting mark on the individuals concerned, even though they do not attain their original goals. Owenism was formulated as a response to certain personal and social problems of the new societies in America and Britain in the period 1815–40. Had the problems been simply material ones the prosperity of the post-1848 era might have been sufficient to make them disappear. But they were more than economic. They arose from the need to evolve an acceptable philosophy of the nature of man and a theory and method of social reform. This had by no means been carried to a satisfactory conclusion by 1848: it continued to exercise the attention not only of Owenites but of the greatest radical intellects of the time from John Stuart Mill downwards. Small wonder then that the Owenites continued their search. Owenism was always weakest on its institutional side and from this quarter the later Owenites could draw little strength. But a stronger legacy was available to them from the ideology and methodology of Owenism. The communities and labour exchanges and halls of science

---

[1] *Propositions of the National Reform League for the Peaceful Regeneration of Society* (London, 1850).

[2] By Martin J. Boon, secretary of the Land and Labour League and a member of the General Council of the First International Working Men's Association (1869–72). Boon advocated republicanism, land nationalization, and currency reform, and republished O'Brien's *State Socialism* and *Rise, Progress and Phases of Human Slavery*. The National Reform League was represented on the First International.

[3] John Campbell, *Theory of Equality* (Philadelphia, Penn. and New York, N.Y., 1848). Campbell was an Irish weaver in Manchester. After his imprisonment for Chartist activities he emigrated to Philadelphia in 1842 and became a bookseller and publisher of law books. In his book he salutes the French revolutionaries of 1848 and quotes extensively from O'Brien and John Francis Bray.

disappeared, but the values of sectarianism and the faith in education were not so easily destroyed.

Sectarianism appeared in the 1850s at the two opposite poles of secularism and spiritualism. Writing to the *Reasoner*, Henry G. Atkinson complained that hundreds of Owenites had been carried away by the delusion of spiritualism.[1] Even if there was some exaggeration here, the interest in spiritualism among Owenites was sufficient to attract the attention of other contemporaries. Owen himself set the example, followed closely by his eldest son, Robert Dale Owen.[2] In the second number of his *Rational Quarterly Review* (1853), Owen suddenly announced:

A great moral revolution is about to be effected for the human race, and by an apparent miracle.

Strange and incredible as it will at first appear, communications, most important and gratifying, have been made to great numbers in America, and to many in this country, through manifestations, by invisible but audible powers, purporting to be from departed spirits.[3]

And he went on to describe how he had spoken with the spirits of Jefferson, Benjamin Franklin, the Duke of Kent and deceased members of his own family. By chance he had called on Mrs Hayden, an American medium who was visiting London, to collect a book on spiritual manifestations written by Adin Ballou, the Universalist minister and communitarian. While conversing with Mrs Hayden Owen heard raps on a table, which proved to be from spirits desiring to communicate with him. Subsequently he had seances with Mrs Hayden and other mediums. Through these experiences and investigation of the reports from America he became a spiritualist: 'I have been compelled, contrary to my previous strong convictions, to believe in a future conscious state of life, existing in a refined material, or what is called a spiritual state.' But he hastened to add that 'these new and extraordinary manifestations have not changed my confidence in the truth of the principles which I have so long advocated'. The spirits of Jefferson and the Duke of Kent merely confirmed the correctness of his plans for the new moral world. Owen's spiritualism was a practical device for ushering in the millennium.

The enthusiasm for spiritualism in the 1850s, beginning in America

[1] *Reasoner*, XXII (1857), 77. H. G. Atkinson was a mesmerist and co-author with Harriet Martineau of *Letters on the Laws of Man's Nature and Development* (London, 1851).

[2] Robert Dale Owen, *Footfalls on the Boundary of Another World* (Philadelphia, Penn., 1860); and *The Debatable Land between This World and the Next* (London, 1871).

[3] *Robert Owen's Rational Quarterly Review*, I (1853), 122. The following quotations in this paragraph are from pp. 123, 125. Owen continued his accounts of his spiritualist experiences in his *New Existence of Man upon the Earth* (London, 1854–55), pt. VI.

and spreading rapidly in Britain, caught hold of Owenites in both countries.[1] In Wisconsin Thomas Hunt and Dr Steel investigated the 'levitation' of tables and listened to lectures on spiritualism by the Fourierist Warren Chase; and Hunt claimed to have conversed with the spirit of Emma Martin, the British Owenite and secularist.[2] In Britain Shepherd Smith appeared as a supporter of the new movement; and working-class Owenites like Thomas Shorter[3] found a new basis for their millennial hopes. The provincial spiritualist societies which flourished in Keighley and Nottingham combined Owenite socialist ideas with preparations for the millennium.[4] Charles Bray elaborated a theory that as our bodies give off heat rays so also they give off thought rays, which form a kind of thought reservoir, with which spirit mediums are in communication; and on this basis he was favourably disposed towards the claims of spiritualism.[5]

Given the millennial and sectarian elements in Owenism it is not difficult to see why Owenites should have been susceptible to the attractions of spiritualism. Past and continuing associations with Swedenborgians, Shakers, Universalists, Transcendentalists and mystics brought them into the orbit from which many spiritualists came. Owenites were not the only reformers to become spiritualists: some Chartists, many Fourierists, and liberals like the Howitts also made the journey. Spiritualism for the intellectuals was not primarily a matter of table-rapping, seances and mediums. Rather, spiritualists were seceders from the orthodox churches, seekers for a rational, non-credal religion which did not offend their scientific interests. Part of the appeal of Owenism had always been that it was a heresy,[6] and spiritualism satisfied the same need. Like

---

[1] A mine of information on the relations of spiritualists to reform movements in Britain and America is the book by Owen's biographer, Frank Podmore, *Modern Spiritualism* (2 vols., London, 1902).

[2] 'Letter of Thomas Hunt to Mr B.', dated Waukesha, Wis., 19 June 1853, in *Robert Owen's Rational Quarterly Review*, pp. 215–22.

[3] Thomas Shorter (1823–1899) was a silver watch case finisher, a Chartist and secretary of the Finsbury Owenites in 1845–46. He was the first secretary of the London Working Men's College, founded by the Christian Socialists in 1854, and was for many years a familiar figure in the college. In 1860 he became the first editor of the *Spiritual Magazine*. He was a contributor to Owenite, Christian Socialist and Spiritualist journals.

[4] J. G. H. Brown was the leader in Nottingham. See Podmore, *Modern Spiritualism*, II, 41–2.

[5] Bray, *On Force, its Mental and Moral Correlates . . . with Speculations on Spiritualism* (London, 1866).

[6] J. C. Farn declared that in Scotland socialism was 'a modern form of heresy, a reaction against their national creed'. *Reasoner*, XXIII (1858), 62. Similarly Adam Harthill of Edinburgh said that Scottish Owenite branches could not exist unless they argued theology. *New Moral World*, 1 June 1844.

phrenology, the significance of spiritualism is not to be underestimated because it was partly fraudulent. Contact with the spirit world was a device which could be put to different purposes, and some Owenites used it in their search for what they had once called the new moral world.

More widespread and lasting than spiritualism was the legacy of education. It had been Owen's earliest enthusiasm, the corner-stone of his plans, and it remained longest with his disciples. Almost all active Owenites at some stage in their careers had been teachers or lecturers or writers. Like Owen they defined education in broad terms. 'Education is not an affair of childhood and youth, it is the business of the whole life',[1] wrote James Hole. For the later Owenites education was important for two reasons. First, it provided an explanation of why the communities and other Owenite institutions had been unsuccessful. 'All our Millenniums have yet failed,' declared Bray, 'because unselfish conduct was expected from people in whom the selfish feelings predominated.'[2] Only when the moral standards of the community have been raised would socialism be possible, and that improvement in morality would come only from education in the broadest sense. Hence the second reason for the importance of education: it provided opportunities for practical activities which would in the long run prepare men for the new moral world.

James Hole saw this clearly when he cited mechanics' institutes as a successful example of the principle of association. For twenty years (1848–67) he worked as honorary secretary of the Yorkshire Union of Mechanics' Institutes, and wrote *An Essay on the History, and Management of Literary, Scientific, and Mechanics' Institutions* (London, 1853). E. T. Craig also became a lecturer for the Yorkshire Union and later was principal of the Rotherham and Mexborough Mechanics' Institute. At the opposite end of the educational spectrum Robert Pemberton[3] founded a 'philosophical model infant school'. This was based on his theory of the 'science of mind formation' and a philosophy which blended together Owenism and Transcendentalism. As they busied themselves with educational activities the older Owenites comforted themselves that they were working towards the goals which had inspired them in their youth. They still believed that socialism was practicable, though not

---

[1] Hole, *Essay on . . . Mechanics' Institutions* (London, 1853), p. 44.

[2] Bray, *Phases of Opinion*, p. 118.

[3] Robert Pemberton was a philanthropist and admirer of John Minter Morgan, whose ideas he partly adopted. In the *Happy Colony* (London, 1854) he outlined a plan for a community in New Zealand. His philosophy was a type of mystical Owenism somewhat like that of J. P. Greaves. He lived in Paris and London and was present during the 1848 French Revolution.

immediately: 'socialism appeals . . . directly to all our higher feelings, and may perhaps be the last form that society will take when the perfectability of man shall have reached a higher range on this earth'. In the meantime the practical tasks were clear: 'What we have now to do then is not to neglect any means which are offered to us for developing and perfecting the individual; among which means Temperance and Education must stand first.'[1]

It is not possible of course to fix a precise date at which the communitarian vision of a new moral world finally disappeared. In various forms it has continued to the present day. Certainly at the last public gathering of Owenites in London in 1871 tribute was paid to the old ideals of the movement.[2] Owenites had always loved to celebrate their founder's birthday and for his centenary they planned a large festival in the Freemasons' Hall. The occasion provided a significant epitaph for Owenism no less than for Robert Owen. It was mainly a middle-class affair: the halfcrown charge for admission excluded 'hundreds of friends and admirers of Mr Owen among the working classes'. No notable figures from outside the Owenite body were present: John Stuart Mill, Henry Fawcett, T. H. Huxley, Jacob (brother of John) Bright, and Viscount Amberley all sent polite refusals. The proceedings were firmly in the hands of the Old Guard: Pare, Travis, Lloyd Jones, Holyoake and Watson. But links with other places and movements were indicated by some of the participants. Mrs Ernestine Le Rose from New York and Moncure D. Conway, the secularist and biographer of Thomas Paine, added a transatlantic touch. Edward Truelove, the secretary of the festival, was a noted secularist bookseller and active in the birth control movement in the 1870s.[3] James Watson and the widow of Henry Hetherington were veterans from the unstamped press and freethought struggles of the 1830s. A great many of the participants were cooperators and secularists.

Between the violin solos and songs ('The Bursting of the Chain' by Miss Eleanor Moore, 'Poor Tom Bowling' by Mr G. Stewart, a man of colour) the main speakers paid tribute to Owen's personal qualities, especially his patience, kindness and charity. But more interesting as showing what was understood to be Owen's intellectual legacy were the

---

[1] Bray, *Philosophy of Necessity* (1863 edn.), p. 412.

[2] Details and quotations are from *Report of . . . the Festival*.

[3] Edward Truelove (1804–1899) was a radical London bookseller. He was secretary of the John Street Institute for nine years, and was resident at Queenwood in 1844–45. In 1878 he was the defendant in the famous birth control trial, having published R. Dale Owen's *Moral Physiology*, and served four months imprisonment. There is an account of the naming of his six-months-old child Mazzini Truelove, by Holyoake in the John Street Institute in 1849. *Reasoner*, VII (1850), 305–7.

three 'sentiments' which were proposed. The first was to Owen's contribution in founding 'a science of man and a science of society'. The second proposed the diffusion of Owen's principles for the organization of a society in which all men would 'become consistently good, highly intelligent, and permanently happy'. The third vowed allegiance to Owen's memory through 'the practice of his principles by communities'. No practical proposals came out of the festival. It was not a meeting for action but for reminiscence and celebration of the past. Those who wanted action turned to the cooperative movement, secularism and the propagation of birth control knowledge. At this point Owenism ceased to be a legacy and became a legend.

2 The Literature of Owenism

Owenism left one legacy of a more tangible kind. As the following bibliography shows, Owenite literature was extensive and varied.[1] More than most social reform movements of the time Owenism was a movement of intellectuals—the class most addicted to articulating their views in print. Owenites did not produce creative works of high literary quality, nor did they make any distinctive contributions in other art forms. There was nothing like the work of William Morris and the artistic socialists of the 1880s, nor was there anything resembling the communitarian architecture and furniture of the Shakers. Perhaps if the Owenite communities had thrived a distinctive style of architecture might have been evolved; as it was, the buildings were either inherited from previous owners or designed in accordance with contemporary taste (even the Owenite parallelogram was a version of the endlessly repeated London square, complained Leigh Hunt). Owenism did not inspire novels[2] or painting, though some poems and hymns were written. The nature of Owenite literature was of course determined by its purpose,

---

[1] The most useful collection of Owenite literature in Britain is in the Goldsmiths' Library, University of London. In America the richest collections are at the Working Men's Institute, New Harmony, Indiana, and Columbia University, but several of the larger university libraries such as Wisconsin and Illinois are also strong in this field. The National Library of Wales has excellent holdings. No one library has anything like a complete collection of Owen's works, still less of Owenites'. Many items have to be tracked down in the local collections of the Public Libraries at Manchester, Leeds, Birmingham and other towns in Britain. The libraries of the Cooperative Union at Manchester and the Cooperative College at Loughborough contain valuable material.

[2] With the possible exception of J. E. Smith's *The Coming Man* (1873).

which was to explain and proclaim as effectively as possible the new views of society. Granted the rationalist premises of Owenism, all that was necessary was to set out the arguments in its favour: granted the millennial attitudes of many Owenites all that was required was to announce the millennium. Owenite literature therefore tended to be expository and didactic, with occasional pieces of romantic or millennial rhetoric. It was not distinctive in style but, like other aspects of Owenism, conformed to the general pattern of the times. For the most part Owenite works are very close to other similarly purposed writings of the period: usually verbose and orotund, but occasionally pointed and pungent. No literary masterpieces were produced but a body of writings remains which faithfully conveys the tone and purposes of the movement. Three categories of this Owenite literature may be conveniently distinguished: the works of Owen himself, the writings of the Owenite school and the periodicals.

Owen's contributions were the largest single element in the collection. He published about 130 separate titles, some of which went into several editions. Many of these were pamphlets or manifestoes which simply repeated what he had already said, often in the original phrases. His most influential works were his earliest, *A New View of Society* and *Report to the County of Lanark*. It is not true, as has sometimes been alleged, that thereafter there was no further development of his ideas, but these two slim volumes (hardly more than pamphlets) always remained the basic statements of Owen's social philosophy. To them was added between 1836 and 1844 the *Book of the New Moral World*, which completed the canon of Owenite orthodoxy. Of the lesser works the *Lectures on Charity* and the *Marriages of the Priesthood* were the most highly regarded within the movement. Owen's reputation as a writer has suffered from charges of verbosity and tediousness; thanks to his biographers the notion is now fairly widespread that Owen's writings are virtually unreadable, that they are in keeping with the characterization of him as a gentle bore. In fact this is hardly fair. The difficulties in reading Owen are the same as in reading most of his contemporaries in the fields of political economy and moral philosophy: unfamiliar terminology, long and involved sentence construction, and painstaking, humourless style of presentation. A modern distaste for nineteenth-century prose style reduces the readability of all but the greatest of the Great Victorians, but if this lack of sympathy can be overcome there are rewards to be found in the lesser writings of the period. Owen's *Letter to the Earl of Liverpool* (1818) is a clear, crisp statement of observations and specific arguments about the employment of children in factories. Or consider the following passage from *A New View of Society*, in which Owen pleads for a national system of education:

the *manner* of giving instruction is one thing, the *instruction* itself another, and no two objects can be more distinct. The *worst* manner may be applied to give the *best* instruction, and the *best* manner to give the *worst* instruction. Were the real importance of both to be estimated by numbers, the manner of instruction may be compared to one, and the matter of instruction to millions: the first is the means only; the last, the end to be accomplished by those means.

If, therefore, in a national system of education for the poor, it be desirable to adopt the best *manner*, it is surely so much the more desirable to adopt also the best *matter*, of instruction.

Either give the poor a rational and useful training, or mock not their ignorance, their poverty, and their misery, by merely instructing them to become conscious of the extent of the degradation under which they exist. And, therefore, in pity to suffering humanity, either keep the poor, if you now can, in the state of the most abject ignorance, as near as possible to animal life, or at once determine to form them into rational beings, into useful and effective members of the state.

Were it possible, without national prejudice to examine into the matter of instruction which is now given in some of our boasted new systems for the instruction of the poor, it would be found to be almost as wretched as any which can be devised. In proof of this statement, enter any one of the schools denominated national, and request the master to show the acquirements of the children. These are called out, and he asks them theological questions to which men of the most profound erudition cannot make a rational reply; the children, however, readily answer as they had been previously instructed; for memory, in this mockery of learning, is all that is required. Thus the child whose natural faculty of comparing ideas, or whose rational powers, shall be the soonest destroyed, if, at the same time, he possess a memory to retain incongruities without connexion, will become what is termed the first scholar in the class; and three-fourths of the time which ought to be devoted to the acquirement of useful instruction, will be really occupied in destroying the mental powers of the children.[1]

One work of Owen's stands apart from his other writing. Partly because of its subject and partly because of the circumstances of its composition his autobiography has a freshness and charm which is very attractive. The *Life* was published in 1857, when Owen was a very old man. Parts of it had appeared earlier, and the volume was to some extent a compilation, with Travis's assistance, of autobiographical fragments

---

[1] *A New View of Society* in Owen, *Life*, I, 318–19. Podmore, *Robert Owen*, pp. 121–3, suggests that Francis Place and James Mill may have helped Owen with *A New View* and this would account for its superior clarity and style. But the evidence is not very conclusive.

from journals and speeches written at various times from 1817 onwards. Like all autobiographers Owen sees his early life through the distorting glass of later interests and experiences: subconsciously he hides part of himself and exaggerates those elements which he thinks substantiate his own self-image. Thus his formative intellectual development is glossed over in an unanalytical fashion, while his religious views at the age of nine or ten are precocious to the point of incredibility. Other passages, however, are more revealing. His description of the interview with Peter Drinkwater in 1792 is unforgettable. Owen had recently left the drapery business and set up as a yarn manufacturer. He then heard that Drinkwater, one of the largest cotton spinners in Manchester, wanted a manager:

his [Drinkwater's] advertisement appeared on a Saturday in the Manchester papers, but I had not seen or heard of it until I went to my factory on the Monday morning following, when, as I entered the room where my spinning machines were, one of the spinners said, 'Mr Lee has left Mr Drinkwater, and he has advertised for a manager.' I merely said, 'What will he do?' and passed on to my own occupation. But (and how such an idea could enter my head I know not) without saying a word, I put on my hat and proceeded straight to Mr Drinkwater's counting house, and boy and inexperienced as I was, I asked him for the situation for which he had advertised. The circumstances which now occurred made a lasting impression upon me, because they led to important future consequences. He said immediately, 'You are too young,' and at that time being fresh coloured I looked younger than I was. I said, 'That was an objection made to me four or five years ago, but I did not expect it would be made to me now.' 'How old are you?' 'Twenty in May this year,' was my reply. 'How often do you get drunk in the week?' (This was a common habit with almost all persons in Manchester and Lancashire at that period.) 'I was never,' I said, 'drunk in my life', blushing scarlet at this unexpected question. My answer and the manner of it made, I suppose, a favourable impression, for the next question was, 'What salary do you ask?' 'Three hundred a year,' was my reply. 'What?', Mr Drinkwater said, with some surprise, repeating the words, 'three hundred a year! I have had this morning I know not how many seeking the situation, and I do not think that all their askings together would amount to what you require.' 'I cannot be governed by what others ask,' said I, 'and I cannot take less. I am now making that sum by my own business.' 'Can you prove that to me?' 'Yes, I will show you the business and my books.' 'Then I will go with you and let me see them,' said Mr Drinkwater. We went to my factory. I explained the nature of my business, opened the books, and proved my statement to his satisfaction. He then said, 'What reference as to past character can you give?' I referred him to Mr Satterfield, Messrs. Flint and Palmer, and Mr McGuffog. 'Come to me on such a day, and you shall have my answer.' This was to give him time to make the enquiries.

I called upon him at the time appointed. He said, 'I will give you the three hundred a year, as you ask, and I will take all your machinery at its cost price, and I shall require you to take the management of the mill and of the work-people, about 500, immediately.' I accordingly made my arrangements.[1]

Unfortunately much of Owen's later writing lacks the vividness of this passage. His millenarian inclinations led him to constant restatements of his original doctrines rather than to the discovery and presentation of new ideas, and his mind was not stored with any wide body of learning upon which he could draw. In his large output of articles and pamphlets he repeated himself without sharpening or refining his arguments. He was not generally very imaginative and literature was for him primarily a technique for propagating truth and combating error. Nevertheless, he was not as insensitive as has sometimes been suggested and he may even have aspired to writing poetry.[2]

The variety of types of Owenite writing is clear from the material used in earlier sections. Best known is the literature of Ricardian socialism, some of which has been reissued in recent years. William Thompson's work tends to be diffuse and involved; John Gray and John Francis Bray wrote with more economy and punch. Most Owenite works in this category are similar in tone and language to the general literature of early nineteenth-century political economy, of which in fact they form a minor branch. The same situation is true for the philosophical and sociological literature of Owenism, though here the contrast between the great classics of the Scottish Enlightenment and utilitarian philosophy, and the second-rate productions of a Charles Bray or a Henry Travis is even more marked. Although Owenism was a movement of intellectuals it failed to attract any really first-rate minds. Its appeal was at the level of members of the middle classes and intelligent self-educated working men who were not very far advanced in their explorations of human nature and society but who were yet anxious for certitude. They were quite happy to accept belief rather than rigorous logic as a basis for their social science, especially belief in progress and man's ability to control human destiny. A good deal of Owenite writing was the thinking aloud of home-spun philosophers, unsophisticated preliminary attempts at working out a social philosophy with a rather limited intellectual equipment. From Owen they had acquired a few basic ideas and principles (such as the

[1] Owen, *Life*, I, 27–8.
[2] In the library of the Kooperativa Forbundet, Stockholm, Sweden, there are three poems in Owen's handwriting, entitled 'Sonnets for Slaves'. It seems possible that they were composed by Owen. See Walter Sjolin, 'New Light on Robert Owen: Poetic Vein in the Reformer's Personality', *Cooperative Review*, February 1955, pp. 38–41.

need to study the whole man functioning in his environment), and they supplemented these with borrowings from phrenology, millennialism, spiritualism or whatever came their way. This was not a formula likely to produce anything intellectually original. Rather the literature which was its outcome provides a composite intellectual biography of a certain type of reformer in the nineteenth century.

All the main forms of Owenite literature were characteristic of writing in general in the period 1820–60. The Owenite series of *Popular Tracts* or *Social Tracts* were the counterpart of the tracts put out by the religious bodies or the Anti-Corn Law League. The self-improvement writings of Rowland Detrosier or William Maclure matched a vast popular literature of this genre. And the sectarian works of Shepherd Smith, John Finch or George Jacob Holyoake were but the fringe of a large body of such writing. The need to communicate with certain groups of people at a particular level of intellectual development largely determined the form and content of Owenite literature. Today the most readable of Owenite writings are, as in the case of Owen himself, the autobiographies. William Lovett, Thomas Frost, Robert Dale Owen, Charles Bray and Holyoake all left reminiscences of their Owenite days; and although by the time they wrote their autobiographies they had moved away from the beliefs of their youth, they were able and willing to recapture something of the spirit of Owenism as it had fired them. They make it possible to understand the appeal of a movement which otherwise from its bibliography would appear to have been chiefly devoted to polemics with the clergy and discussions of moral responsibility.

Even more valuable than the autobiographies for a close focus of Owenism is the third category of its literature, the periodicals. Over a hundred journals were published which were either avowedly Owenite or in which substantial space was devoted to Owenism. Many of these papers were short-lived and probably had only a minute circulation. But from 1820 to 1860 there was an almost continuous run of a central Owenite organ. Owen's first attempt at a journal, the *Mirror of Truth* in 1817, lasted for only two months. His followers were more successful with the *Economist* and the *Cooperative Magazine*, and in 1825 the *New Harmony Gazette* began the long series which continued through the *Crisis* and the *New Moral World* to the *Reasoner*. Colaterally with the main journal were other papers produced by a particular community or some special section of the movement such as secularism or the labour exchanges. Again, in the radical reform journals of Hetherington, Carpenter and O'Brien Owenite concerns were treated at length. The role of the Owenite periodical was crucial in a movement in which other institutions were relatively weak. It provided a main channel of communication between the branches and the central leadership. It supplemented the lecture and the debate as a forum for the discussion and extension of the new view of society. Each week reports from the branches and lectures by the social missionaries were printed, and the sense of belonging to a movement larger than a local community or hall of science was strengthened.

Within the pages of the *New Moral World* news of the movement occupied substantial space but by no means the bulk of the paper. Pride of place on the front page was usually given to Owen's most recent lecture or failing that to the latest Sunday address delivered at the central Owenite institute in London. Letters from correspondents, snippets of improving information culled from other journals, and accounts of the tours of the social missionaries made up the rest. There was also a large amount of reprinting of Owen's earlier writings, together with some poetry and occasional fables or semi-fictional pieces. The whole was well tuned to the taste of the seriously-minded shopkeeper or artisan, with a sufficient sprinkling of the bizarre and *outré* to satisfy advanced liberals. In general, the *New Moral World* was closer to papers of the type of *Howitts' Journal* than to the *Poor Man's Guardian* or John Cleave's penny serials.

The literature of Owenism constituted a rich legacy, but it was a legacy which was little used. There is no evidence to suggest that Owen and the Owenites were much read after the 1850s. Their writings were regarded as ephemeral, tracts for times which were past. Neither in Britain nor in America did socialists of the later nineteenth century turn to Owen. There was no rediscovery of *A New View of Society* as there was of the *Communist Manifesto* in the 1880s. Nor did social scientists have much use for the legacy of Owenite writings. Under the tutelage of Herbert Spencer, Darwin and the positivists a generation emerged which did not find Owenism in any way helpful for exploring the questions they were interested in. Owenite literature lay forgotten in the little libraries of the cooperative societies, secular halls and working men's institutes. It had come to be regarded not as a legacy but as a relic.

PROTESTANTISM VERSUS SOCIALISM,
OR THE REVIVAL OF GOOD OLD TIMES.

37. Cartoon from *The Penny Satirist*, 1840

The Goblin Sprite, or the Old Women and the Bugaboo.

Mother Fillpurse.—Ah, here it is! the deuce is in the imp, it's *here*, *there*, and *everywhere* in a moment, and *not a blow* can we give it.

Mother Blightfield.—Curse it! when we try to *hit it*, we only *hit ourselves*. Here it is; ha! it's gone again! and bids us defiance, too!

Mother Cantaway.—What shall we do to destroy it? If it is suffered to run about our *holy house*, it will soon corrupt the *morals* of our children, to say nothing of our own. Mother Wellington, you've been along of the sogers, perhaps you know of the best method to put an end to the varmint.

Mother Wellington.—Why, the best way I know of to kill all these unorthodox devils is with a mixture of *dry powder*, *leaden pills*, and *steel lozenges*, strewed about; but I'm afraid, if great tact is not observed, the *experiment* will prove rather *dangerous* to ourselves.

38. Cartoon from *The Penny Satirist*, 1840

A Bibliography of
Robert Owen and
the Owenite Movement
in Britain and America

S

Bibliographies

1 Bibliographies of Robert Owen and Owenites

GOSS, CHARLES WILLIAM F. *A Descriptive Bibliography of the Writings of George Jacob Holyoake, with a Brief Sketch of His Life.* London, 1908.

GOTO, SHIGERU. *Robert Owen, 1771–1858: a New Bibliographical Study.* 2 vols. Osaka, Japan, 1932–34. [In Japanese and English.]

NATIONAL LIBRARY OF WALES. *A Bibliography of Robert Owen, the Socialist, 1771–1858.* Aberystwyth, 1914.
[2nd edn.] Aberystwyth, London, 1925.

UNIVERSITY OF LONDON. *Robert Owen, 1771–1858. Catalogue of an Exhibition of Printed Books Held in the Library of the University of London, October–December 1958.* London, 1959.

2 Other Works containing substantial Bibliographies of Robert Owen and the Owenite Movement

BESTOR, ARTHUR EUGENE, JR. *Backwoods Utopias: the Sectarian and Owenite Phases of Communitarian Socialism in America: 1663–1829.* Philadelphia, Penn., 1950.

EGBERT, DONALD DREW, and STOW PERSONS. *Socialism and American Life.* 2 vols. Princeton, N.J., 1952.

LEOPOLD, R. W. *Robert Dale Owen.* Cambridge, Mass., 1940.

London Bibliography of the Social Sciences. 4 vols. and 2 supplements. London, 1931–37.

MENGER, ANTON. *The Right to the Whole Produce of Labour,* trans. M. E. Tanner. London, 1899. [Introd. and bibliography by H. S. Foxwell.] [Reprinted] New York, 1962.

REESE, RENA. *List of Books and Pamphlets in a Special Collection in the Library of the Workingmen's Institute.* New Harmony, Ind., 1909.

STAMMHAMMER, J. *Bibliographie des Socialismus und Communismus.* 3 vols. Jena, Germany, 1893–1909.

WHEELER, JOSEPH MAZZINI. *Dictionary of Free Thinkers.* London 1889.

Works by and about Robert Owen

1 Manuscript Collections

MS. letters and documents. Cooperative Union, Manchester [numbered 1–2964, and dated 1821–54. This is the main collection of Owen's personal papers, but none of it relates to his early life. The collection begins where his autobiography ends].

MS. letters. There are scattered letters by and to Owen in the British Museum, the International Institute of Social History, Amsterdam, Netherlands, and in several of the collections listed on pp. 287-5.

MS. copy. Report to the County of Lanark, pts. II and III. University of London Library, MS. 692. [Pt. II is in Robert Owen's hand, and Pt. III has corrections by him. Pt. I and the Appendices are missing.]

2 Writings of Robert Owen

[This list includes printed books, pamphlets and broadsheets, but does not include articles in periodicals unless they were also published as separate titles.]

Additional Statements respecting Mr Owen's Plan for the Support of the Unemployed Working Classes by their own Labour. [n.p.] 1819.

An Address by Robert Owen on His System Delivered at the City of London Tavern, April 12th, 1830. London, 1830.

Address delivered by Robert Owen, at a Public Meeting at the Franklin Institute in Philadelphia . . . June 25th, 1827. Philadelphia, Penn., 1827.

Address delivered to the Inhabitants of New Lanark, on Jan. 1st, 1816, at the Opening of the Institution established for the Formation of Character. London, 1816.
[2nd edn.] London, 1816.
[3rd edn.] London, 1817.
[4th edn.] London, 1819.
[Another edn.] London, 1841.

Address of Robert Owen, delivered at the great Public Meeting, held at the National Equitable Labour Exchange . . . on 1st May, 1833, Denouncing the Old System of the World and Announcing the Commencement of the New. [n.p.] 1833.

Address of Robert Owen to the Profession of Arms, from the Commander in Chief to the Private. [n.p.] 1857. [Broadsheet.]

Address On Leaving the United States for Europe, June 1st, 1845. New York, 1845. [Broadsheet.]

Address On Spiritual Manifestations. [n.p.] 1855.

Address to All Classes in the State From the Governors, Directors, and Committee of the Association [for Removing the Causes of Ignorance and Poverty By Education and Employment]. London, 1832.

Address to Her Royal Highness the Princess Victoria and to Her Majesty the Queen of Great Britain and Ireland. London, 1837.

An Address to the Agriculturalists, Mechanics, and Manufacturers of Great Britain and Ireland, Both Masters and Operatives. Bury, 1827.

Address to the Electors of Great Britain and Ireland But Especially to the Electors of the Metropolis of the British Empire and of the World. [n.p.] 1857.

An Address to the Master Manufacturers of Great Britain On the Present Existing Evils in the Manufacturing System. Bolton, 1819.

Address to the National Association for the Promotion of Social Science, On Its Second Annual Meeting. [n.p.] 1858.

Address to the Operative Manufacturers and Agricultural Labourers in Great Britain and Ireland. [n.p.] 1830.

Address to the Socialists, Being the Substance of Two Lectures Delivered in London, Previous to the Congress in May, 1843. [n.p., 1843?]

An Address to the Socialists On the Present Position of the Rational System of Society: and the Measures Required to Direct . . . the Operations of the Universal Community Society of Rational Religionists: Being the Substance of Two Lectures Delivered . . . in May, 1841. London, 1841.

Address to the Tories, Whigs, Radicals . . . to All Producers of Wealth, and Non-producers in Great Britain and Ireland; On the Necessity of Providing a Sound Practical Education . . . for the Population. . . . London, 1841.

The Addresses of Robert Owen (as Published in the London Journals), Preparatory to the Development of a Practical Plan for the Relief of All Classes, Without Injury to Any. London, 1830.

Addresses to the Delegates of the Human Race at the World's Fair, in the Crystal Palace . . . to Which Are Added a Petition . . . to Both Houses of Parliament and a Letter to the Editors of the Christian Socialist. London, 1851.

Adresse à l'Assemblée Nationale de France. Paris, 1848. [Handbill.]

Adresse aux Souverains à Aix-la-Chapelle et aux Gouvernements Européens, trans. M. le Comte de Lasteyrie. Paris, 1819.

The Advantages and Disadvantages of Religion, containing an Address delivered by Robert Owen, to a Public Meeting in London, on Wednesday, October 20th, 1830. Glasgow, 1830.

An Attempt to Explain the Cause of the commercial and other Difficulties which are now experienced in the Civilized Parts of the World; and to develop the Means by which they may be removed. Norwich [1821].

The Book of the New Moral World, containing the Rational System of Society. Pt. I. London, 1836.
[Another edn.] Glasgow, 1837.
[Abridged edn.] *Human Nature, or the Moral Science of Man.* London, 1838. [Abstract of Pt. I, by Samuel Cornish.]
[Another edn.] Glasgow, 1840.
[French trans.] *Le Livre du Nouveau Monde Moral.* [Paris, 1838?]
[German trans.] *Das Buch der Neuen Moralischen Welt.* Nordhausen, 1840.

The Book of the New Moral World. Pts. II, III. London, 1842.

The Book of the New Moral World. Pts. IV–VII. London, 1844.
[1st American edn.] New York, 1845.
[Another edn., of complete work issued in seven parts, each separately
paginated.] London, 1849.
[French trans.] *Le Livre du Nouveau Monde Moral . . . Abregé et
traduit de l'Anglais par T. W. Thornton.* Paris, 1847.
[Italian trans.]. *Il Libro del Nuovo Mondo Morale.* [n.p.] 1882.

*Calculations showing the Facility with which the Paupers and Unemployed may
be enabled to support themselves within most desirable Circumstances by
Co-operation.* London, 1851.

The Catechism of the New Moral World. Manchester, 1838.
[2nd edn.] Leeds, 1838.
[Another edn.] Manchester, 1840.

Catechism of the Rational System of Society and Proclamation. London
[1850?]

*A Development of the Origin and Effects of Moral Evil, and of the Principles and
Practices of Moral Good.* Manchester, 1838.

*A Development of the Principles and Plans on which to establish Self-supporting
Home Colonies.* London, 1841.
[2nd edn.] London, 1841.

*Dialogue entre les Membres de la Commission Exécutive, les Ambassadeurs
d'Angleterre, de Russie, d'Autriche, de Prusse, de Hollande, des États-Unis,
et Robert Owen.* Paris, 1848.

*A Dialogue, in Three Parts, Between the Founder of the 'Association of All
Classes of All Nations' and a Stranger Desirous of Being Accurately Informed Respecting Its Origin and Objects.* Manchester, 1838.

*Dialogue Sur le Système Social . . . Entre la France, le Monde, et Robert Owen,
Sur la Necessité d'un Changement Total dans Nos Systèmes d'Éducation et
de Gouvernement.* Paris, 1848.

*An Explanation of the Cause of the Distress Which Pervades the Civilized Parts of
the World, and of the Means Whereby It May Be Removed.* London,
1823.
[Another edn.] London, 1823.

Exposition of Mr Owen's Views on the Marriage Question. Coventry, [1838?]
[Small broadsheet.]

A Farewell Address Delivered at the Scientific Institution . . . on 9th June, 1850.
London, 1850.

The Future of the Human Race; Or, a Great Glorious and Peaceful Revolution, Near at Hand, To Be Effected Through the Agency of Departed Spirits of Good and Superior Men and Women. London, 1853.
[2nd edn.] London, 1854.

Great Preliminary Meeting On the First Day of the Year 1855, in Which By His Previous Advertisement Mr. Owen Had Announced That the True Millenial State of Human Existence Should Commence. With His Reasons For Calling These Meetings. London, 1855.
[2nd edn.] London 1855.
[3rd edn.] London, 1855.

The Inauguration of the Millenium, May 14th, 1855, being the Report of two Public Meetings, with an Introduction. London, 1855.

Institution of the Intelligent and Well-disposed of the Industrious Classes. Prospectus of the System of Education to be pursued in the Schools attached to the Institution. London [1833?].

A Lecture delivered in the Mechanics' Institute, London, on the 30th March, 1840 . . . in Reply to the Errors and Misrepresentations in . . . Parliament, by the London City Mission, by a large Portion of the Daily Press. . . . [London, n.d.].
[2nd edn.] London [1841?]

Lectures on an entire New State of Society: comprehending an Analysis of British Society, relative to the Production and Distribution of Wealth; the Formation of Character; and Government, Domestic and Foreign. London [1830?]
[Another edn.] *Twelve Lectures on an entire New State of Society, delivered in London in 1830; with a Memoir and Writings of Miss Owen; and an Address to the Inhabitants of New Harmony.* London, 1841.

Lectures on Charity; delivered by Robert Owen at the Institution of New Lanark, upon Ch. XIII of I Corinthians, nos. 1–6. London, 1833–34.
[Another edn.] *Six Lectures on Charity. . . .* London [1834?]

Lectures on the Marriages of the Priesthood of the Old Immoral World, delivered in the Year 1835, before the Passing of the New Marriage Act. Leeds, 1835.
[2nd edn.] *The Marriage System of the New Moral World: with a faint Outline of the present very irrational System, as developed in a Course of Ten Lectures.* Leeds, 1838.
[3rd edn.] Leeds, 1839.
[4th edn.] *Lectures on the Marriages of the Priesthood . . . with an Appendix containing the Marriage System of the New Moral World.* Leeds, 1840.

Lectures on the Rational System of Society, derived solely from Nature and Experience, as propounded by Robert Owen, versus Socialism, derived from Misrepresentation, as explained by the Lord Bishop of Exeter and Others; and versus the present System of Society. . . . London, 1841.

[Another edn.] *Syllabus of Four Morning and Four Evening Courses of Lectures at the Egyptian Hall . . . on the Rational System of Society.* London, 1841.

A Letter addressed to the Potentates of the Earth in whom the Happiness and Misery of the Human Race are now invested. . . . [n.p.] 1857.

A Letter to the Archbishop of Canterbury on the Union of Churches and Schools. [n.p.] 1818.

Letter to the Earl of Lauderdale, May 27th, 1824. [n.p., n.d.]

A Letter to the Earl of Liverpool on the Employment of Children in Manufactories. [n.p.] 1818.

A Letter to the Moderator of the General Assembly Upon the Late Attack of the Christian Instructor Upon Mr. Owen. [n.p.] 1823.

Letter to the President and Members of the New York State Convention, Appointed To Revise the Constitution of the State. [n.p.] 1846.

Letters on Education . . . Addressed to the Teachers of the Human Race in All Countries. London, 1849.
[Another edn., n.p.] 1851.

Letters on Government As It Is and As It Ought To Be Addressed to the Government of the British Empire. [n.p.] 1851.

Life and Death Society. [n.p.] 1857. [Broadsheet.]

Life of Robert Owen. Written By Himself. With Selections From His Writings and Correspondence. Vol. I. London, 1857.
A Supplementary Appendix to the First Volume of the Life of Robert Owen, Containing a Series of Reports, Addresses, Memorials, and Other Documents Referred To In That Volume. Vol. IA. London, 1858.
[Another edn.] *Life of Robert Owen, By Himself,* with an introduction by M. Beer. London, 1920.
[American edn.] *Life, by Himself.* New York, 1920.

Manifesto . . . addressed to all Governments and People who desire to become civilized, and to improve permanently the Condition of all Classes in all Countries. Washington, D.C., 1844.

Manifesto of Robert Owen, the Discoverer and Founder of the Rational System of Society, and of the Rational Religion. London, 1840.
[5th edn.] London, 1840.

[6th edn.] ... *to which are added a Preface and Appendix.* London, 1840.

[7th edn.] London, 1840.

[8th edn.] *Manifesto of Robert Owen, in Reply to the Bishop of Exeter; with a Preface; and an Appendix; containing Mr. Owen's Petition to Parliament in February, 1840; his Memorials to the Governments of Europe and America. ...* London, 1841.

Manifesto of Robert Owen to the Civilized World: a Solution of the Great Problem of the Age. [New York, 1847.]

Memorial of Robert Owen to the Mexican Republic, and to the Government of the State of Coahuila and Texas. Philadelphia, Penn., 1827.

[Another edn.] London, 1828.

The Millenium in Practice. [n.p.] 1855.

Mr. Owen's proposed Arrangements for the distressed Working Classes, shown to be Consistent with sound Principles of Political Economy: in Three Letters addressed to David Ricardo. ... London, 1819.

Mr. Owen's Report to the Committee of the Association for the Relief of the Manufacturing and Labouring Poor ... accompanied by his Address ... at a Public Meeting expressly convened to consider a Plan ... to reduce the Poor's Rate, and to gradually abolish Pauperism. London, 1817.

Mr Owen's Sunday Morning Lectures. [London, 1830? Small broadsheet notice of lectures in Mechanics' Institution, Southampton Buildings, Holborn, London.]

The New Existence of Man upon the Earth. To which are added an Outline, and an Appendix containing his Addresses published in 1815 and 1817 [8 parts separately published]. London, nos. 1–5, 1854; nos. 6–8, 1855.

New Lanark. [n.p.] 1849. [Broadsheet.]

The New Religion: or, Religion founded on the Immutable Laws of the Universe, contrasted with all Religions founded on Human Testimony, as developed in a Public Lecture ... 20th October, 1830. London, 1830.

New State of Society. Mr. Owen's Second Address, delivered at the 'City of London Tavern' on Thursday, August 21st, 1817. ... [n.p.] 1817.

A New View of Society; or, Essays on the Principle of the Formation of Human Character. [First Essay.] London, 1813.

[2nd Essay.] London, 1813.

[Another edn.] London, 1813.

[3rd Essay.] London, 1814.

[4th Essay.] London, 1814.

[2nd edn., of the complete work] London, 1816.

[3rd edn.] London, 1817.

[4th edn.]   London, 1818–19.

[1st American edn., from the 3rd London edn.]   New York, 1825.

[Another American edn., from the 4th London edn.]   Cincinnati, Ohio, 1825.

[Another edn.]   Edinburgh, 1826.

[Another edn.]   *Essays on the Formation of Human Character.*   London, 1834.

[Another edn.]   Manchester, 1837.

[Another edn.]   Manchester, 1840.

[Another edn.]   London, 1840.

[Another edn.: Everyman's Series.]   *A New View of Society and Other Writings.*   Introd. by G. D. H. Cole. London, 1927.

[Another edn., unchanged reprint from 1927 Everyman's edn.]   New York, 1963.

New View of Society. No. 1. Extracted from the London daily Newspapers of the 30th of July, and the 9th and 11th of August, 1817. With Reference to a Public Meeting held at the City of London Tavern, on Thursday, 14th August, 1817. . . .   London, 1817.

New View of Society. No. 2. Mr. Owen's Report to the Committee of the Association for the Relief of the Manufacturing and Labouring Poor . . . accompanied by his Address delivered . . . on Thursday, 14th August, 1817. . . .   [n.p.] 1817.

New View of Society. No. 3. Mr. Owen's Second Address delivered at the City of London Tavern, 1817.   [n.p.] 1817.

New View of Society. Tracts relative to this Subject; viz. Proposals for raising a Colledge of Industry of all useful Trades and Husbandry. By John Bellers (Reprinted from the Original, published in the Year 1696), Report to the Committee of the Association for the Relief of the Manufacturing and Labouring Poor, A Brief Sketch of the religious Society of People called Shakers (Communicated . . . by W. S. Warder). With an Account of the Public Proceedings connected with the Subject which took place in London in July and August, 1817.   London, 1818.

Notice to All. To new-form Man and new-form Society. . . .   [n.p.] 1857. [Broadsheet.]

Observations on the Cotton Trade of Great Britain and on the late Duties on the Importation of Cotton Wool.   Glasgow, 1803.

Observations on the Effect of the Manufacturing System: with Hints for the Improvement of those Parts of It which are most injurious to Health and Morals.   London, 1815.

[2nd edn.]   London, 1817.

[Another edn., privately printed, without author's name and date] ... *To which are added two Letters on the Employment of Children in Manufactories and a Letter on the Union of Churches and Schools.* London, 1818.

On the Employment of Children in Manufactories. [New Lanark, 1848.]

Oration containing a Declaration of Mental Independence delivered at New Harmony, Indiana. New Harmony, Ind., 1826.

Outline of the Rational System of Society. . . . [London?] 1830.
[Another edn.] London, 1831.
[Another edn.] *An Outline of the Rational System of Society, founded on demonstrable Facts developing the Constitution and Laws of Human Nature being the only effective Remedy for the Evils experienced by the World: the immediate Adoption of which would tranquilize the present agitated State of Society.* . . . Manchester, London [1836?]
[French trans.] *Propositions fondamentales du Système Social, de la Communauté des Biens* . . . traduit de l'Anglais par Jules Gay. Paris, 1837.
[Another edn.] *Social Tracts, No. 7.* London, 1838.
[Another edn.] Birmingham, 1839.
[Another edn., n.p.] 1840.
[6th edn.] Leeds, 1840.
[Another edn., in] *Social Hymns.* Leeds, 1840.
[Another edn.] Manchester [1840?]
[Another edn.] London, 1841.
[Welsh trans.] *Talfyriad O'r Gyfundrefn Resymol Sefydledig Ar Ffeithiau Diwrthed-brawf, yn Amlygu Cyfansoddiad a Deddfau y Natur ddynol.* . . . Bangor, 1841.
[Another edn.] London, 1842.
[Another edn.] *Social Bible; or an Outline.* . . . Manchester, London [n.d.]
[French trans.] *Courte Exposition d'un Système Social Rationnel.* . . . Paris, 1848.
[Another edn.] London, 1851.
[Another edn., in] *Report of the Proceedings of the Festival in Commemoration of the Centenary Birthday of Robert Owen.* . . . London, 1871.
[Another edn.] London, 1872.

Papers sent to the National Association for the Promotion of Social Science at the First Meeting, 1857. London, 1857.

Peace on Earth—Good Will towards Men: Development of the Plan for the Relief of the Poor, and the Emancipation of Mankind. London, 1817.

Preliminary Charter of the Rational System, by the Founder of the System (no. 3). London, 1843. [Handbill.]

Proclamation au Peuple français, aux Militaires et aux Civils de toutes les Classes, de tous les Partis, de toutes les Religions. Paris, 1848.

Proclamation by Robert Owen. London, 1856 [re Congress of the Reformers of the World].

Proclamation of Robert Owen. [n.p.] 1848. [Broadsheet.]

Proclamation (of the World's Convention or Congress of Delegates, to be held in St. Martin's Hall. . . .) [n.p.] 1855. [Broadsheet.]

Reasons for each Law of the Constitution to be introduced into the State of New York. Washington, D.C., 1846.

Report of the Meetings of the Advanced Minds of the World, convened by Robert Owen. . . . London, 1857.
[2nd edn.] London, 1857.

Report of the Proceedings at the several Meetings held in Dublin by Robert Owen, Esq., on the 18th March, 12th April, 19th April, and 3rd May; preceded by an introductory Statement of his Opinions and Arrangements at New Lanark, extracted from his 'Essays on the Formation of Human Character'. Dublin, 1823.

Report to the Committee of the Association for the Relief of the Manufacturing and Labouring Poor . . . laid before the Committee of the House of Commons on the Poor Laws. [n.p., 1817.]

Report to the County of Lanark of a Plan for relieving Public Distress and removing Discontent. . . . Glasgow, 1821.
[Another edn.] London, 1832.

The Revolution in the Mind and Practice of the Human Race. London, 1849.
[Supplement]. *A Supplement to the Revolution in the Mind. . . .* London, 1849
[Another edn., with Supplement., n.p.] 1850.

Robert Owen and the Exhibition of 1851. Second Address. To the Social Reformers of Great Britain. [n.p., n.d.; broadsheet.]

Robert Owen on Marriage, Religion, and Private Property, and on the Necessity of immediately carrying into Practice the 'Rational System of Society', to prevent the Evils of a Physical Revolution. London, 1839. [Broadsheet.]

Robert Owen's Address delivered at the Meeting in St. Martin's Hall, Long Acre, London, on the 1st of January, 1855. London, 1855.

Robert Owen's Address to the Human Race on his Eighty-fourth Birthday, May 14th, 1854; with his Last Legacy. . . . London, 1854.

Robert Owen's Address to the Ministers of All Religions . . . as delivered by him in the Chinese Museum . . . December 21st, 1845. Philadelphia, Penn., 1845. [Broadsheet.]

Robert Owen's Congress of Advanced Minds. Addresses of Robert Owen. . . . London, 1857. [Five broadsheets.]

Robert Owen's Letter to the Senate of the 28th Congress . . . requesting Permission to deliver a Course of Lectures in its Chamber. . . . Washington, D.C., 1845.

Robert Owen's Opening Speech, and his Reply to the Rev. Alex. Campbell . . . also Mr. Owen's Memorial to the Republic of Mexico . . . as explained in the above Debate with Mr. Campbell. . . . Cincinnati, Ohio, 1829.

Robert Owen's Reply to the Question 'What Would You Do, if You Were Prime Minister of England?' [2nd edn.] Stockport [1832?]

Robert Owen's Tracts for the World's Fair. [n.p.] 1851. [Six handbills.]

The Royal Consort's Schools for All Classes. . . . London, 1857. [Broadsheet.]

Second Lecture on the New Religion: or Religion founded on the Immutable Laws of the Universe . . . as developed in a Public Lecture . . . by Mr. Owen . . . December 15th, 1830. London, 1830.

The Signs of the Times; or, the Approach of the Millenium. London, 1841. [Issued as an appendix to *A Development of the Principles and Plans.*]

Six Lectures delivered in Manchester previously to the Discussion between Mr. Robert Owen and the Rev. J. H. Roebuck. And an Address delivered at the Annual Congress of the 'Association of All Classes of All Nations'. Manchester, 1837.
[Another edn.] Birmingham, 1838.
[Another edn.] Manchester, 1839.

'Socialism', in *Cyclopedia of Religious Denominations.* London, Glasgow [1853?; 3rd edn., separately paginated].

Socialism Misrepresented, and truly Represented. [n.p.] 1848.

Socialism, or the Rational System of Society. Three Lectures, delivered . . . 30th March, 3rd and 6th April, 1840. [First Lecture.] London, 1840. [2nd edn.] London, 1841.

Société fraternelle centrale. *7ᵉ et 8ᵉ Discours du Citoyen Cabet sur les Élections. Discours de Robert Owen.* Paris, 1848.

Speech by Robert Owen at New Harmony, April 27th, 1825. [n.p., n.d.]

Speeches delivered by Robert Owen at the Breakfast given in Anticipation of his Departure for America . . . August 11, 1844. [n.p., n.d.]

A Statement regarding the New Lanark Establishment. Edinburgh, 1812.

Statement submitted to the Most Noble Marquis of Normanby, Secretary of State for the Home Department, relative to the Principles and Objects of the Universal Community Society of Rational Religionists. London [n.d.]

System, as developed in a Public Lecture, . . . to take into consideration the Best Mode of rationally Educating, Employing, and Uniting the People, in Order to prevent the Necessity for the distressing Occurences which have Lately taken Place in France. . . . London, 1832.

Temple of Free Inquiry. A Report of the Proceedings Consequent on Laying the Foundation Stone of the Manchester Hall of Science, with an Address by Robert Owen. Leeds, 1839.

Ten Lectures on the Evils of Indissoluble Marriage. [Leeds, 1840?]

To Her Majesty, Victoria . . . and to Her Responsible Advisers. [London, 1849; Broadsheet.]

To Lords John Russell and Stanley, Sir Robert Peel, and Messrs. Cobden, and Feargus O'Connor. [London, 1849; broadsheet.]

To the Electors of Great Britain and Ireland. London [1841?; handbill.]

To the Electors of Oldham. [n.p., 1852?; broadsheet.]

To the Electors of the Borough of Marylebone. [n.p.] 1846. [Broadsheet.]

To the President of the United States, and to His Cabinet. Washington, D.C., 1845. [Broadsheet.]

To the Senate and House of Representatives of the Congress of the United States . . . and Petition to the House of Commons. London, 1852. [Broadsheet.]

Tract No. 1. To the Inhabitants of Manchester and Salford, and to the Strangers Who Attend the Grand Festival, as It is called. [n.p., n.d.]

Tracts for the World's Fair. Nos. 1–6. [n.p.] 1851.

Tracts on the Coming Millenium. Two series. [n.p.] 1855.

The Twelve Fundamental Laws of Human Nature, in which Robert Owen predicates a Change of Society that will form an entire New State of Existence, as read in the Debate between him and Mr. Campbell, . . . on the 13th April, 1829. [n.p., n.d.; broadsheet.]

Two Discourses on a New System of Society, as delivered in the Hall of Representatives of the United States . . . on the 25th February and 7th March, 1825. . . . Louisville, Ky., 1825.

NEW HARMONY – All Owin' – No payin'

39. Cartoon from *The Comic Almanac*, 1843, by George Cruikshank

FREEMASONS' HALL,

GREAT QUEEN STREET, LINCOLN'S-INN FIELDS.

PROGRAMME

OF THE

CELEBRATION of the HUNDREDTH ANNIVERSARY
of the BIRTHDAY of

ROBERT OWEN,

the PHILANTHROPIST,

[Born at Newtown, Montgomeryshire, Wales, on the 14th of May, 1771 :
Died 17th November, 1858, and buried at his Birthplace],

On TUESDAY, MAY 16th, 1871.

Vocalists :

Miss ELEANOR MOORE.   Miss MARIA LANGLEY.
Miss BLANCHE OWEN.   Mrs. JENNINGS.
Mr. GEORGE STEWART.   Mr. GANNEY.
Mr. J. H. JENNINGS. Mr. HARRY THOMAS.

Reciters :

Mrs. AUSTIN HOLYOAKE.   Mr. E. J. ELKINGTON.

Instrumentalists :

Violin . . . . . . Mr. VIOTTI COLLINS.

Pianistes . . . . . . { Miss LUCY THOMAS.
(Pupil of Miss Elizabeth Stirling).
Mr. J. L. KING.

Conductor . . Mr. CHARLES CLEMENTS.

TICKETS:

SINGLE (including Tea) .... 2s. 6d.
DOUBLE (for Lady and Gentleman, or Two Ladies) .... 3s. 6d.

DOORS OPEN at SIX o'Clock ; Concert to commence at Half-past.

WILLIAM PARE, F.S.S.—*Chairman.*
EDWARD TRUELOVE—*Honorary Secretary.*

40. Centenary Celebration, 1871

[Another edn.] Philadelphia, Penn., 1825.
[Another edn.] Pittsburgh, Penn., 1825.
[Another edn.] Washington, D.C., 1825.
[English edn.] London, 1825.

Two Memorials on Behalf of the Working Classes; the First presented to the Governments of Europe and America, the Second to the Allied Powers assembled . . . at Aix-la-Chapelle. Lanark, 1818.

The Universal Permanent Government, Constitution, and Code of Laws . . . for the World. . . . [London, 1848?]

The World's Convention of Delegates from the Human Race will be held in St. Martin's Hall . . . on May 14th, when will be explained the Divine Millenial State of Life upon Earth. . . . [n.p.] 1855. [Broadsheet.]

and JOHN BRINDLEY. *What Is Socialism? . . . a correct Report of the Public Discussion between Robert Owen and Mr. J. Brindley . . . January, 1841. . . .* London, 1841.
[Another edn.] Birmingham, 1841.

and ALEXANDER CAMPBELL. *Debate on the Evidences of Christianity; held in the City of Cincinnati . . . from the 13th to the 21st of April, 1829, between R. Owen and A. Campbell. . . .* 2 vols. Bethany, Va., 1829.
[2nd edn.] Cincinnati, Ohio, 1829.
[Another edn.] *Public Discussion. . . .* London, 1839.
[3rd edn.] *The Evidences of Christianity.* Cincinnati, Ohio, 1854.
[5th edn.] Cincinnati, Ohio, 1858.
[Another edn.] *Evidences of Christianity. . . .* New York [1900?]

and REV. WILLIAM LEGG. *Report of the Discussion between Robert Owen, and the Rev. Wm. Legg, . . . March 5th and 6th, 1839, on Mr. Owen's New Views of Society.* Birmingham, 1839.

and REV. J. H. ROEBUCK. *Public Discussion between Robert Owen . . . and the Rev. J. H. Roebuck, of Manchester. Revised and authorized by the Speakers. . . .* Manchester, London, 1837.

in Parliamentary Papers

Report of the Select Committee on Education of the Lower Classes in the Metropolis. IV:1816. [Owen's evidence: pp. 238–42.]

Report of the Select Committee on the State of Children employed in the Manufactories of the United Kingdom. III:1816. [Owen's evidence: pp. 20–8; 36–40; 86–95.]
[Reprinted in evidence of] *House of Lords Committee on Cotton Factories Bill, 1818–1819.*

Report of the Select Committee on Employment of the Poor in Ireland. I:1823. [Owen's evidence: pp. 70–103, 156–7.]

T

3 Secondary Works on Robert Owen

(i) *Unpublished*

DOUGLAS, PAUL H. 'Some New Material on the Lives of Robert and Robert Dale Owen'. [A paper presented to the Chicago Literary Club, 2 February, 1942. Typescripts in LC and the Newberry Library, Chicago.]

SILVER, HAROLD. 'Robert Owen and the Concept of Popular Education'. [M.Ed. thesis, University of Hull, 1964.]

(ii) *Books and Pamphlets*

BARNES, GEORGE N. *Life and Work of Robert Owen: a Lecture delivered . . . to the Montgomeryshire Society at the University of London . . . 10th October, 1928.* (Reprinted from the *Montgomeryshire Express and Radnor Times,* 23 October, 1928.) [n.p.] 1928.

BOOTH, ARTHUR JOHN. *Robert Owen, the Founder of Socialism in England.* London, 1869.

BRADLAUGH, CHARLES. *Five Dead Men Whom I Knew.* London, 1884. [Includes Robert Owen.]

BRIGGS, ASA. *Robert Owen in Retrospect.* Cooperative College Papers, no. 6. Loughborough, 1959.

BROWN, WILLIAM HENRY. *A Century of Liverpool Cooperation.* Liverpool, 1930. ['Robert Owen and Liverpool'.]

CLAYTON, JOSEPH. *Robert Owen, Pioneer of Social Reforms.* London, 1908.

COHN, WILLY. *Ein Lebensbild von Robert Owen.* Breslau, 1924.

COLE, GEORGE DOUGLAS HOWARD. *Robert Owen.* London, 1925. [2nd edn.] *Life of Robert Owen.* London, 1930. [3rd edn., with new introduction by Margaret Cole.] London, 1965.

COLE, MARGARET. *Robert Owen of New Lanark, 1771–1858.* London, 1953. [Another edn.] New York, 1953.

DAVIES, SIR ALFRED T., ed. *Robert Owen: Pioneer Social Reformer and Philanthropist.* Manchester, 1948.

DAVIES, R. E. *The Life of Robert Owen. . . .* London, 1907.

DEBORIN, A. M. 'The Ideas of Robert Owen', *I\z Istorii Rabochego Klassa i Revolutsii Novogo Dvi\zheniya* (A. M. Pankratova Memorial Volume), 1958.

DERRY, JOHN W. *The Radical Tradition: Tom Paine to Lloyd George.* London, 1967. [Chap. 4 on Owen.]

DOLLÉANS, ÉDOUARD. *Robert Owen, 1771–1858.* Paris, 1905. [2nd edn.] *Individualisme et Socialisme.* Paris, 1907.

DOMMANGET, MAURICE. *Robert Owen.* Paris, 1956.

DOWD, DOUGLAS FITZGERALD, and anon., in the *Encyclopedia Britannica*, vol. XVI. London, Chicago, 1964. [Article on Owen.]

FABRE, AUGUSTE. *Deux Épisodes de la Vie de Robert Owen, . . .* Nîmes, 1894.
Un Socialiste Pratique, Robert Owen. Nîmes, 1896.

FICHTER, JOSEPH H. *Roots of Change.* New York, 1939. ['Energetic Dreamer'.]

GILMAN, N. P. *A Dividend to Labor.* Boston, New York, 1899. ['Robert Owen the Manufacturer'.]

GLASSE, JOHN. *Robert Owen and His Life Work.* London, 1900.

GREENING, EDWARD OWEN. *Memories of Robert Owen and the Cooperative Pioneers.* Manchester, 1925.

GÜNTHER, KURT-HEINZ, ed. *Robert Owen: Pädagogische Schriften.* Berlin, 1955.

HALL, SPENCER T. *Biographical Sketches of Remarkable People.* London, 1873. [Includes account of meeting with Owen.]
[Another edn.] Burnley, 1881.

HARVEY, ROWLAND HILL. *Robert Owen: Social Idealist*, ed. John Walton Caughey. Berkeley and Los Angeles, Cal., 1949.

HOLYOAKE, GEORGE JACOB. *Life and Last Days of Robert Owen of New Lanark. . . .* London, 1859.
[2nd edn.] London, 1859.
[3rd edn.] London, 1866.
[Another edn.] London, 1871.
Robert Owen Co-operative Memorial at Newtown. The Unveiling Ceremony on July 12th, 1902. Address by Mr. G. J. Holyoake. Manchester [1902].
Robert Owen, the Precursor of Social Justice. In Justification of the Newtown Memorial. Written at the Request and Issued by the Owen Memorial Committee. Manchester [1900].

HUTCHINS, B. L. *Robert Owen: Social Reformer.* Fabian Tract No. 166. Biographical Series no. 2. London, 1912.
[Reprinted] London, 1923.
[Another edn.] London, 1928.

JOAD, CYRIL EDWIN M. *Robert Owen: Idealist.* Fabian Tract no. 182. London, 1915.
[Reprinted] London, 1917, 1922.
[Another edn.] London, 1928.

JONES, LLOYD. *The Life, Times, and Labours of Robert Owen,* ed. William Cairns Jones. 2 vols. London, 1889–90.
[Another edn., 2 vols. in 1] London, 1890.
[2nd edn.] London, 1895.
[American edn.] New York, 1895.
[3rd edn.] London, 1900.

KAMENSKI, A. B. *Robert Owen; ego zhizn i obshchestvennaya deyatel nost.* St Petersburg, 1893.

KNORTZ, KARL. *Robert Owen und sein Weltverbesserungsversuche.* Leipzig [1910].

LIEBKNECHT, WILHELM. *Robert Owen, sein Leben und Sozialpolitisches Wirken: zwei Ausgegrabene Skizzen.* Nürnberg, 1892.

MARTINEAU, HARRIET. *Biographical Sketches.* London, 1869. [Contains obituary notice of Owen.]
[4th edn.] London, 1876.
[Another edn.] London, 1877.

McCABE, JOSEPH. *Robert Owen.* London, 1920.

MAY, HENRY J. *The Life and Work of Robert Owen.* Manchester, 1901.

MORTON, A. L. *The Life and Ideas of Robert Owen.* London, 1962.
[Introduction, and selections from Owen's writings.]

NIEUWENHUIS, F.D. *Robert Owen in Zijn Leven en Werken Geschetst (1771–1858).* Amsterdam [1908?]

PACKARD, FREDERICK A. *Life of Robert Owen.* Philadelphia, Pa., 1866.
[2nd edn.] Philadelphia, Pa., 1868.

PODMORE, FRANK. *Robert Owen: A Biography.* 2 vols. London, 1906.
[American edn.] New York, 1906.
[Another edn., 2 vols. in 1] London, 1923.

PUGH, THOMAS. *Nodiadau Hanesyddol a Beirniadol ar Fywyd a Gwaith Robert Owen, o'r Drefnewydd.* Treffynnon, 1907.

REES, THOMAS MARDY. *Notable Welshmen, 1700–1900.* Caernarvon, 1908. [Includes Owen.]

ROBERTS, RICHARD. *Robert Owen.* 2 vols. Caernarfon, 1907. [In Welsh.]

ROBERTS, R. O. *Robert Owen o'r Dre' Newydd.* [n.p.] 1948.

ROGERS, J. D., in *Dictionary of Political Economy,* ed. R. H. Inglis Palgrave. London, 1899. [Article on Owen.]

SADLER, SIR MICHAEL E. *Owen, Lovett, Maurice and Toynbee: Their Work for Adult Education in England.* London, Manchester, 1907.

SARGANT, WILLIAM LUCAS. *Robert Owen and His Social Philosophy.* London, 1860.

SIMON, HELENE. *Robert Owen und der Sozialismus.* Berlin, 1919.
Robert Owen. Sein Leben und Seine Bedeutung für die Gegenwart. Jena, 1905.

STEPHEN, LESLIE. 'Robert Owen', in the *Dictionary of National Biography.* London, 1895–1900.

TAWNEY, R. H. *The Radical Tradition,* ed. Rita Hinden. London, 1964. [Includes essay on Owen.]

TAYLOR, GEORGE ROBERT STIRLING. *Leaders of Socialism.* London, 1908. [Includes Owen.]

THOMAS, WILLIAM JENKYN. *Heroes of Wales.* London, 1909. [Includes Owen.]

URWICK, L., and E. F. L. BRECH. *Making of Scientific Management.* 3 vols. London, 1946. [Vol. I includes 'The Pioneer of Personnel Management: Robert Owen, 1771–1858'.]

WAGNER, R. R. *Robert Owen, Lebensroman eines Menschengläubigen.* Zurich, 1942.

WALLAS, GRAHAM. 'Robert Owen', in *Men and Ideas.* London, 1940. [First published in *Sociological Review,* Jan. 1910, as 'The Beginning of Modern Socialism'.]

WEBB, CATHERINE. *Lives of Great Men and Women.* London, 1929. [Includes Owen.]

WILLIAMS, RICHARD. *Montgomeryshire Worthies.* Newtown, 1884. [Includes Owen.]
[Another edn.] Newtown, 1894.

WOLBERS, JULIEN O. *Robert Owen de Vader van het Socialisme in Engeland.* Utrecht, 1878.

WYMER, NORMAN. *Lives of Great Men and Women.* Five series. London, 1954–55. [First series, on 'Social Reformers', includes Robert Owen.]

(iii) *Articles*

BLACK, WILLIAM GEORGE. 'Robert Owen of New Lanark', *Notes and Queries,* VII (1901).

CARLTON, F. J. 'Robert Owen—Educator', *School Review* (Chicago, March 1910).

CHALONER, W. H. 'Robert Owen, Peter Drinkwater and the Early Factory System in Manchester, 1788–1800', *Bulletin of the John Rylands Library,* Manchester, XXXVII (1954–55).

COLE, GEORGE DOUGLAS HOWARD. 'The Educational Ideas of Robert Owen', The *Hibbert Journal,* XXIII, 1 (October 1924).

COLLINSON, JOSEPH. 'The Queen and Robert Owen', *Notes and Queries,* III (1893).

DAVIES, R. E. 'Robert Owen: a Eulogy and an Appreciation', *Millgate Monthly,* I (May–July 1906).

DEBORIN, A. M. 'Robert Owen's Utopian Communism and the Chartist Movement', *Vestnik Istorii Mirovoy Kultury,* VI (1959).

EDWARDS, EDWARD. 'Robert Owen', *University College of Wales Magazine,* XV (1893). [In Welsh.]
'Robert Owen, o'r Dre' Newydd', *Cymru,* IV (1893).

FRASER, E. M. 'Robert Owen in Manchester, 1787–1800', *Memoirs and Proceedings of the Manchester Literary and Philosophical Society,* LXXXII (1937–38).

FROWE, E. 'Robert Owen', *Marxism Today* (October 1958).

GORB, PETER. 'Robert Owen as a Business Man', *Bulletin of the Business Historical Society,* XXV (1951).

GRANT, BETTY. 'Robert Owen and Cooperative Production', *Marxism Today* (November 1958).

HULME, ARTHUR. 'An Early Business Letter by Robert Owen. A Memorable Interview Recalled', *Millgate Monthly* (May 1924).

LEWIS, W. 'Robert Owen at New Lanark', *Arena,* II (1890).

MARSHALL, EDWARD H. 'The Queen and Robert Owen', *Notes and Queries,* III (1893).

MILIBAND, RALPH. 'The Politics of Robert Owen', *Journal of the History of Ideas*, XV, ii (April 1954).

MURPHY, JAMES. 'Robert Owen in Liverpool', *Transactions, Historic Society of Lancashire and Cheshire*, CXII (1961).

NODAL, J. H. 'Coleridge and Robert Owen in Manchester', *Notes and Queries*, VII (1877).

OLIVER, W. H. 'Robert Owen and the English Working Class Movements', *History Today* (November 1958).

PODMORE, FRANK. 'Robert Owen and Co-operation', *Economic Journal*, XV (1905).

READE, ALEYN LYELL. 'Robert Owen of New Lanark: His Family', *Notes and Queries*, VIII (1907).

'Robert Owen and English Socialism', anon., *Leisure Hour*, XXVII (1878).

'Robert Owen and John Bellers', anon., *Cambrian Gleanings*, I, viii (August 1914).

'Robert Owen Memorial at Newtown', anon., *Labour Co-partnership*, VIII (1902).

ROCH, WALTER FRANCIS. 'Robert Owen', *Socialist Review*, V, xxix (July 1910).

SARGENT, IRENE. 'Robert Owen and Factory Reform', *Craftsman* (New York), I, v (February 1902).

SJOLIN, WALTER. 'New Light on Robert Owen. Poetic Vein in the Reformer's Personality', *Cooperative Review*, XXIX, 2 (February 1955).

TIMMONS, WILBERT H. 'Robert Owen's Texas Project', *Southwestern Historical Quarterly*, LII (January 1949).

VOLWILER, ALBERT T. 'Robert Owen and the Congress of Aix-la-Chapelle, 1818', *Scottish Historical Review*, XIX (January 1922).

WILLIAMS, HENRY B. 'Robert Owen and His Labour Exchanges', *Workers' Union Record* [Birmingham] (October–November 1917).

Works on Owenism

1 Manuscripts and Collections

[See also p. 265, Robert Owen Papers, Cooperative Union, Manchester].

ASSOCIATION OF ALL CLASSES OF ALL NATIONS. Minute Book of the Central Board, 26 May 1838—13 April 1840.
  Minute Book of Directors of the National Community Friendly Society, 4 June 1838—28 September 1843.
  Minute Book of the Directors of the Rational Society, 1 October 1843—26 February 1845. International Institute of Social History, Amsterdam, Netherlands. [These three vols. are a continuous record of the central Owenite organization, 1838–45.]

BRAY, JOHN FRANCIS. MSS., drafts, and cuttings, Seligman Collection, Columbia University, New York.

BROWN, PAUL. 'The Woodcutter; or, a Glimpse of the 19th Century at the West. [MS.] Illinois State Historical Library.

COMBE, GEORGE. MS. papers. National Library of Scotland, Edinburgh.

DURANT, THOMAS J. MS. papers of – – –, and MOSES GREENWOOD. [Filed under New Orleans.] New York Historical Society. [Includes letters to R. D. Owen and Albert Brisbane.]

EATON, PETER. Library of Robert Owen and the Cooperative Movement. Hitotsubashi University, Japan. [Includes MSS.]

FELLENBERG, PHILIPP EMANUEL VON. MSS., in Burgerbibliothek, Bern, Switzerland. [Includes twenty letters from Robert Owen, R. D. Owen, David Dale Owen, Richard Owen, 1818–35.]

HAMILTON, ARCHIBALD JAMES. Letters, autobiography, accounts, memoranda, including correspondence from Robert Owen, Abram Combe, etc., re the Orbiston community. Hamilton Papers, Motherwell Public Library, Scotland.

HOLE, JAMES. MS. letters. Solly Collection, British Library of Political and Economic Science.

HOLYOAKE, GEORGE JACOB. Diary, 1835–1905. George Howell Collection, Bishopsgate Institute, London.
  MSS., letters, papers. Cooperative Union Library, Manchester.

LEEDS COOPERATIVE SOCIETY. MS. Minute books from 1847. Leeds Industrial Cooperative Society, Leeds.

MACDONALD, A. J. MSS. and collections. Yale University Library, New Haven, Conn.

NEW HARMONY. MSS. Workingmen's Institute, New Harmony, Ind. [For details, see Bestor, *Backwoods Utopias*.]

Owen-Dorsey Papers. Indiana Historical Society.

William Augustus Twiggs Papers. Indiana Historical Society.

NEW LANARK. MSS. at New Lanark Mills, Scotland. (Includes visitors' books, 1795–1832, account books, order and letter books, etc.)

MS. cash-book of the New Lanark Institution, 1816–1825. Edinburgh University Library, Scotland.

OWEN, J. MS. account of the last days, death, and burial of Robert Owen. National Library of Wales.

OWEN, JANE. Scrapbook of newspaper cuttings, etc., 1815–1825. Robert Owen Museum, Newtown, Wales.

OWEN, RICHARD. 'Brief History of the Social Experiment at New Harmony, Indiana'. MS. Albert C. Porter Collection, Indiana State Library, Indianapolis, Ind.

MS. draft of ten essays on progressive education, written in winter of 1840–41. Workingmen's Institute, New Harmony, Ind.

OWEN, ROBERT DALE. MS. diary of 1824 and other items. Purdue University Library, Ind.

MSS. Stone Papers (privately owned). [Includes diary of R. D. Owen, 1825; documents on New Harmony; account of last hours of Robert Owen at Newtown; love letters of R. D. Owen to his wife, 1832–33.]

OWEN, WILLIAM. MS. letters to Robert Owen. Workingmen's Institute, New Harmony, Ind.

PARE, WILLIAM. Collection of broadsides and newspaper cuttings, relating to Owenite cooperation, 1828–42, mostly from the *Weekly Free Press*. University of London Library.

Scrapbook containing printed and MS. material on Robert Owen, collected by W. Pare. University of London Library, MS. 578.

STEEL, THOMAS. Papers. Wisconsin State Historical Society Library.

TINKER, THOMAS C. Papers (MS. letters). Wisconsin State Historical Society Library.

WARREN, JOSIAH. MS. notebook. New Harmony, 1840. [Parts of book written later, i.e., 1860–73; also contains a New Harmony Labor note (undated), signed 'James Promise'.] Workingmen's Institute, New Harmony, Ind.

MSS. and printed materials. Labadie Collection, University of Michigan Library, Ann Arbor, Mich.

2 Works by Owenites and Contemporaries

[This section includes only books, pamphlets and broadsheets relating to the Owenite movement. Years of birth and death, if known are given for authors who at some time in their careers identified themselves as Owenites. Other writings on radicalism, reform and social conditions are excluded except when they relate directly to Owenism. Articles in periodicals are not included unless they were also published as separate titles.]

The Address of the Working Classes of Devonshire, to their Fellow Labourers throughout Great Britain and Ireland. . . . Exeter [1830?; broadsheet.]

An Address to the Working Classes of Walsall on the Objects and Advantages oj Societies or Working Unions, established on the Principles of Mutual Co-operation. By a member of the Walsall Co-operative Society. [n.p.] 1830.

Address to the Working Classes on the Joint System of Exclusive Dealing; and the Formation of Joint-Stock Companies; showing how the People may free Themselves from Oppression. By a Member of the Nottingham Co-operative Store. Nottingham, 1840.

AINSLIE, REV. ROBERT. *An Examination of Socialism: the Last of a Series of Lectures against Socialism* . . . *27th February, 1840, under the Direction of the Committee of the London City Mission.* London, 1841.
Is There a God? London, 1840.

AITON, REV. JOHN. *Mr. Owen's Objections to Christianity and New View of Society and Education, refuted, by a plain Statement of Facts, with a hint to Archibald Hamilton, Esq., of Dalziel.* Edinburgh, 1824 [2nd edn.]

ALLEN, WILLIAM. *Colonies at Home: or, the Means for rendering the Industrious Labourer independent of Parish Relief; and for providing for the Poor Population of Ireland by the Cultivation of the Soil.* Lindfield, 1826.
[Another edn.] Lindfield, 1828.
[Another edn., with additions.] Lindfield, 1832.
Life of William Allen, with Selections from his Diaries and Correspondence. 3 vols. London, Brighton, 1846–47.
[American edn., in 2 vols.] Philadelphia, Penn., 1847.
A Plan for diminishing the Poor's Rate in agricultural Districts. London, 1833.
Reply on Behalf of the London Proprietors to the Address to the Inhabitants of New Lanark. London, 1818.

An Analysis of Human Nature: a Lecture delivered to the Members and Friends of the Association of All Classes of All Nations by One of the honorary Missionaries to that Institution. Leeds, 1838.

ANDREWS, STEPHEN PEARL. *The Science of Society. No. 1. The True Constitution of Government in the Sovereignty of the Individual as the final Development of Protestantism, Democracy, and Socialism.* New York, 1851.
[2nd edn., with] *No. 2. Cost the Limit of Price: a scientific Measure of Honesty in Trade.* New York, 1853.
[And later edns.]

An Answer to the Reply of the Rev. G. Hallatt to the Socialists' Address. By a Yarmouth Socialist. Yarmouth, 1839.

Argument against Socialism; or, the pernicious Principles of Robert Owen completely exposed, by a Clerical Gentleman. London, 1840.

ARISTARCHUS [pseud.] *Internal Free Trade and Capitalists' Trades' Unions. The only Conservative System of Joint Stock Commercial and Industrial Association.* [London, 1842.]

ARMAGH CO-OPERATIVE SOCIETY. *Words of Wisdom, addressed to the Working Classes to which are subjoined the Laws of the First Armagh Co-operative Society.* Armagh, 1830.

ASSOCIATION FOR PROMOTING INDUSTRIAL AND PROVIDENT SOCIETIES. *Strikes Superseded by Self-Employment; an Address to the Operatives of Great Britain, with a Plan for the Formation of Industrial Societies, by the Present Trade Societies or a similar Organization.* London, 1853.

ASSOCIATION FOR REMOVING IGNORANCE AND POVERTY. *Address to All Classes in the State From the Governor, Directors, and Committee of the Association for removing Ignorance and Poverty by Education and Employment.* [London] 1832.

ATKINSON, WILLIAM. *Lecture upon Home Colonization.* . . . Leeds, 1832.
Popery Unmasked, and Her Supporters Exposed. . . . Leeds, 1828.
Principles of Political Economy: or, the Laws of the Formation of National Wealth, developed by Means of the Christian Law of Government; being the Substance of a Case delivered to the Handloom Weavers Commission. London, 1840.
[Another edn., with introduction by Horace Greeley.] New York, 1843.
The State of the Science of Political Economy Investigated, wherein is shown the defective Character of the Arguments advanced for elucidating the Laws of the Formation of Wealth. London, 1838.

Authentic Disclosures of the Introduction of . . . *Robert Owen at St. James's Palace.* . . . London [1839].

BACON, R. N. *A Report of the Transactions at the Holkham Sheep-Shearing.* Norwich, 1821.

BAILEY, JAMES NAPIER. *Essays on miscellaneous Subjects: Historical, Moral, and Political.* Leeds, 1842.
Social Reformers' Cabinet Library. Leeds, 1841. [6 parts in 1 vol., viz:]
Lycurgus and the Spartans historically considered. . . .
A Brief Survey of the principal Features of Character exhibited by the Aborigines of North America. . . .
Preliminary Discourse on the Objects, Pleasures, and Advantages of the Science of Society. . . .
The Pleasures and Advantages of Literature and Philosophy briefly illustrated and explained.
Gehenna: its Monarch and Inhabitants. . . .
Sophistry unmasked. An Examination of the Arguments contained in a Book written by John Brindley and purporting to be a judicious Summary of the Evidences of Natural Theology and Revealed Religion.
[Another edn.] London, 1848.

BAINES, EDWARD. *Mr. Owen's Establishment at New Lanark, a Failure!! As proved by Edward Baines . . . and other Gentlemen deputed with him . . . to visit and inspect that Establishment.* . . . Leeds, 1838 [signed by Baines, Robert Oastler, and John Cawood, and dated 14 September 1819].
[Another edn., in] R. Owen, *Life*, IA. London, 1858.
The Socialists, a Society of Beasts. Important and interesting Proposal addressed to Robert Owen, Esq. Edinburgh [1840?]

BAKER, REV. F. *First Lecture on Cooperation . . . April 19th, 1830 . . . at Bolton.* (Reprinted from 'The Bolton Chronicle') London, 1830. (The *Universal Pamphleteer*).
Second Lecture . . . May 3rd, 1830. . . . (Reprinted from 'The Bolton Chronicle') London, 1830. (The *Universal Pamphleteer*).

BANKS OF INDUSTRY. *Objects and Intentions of Banks of Industry: to the thinking and reflecting Portion of the Public.* No. 3. [London, 1845; originally published, 1821.]

BANNISTER, REV. J. T. and ALEXANDER CAMPBELL. *Socialism, Public Discussion between.* . . . Coventry, 1839.

BARHAM, THOMAS FOSTER. *Philadelphia: or, the Claims of Humanity. A Plea for Social and Religious Reform.* London, 1858.

BARKER, JOSEPH. *Abominations of Socialism exposed, in Reply to the Gateshead Observer.* Newcastle, 1840.
Confessions of Joseph Barker, a Convert from Christianity. London, 1858.
The Gospel Triumphant; or, a Defence of Christianity against the Attacks of the Socialists; and an Exposure of the infidel Character and mischievous Tendency of the Social System of Robert Owen. Newcastle, 1839.
History and Confessions of a Man, as put forth by himself. Wortley, 1846.

Lectures on the Origin, the Character and the Tendency of Christianity, in Reply to G. J. Holyoake, delivered at Halifax on 14th and 15th February, 1848. [n.p.] 1848.

Life of Joseph Barker, written by himself, ed. John Thomas Barker. London, 1880.

Modern Skepticism: a Journey thro' the Land of Doubt and back again. A Life Story. Philadelphia, Penn., 1874.

The Overthrow of Infidel Socialism. . . . London, 1840.

[Another edn.]   Oldham [1841?]

Report of a Public Discussion between Joseph Barker and the Rev. Brewin Grant, held at Halifax. . . . Glasgow, 1855.

Socialism and its Advocates: a Letter from Mr. J. B. of America, with the Reply of the Editor of the Reasoner. London, 1853.

Teachings of Experience; or, Lessons I have learned on my Way through Life. London, 1869.

ed.   *Works on Phrenology, Physiology, etc., by O. S. Fowler.* London, Wortley, 1850.

and ALEXANDER CAMPBELL.   *Condensed Report of Four Lectures on . . . Christianity and Socialism.* . . . Hanley, 1839.

and LLOYD JONES.   *Report of a Public Discussion which took place at Oldham on the Evenings of Tuesday and Wednesday, February 19th and 20th, 1839 . . . on the Influence of Christianity.* Manchester, 1839.

BARMBY, JOHN GOODWYN (1820–1881), ed.   *The Communist Miscellany. A Collection of Tracts, Religious, Political, and Domestic.* London [1843].

The Outlines of Communism, Associality, and Communisation. London, 1841.

BEARD, JOHN RELLY.   *The Religion of Jesus Christ defended from the Assaults of Owenism, . . . in Nine Lectures.* London, 1839.

[Another edn.]   *The Religion of Jesus Christ defended from the Assaults of English Chartism.* . . . London, Manchester, 1839.

BEATSON, JASPER.   *An Examination of Mr. Owen's Plans for relieving Distress, removing Discontent, and 'recreating the Character of Man'.* Glasgow, 1823.

BEGG, W. G.   *A Review of the Sermon preached by the Rev. Newman Hall . . . November 3rd, 1844, in which many false Accusations and Charges were made against Infidels in General and Socialists in Particular.* Hull, 1844.

BIRCH, REV. EDWARD.   *Remarks on Socialism, designed to show the true Character and licentious Tendency of that System of Infidelity.* . . . London, 1839.

BLANDATA [pseud.]   *Intercepted Letter from Signor Blandata to Count Caskovwhiski, in which are given some Matters of Interest to the Owenites.* . . . Manchester, 1838.

BLATCHLY, CORNELIUS CAMDEN (1773–   ). *An Essay on Common
    Wealths.* New York, 1822.
    Part 1. *The Evils of exclusive and the Benefits of inclusive Wealth.*
    Part 2. *Extracts from Robert Owen's New View of Society.*
    Part 3. *Melish's Account of the Harmonists.*
*Some Causes of popular Poverty, derived from the enriching Nature of Interests,
    Rents, Duties, Inheritances, and Church Establishments, investigated in
    their Principles and Consequences, and Agreement with Scripture.* Phila-
    delphia, Penn., 1818. [This is the 2nd edn.; the first (1817) was appended
    to Thomas Branagan's *The Pleasures of Contemplation.*]

BOON, MARTIN JAMES. *Home Colonization, including a Plan showing how
    all the Unemployed might have profitable Work . . . also containing the
    Objects of the National Rational League, based upon the Social System of
    Robert Owen, and the political Programme of J. B. O'Brien.* London
    [1869].
*How to construct Free-State Railways and other national and municipal
    Works of Utility without Loans, Bonds, Mortgages, or the Burden of
    Interest. . . .* London, 1884.
*How to nationalize the Commons and Waste Lands, Railroads, Tramways,
    Malt-works, Gas-works, Public Buildings and other Works throughout
    England and the Colonies without the Burden of Interest, by Means of
    National Money. . . .* London, 1873.
*Important to the Rate-payers: the Object of the Costless Public Works Associa-
    tion.* London [c. 1870?]
*Land Usurpers and Money Changers. Dedicated to the People by a National
    Reformer* [by James Bronterre O'Brien or M. J. Boon?] London [1870].
*Malthusian Quackery: the true allegorical and categorical History of Brassy
    Cheek and Breezy Bouncer. By Herr von Schlagschurke.* London [1884].
*National Paper-Money the one and only Remedy for outcast London and all
    other Cities. . . .* London, 1885.
*A Protest against the present Emigrationists, including Remedies for the
    present Stagnation of Trade. . . .* London [1869].

BOWER, SAMUEL. *Competition in Peril; or, the present Position of the
    Owenites, or Rationalists, considered; together with Miss Martineau's
    Account of Communities in America.* Leeds [1837].
*The Peopling of Utopia; or, the Sufficiency of Socialism for Human Happiness:
    being a Comparison of the Social and Radical Schemes.* Bradford, 1838.
A Sequel to the Peopling of Utopia. . . . Bradford, 1838.

BOWES, REV. JOHN. *The right Use of Money Scripturally stated; or, an
    Answer to the Question, 'Ought Christians to save Money?'.* Dundee,
    1833.
The Social Beasts; or, an Exposure of the Principles of Robert Owen. Liver-
    pool, 1840.

and LLOYD JONES. *Report of the Discussion on Marriage, as advocated by Robert Owen. Between L. Jones and J. Bowes ... on Wednesday, 27th May, 1840.* Liverpool, 1840. [Reprinted from the *Liverpool Journal.*]

BOYD, SIR WILLIAM. *A Patriot's Fourth Letter to the British People; more particularly addressed to the Operatives of the United Kingdom, on the Advantages and Importance of a System of Co-operative Residence.* London, 1840. [2nd edn.]

BRAY, CHARLES (1811–1884). *Communism.* Coventry, 1848. [Reprinted from the *Coventry Herald*, 31 March 1848.]
The Education of the Body, an Address to the Working Classes. Coventry, 1837.
[2nd edn., n.p.] 1847.
The Education of the Feelings. London, 1838.
[2nd edn.] London, 1849.
[and later edns.]
An Essay upon the Union of Agriculture and Manufactures and upon the Organization of Industry. London, 1844 [originally the introduction to Mary Hennell's *Outline*, etc.].
The Income of the Kingdom and the Mode of its Distribution. London, 1857.
The Industrial Employment of Women, being a Comparison between the Condition of the People in the Watch Trade in Coventry, in which Women are not employed, and the People in the Ribbon Trade in which they are employed. . . . London, 1857.
On Force, its Mental and Moral Correlates . . . with Speculations on Spiritualism. London [1866].
Phases of Opinion and Experience during a long Life. London, 1879.
[Another edn.] London, 1884.
The Philosophy of Necessity. 2 vols. London, 1841. [With an appendix on Social Systems by Mary Hennell.]
[2nd edn., revised in 1 vol.] London, 1863.
[3rd edn., revised and abridged.] London, 1889.
The Science of Man: a Bird's Eye View of the wide and fertile Field of Anthropology. London, 1868.
[JONATHAN JONATHAN.] *Socialism. A Commentary on the Public Discussion on the Subjects of Necessity and Responsibility, between Mr. A. Campbell, Social Missionary, and the Rev. J. T. Bannister, of Coventry.* Coventry, 1839.
Toleration: with some Remarks on Prof. Tyndall's Address at Belfast. London, 1875.

BRAY, JOHN FRANCIS (1809–1897). *American Destiny. What Shall It Be, Republican or Cossack? An Argument Addressed to the People of the Late Union of North and South.* New York, 1864.

Labour's Wrongs and Labour's Remedies: or the Age of Might and the Age of Right. Leeds, 1839.

[Another edn., of chap. 2 only, was published as no. 4 of the Labourer's Library]. Leeds, 1842.

BRIANCOURT, MATHEW. *The Organization of Labor and Association,* trans. Francis George Shaw. New York, 1847.

BRIDGE, JOHN. *Arguments Addressed to Lord John Russell and Lord Melbourne on the Imprudence of Lending Their Great Names to Revolutionists and Infidels.* Manchester, 1843.

Brief History of the Proceedings of the Operative Builders' Trades Unions. [Manchester?] 1833.

BRINDLEY, JOHN. *An Answer to Mr. Owen's Denunciation of Marriage.* Birmingham [1840].

The Blasphemies of Socialism. Birmingham Tract I. Birmingham [1840].

The Immoralities of Socialism: being an Exposure of Mr. Owen's Attack upon Marriage. . . . Birmingham, 1840.

[Another edn.] *A Reply to Robert Owen's Attack upon Marriage.* Birmingham [n.d.]

A Reply to Robert Owen's Fundamental Principles of Socialism. Birmingham [1840].

[2nd edn.] Birmingham [1840].

A Reply to the Infidelity and Atheism of Socialism. Birmingham [1841].

Tract I. A Refutation of Robert Owen's Fundamental Principles of Socialism; proving the Free Agency of Man. Birmingham, 1840.

A Voice from Tytherly: being a faithful Account of the Explosion of the Hampshire Heaven! . . . Macclesfield, 1840.

and ALEXANDER CAMPBELL. *A Report of a Public Discussion on Socialism, held in the Theatre, Sheffield. . . .* Sheffield, 1840.

and FREDERICK HOLLICK. *Public Discussion on Socialism, held at the New Theatre, Leicester, . . . April 14 and 15, 1840, between Mr. Brindley and Mr. Hollick.* Leicester, 1840.

BROMILY, ARTHUR. *Proposals for an Experiment intended to determine and illustrate the Leading Principles of Social Physics.* Manchester, 1852.

A Social Theory: or, a brief Exposition of the Primary Law in Nature, affecting Social Development. Also an Appendix containing an Outline of a Scheme framed in Accordance with the above mentioned Law. London, Manchester, 1851.

BROUGHAM, LORD HENRY. *Mr. Brougham's Speech on Sir William De Crespigny's Motion to enquire into Mr. Owen's Plan. December 16th, 1820.* London [1820?].

BROWN, DAVID. *A Complete Refutation of the Principles of Socialism or Owenism . . . also an Investigation of the Book of the New Moral World.* Glasgow, 1840.

BROWN, JOHN. *Remarks on the Plans and Publications of Robert Owen Esq. of New Lanark.* Edinburgh, 1817.

BROWN, PAUL. *A Dialogue on Commonwealths.* Cincinnati, Ohio, 1828.
A Disquisition on Faith. Washington, D.C., 1822.
An Enquiry concerning the Nature, End, and Practicability of a Course of Philosophical Education. Washington, D.C., 1822.
Twelve Months in New Harmony: presenting a faithful Account of the principal Occurrences which have taken Place there within that Period. . . . Cincinnati, Ohio, 1827.

BUCHANAN, ROBERT (1813–1866). *A Concise History of Modern Priest-craft. . . .* Manchester, 1840.
[2nd edn.] Manchester, 1840.
Exposure of the Falsehoods, Calumnies and Misrepresentations of a Pamphlet entitled 'The Abominations of Socialism Exposed', being a Refutation of . . . the Rev. Joseph Barker and all Others who have adopted a similar Mode of opposing Socialism. Manchester, 1840.
The Origin and Nature of Ghosts, Demons, Spectral Illusions. [n.p.] 1840.
The Past, the Present, and the Future. A Poem. Manchester, 1841.
The Religion of Past and Present Society founded upon a false Principle . . . a Lecture . . . Social Institution, Salford . . . 10th March, 1839. [n.p.] 1839.
Socialism vindicated in a Reply to a Sermon entitled 'Socialism Denounced as an Outrage upon the Laws of God and Man', Preached by the Rev. W. J. Kidd . . . on July 12th, 1840. Manchester, 1840.

BUCKINGHAM, JAMES SILK. *National Evils and Practical Remedies, with the Plan of a Model Town. Accompanied by an Examination of some important Moral and Political Problems.* London, 1849.

A Budget for the Socialists, containing The Female Socialist: a Doggerel worthy of its Burthen: also the Lord's Prayer of the Owenites, and the Gospel according to St. Owen. London, 1840.

BULL, REV. GEORGE STRINGER. *Mr. Bull and the Regeneration Society. To the . . . Leeds Times.* [Bradford?] 1834.

BURET, EUGÈNE. *De la Misère des Classes Laborieuses en Angleterre et en France.* 2 vols. Paris, 1840.

BYLLESBY, LANGTON (1789–1871). *Observations on the Sources and Effects of Unequal Wealth.* New York, 1826.
[Another edn., with introduction by Joseph Dorfman] New York, 1961.

Calculations showing the Facility with which the Paupers and Unemployed, or any other Portion of the Population, may be enabled to support themselves within most desirable Circumstances, by Co-operation. London [1850?].

CAMERON, WILLIAM. *An Address to the Disciples of Robert Owen, on the Importance and Necessity of speedily accomplishing a Bond of Union of Mutual Interests, for gradually carrying into Operation the New Science of Society.* London, 1832.
The Second Trumpet, a Satirical and Instructive Poem. London, 1835.

CAMPBELL, ALEXANDER (1796–1870). *Address on the Progress of the Co-operative System.* [Glasgow?] 1831.
Trial and Defence of A. Campbell, Operative, before the Exchequer Court, Edinburgh, for printing and publishing 'The Tradesman' contrary to the infamous Gagging Act. Glasgow, 1835.
and WILLIAM PROWTING ROBERTS. *Authentic Report of the Discussion at the Guildhall, Bath, on . . . the 13th, 14th, and 15th of September, 1838, between Mr. A. Campbell and Mr. W. P. Roberts, on the Principles of Mr. Robert Owen.* Bath, 1838.

CAMPBELL, JOHN. *A Theory of Equality or the Way to make every Man act honestly.* Philadelphia, Penn., 1848.

'CAPYS'. *Theron, the Socialist: a Poem in 6 Cantos.* London [n.d.].

CARLILE, RICHARD. *A View and Review of Robert Owen's Projects; or, the Manspel, according to Robert Owen, criticised by the Gospel according to Richard Carlile.* London [183?].

CARPENTER, WILLIAM (1797–1874). *An Address to the Working Classes on the Reform Bill.* London [1831].
Can the Tories become Reformers? London, 1834.
The Corporation of London, as it is, and as it should be. London, 1847.
The Elector's Manual; comprising . . . Information . . . connected with the Exercise of the Franchise. . . . London, 1832.
Machinery, as it affects the Industrial Classes; and the Employment of Children in Factories. London [1844–45?].
The Necessity and Efficiency of the Ballot Discussed. London, 1838.
Peerage for the People. [n.p.] 1837.
ed. *The People's Book, comprising their Chartered Rights and Practical Wrongs.* London, 1831.
The Perils of Policy Holders. London, 1860. [3rd edn.]
Political Letters and Pamphlets. London, 1830–31.
The Political Text Book; . . . London, 1833.
Political and Historical Essays. . . . London, 1831. [Including the] *Political Tracts,* nos. 1–9:
No. 1. *The Advantages of Parliamentary Reform.*

No. 2. *Natural and Civil Rights.*

No. 3. *Origin and Objects of Civil Government.*

No. 4. *Popular Remedies for Popular Ends.*

No. 5. *Advantages of Trade Unions.*

No. 6. *Progress and Influence of Knowledge.*

No. 7. *Alleged Benefits of Emigration Examined and Refuted.*

No. 8. *Historical Sketch of the State of Ireland.*

No. 9. *Historical Sketch.* . . . [concluded.]

Relief for the Unemployed: Emigration and Colonization considered, with special Reference to the Australian Colonies of South Australia and New Zealand. . . . London, 1841.

A Reply to William Howitt's Preface to the Abridged History of Priestcraft. London, 1834.

CARTER, JOHN H. *The Voice of the Past; written in Defence of Christianity and the Constitution of England . . . being a Reply to the Manifesto of Mr. Robert Owen.* Portsea, 1840 [2nd edn.]

CHAMBERS, WILLIAM. *Co-operation in Its Different Branches.* Chambers's Social Science Tracts, no. 1. London, Edinburgh, 1860.

Charter of the Rights of Humanity, passed at a Great Public Meeting of the Producers of Wealth and Knowledge, held in the Metropolis on Wednesday, February 12th, 1834. [n.p.] 1834. [Broadsheet.]

CHEVALIER, JULES ST ANDRE. *Five Years in the Land of Refuge: a Letter on the Prospects of Cooperative Associations in England.* London, 1851.

A CHRISTIAN SOCIALIST. *Religion as now practiced Opposed to the Laws of God, or Remarks on the Necessity of immediately reviving Primitive Christianity, and Community of Goods.* Manchester, 1838.

CHRISTIANUS [MORGAN, JOHN MINTER?] *Mr. Owen's proposed Villages for the Poor shown to be highly favourable to Christianity: in a Letter to William Wilberforce.* . . . London, 1819.

A CITIZEN. *The Days of Queen Victoria; or, a Sketch of the Times.* Bath, 1838.

CLARKE, J. G. *The Christian's Looking Glass, or, a Reply to the Animadversions of the Rev. Dr. Redford, . . . and the Clergy of All Denominations, who attempt to Oppose the Religion of Charity as propounded by Robert Owen, being a Lecture delivered in the Social Institution, Manchester.* Hulme, 1838.

Letters to Dr. Adam Clarke; or, a critical Review of the Life, Character, Miracles, and Resurrection of Jesus Christ. London, Leeds [1838?].

Marriage Calmly and Philosophically Considered. Manchester [1840?].

A CLERICAL GENTLEMAN. *A Concise and convincing Argument against Socialism: or, the pernicious Principles of Robert Owen Completely Exposed.* London, 1840.

CLINTON, HENRY. *Associated Homes. An Address to the Shareholders of the Mutual, Land, Emigration and Cooperative Colonization Society, delivered at the Eclectic Institute . . . April 24th, 1870.* London, 1871.
The Best Possible Government at the least possible Cost impossible until Commerce is regulated. London, 1857.
The 'Screw Loose' in the Machinery of Society. [n.p.] 1859. [Broadsheet.]
and E. V. NEALE. *Letters on Associated Homes.* London, 1861.

CLISSOLD, HENRY. *Prospectus of a Central, National Institution of Home Colonies: designed to instruct and employ distressed, unoccupied Poor, on Waste Lands, in Spade Husbandry.* London, 1830.

COLLET, SOPHIA DOBSON. *George Jacob Holyoake and Modern Atheism: a Biographical and Critical Essay.* London, 1855.

COMBE, ABRAM (1785–1827). *An Address to the Conductors of the Periodical Press upon the Causes of religious and political Disputes, with Remarks on the . . . Definition of certain Words and Terms which have often been the Subject of Controversy.* Edinburgh, 1823.
Life and Dying Testimony of Abram Combe in Favour of Robert Owen's New Views of Man and Society, ed. Alexander Campbell. London, 1844.

[COMBE, ABRAM.] *The New Court. No. 1. The Records of the New Court, established by the First Society . . . for the Extinction of Disputes, 22nd March, 1825.* [n.p., n.d.]

COMBE, ABRAM. *Metaphorical Sketches of the Old and the New Systems, with Opinions on Interesting Subjects.* Edinburgh, 1823.
Observations on the Old and New Views, and their Effects on the Conduct of Individuals, as manifested in the Proceedings of the Edinburgh Christian Instructor and Mr. Owen. Edinburgh, 1823.
A Proposal for Commencing the Experiment of Mr. Owen's System, in a Way which is not altogether opposed to the prevailing Prejudices of Mankind. [First published in the *Edinburgh Observer,* 31 January 1824. Reprinted in the *Orbiston Register,* II, 19–32 (14 February, 14 March 1827).]
The Religious Creed of the New System, with an Explanatory Catechism, and an Appeal in Favour of True Religion, to the Ministers of All religious Persuasions and Denominations. Edinburgh, 1824.
The Sphere for Joint-stock Companies: or, the Way to increase the Value of Land, Capital, and Labour. With an Account of the Establishment at Orbiston. . . . Edinburgh, 1825.

Competitive versus Co-operative Labour; or, Labour as it is, and Labour as it ought to be. London, 1837.

Complete Defeat of Robert Owen and Socialism in the Staffordshire Potteries.
Birmingham, 1840. [Broadsheet.]

COMPREHENSIONISTS, SECRETARY OF THE. *Poetry of the Pavement.*
London [n.d.]

CONCORDIUM. *A Brief Account of the First Concordium, or Harmonious
Industrial College. A Home for the Affectionate, Skilful, and Industrious.*
Ham Common [1843].
*A Prospectus for the Establishment of a Concordium or an Industry Harmony
College.* London, 1841.

A CONFUCIAN. *Sectarianism explained, and the Force of the Imagination
displayed.* London, 1836.

CONINGHAM, WILLIAM. *The Self-organized Cooperative Associations in
Paris and the French Republic. A Public Lecture . . . Brighton, July 28,
1851.* London, 1851.

COOPER, ROBERT (1819–1868). *Christianity a Failure! a Lecture . . .
Sunderland . . . November 19th, 1841.* Sunderland, 1841.
*A Contrast between the New Moral and the Old Immoral World; a Lecture
delivered in the Social Institution, Salford.* Hulme, 1838.
*Death-Bed Repentance; Its Inconclusiveness and Absurdity when applied as a
Test of the Truth of Opinion. A Lecture, delivered in the Hall of Science, . . .
Manchester . . . November 1st, 1840.* Leeds, 1840.
*The 'Holy Scriptures' analyzed, or, Extracts from the Bible, shewing its
Contradictions, Absurdities, and Immoralities.* Hulme, 1839.
[2nd edn.] Hulme, 1840.
A Lecture on Original Sin, delivered in the Social Institution, . . . Salford.
Manchester, London, Hulme, 1838 [2nd edn.]
[4th edn.] Manchester, 1839.
Two Lectures on Free Agency versus Orthodoxy. . . . Edinburgh, 1845.

*Co-operation: Dialogue between a Shoemaker and a Tailor . . . by a Member of
the Metropolitan Cooperative Trading Association.* London, 1830.
[2nd edn.]

A COOPERATOR. *The Circulating Medium, and the Present Mode of Ex-
change, the Cause of increasing Distress among the Productive Classes—
Labour Exchange Banks the only Remedy.* London, 1832.
*Remarks on the Rational System as developed by Robert Owen, Esq., and on
the Prospects of Society in Reference to Its Introduction into Practice.*
London, 1832.

CORNISH, SAMUEL. *The Rationalist, or, an Inquiry into the Nature, Progress, and Prospects of Man, Nos. I–II.* London [1834?].
ed. *Social Tracts.* London, 1837–38.
No. 1. *Observations on Political and Social Reform. . . .*

No. 2. *A Calculation of the Result of the Industry of 500 Persons.* . . .
No. 3. *The Pull All Together.*
No. 4. *Man the Creature of Circumstances.*
No. 5. *Human Nature.* . . .
No. 6. *The Religion of the New Moral World.*
No. 7. *Outline of the Rational System of Society.* . . .

CORVAJA, BARON JOSEPH. *Perpetual Peace to the Machine by the Universal Millennium,* . . . London, 1855.

CORY, I. P. *Competition: its Abuse, and the Present Distress.* [n.p.] 1842.

COURTAULD, GEORGE. *Address to Those who may be disposed to remove to the United States* . . . *on the Advantages of Equitable Associations of Capital and Labour, in the Formation of Agricultural Establishments in the Interior Country. Including Remarks on Mr. Birkbeck's Opinions upon this Subject.* Sudbury, 1820.

COWARD, W. C. *Victoriaism; or, a Reorganization of the People: Moral, Social, Economical, and Political: suggested as a Remedy for the present Distress.* . . . London, 1843.

CRAIG, EDWARD THOMAS (1804–1894). *Competitive Society illustrated, showing how the Producers of Wealth are fleeced by the Non-producing Consumers.* London, 1885.
Health and Length of Life; or, the Social and Domestic Affections, and an important Discovery in Relation to the Influence of Ventilation on Longevity. A Lecture with Ten Illustrations. [n.p., 1856?]
The Irish and Labour Question illustrated in the History of Ralahine and Co-operative Farming. London, 1882.
[Another edn.] London, 1893.
[Another edn.] *Histoire de l'Association agricole de Ralahine,* résumé et traduit par Marie Moret. Saint Quentin, 1882.
[Another edn.] *An Irish Commune. The History of Ralahine. Adapted from the Narrative of E. T. Craig.* Introduction by A. E. Notes by D. O'Cobhthaigh. Dublin [1919].
[Another edn.] Dublin, 1920.
Memoir and In Memoriam of Henry Travis, M.D., English Socialist. Manchester [1884].
Palmistry and Phrenology—a Reply to the Editor of the Daily News. [From the *Phrenological Magazine,* 1886; n.p., n.d.]
Phrenological Chart of the Propensities, Moral Sentiments, and intellectual Faculties of the Human Mind. London [1845?].
Ralahine; or, the History of important practical Experiences made by the Ralahine Agricultural and Manual Labour Association. . . . [n.p.] 1838. [Reprinted from the *Star in the East.*]

Shakespeare and Art, Portraiture of the Poet and Heritage of Genius.
London, 1865 [2nd edn.].
The Portraits, Bust and Monument of Shakespeare. [n.p.] 1886.
Shakespeare's Portraits Phrenologically considered. Philadelphia, Penn.,
1875. [Originally published as an article, 1864.]
Sophistry unmasked, being an Answer to Mr. E. Thornby. Manchester, 1841.
*Ventilation; or, a new Reading of the Returns of the Registrar-General, on
Life, Health, Disease, and Drainage.* [n.p., 1869?; broadsheet.]
Work and Wages; or, Capital, Currency, and Production. London [1865?].

[CROSSLEY, D.] *Three Letters . . . to the Rev. Enoch Mellor, Independent
Minister of Halifax, by the Friends of Robert Owen, the Founder of Infant
Schools.* Halifax, 1854.

CROWTHER, RICHARD. *A Letter to the Socialists, on the Doctrine of Irresponsibility.* . . . Manchester, 1838.

CUBITT, GEORGE. *The Power of Circumstances: being the seventh of a Series
of Lectures against Socialism.* . . . London, 1840.

CUNNINGHAM, ABNER. *An Address submitted to the Consideration of R. D.
Owen, Kneeland, Houston, and Others of the Infidel Party.* New York,
1833.
*Practical Infidelity portrayed . . . an Address submitted to the consideration of
R. D. Owen.* [n.p.] 1836.

D. *Ode to Mr. Owen.* [n.p., n.d.]

DALTON, REV. T. *The Responsibility of Men for their Belief.* London,
Salford, Todmorden, 1840.
and LLOYD JONES. *Socialism Examined. Report of a Public Discussion
which took place at Huddersfield, on . . . 13th, 14th, and 15th December,
1837, . . . upon 'The Five Fundamental Facts, and the Twenty Laws of
Human Nature, as found in the Book of the New Moral World, written by
Robert Owen, Esq.'* Manchester, 1838.

DAVENPORT, ALLEN (1775–1846.) *The Life and literary Pursuits of Allen
Davenport.* [n.p., c. 1846?]
Life, Writings, and Principles of Thomas Spence. London, 1836.
The Muse's Wreath; composed of original Poems. London [1830?].
Origin of Man and the Progress of Society. London, 1846.

DAVIDSON, W. *History of Lanark and Guide to the Scenery, with List of
Roads to the principal Towns.* Lanark, 1828. [Includes description of
New Lanark, pp. 160–83.]

DAVIES, . *A short Sketch of the Scripturian's Creed.* [Manchester] 1839.

DEBATE ON SOCIALISM. *Reprint of the Debate in the Lords on Socialism, from 'The Times' of 5th February, 1840. For the especial Use of the Members of the Universal Community Society of Rational Religionists.* Leeds, 1840.

The Democratic and Social Almanac for 1850: presented to the Readers of the 'Weekly Tribune' of December 8th, 1849. London [1849].

DEMOCRITUS. *What is God? Or, the Laughing Philosopher's Conversation with a Protestant Clergyman.* Manchester [n.d.].

The Deplorable Effects of Sectarian Training . . . as illustrated in the Life and Proceedings of the notorious John Brindley. Manchester [1841].

DETROSIER, ROWLAND (1800–1834). *An Address delivered at the New Mechanics' Institution, . . . Manchester, . . . December 30, 1829.* Manchester [1829].
Address delivered to Members of the New Mechanics' Institution, Manchester, on March 25, 1831, on the Necessity of an Extension of Moral and Political Instruction among the Working Classes. London, Manchester, 1831.
[Another edn.] *. . . with a brief Memoir of the Author* [by Shuttleworth]. London, 1832.
[Another edn.] London, 1835.
An Address on the Advantages of the Intended Mechanics' Hall of Science, delivered at the Manchester New Mechanics' Institution, . . . Manchester, 1831.
The Benefits of General Knowledge, more especially the Sciences of Mineralogy, Geology, Botany, and Entomology; Being an Address . . . at the Opening of the Banksian Society, Manchester, on Monday, January 5th, 1829. London [n.d.]
Lecture on the Utility of Political Unions for the Diffusion of sound Moral and Political Information amongst the People, on the Necessity for that Information, and on the Political Influence of Scientific Knowledge. Delivered to . . . the National Political Union . . . March 26, 1832. London, 1832.

A Diagram illustrative of the Formation of Human Character suggested by Mr. Owen's Development of a New Society. [n.p.] 1824.

DICK, ROBERT. *Evils and Anomaly of Individuals being Landlords, and Nations Tenants.* [n.p., n.d.]
Labour: Its unequal Distribution and unnecessary Excess. London, 1858.
Marriage and Population; their Natural Laws. London, 1858.
Physiology: Its Politico-moral Teachings. [n.p., n.d.]

Divine Revelation Examined. Manchester [n.d.]

[DOHERTY, JOHN (1789–   )?] *Address . . . to the Workmen of the United Kingdom.* Manchester, 1830.

DOHERTY, JOHN. *A Letter to the Members of the National Association for the Protection of Labour.* Manchester, 1831.
The Ten Hours Bill. A Letter to the Factory Operatives of Lancashire, on the Necessity of petitioning Parliament in favour of the Ten Hours Bill. Manchester, 1845.

The Drones and the Bees: A Fable. Edinburgh, 1831.

DUNCAN, JAMES. *Animadversions on the Principles of the New Harmony Society.* Indianapolis, Ind., 1826.
A Dialogue between an Atheist and a Theist. Indianapolis, Ind., 1826.

DUNCAN, JAMES ELMSLIE. *Flowers and Fruits; or, Poetry, Philosophy, and Science.* London [1843?].
Pe-ans for the People. London, 1848. [Broadsides.]

DUNLOP, JOHN. *The Universal Tendency to Association in Mankind analyzed and illustrated. . . .* London, 1840.

EDGAR, HENRY. *Modern Times, the Labor Question, and the Family. A brief Statement of Facts and Principles.* New York [1855].

The Educational Circular: for all Sects and Parties. Cheltenham [c. 1841].

Effects of Machinery on manual Labour, and on the Distribution of the Produce of Industry (reprinted from Carpenter's Political Magazine). London [1832].
[Another edn.] London, 1835.

ELLIS, JOHN. *A Letter to the Rev. Jas. Acworth, . . . being a Reply to a slanderous Letter written by his Reverence to one of his Christian Brethren at Oldham.* Manchester [185?].
Marriage: as practiced by the Priesthood in all Ages, contrasted with the Principles of Reason, and the Views of the Rational Society. An Address delivered in the Institution, . . . Tottenham Court Rd. London [1845].

The Emigrants of the nineteenth Century. London, 1828.

ENSOR, GEORGE. *Of Property, and of its equal Distribution, as promoting Virtue, Population, Abundance.* London, 1844.

An Epitome of Mr. Owen's Social System. . . . [n.p.] 1831.

Equality. [n.p.] 1831. [A poem written against Wilmot Horton's views.]

An Essay, in Answer to the Question, whether does the Principle of Competition . . . or, the Principle of united Exertions, . . . form the most secure Basis for the Formation of Society? London, 1834.

Essays and Articles on Subjects connected with popular Political Economy, illustrative of the Condition and Prospects of the Working Classes. Birmingham, 1833.

ETHNICUS. *Why am I a Socialist? or, a Defence of Social Principles; in a Letter to a Christian Friend.* Glasgow, 1840.

ETZLER, JOHN ADOLPHUS. *Description of the naval Automation invented by J. A. Etzler. . . .* London, 1844.

Dialogue on Etzler's Paradise: between Messrs. Clear, Flat, Dunce, and Grudge. By the Author of 'Paradise within the Reach of all Men'. [London] 1843.

Emigration to the Tropical World for the Melioration of all Classes of People of all Nations. Ham Common, 1844.

Mechanical System in its greatest Simplicity, for agricultural Works, Formation of Ditches, Canals, Dams, and any other Works. London, 1844.

The New World or Mechanical System, to perform the Labours of Man and Beast by inanimate Powers, that cost Nothing . . . as a Sequel of his 'Paradise'. Philadelphia, Penn., 1841.

The Paradise within the Reach of all Men, without Labour, by Powers of Nature and Machinery. An Address to all intelligent Men. 2 parts. Philadelphia, Penn., 1833. [2 vols. in 1.]

[Another edn.] London, 1836.

[2nd English edn.] London, 1842.

Two Visions of J. A. Etzler . . . a Revelation of Futurity. Ham Common, 1844.

EVANS, THOMAS. *Address of the Society of Spencean Philanthropists to all Mankind, on the Means of promoting Liberty and Happiness.* [London] 1817.

[EVANS, THOMAS]. *Christian Policy in full Practice among the People of Harmony, a Town in the State of Pennsylvania . . . to which are Subjoined a concise View of the Spencean System of Agrarian Fellowship. . . .* [London, 1818.]

EVANS, THOMAS. *Christian Policy, the Salvation of the Empire.* London, 1816. [2nd edn.]

The Petition of Thomas Evans, Librarian to the Spencean Philanthropist Society . . . to the . . . House of Commons, 28th February, 1817. [London] 1817.

EVELYN, JOHN. *Co-operation. An Address to the Labouring Classes, on the Plans to be pursued and the Errors to be avoided in conducting Trading Unions.* London, 1830.

EVERETT, L. S. *An Exposure of the Principles of the 'Free Inquirers'.* Boston, Mass., 1831.

An Examination of Mr. Robert Owen's Doctrines of Human Responsibility. . . . London [1840].

An Exposure of a New System of Irreligion, which is in Opposition to the Holy Scriptures, and is called the New Moral World. Promulgated by Robert Owen, Esq., whose Doctrine proves him a Child of the Devil, and is here exploded by the Christian Philosopher. Newcastle-on-Tyne [n.d.].

An Exposure of Joseph Mather's Pamphlet entitled 'Socialism exposed: or, the Book of the New Moral World examined, and brought to the Test of Fact and Experience'. By a Lover of Practical Christianity. Bilston [1839?].

EYRE, C.S. *A Few Words on Socialism.* Coventry, 1840.
Socialism Examined. [n.p.] 1839.

FAIRPLAY, JOHN [pseud.?] *Remarks on a Sermon . . . entitled 'The Use of the Church Service on a Late Occasion defended, and Socialist Crimes exposed, by the Rev. John Craig, . . .'* Coventry, 1840.

FALLAS, THOMAS. *The People's Rights, and how to get them. By the Poor Man's Friend.* [n.p., c. 1844.]

False Sanctity: or, the Modern Tartuffes. London, 1831. [Verse.]

FARN, JOHN COLIER (1815–). *Pictures of Controversy; or, the Conflicts of Faith and Scepticism.* London, 1857.

Farther Address of the Committee on Mr. Owen's Plan for providing Employment for the Poor. 1 December, 1819. [n.p.; n.d.]

FERRALL, SIMON A. [O'FERRALL]. *Ramble of Six Thousand Miles Through the United States of America.* London, 1832. [Contains description of New Harmony.]

FEUERBACH, A. VON. *Caspar Hauser: an Account of an Individual kept in a Dungeon, separated from all Communication with the World, from early Childhood to about the Age of Seventeen. . . .* [n.p.] 1834.

FIELDEN, JOHN. *The Curse of the Factory System: or, a short Account of the Origin of Factory Cruelties.* Halifax, 1836.
and others. *National Regeneration:—*
   1. *Letter from Mr. Fitton to Mr. Fielden.*
   2. *Letter from Mr. Fielden to Mr. Fitton.*
   3. *Letter from Mr. Holt to Mr. Fielden.*
Which Letters contain a Development of all the Principles and all the Views connected with this important Change in the manufacturing Affairs of the Country. London, 1834.

FINCH, JOHN (1783–1857). *Important Meeting of the Working Classes: Delegates from Fifty Cooperative Societies.* [n.p., 1831?]

The Millennium. The Wisdom of Jesus, and the Foolery of Sectarianism, in Twelve Letters. Liverpool, 1837.

Moral Code of the New Moral World . . . *corrected, revised, and approved by Robert Owen.* Liverpool, 1840.

A Reformed Established Church. Liverpool, 1841.

[FINCH, JOHN.] *Society as it is, and Society as it ought to be; or, Social Diseases and Social Remedies,* . . . *by a Liverpool Merchant.* Liverpool, 1847.

FINCH, JOHN. *Temperance Tracts.* Liverpool, 1836.

Town Dues and Currency, Free Trade and Protection. Liverpool, 1850.

[FINCH, JOHN, ed.?] *The Book of the inspired British Prophet of the Seventeenth Century, containing the Religion of the Millennium, New Law of Righteousness, and most remarkable Prophecies* . . . *concerning the Deliverance and Salvation of the Working People* . . . *and the immediate and Universal Establishment of the Millennium.* Part I. Liverpool, 1842. [First published in 1649.]

FINCH, JOHN, ed. *The Seven Seals broke open; or, the Bible of the Reformation Reformed.* London, 1853. [3 vols. in 7 books.]

FINCH, JOHN, JR. *Statistics of Vauxhall Ward, Liverpool, showing the actual Condition of more than Five Thousand Families, being the Result of an Inquiry* . . . *at the Request of the Liverpool Anti-Monopoly Association.* . . . Liverpool, 1842.

FINCH, WILLIAM STAFFORD. *The Present Circumstances of the Poor displayed, and the Means suggested for their Improvement: in Accordance with the Plans of the Church of England Self-Supporting Village Society.* [n.p.] 1850.

FINLAY, THOMAS. *Defence of Thomas Finlay, charged* . . . *with vending Blasphemy, and printed by Order of 'The Scottish Anti-Persecution Union'.* Edinburgh, 1843.

[FISHER, WILLIAM LOGAN.] *An Examination of the New System of Society by Robert Owen, showing its Insufficiency to reform Mankind. With Observations on the Operation of the Principle of Virtue in the Mind of Man.* Philadelphia, Penn., 1826.

[FLEMING, GEORGE ALEXANDER.] *A Day at New Lanark by the Editor of the New Moral World.* Birmingham, 1839.

FLEMING, GEORGE ALEXANDER. *A full Account of the Farewell Festival given to Robert Owen, Esq., on his Departure for America, with Reports of the Speeches of Messrs.* . . . *Fleming,* . . . London, 1844.

Infidelity of professed Christianity. . . . *Lecture* . . . *at Salford.* Manchester [n.d.].

The Right Application of Science: an Address delivered at the Opening of the Huddersfield Hall of Science, on . . . November 3rd, 1839. Leeds, 1839.
A Vindication of the Principles of the Rational System of Society as proposed by Robert Owen. Manchester [1838?].

FOURIER, CHARLES. *Piéges et Charlatanisme des deux Sectes Saint-Simon et Owen, qui promettent l'Association et le Progrès. . . .* Paris, 1831.
Political Economy made easy, a Speech, . . . presented to the London Co-operative Society, by the Translator. London, 1828.

FOX, REV. JOHN. *Animadversions on Robert Owen's Five Fundamental Facts. . . .* Manchester, 1837.
[2nd edn.] Leeds, 1839.

Frances Wright unmasked by her own Pen. Explanatory Notes, respecting the Nature and Objects of the Institution of Nashoba. New York, 1830.
[3rd edn.]

FRANCIS, SAMUEL. [Bishop] *Watson refuted, in a Series of Letters.* London [n.d.].

[FREARSON, JOHN.] *The relative Rights and Interests of the Employer and Employed discussed; and a System proposed, by which the conflicting Interests of all Classes of Society may be reconciled. By M. Justitia.* London, 1855.

[FREARSON, JOHN.] *An Essay bearing the Motto 'Anti-Equality', showing how the 'Surplus Funds' of the Amalgamated Society of Engineers . . . may be practically employed in 'Associative Industry'; . . . by Meritum Justitia, Mechanical Engineer.* London, Birmingham, Manchester [1855].

FROST, THOMAS (1821–1908). *Forty Years' Recollections. . . .* London, 1880.

[FROST, THOMAS.] *Social Utopias,* in *Chambers's Papers for the People,* III. Edinburgh, 1850.

A Full and complete Exposure of the atrocious and horrible Doctrines of the Owenites. . . . London [1840].

The 'Fundamental Facts' of Socialism examined. London, 1839.

FYFE, WILLIAM W. *Robert Owen in his true Colours. . . .* [n.p., n.d.]

GARWOOD, JOHN. *The Force of Circumstance, a Poem.* Birmingham, 1838. [Dedicated to Robert Owen.]

GARWOOD, REV. JOHN. *Is the Bible of Divine Authority? The Second of a Series of Lectures against Socialism.* London, 1840. [2nd edn.]

GAY, JULES. *Le Socialisme rationnel et le Socialisme autoritaire.* Geneva, 1868.

GIBBONS, WILLIAM. *An Exposition of Modern Scepticism, in a Letter addressed to the Editors of the Free Enquirer.* Wilmington, Del., 1830. [3rd edn.]

GILBERT, AMOS. *Memoir of Frances Wright.* Cincinnati, Ohio, 1855.

GILES, REV. JOHN EUSTACE. *Socialism as a Religious Theory, irrational and absurd: the First of Three Lectures on Socialism (as propounded by Robert Owen and Others). Delivered in the Baptist Chapel, . . . Leeds, September 23, 1838.* Leeds, 1838.
[Another edn.] *Second Thousand.* London, 1838.
[Another edn.] London, 1839.
Socialism in its Moral Tendencies compared with Christianity. The Second of Three Lectures on Socialism, delivered in . . . Leeds, 30th September, 1838. London, 1838.
[Another edn.] *Third Thousand.* London, 1839.
The Suffrage demonstrated to be the Right of All Men, By an Appeal to Scripture and Common Sense, being the Substance of a Lecture delivered in March, 1843. [London, 1843?]

GODWIN, REV. B. *Lectures on the Atheistic Controversy; delivered in the Months of February and March, 1834, . . . Bradford, Yorkshire.* [London] 1834.

GODYER, REV. D. G. *Acquisitiveness; its Uses and Abuses; a Prize Essay.* Leeds [1838?].

GOURARD, CHARLES. *Socialism unmasked: a plain Lecture from the French.* London, 1850.

GRANT, REV. BREWIN. *An Apology for Christianity: or, Modern Infidelity examined in a Series of Letters to Robert Owen.* London [1840].
'Is Man responsible for his Belief?' A Lecture delivered in the City Hall, Glasgow, on 23rd October, 1854. Glasgow, 1854.

[GRANT, JAMES.] *Portraits of Public Characters, by the Author of Random Recollections of the Lords and Commons.* 2 vols. London, 1841. [Includes a study of Owen and his aims.]

GRAY, JOHN (1799–1883). *The Currency Question. A rejected Letter . . . to The Times. Challenge to The Times to discuss the Subject for the Sum of 500 Guineas.* Edinburgh, London, 1847.
Edinburgh Monetary Reform Pamphlet, No. 1. Committee of Enquiry into the Validity of the monetary Principle advocated in Gray's Lectures. . . . Edinburgh, 1849.

An Efficient Remedy for the Distress of Nations. Edinburgh, 1842.

A Lecture on Human Happiness; being the First of a Series of Lectures on the Causes of the existing Evils of Society. To which are added the Articles of Agreement recommended by the London Co-operative Society. London, 1825.

[Another edn.] *A Lecture on Human Happiness; . . . to which are added the Preamble and Constitution of the Friendly Association for Mutual Interests, Located at Valley Forge (near Philadelphia).* Philadelphia, Penn., 1826.

[Another edn., reprinted facsimile.] London, 1931.

Lectures on the Nature and Use of Money. Edinburgh, 1848.

The Social System: a Treatise on the Principle of Exchange. Edinburgh, 1831.

A Word of Advice to the Orbistonians on the Principles which ought to regulate their present Proceedings. 29th June, 1826. [n.p.] 1826.

The Great Millennium Humbug. The Shevvild Chaps Opinion of Robert Owen's Socialism as exhibited in the Social Bible. Sheffield, 1838.

GREAVES, JAMES PIERREPONT. *Exposition of the Principles of conducting Infant Education.* [n.p., n.d.]

Letters and Extracts from the Manuscript Writings of . . . ed. Alexander Campbell. 2 vols. Ham Common, 1843; London, 1845.

The New Nature in the Soul. From the Journal of J. P. Greaves. London, 1847.

New Theosophic Revelations. From the Manuscript Journal of J. P. Greaves. London, 1847.

Physical and Metaphysical Hints for Every Body. [n.p.] 1827. [With additions and alterations by E. Biber.]

[GREAVES, JAMES PIERREPONT.] *The Sentiments of Robert Owen and J. P. Greaves, as contrasted by the Latter in the Margins of the 'Book of the New Moral World'.* Ham Common, 1844.

GREAVES, JAMES PIERREPONT. *Three Hundred Maxims for the Consideration of Parents.* [n.p.] 1827. [With additions and alterations by E. Biber.]

[Another edn., n.p.] 1837.

Triune-Life Divine and Human. London, 1880 [with introduction by A. M. H. W.]

and C. WALTON. *Behmen, Law and other Mystics.* [n.p.] 1847.

GREEN, DAVID. *Claims of the Redemption Society considered and enforced.* Leeds [n.d.].

Community practicable and practiced. Leeds [n.d.].

GREEN, JOHN. *Caspar Hauser: or, the Power of external Circumstances exhibited in forming the Human Character, with Remarks.* Manchester, London [1840?].

The Emigrants; a Lecture delivered in the Social Institution, Liverpool ...
August, 1838. Manchester, London [1838?].

and RICHARD CARLILE. *A Report of the Public Discussion held in ...*
Norwich, August 24th and 25th, 1837. ... Manchester [n.d.].

GREENING, EDWARD OWEN. *How far is it desirable and practicable to ex-*
tend Partnerships of Industry? ... London, 1870.
The present Position and Prospects of Partnerships of Industry: a Paper
prepared at the Request of the Economy and Trade Section of the Social
Science Association. ... Manchester, 1866.

GREGG, WILLIAM RATHBONE. *Essays on Political and Social Science,*
contributed chiefly to the Edinburgh Review. 2 vols. London, 1853.
Mistaken Aims and attainable Ideals of the Artizan Class. London, 1876.

GRESLEY, WILLIAM. *Charles Lever; or, the Man of the XIXth Century.*
London, 1841.

GRIFFITHS, REES. *The Protestant's Progress from Church of Englandism to*
Infidelity. ... London [c. 1840].

GRISCOM, JOHN. *A Year in Europe: comprising a Journal of Observations*
in England, Scotland, Ireland ... in 1818 and 1819. 2 vols. New
York, 1823. [Includes visit to New Lanark and Robert Owen.]

[HALE, GEORGE.] *A Reasonable and just Invitation or Challenge to the*
Founder of Socialism. By a Christian. [n.p.] 1840.

HALL, CHARLES. *The Effects of Civilization on the People of the European*
States. London, 1805.
[2nd edn.] *An Enquiry into the Cause of the present Distress of the People.*
London, 1813.
[Another edn., referred to as the 2nd edn.] London, 1820.
[Another edn., in Phoenix Library]. London, 1850.
Observations on the principal Conclusion in Mr. Malthus's Essay on Popu-
lation. London, 1805.

HALL, THEODORE. *The Gordian Knot untied ... being an Answer to ... the*
Rev. W. J. Kidd. Manchester [1841].

HALL, WILLIAM. 'From England to Illinois in 1821; the Journal of William
Hall', ed. Jay Monoghan, in *Journal*, State Historical Society of Illinois.
XXXIX (1946).

HAMILTON, JAMES. *Owenism rendered consistent with our civil and religious*
Institutions; or, a Mode of forming Societies for Mutual Benefit on rational
and practical Principles, without the Assistance of the Rich. [n.p.]
1825.

HANCOCK, EDWARD. *Robert Owen's Community System, ... and the horrid Doings of the St. Simonians, in Beaumont Square, ... a new Sect from France. Letter Third.* London [1837].

A true Exposure of the noted Robert Owen. Concerning his late Visit to the Queen ... and showing up his Doctrines. The dark Scenes, and midnight Revels that were carried on, in a Male and Female 'Co-operative Society'. With an Account of the Victims of Seduction and his New Moral Marriage System. London [n.d.].

HANSOM, JOSEPH (1803–1882). *A Statement of Facts relative to the Birmingham Town Hall, with an Appeal to the Rate-payers and Inhabitants of Birmingham.* Birmingham, 1834.

HANSON, JOHN. *The Dissection of Owenism dissected; or, a Socialist's Answer to Mr. Frederic R. Lees's Pamphlet entitled, 'A calm Examination of the fundamental Principles of Robert Owen's misnamed Rational System'.* Leeds, 1838.

[2nd edn.] Leeds, 1839.

Lectures to the Working Classes, delivered ... in the Theatre, Huddersfield, during the Winter of 1858–59. Ser. 2. Huddersfield, 1859.

The Owenite's Escape from the Charnel-House, and Blow-up of the Ostamachia; being a Reply to Mr. F. R. Lees's Pamphlet entitled, 'The Owenite Anatomized'. Manchester, 1838.

HARPER, ROBERT. *Co-operation as contrasted with Competition: a Letter to the Working Men of Birmingham.* Birmingham, 1867.

HASLAM, C. J. *A Defence of the Social Principles, delivered in the Social Institution, Salford ... being an Answer to a Lecture by the Rev. J. R. Beard ... on Sunday, April 30th, 1837.* Manchester [1837].

The Evils of private Property, being an Answer to a Letter ... by the Rev. J. Barker. Hulme, 1838.

Letters 1 to 12 to the Clergy of all Denominations, showing the Errors, Absurdities, and Irrationalities of their Doctrines. London [1839?].

The Necessity of a Change; or, an Exposure of the Errors and Evils of the present Arrangement of Society; with a partial Development of a New Arrangement. Manchester [1837?].

[2nd edn.] Manchester, London [1837?].

[4th edn.] Manchester, 1841.

Who are the Infidels, those who call themselves Socialists, or Followers of Robert Owen; or those who call themselves Christians, or Followers of Jesus Christ? Manchester [n.d.; 2nd edn.].

[3rd edn.] Manchester [1840?].

HAZELRIG, EDWARD [pseud.], and D. WINGATE. *Attic Stories; or, the Opinions of E. H.* [ed. by E. H. and D. W.]. Glasgow, 1817–18.

X

[Nos. 5 and 6 (except for a poem at the end of part 6) are entirely devoted to Robert Owen.]

[HEATH, WILLIAM.] *Paul Pry's Ramble through the 'New Moral World'*, *with 'First Impressions'*. Doncaster, 1838.
Paul Pry's Second Ramble through the 'New Moral World', with Rhymes and Reflections on 'The Rights of Woman'. Doncaster, 1839.
Paul Pry's Third Ramble through the 'New Moral World'. With 'Gatherings by the Way'. Doncaster, 1840.

HEBERT, WILLIAM. *A Visit to the Colony of Harmony in Indiana . . . recently purchased by Mr. Owen for the Establishment of a Society for Mutual Cooperation and Community of Property . . . also a Sketch for the Formation of a Cooperative Society*. London, 1825.
[Another edn.] 'A Visit to the Colony of Harmony in Indiana', in Harlow Lindley, *Indiana as seen by early Travelers*. Indianapolis, Ind., 1916.

[HEIGHTON, WILLIAM.] *An Address to the Members of the Trade Societies, and to the Working Classes generally; being an Exposition of the relative Situation, Condition, and future Prospects of the Working People in the United States . . . together with a Suggestion and Outlines of a Plan . . . by a Fellow Labourer*. Philadelphia, Penn., 1827.
[Another edn.] London, 1827.
[Another edn.] *An Address to Members of Trade Unions, and to the Working Classes generally: . . . by a Journeyman Bootmaker*. London, 1833.
[Another edn.] *An Address to the Socialists, Radicals, Trades Unions, and the Working Classes generally. . . .* London, Manchester, 1839.

HENNELL, MARY (1802–1843). *An Outline of the various Social Systems and Communities which have been founded on the Principle of Cooperation. With an introductory Essay, by the Author of 'The Philosophy of Necessity'*. Coventry, 1844. [First published in 1841, as appendix to Bray's *Philosophy of Necessity*.]
[Another edn.] London, 1844.

HETHERINGTON, HENRY (1792–1849). *Cheap Salvation; or, an Antidote to Priestcraft; being a succinct, practical, essential, and rational Religion, deduced from the New Testament. . . .* London [1843; 2nd edn.].

[HETHERINGTON, HENRY.] *A full Report of the Trial of H. H. on an Indictment for Blasphemy . . . December, 1840, for selling Haslam's Letters to the Clergy of all Denominations: with the Whole of the Authorities cited in the Defence, at full Length*. London, 1840.

HETHERINGTON, HENRY. *The Last Will and Testament of H. H. In the Presence of G. J. Holyoake, H. A. Ivory, J. Kenny*. [n.p., n.d.]

Principles and Practice contrasted; or, a Peep into 'the only true Church of God upon Earth', commonly called Freethinking Christians. London, 1828. [2nd edn.]

HEYWOOD, BENJAMIN. *An Address . . . at the Opening of the Manchester Mechanics' Institution . . . March, 1825*. Manchester, 1825.
Addresses delivered at the Manchester Mechanics' Institution. [n.p.] 1843.

HIBBERT, JULIAN (1801–1834). *Advice to Labourers*. London, 1829.
trans. *Système de la Nature . . .*, by Baron Paul H. D. Holbach. London, 1834.

HILL, JAMES. *The Commonweal No. 1. Development of a Measure for advancing the political, social, and domestic Condition of the Working Classes*. [n.p.] 1845.
The Defeater defeated: being a Refutation of Mr. Day's Pamphlet entitled 'Defeat of the Anti-Corn Law League in Huntingdonshire'. London, 1843. [6th edn.]

Histoire de Communisme, ou Réfutation historique des Utopies Socialistes. Paris, 8149.
[4th edn.] Paris, 1850.
[5th edn.] Paris, 1856.

History of the Diabolical Handbills. Manchester, 1823.

HOBSON, JOSHUA (1810–1876). *Socialism as it is! Lectures in Reply to the Fallacies and Misrepresentations of the Rev. John Eustace Giles. . . .* Leeds, 1838.

HOLE, JAMES (1820–1895). *An Essay on the History and Management of Literary, Scientific, and Mechanics' Institutions; . . .* London, 1853.
The Homes of the Working Classes, with Suggestions for their Improvement. London, 1866.
Lectures on Social Science and the Organization of Labor. London, 1851.

[HOLE, JAMES], trans. *The Life of Jesus*, by Ernest Renan. London, Paris, 1864.
[Another edn.] London, 1865.

HOLE, JAMES. *Light, more Light!—on the present State of Education amongst the Working Classes of Leeds, and how it can best be improved*. London, 1860.
[2nd edn.] London, 1863.
National Railways: an Argument for State Purchase. London, 1893.
[2nd edn.] London, 1895.

HOLLICK, FREDERICK (1813–   ). *What is Christianity? and have the Persons calling themselves Christians any Right to interfere with the free Expression of Opinions by other Parties?* Liverpool, 1840.

and REV. JOSEPH BAYLEE. *The Substance of the Two Nights Discussion in the Social Institution, . . . London, on Friday and Saturday, 14th and 15th of December.* London, 1839.

HOLMES, JOHN. *The Coal Question: a Correspondence between H. Briggs . . . and John Holmes on the Differences existing betwixt the Coal-masters and their Men. . . .* Leeds [1863].
The economic Advantages of Co-operation substantiated. A Letter addressed to the Rev. Norman Macleod, proving the Truth of the large Profits from Cooperative Economy, as stated at the Glasgow Meeting of the Association for the Promotion of Social Science; Reply to the Objections of a practical Miller. . . . Leeds, 1860.
The Economic and Moral Advantages of Cooperation in the Provision of Food, instanced in the People's Flour Mill Society at Leeds, and in the Rochdale Cooperative Pioneers' Store. Leeds [1857].

[HOLMES, JOHN.] *A few plain Words of Advice respecting the future Conduct of the Members of the Leeds District Flour and Provision Society towards each other, as well as several Hints and Suggestions, which may be of some Service to the Reader, if he should think proper to make Use of them; . . .* Leeds, 1860.

HOLMES, JOHN. *Political Economy versus Co-operation.* Manchester, 1880.
The Second great Step of Cooperative Beneficence (a Paper read at Leeds, December 13, 1873). Manchester [n.d.].

[HOLMES, JOHN.] *The Wealth Man made: a Parody* [on This is the House That Jack Built], *by One who loves the Man more than the Wealth.* [Leeds, 1850?]

HOLYOAKE, GEORGE JACOB (1817–1906). [For a full bibliography see C. W. F. Goss, *A Descriptive Bibliography of George Jacob Holyoake: with a brief Sketch of his Life.* London, 1908.]
The Advantages and Disadvantages of Trades' Unions. Sheffield, 1841.
British Secular Institute of Communication and Propagandism: Report of the Fleet Street House, Part II, for 1857. London, 1858.
Bygones worth Remembering. 2 vols. London, 1905.
[Another edn., 2 vols. in 1]. London, 1915.
Cabinet of Reason. London, 1851–54. [Series of reprints of works relating to Secularism, by G. J. H., Spinoza, C. R. Pemberton and others.]
The Case of Thomas Pooley, the Cornish Well-sinker, sentenced to a Year and Nine Months' Imprisonment for writing on a Clergyman's Field-gate. London, 1857.
Christianity and Secularism: Report of a Public Discussion between the Rev. Brewin Grant, . . . and G. J. Holyoake . . . held in the Royal British Institution, . . . London, . . . commencing January 20th, and ending February 24th, 1853. London, 1853.

Christianity versus Secularism: a Public Discussion in Newcastle-Upon-Tyne between the Rev. J. H. Rutherford and Mr. G. J. Holyoake, on the Evenings of 1st, 3rd, and 5th August, 1853. London, 1854.
Collected Writings. 2 vols. London, 1875.

[HOLYOAKE, GEORGE JACOB], ed. *The Confessions of Rousseau; with a Preface by the Editor of the Reasoner.* London, 1857. [Abridged from 1796 edition.]

HOLYOAKE, GEORGE JACOB. *The Co-operative Movement Today.* London, 1891.

[HOLYOAKE, GEORGE JACOB.] *Dr. Brindley and the Vote of Censure.* [n.p.] 1861. [A leaflet signed 'Ion'.]

HOLYOAKE, GEORGE JACOB. *Friends of Mental Liberty.* Sheffield, 1841.
The History of Co-operation in England: its Literature and its Advocates. 2 vols. London, 1875–79.
Vol I: *The Pioneer Period: 1812–1844* [published, 1875].
Vol. II: *The Constructive Period: 1845–1878* [published, 1879].
[American edn.] *Manual of Co-operation; being an Epitome of Holyoake's 'History of Co-operation' arranged by the Sociologic Society of America.* New York, 1885.
['Complete' edn., 2 vols., containing Part III, 1876–1904]. London, 1906.
[Another edn., in 1 vol.] London, 1908.
The History of Co-operation in Halifax and of some other Institutions around It. London, 1867.
The History of Fleet Street House: a Report of Sixteen Years. London, 1856.
The History of the Last Trial by Jury for Atheism in England: a Fragment of Autobiography. London, 1850.
[And later edns.]
The Jubilee History of the Leeds Industrial Co-operative Society, from 1847 to 1897, traced Year by Year. Leeds, 1897.
The Last Days of Mrs. Emma Martin, Advocate of Free Thought. London, 1851.
Letter to the Rev. Joseph Barker, now a Preacher among Unitarians. London, 1847.
The Life and Character of Henry Hetherington ... the Oration at Kensal Green Cemetery. London, 1849. [An abridgment of Thomas Cooper's *Eloge* of 26 August 1849.]
The Life and Character of Richard Carlile. London, 1849.
[Another edn.] London, 1858.
[Another edn.] London, 1870.
Life of the Rev. Joseph Rayner Stephens. London, 1881.
The Limits of Atheism; or, why should Sceptics be Outlaws? London, 1861.

313

The Logic of Death; or, why should the Atheist fear to die?   London, 1850.
   [Originally appeared in the *Reasoner*.]
[And later edns.]

ed. '*The Man Paterson*'. *God versus Paterson: the extraordinary Bow Street Police Report*.   London, 1843.

Moral Errors endangering the Permanence of Co-operative Societies. . . . Paper read at Social Science Congress, Guildhall, London, 1862.   [n.p.] 1862. [5th edn.]

Organization: not of Arms . . . but Ideas.   London, 1853. [Part of the *Cabinet of Reason*.]

The Organization of Freethinkers.   London, 1852.

The Origin and Nature of Secularism; showing that where Freethought commonly ends, Secularism begins.   London, 1896.

[Another edn.]   *English Secularism: a Confession of Faith.*   Chicago, Ill., 1896.

Paley refuted in his own Words.   London, 1843.
[And later edns.]

Partnership of Industry: a Statement of the Co-operative Case divested of Sentimentality.   London, 1865.

ed. and revised by.   *The Path I took and where it led me; an Autobiography and Argument. By a Monmouthshire Farmer.*   London, 1897.

Principles of Secularism briefly explained.   London, 1859.

Propagandism.   London, 1847.

Rationalism; a Treatise for the Times.   London, 1845.

Rationalism, the legitimate Opponent of Catholicism.   London, 1851.

ed.   *The Reasoner Tracts.* Nos. 1–58 (10 April 1850–14 May 1851).

Reply to 'Infidelity developed' by the Rev. E. Fice of Ipswich.   London, 1850.
   [*Reasoner Tracts* No. 12.]

Secularism distinguished from Unitarianism.   London, 1855.

Secularism, the practical Philosophy of the People.   London, 1854.

[Another edn.]   *Secularism, the affirmative Philosophy of the People.*   London, 1854.

Self-help a Hundred Years ago.   London, 1888.
[2nd edn.]   London, 1889.
[3rd edn.]   London, 1891.

Self-Help by the People: History of Co-operation in Rochdale. Part I. 1844–1857.   London, 1858. *Part II. 1857–1877.* London, 1878.
[For the many edns. of this work, see Goss.]

A short and easy Method with the Saints.   London, 1843.

Sixty Years of an Agitator's Life. 2 vols.   London, 1892.
[2nd edn., 2 vols.]   London, 1893.
[3rd edn., 2 vols.]   London, 1893.
[Another edn., 4th impression; 2 vols.]   London, 1900.
[5th impression, 2 vols.]   London, 1902.

[6th impression, 2 vols.] London, 1906.

A Sketch of the Life and a Few of the Beauties of Pemberton, compiled and selected chiefly with a View of developing the Causes which generated the Talent and Moral Greatness of this extraordinary Man. Leeds, 1842.

The Spirit of Bonner in the Disciples of Jesus; or, the Cruelty and Intolerance of Christianity displayed, in the Persecution for Blasphemy, of Charles Southwell, Editor of 'The Oracle of Reason': a Lecture. London, 1842.

Thomas Cooper delineated as Convert and Controversialist: a Companion to his missionary Wanderings. London, 1861.

The Trial of George Jacob Holyoake, on an Indictment for Blasphemy, before Mr. Justice Erskine and a Common Jury, at Gloucester, August the 15th, 1842, from Notes specially taken by Mr. Hunt. London, 1842.

The Trial of Theism. London, 1858.

[Another edn.] London, 1877.

[HOLYOAKE, GEORGE JACOB.] *The Trial of Thomas Paterson for Blasphemy before the High Court of Justiciary, Edinburgh . . . also the Trials of Thomas Finlay and Miss Mathilda Roalfe (for Blasphemy); with Notes and a special Dissertation on Blasphemy Prosecutions in general, by the Secretary of the Anti-Persecution Union.* London, 1844.

HOLYOAKE, GEORGE JACOB. *The Value of Biography in the Formation of Individual Character, illustrated by the Life and Writings of Charles Reece Pemberton.* London, 1845.

A Visit to Harmony Hall. (Reprinted from the 'Movement') With Emendations and a new and curious vindicatory Chapter. Dedicated to the Socialists of England and Scotland. London, 1844.

Why do the Clergy avoid Discussion and the Philosophers discountenance it? London, 1852.

and JOHN BOWES. *The Report of the Four Nights Public Discussion, at Bradford, between George J. Holyoake . . . and John Bowes . . . on 'The Truth of Christianity and the Folly of Infidelity', 22nd, 23rd, and 24th, April 1850: 'The Free Agency of Man and the Formation of Character', on the 25th. Taken down by a Reporter and revised by both Speakers.* London, 1850.

and BREWIN GRANT. *Report of a Public Discussion between the Rev. Brewin Grant, . . . and George Jacob Holyoake, Esq., held in the City Hall, Glasgow, on Monday and Thursday Evenings, commencing October 2nd, and ending October 19th, 1854.* Glasgow, 1854.

and DAVID KING. *A Report of the Public Discussion between George J. Holyoake and David King, held in the Hall, John Street, Tottenham Court Road, London, on Three Evenings in September, 1850.* London, 1850

and AMOS SCOTTEN. *The Jubilee History of the Derby Co-operative Provident Society, Limited, 1850–1900.* Manchester, 1900.

HOME COLONIZATION SOCIETY. *Prospectus.* [n.p.; dated January, 1842.]

HOPPER, JOHN. *Remedial Measures: or, the Workman's Path to Independence. A Tract for all Classes of Workmen.* London [n.d.].
The Rights of Working Men: or, Working Men's Christian Unions. A Tract for the Times. London, 1852.

[HOPPER, JOHN.] *Operative Shipwright. A Defence of Trade Unions in general; and the Sunderland Shipwrights Society in particular; addressed to the Clergy and all who oppose such Unions: being a Reply to the Rev. D. R. Falconer, Curate of Bishopwearmouth.* Sunderland, 1857.

HOPPUS, JOHN. *The Province of Reason, in Reference to Religion; considered in a Lecture against Socialism. . . .* London, 1840.

The horrible Effects of the Social System, with an Account of the cruel Seduction of the three unfortunate Sisters, Mary, Elizabeth, and Catherine Johnson, and the death bed Scene of their wretched Father. [n.p., n.d.]

HORTON, HARRY HOWELLS. *A brief Survey of the Effects of Christianity in the World, in Reply to a Lecture delivered by the Rev. Hugh Stowell, A.M., and addressed to the Working Classes.* London, 1838.
Community the only Salvation for Man. A Lecture delivered in the Social Institution, Salford, . . . 16th September, 1838. Manchester, London, Hulme, 1838.

[HOUSTON, GEORGE?] *Robert Owen unmasked by his own Pen.* New York, 1830.

HUBER, VICTOR AIMÉ. *Ueber die Cooperativen Arbeiter-Associationen in England.* Berlin, 1852.

HUDSON, T. H. *Christian Socialism, explained and enforced, and compared with infidel Fellowship, especially, as propounded by Robert Owen, Esq., and his Disciples.* London, Hull, Leicester, Halifax, 1839.

HUGHES, REV. HENRY. *What am I? The Fourth of a Series of Lectures against Socialism. . . .* London, 1840.

The Human Eccaleobion; or the New Moral Warren: being a concise but faithful Exposition of Socialism, instituted by Robert Owen. . . . London, 1842. [In verse.]

HUNT, THOMAS. *Chartism, Trades Unionism, and Socialism; or, which is the best calculated to produce permanent Relief to the Working Classes? A Dialogue.* London, 1840.
Report to a Meeting of intending Emigrants, comprehending a practical Plan for founding co-operative Colonies of United Interests in the North-western Territories of the United States. London, 1843.

HUTCHISON, GRAHAM. *An Exposition of the erroneous Nature of Mr. Owen's Plan for ameliorating the Condition of Mankind. . . .* Glasgow, 1835.

A Treatise on the Causes and Principles of meteorological Phenomena. Also Two Essays, the One 'On Marsh Fevers', the Other, 'On the System of Equality, proposed by Robert Owen. . . .' Glasgow, 1835.

An impartial Statement of the Proceedings of the Members of the Trades Union Societies. Liverpool, 1833.

INDEPENDENT EXCHANGE BAZAAR. *Commercial Trading Chamber. Established for the Interchange of all Kinds of useful Property.* London [1840].

INVESTIGATOR. *Letter to the Editor of the Edinburgh Beacon.* [n.p., n.d.; a defence of Robert Owen.]

IRONSIDE, ISAAC (1808–1870). *Brindley and his lying Braggadocio.* Sheffield, 1840.

ISHAM, RICHARD. *Land, Common Property. The People's Right to Land. What 'Commonality' is, and its perpetual Existence. By Terrigenous.* London [1848?].
[3rd edn., London] 1852.
[Another edn.] London, 1882.

ISMAR, F.A. *The School of Industry at New Harmony, State of Indiana, and Madame Maria Duclos Fretageot; a Letter to Mr. William Maclure.* New Harmony, Ind., 1830.

JENNINGS, JAMES. *The Family Cyclopaedia; or, Manual of useful and necessary Knowledge. . . .* London, 1821.
An Inquiry concerning the Nature and Operations of the Human Mind, in which the Science of Phrenology, the Doctrine of Necessity, Punishment, and Education, are particularly considered. (A Lecture delivered at the Mechanics' Institution, London). . . . London, 1828.
A Lecture on the History and Utility of Literary Institutions. Delivered at the Surrey and Russell Institutions, London, in December and November, 1822. . . . London, 1823.

[JENNINGS, JAMES?] *A Letter to Sir James Graham, Bart., M.P., alias 'a Cumberland Landowner'; in Reply to certain Positions contained in a Pamphlet entitled 'Free Trade in Corn the real Interest of the Landlord and the true Policy of the State. . . .'* London, 1828. [Defence of Owen and Orbiston.]

JENNINGS, JAMES. *Observations on some of the Dialects of the West of England, particularly Somersetshire. . . .* London, 1825.
Ornithologia; or, The Birds: a Poem in Two Parts; with an Introduction to their natural History. . . . London, 1828.

JONES, LLOYD (1811–1886). 'Cooperative Stores', in *Transactions of the Cooperative League* (1852).

The Freaks of Faith; or, an Account of some of the many Messiahs who have deluded Mankind. Manchester, 1840.

A Reply to Mr. R. Carlile's Objections to the Five Fundamental Facts as Laid down by Mr. Owen. An Answer to a Lecture delivered in his Chapel, 27th November, 1837. Manchester, 1837.

and W. PALLISTER. *Report of the Discussion on Owenism... Sheffield ... March, 1839, between Mr. Lloyd Jones ... and Mr. W. Pallister. ...* Sheffield, 1839.

and GEORGE TROUP. *Report of the Discussion between Mr. Troup ... and Mr. Lloyd Jones ... in the Watt Institute Hall, Dundee ... 17th and 18th September, 1839, on the Propositions (I) That Socialism is atheistical; and, (II) That Socialism is incredible and absurd.* Dundee, 1839.

JUNIUS [pseud.]. *Six Letters on the Theory and Practice of Socialism, Addressed to All Classes of the Population of Great Britain.* London [1840].

KERR, GEORGE. *Kerr's Exposition of Legislative Tyranny and Defence of the Trades Union.* Belfast, 1834.

KIDD, REV. WILLIAM JOHN. *The Gordian Knot of Infidelity.* London, 1839.
The People armed against Socialism. ... Manchester, 1839.
Socialism denounced as an Outrage ... a Sermon ... Manchester ... July 12, 1840. London, 1840.

[KING, WILLIAM.] *Currency; or, the Money Juggle.* [n.p., n.d.]

KING, WILLIAM. *Gothic Hall Labour Bank.* [n.p., n.d.]
London Bank of Industry, No. 8, Margaret Street. [n.p., n.d.]

[KING, WILLIAM.] *Money Dialogue: or, a Catechism on Currency, Exchanges, etc. By a Member of the Bank of Industry.* London, 1845.
A Note of the London Bank of Industry, Margaret Street. William King, Manager. [n.p., 1845?]
(Bank of Industry Tracts.) *Reasons Why Orders Are Not Useful in Promoting the Progressive Extension and Concentration of Banks of Interest.* [n.p., 1845?]
To the Thinking Public. No. 3. Bank of Industry, Margaret Street. [n.p., 1845?]

KING, WILLIAM. *Owenite Leaflets.* [n.p., 1831; including:]
  1. *The Workings of Money.*
  2. *The Workings of Money Capital.*
  3. *The Workings of Capital, at Present, represented by Money. Part II.*
  4. *To the Makers of all Wealth, the Useful Working Population.*
  5. *To the Useful Classes.*
  6. *From my Uncle Toby's Portfolio: 'Gentility'.*
  7. *A Riddle.*

KING, DR WILLIAM. *An Important Address to Trade Unions.* Manchester [1831?].

KNIGHT, HENRY L. *A Lecture on Irresponsibility, Moral and Natural . . . delivered in the Social Institution, Oldham.* Hulme, 1838.
The 'Nuts' Cracked, being an Answer to Questions on the Five Facts, and the Religion of the New Moral World, 'by a sincere Inquirer after the Truth'. . . . Rochdale [1838?].

KNIGHT, JAMES. *America or England, containing Observations illustrative of the Subject of Emigration to the United States . . . with Extracts from Several Writers, particularly from the Pamphlet of Mr. G. Courtauld, on the Formation of an Equitable Association of Capital and Labour in the State of Ohio.* London, 1820.

The Labourer's Library. Leeds, 1841–42.
No. 1 William Cobbett. *The Right of the Poor to the Suffrage of the People's Charter. . . .* Leeds, 1841.
Nos. 2, and 3. Feargus O'Connor. *The Remedy for National Poverty and Impending National Ruin.* Leeds, 1841.
No. 4. John F. Bray. *Government and Society Considered in Relation to First Principles.* Reprinted from *Labour's Wrongs and Labour's Remedy.* Leeds, 1842.

LALOR, JOHN. *Money and Morals: a Book for the Times.* London, 1852.

LANE, CHARLES. *A Classification of Science and Arts; or, a Map of Human Knowledge.* London, 1826.
Temper and Diet (Extracted from the New Age, July 1, 1843). Ham Common, 1843.

LANGFORD, JOHN ALFRED. *Christianity, Not Secularism the practical Philosophy of the People: a Reply to G. J. Holyoake's Tract. . . .* London, 1854.

The Law of Reason, embracing the Subjects of Utility, of Free Discussion, Elements of Metaphysics . . . also an Epitome of Mr. Owen's Social System . . . Mr. Owen's Opinion of Jesus Christ. . . . London, 1831.

LAWSON, WILLIAM, CHARLES D. HUNTER and others. *Ten Years of Gentleman Farming at Blennerhasset, with Cooperative Objects.* London, 1874.

LECHEVALIER, JULES. *Prospects of Cooperative Associations in England.* London, 1854.

Lectures against Socialism. Correspondence between the London District Board of the Universal Community Society of Rational Religionists and the Committee of the London City Mission. Leeds, 1839.

LEEDS REDEMPTION SOCIETY. *Fourteen Days Propagandism. What to say.* [n.p., 1851.]

LEES, FREDERIC RICHARD. *The Burial of the Owenite. . . .* London, Leeds, 1839.
    The Metaphysics of Owenism dissected. . . . London, 1842. [Consists of a reissue of *Owenism dissected. . . .* (Leeds, 1839, 2nd edn.), and *Owenite anatomized.* (Leeds, 1838).]
    Owenism dissected: a calm Examination of the Fundamental Principles of Robert Owen's misnamed Rational System. . . . Leeds, 1838.
    [2nd edn.] Leeds, 1839.
    The Owenite anatomized: an Analysis of the Blunders and Fallacies put forth by one John Hanson in his mis-styled Answer to 'Owenism dissected'. London, Leeds, 1838.

A Letter containing some Observations on the delusive Nature of the System proposed by Robert Owen . . . for the Amelioration of the Condition of the People of Ireland, as developed by him . . . in Dublin, 18th March. Dublin, 1823.

A Letter to Robert Owen . . . by a Son of the Mist. Philadelphia, Penn., 1825.

A Letter to the Human Race. By a Brother. London [1840?].

A Letter to the Moderator of the General Assembly, requesting his Attention to the Complexion of the Times, to the Late Attack of the Christian Instructor upon Mr. Owen, and to the Manner in which Religious Controversies are generally conducted. Edinburgh, 1823.

A Letter to the Rev. W. L. Pope, . . . in Reply to Two Sermons preached by him on the Subject of Co-operation. Tunbridge Wells, 1829.

Letter to the Right Honourable Lord Viscount Melbourne, on the Presentation of Mr. Robert Owen at Court. By a Member of the Church of England. London, 1840.

Liberal Tracts. Nos. 1–8. New York [c. 1822; ed. George Houston?].

LIBERIUS FORTINBRAS [pseud.]. *Sketch of a Proposed Plan for the Formation of a National Agricultural Banking Company; with Remarks on the Plans of Mr. Owen. . . .* London, 1818.

LINTON, W. J. *G. J. Holyoake Exposed: a Supplement to the Reasoner of 9th November, 1853.* London, 1853.
    Holyoake versus Garrison: a Defence of Earnestness. London, 1853.
    James Watson, a Memoir. Manchester, 1880.
    Memories. London, 1895.
    The People's Land, and an Easy Way To Recover It. Three Letters to the Editor of the 'Nation'. . . . London, 1850.

LONDON CITY MISSION. *Lectures against Socialism.* London, 1840. [For separate titles, see under authors, viz., Robert Ainslie, Rev. John Garwood, Rev. B. W. Noel, Rev. Henry Hughes, Rev. George Cubitt, John Hoppus, R. Matthews, Isaac Taylor.]

LOVETT, WILLIAM (1800–1877). *An Address from the National Association for Promoting the Political and Social Improvement of the People . . . on the Subject of the Militia, etc. . . .* London, 1846.
Address of the National Association, London, to the People of Ireland. London, 1843.
The Council of the National Complete Suffrage Union to Political Reformers of all Shades of Opinion. Birmingham, 1842.
Enrolment of the Militia for immediate Service. London, 1846.
Justice safer than Expediency: an Appeal to the Middle Classes on the Question of the Suffrage. London, 1848.
Letter from Mr. Lovett to Messrs. Donaldson and Mason. Containing his Reasons for refusing to be nominated Secretary of the National Charter Association. London, 1843.
A Letter to Daniel O'Connell . . . in Reply to the Calumnies he put forth in the Corn Exchange, August 8th, in Answer to the Address of the National Association to the People of Ireland. London, 1843.
The Life and Struggles of William Lovett in his Pursuit of Bread, Knowledge, and Freedom. With some . . . Account of the Different Associations he belonged to. . . . London, 1876.
[Another edn., in 2 vols., with introd. by R. H. Tawney.] London, 1920.
The Peace Principle, the great Agent of Social and Political Progress, being a short Review of the Peace Doctrines of the 'Family Herald'. London, 1849.
The People's League. To the People of London and its Vicinity. London, 1848.
A Proposal for the Consideration of the Friends of Progress. [n.p., 1847.]
Social and Political Morality. London, 1853.
and JOHN COLLINS. *Chartism; a New Organization of the People, embracing a Plan for the Improvement of the People, politically and socially . . . written in Warwick Gaol.* London, 1840.
[2nd edn.] London, 1841.
and HUGH CRAIG. *Manifesto of the General Convention of the industrious Classes.* London, 1839.

LUDLOW, JOHN MALCOLM FORBES, and LLOYD JONES. *Progress of the Working Class, 1832–1867.* London, 1867.

[LUDLOW, WILLIAM.] *The Belief of the Rational Brethren of the West.* Cincinnati, Ohio, 1819.

LUNN, EDWIN. *Divine Revelation examined; or, Lecture on the Nature and Attitudes of the Deity . . . or the Truth of the First Article of the Creed of the New Moral World demonstrated, . . . delivered in the Social Institution, Huddersfield.* Manchester [c. 1840].

A Lecture on Prayer, its Folly, Inutility, and Irrationality, demonstrated. Delivered in the Social Institution, . . . Huddersfield, March 31st, 1839. Manchester, London, 1839.

MACAULEY, ELIZABETH WRIGHT. *Address to the King, Legislature, and Population of the United Kingdom, on the Subject of an improved System of mental Cultivation, claiming the particular Attention of Parents, but most especially of young Mothers: delivered . . . September 30th, 1828.* London, 1828.

Lecture addressed to the Inhabitants of Surrey and Southwark, delivered at the New Surrey and Southwark Institution . . . July 29th, 1832. London, 1832.

MACCALL, WILLIAM. *Agents of Civilization.* London, 1843.
Outlines of Individualism. London, 1853.

MACCONNELL, REV. THOMAS. *A Lecture on the Signs of the Times: delivered in the Great Lecture Room of Robert Owen's Institution, . . . November 18th, 1832.* London, 1832.

The Prize Essay on 'The present Condition of the People of this Country, and the best Means of improving it'. London, 1838.

MACCORMAC, HENRY (1800–1886). *An Appeal in Behalf of the Poor; . . .* Belfast, 1830.

Aspirations from the Inner, the Spiritual Life, aiming to reconcile Religion, Literature, Science, Art, with Faith, and Hope, and Love, and Immortality. London, 1860.

The Conversation of a Soul with God: a Theodicy. London, 1877.

Moral-Sanatory Economy . . . Education, Health, Order, Progress, Competence. London, 1853.

On Synthesis as taking Precedence of Analysis in Education. London, 1867.

On the best Means of Improving the Moral and Physical Condition of the Working Classes. Being an Address . . . Belfast Mechanics' Institute. London, 1830.

The Philosophy of Human Nature, in its Physical, Intellectual and Moral Relations; with an Attempt to demonstrate the Order of Providence in the Three-fold Constitution of our Being. London, 1837.

Plan for the Relief of the Unemployed Poor. Belfast, 1830.

Unsectarian, as contrasted with Denominational Education: in Relation to the Queen's University in Ireland. Belfast, 1866.

[MACCORMAC, HENRY.] *Words of Wisdom, addressed to the Working Classes; containing simple Directions, . . . to which are subjoined the Laws of the First Armagh Co-operative Society.* Armagh, 1830.

MACDONALD, DONALD. *The Diaries of Donald Macdonald, 1824–1826* (with an introduction by Caroline Dale Snedeker), in Indiana Historical Society *Publications*, XIV, no. 2, Indianapolis, Ind., 1942.

MACGAVIN, WILLIAM. *The Fundamental Principles of the New Lanark System Exposed.* . . . Glasgow, 1824.
Letters on Mr. Owen's New System. Seven Letters in 4 Parts. Glasgow, 1823.

MACKINTOSH, THOMAS SIMMONS. *An Inquiry into the Nature of Responsibility, as deduced from savage Justice, Civil Justice, and Social Justice.* Birmingham [1840].

M'KNIGHT, JAMES. *A Discourse exposing Robert Owen's System, as practised by the Franklin Community at Haverstraw.* New York, 1826.

MACLURE, WILLIAM (1763–1840). *Opinions on Various Subjects, dedicated to the industrious Producers.* 3 vols. New Harmony, Ind., 1831–38.
[Largely printed from the *Disseminator*, New Harmony, 1828–35.]
and MARIE D. FRETAGEOT. *Education and Reform at New Harmony: Correspondence of William Maclure and Marie Duclos Fretageot, 1820–1833,* ed. Arthur E. Bestor, Jr. Indianapolis, Ind., 1948.

MACKIE, ALEXANDER. *An Extinguisher to Atheism and Infidelity; being a Reply to Mr. Southwell's Roland for (what he calls) Mr. Massie's Oliver.* . . . Manchester, 1845.
A Word to the Dupes of Mrs. Martin, Messrs. Buchanan, Southwell, and Co., of the Hall of Science, Manchester, and a Receipt for making Money without Working. Manchester [1845].

MACNAB, HENRY GREY. *First Lines of a System of Universal Education founded on the immutable Laws and Elements of Science and of Religion.* . . . [n.p.] 1819.
The New Views of Mr. Owen of Lanark impartially examined, as rational Means of ultimately promoting the productive Industry, Comfort, Moral Improvement, and Happiness of the Labouring Classes of Society, . . . *also Observations on the New Lanark School.* . . . London, 1819.
[French edn.] *Examen impartial des Nouvelles Vues de* . . . *Robert Owen et ses Etablissements à New Lanark* . . . traduit par Laffon de Ladebat. . . . Paris, 1821.

Manifesto of the Productive Classes of Great Britain and Ireland, to the Governments and Peoples of the Continents of Europe, and of North and South America (passed unanimously at the Great Public Meeting held at the National Equitable Labour Exchange, . . . *London, on 13th May, 1833).* [n.p., 1833; broadsheet.]

MANNING, WILLIAM. *The Wrongs of Man exemplified.* . . . London, 1838.

Man's Appeal to Woman. London, 1842.

The Marriage System of Socialism freed from the Mis-representations of its Enemies. Chester, 1841.

MARRIOTT, REV. JOSEPH. *A Catechism on Circumstances; or, the Foundation Stone of a Community.* London, 1840.
[2nd edn.] Manchester, 1841.
[Another edn.] Salford [184?].
Community: a Drama. Manchester, London, 1838.
On Ragged Scientific Institutes: or, Societies for diffusing useful Information among the Poor and Miserable. Islington, London, [1848?].

MARTIN, EMMA (1812–1851). *Baptism: a Pagan Rite.* London, 1844.
The Bible no Revelation. London [1850?].
A Funeral Sermon, occasioned by the Death of Richard Carlile, preached at . . . London on . . . the 26th of February, 1843. London [n.d.].
The Punishment of Death. London [1849].
Religion superseded: or, the Moral Code of Nature sufficient. . . . London [1850?].

MARTIN, WILLIAM. *An Exposure of a New System of Irreligion, which is . . . called 'The New Moral World', promulgated by Robert Owen. . . .* Newcastle-on-Tyne, 1839.

MARTINEAU, HARRIET. *Society in America.* 3 vols. London, 1837.
[Includes accounts of communitarian experiments.]

MARX, KARL, and FRIEDRICH ENGELS. *Manifesto of the Communist Party* (1848), trans. Samuel Moore in collaboration with F. Engels. London, 1888.

MASQUERIER, LEWIS (1802–18?). *Sociology; or, the Reconstruction of Society, Government, and Property.* New York, 1877.

MATHER, REV. JOSEPH. *Socialism exposed; or, the Book of the New Moral World examined, and brought to the Test of Fact and Experience. . . .* London, 1839.
[2nd edn.] London, 1839.
[Another edn., abridged.] London [1840].

MATTHEWS, RICHARD. *Is Marriage worth perpetuating? The Ninth of a Series of Lectures against Socialism. . . .* London, 1840.

MELISH, JOHN. *Travels in the United States . . . in the Years 1806 and 1807, and 1809, 1810, and 1811.* 2 vols. Philadelphia, Penn., 1812.
[With an account of the society at Harmony.]
[Reprint of the section on Harmony.] *Account of a Society at Harmony, Pennsylvania, . . .* [n.p.] 1815.
[Another reprint of above, n.p.] 1820.

A MEMBER OF THE CO-OPERATIVE AND ECONOMICAL SOCIETY OF EDINBURGH. [Letter] *To the Editor of the Caledonian Mercury, 20 December, 1822.* Edinburgh [n.d.].

Memoir of E. T. Craig, one of the Originators of the Co-operative Movement, Founder and Historian of Ralahine. [n.p., n.d.; apparently from Craig's own articles 'English Socialism, Historical Reminiscences' in the *American Socialist*, II–III (1877–78).]

Mr. Robert Owen. A Letter on His Presentation at Court. [n.p.] 1840.

MORGAN, JOHN MINTER (1782–1854). *Address ... at the Theatre of the Mechanics' Institution, on Thursday, 6th May, 1830.* London, 1830.
Address to the Proprietors of the University of London. London, 1833.
Brief Account of the Stockport Sunday School with Thoughts on the Extension and Improvement of Sunday Schools in General and more especially in the Rural Districts. London, 1838.
The Christian Commonwealth. London, 1845.
[Another edn.] London, Paris, 1845.
[Another edn., for the Phoenix Library, including] *An Inquiry respecting Private Property ... from a Periodical of 1827.* London, 1850.
[2nd edn.] Edinburgh, 1854.
[French edn.] *Colonie Chretienne. ...* [n.p.] 1846.

[MORGAN, JOHN MINTER.] *The Church of England Self-Supporting Village, for promoting the Religious, Moral, and General Improvement of the Working Classes, by forming Establishments of Three Hundred Families on the Land, and combining agricultural with manufacturing Employment. ...* London [1850].
Colloquies on Religion and Religious Education; being a Supplement to Hampden in the Nineteenth Century. London, 1837.

MORGAN, JOHN MINTER. *The Critics Criticized; with Remarks on a Passage in Dr. Chalmer's Bridgewater Treatise.* London, 1834.
Extracts for Schools and Families. London [n.d.].
ed., trans. *Extinction of Pauperism* by Napoleon III. London [1849?].
Hampden in the Nineteenth Century; or, Colloquies on the Errors and Improvement of Society. 2 vols. London, 1834.
An Inquiry respecting Private Property and the Authority and Perpetuity of the Apostolic Institution of a Community of Goods. [n.p.] 1827.
A Letter to the Bishop of London suggested by that Prelate's Letter to the Inhabitants of London and Westminster on the Profanation of the Sabbath. London, 1830.
Letters to a Clergyman on Institutions for Ameliorating the Condition of the People. Chiefly from Paris, in ... 1845. London, 1846.
[Another edn., for Phoenix Library.] London, 1850.
ed. *Pestalozzi's Letters on Early Education with a Memoir of the Author.* London, 1850. [Phoenix Library.]
The Phoenix Library: a Series of Original and Reprinted Works, bearing on the Renovation and Progress of Society, in Religion, Morality, and Science. Selected by J. M. Morgan. London, 1849–50. [Reprints].

Religion and Crime; or, the Distresses of the People, and the Remedies. [2nd edn., enlarged.]   London, 1840.
[Another edn.]   London, 1849.
Religion and Religious Education.   London [n.d.].

[MORGAN, JOHN MINTER.]   Remarks on the Practicability of Robert Owen's Plan . . . to improve the Condition of the Lower Classes. By Philanthropos.   London, 1819.
[Another edn., in Phoenix Library.]   London, 1849.

MORGAN, JOHN MINTER.   The Reproof of Brutus. London, 1830. [In verse].
The Revolt of the Bees.   London, 1826.
[Other edns.]   London, 1828, 1830, 1839.
[Another edn., in Phoenix Library.]   London, 1849.
Tour through Switzerland and Italy, in the Years 1846–47.   London, 1850. [Phoenix Library.]
Tracts: originally published at various Periods, from 1819–1838. With an Appendix.   London, 1849. [Phoenix Library.]
[Another edn.]   London, 1850.
[2nd edn.]   London, 1851.
The Triumph, or the coming Age of Christianity.   [n.p.] 1851.

MORRISON, CHARLES.   An Essay on the Relations between Labour and Capital.   London, 1854.

MORRISON, FRANCES.   The Influence of the present Marriage System upon the Character and Interests of Females contrasted with that proposed by Robert Owen, Esq., A Lecture delivered in the Social Institution, . . . Manchester, . . . 2nd September, 1838.   Manchester [1838].

MORTON, SAMUEL GEORGE.   A Memoir of William Maclure, Esq. Philadelphia, Penn., 1841.
[2nd edn., n.p.]   1844.

MUDIE, GEORGE.   A Few Particulars respecting the secret History of the Late Forum.   Edinburgh, 1812.
The Grammar of the English Language truly made easy and amusing by the Invention of Three Hundred moveable Parts of Speech.   London, 1840.

[MUDIE, GEORGE.]   Report of the Committee appointed at a Meeting of Journeymen, chiefly Printers, to take into Consideration certain Propositions, submitted to them by Mr George Mudie, having for Their Object a System of Social Arrangement, calculated to effect essential Improvements in the Condition of the Working Classes. . . .   London [n.d.].
[2nd edn.]   London, 1821.

MUDIE, GEORGE.   A Solution of the portentious Enigma of modern Civilization . . . addressed to Charles Louis Napoleon Bonaparte . . . Author of a Work on the Extinction of Pauperism.   London, 1849.

[MULLINS.] *The Scheme of Universal Brotherhood.* London, 1842.

[MURPHY, JOHN LOWTHER.] *The Elements of Socialism: compiled by the Author of 'An Essay towards a Science of Consciousness'.* Birmingham, 1840.

MURPHY, JOHN LOWTHER. *An Essay towards a Science of Consciousness, more particularly illustrative of the Phenomena of Human Knowledge, Feeling, and Action.* London, Birmingham [n.d.].

MURRAY, CHARLES. *A Letter to Mr. George Jacob Holyoake; containing a brief Review of that Gentleman's Conduct and Policy as a Reformer, with especial Reference to his Reply to Mr. Linton and the 'Boston Liberator'.* .... London, 1854.

The Nature and Reasons of Co-operation, addressed to the Working Classes. [Brighton?, 1828.]

NEALE, EDWARD VANSITTART. *The Characteristic Features of some of the principal Systems of Socialism: a Lecture.* London, 1851.
Prize Essay. On the best Means of employing the surplus Funds of the Amalgamated Society of Engineers ... in Associative or other productive Objects. London, 1855.
Memoir relating to the Position and Prospects of the Associations. For the Consideration of the Promoters and Associates. London, 1850.

NEEF, JOSEPH. *The Logic of Condillac translated by Joseph Neef, as an Illustration of the Plan of Education established at his School near Philadelphia.* Philadelphia, Penn., 1809.
The Method of instructing Children rationally, in the Arts of Writing and Reading. Philadelphia, Penn., 1813.
Sketch of a Plan and Method of Education. Philadelphia, Penn., 1808.

The New Political Economy of the Honey-Bee. By the Author of the Emigrants. [n.p., 1828?].

A New State of Society. A Dialogue between Theophilus and Amida. [n.p., n.d.].

A new Theory of moral and social Reform; founded on the principal and most general Facts of Human Nature; or, Essays to establish a universal Criterion of moral truth ... and to found thereon a Plan of voluntary Association and Order ... by a Friend of the Utmost Reform. .... London, 1823.

[NICHOLSON, WILLIAM?]. *The Doubts of Infidels; or, Queries relative to Scriptural Inconsistencies and Contradictions, submitted to the Bench of Bishops. By a weak but sincere Christian.* London [1840, 2nd edn.].

NIGHTINGALE, J. *The Bazaar.* [n.p.] 1816. [On co-operative bazaars.]

NOEL, BAPTIST W. *What is Christianity? The Third of a Course of Lectures addressed to Socialists, delivered at the London Mechanics' Institution, ... February, 1840.* London, 1840.

327

NOYES, JOHN HUMPHREY. *History of American Socialisms.* Philadelphia, Penn., 1870.
[Another edn.] New York, 1961.

OASTLER, RICHARD. *A Few Words to the Friends and Enemies of Trade Unions.* Huddersfield, 1834.
Mr. Oastler's Three Letters to Mr. Hetherington. London, 1835.
A Serious Address to the Millowners, Manufacturers, and Cloth-dressers of Leeds, who have organized themselves into a 'Trades Union' to compel their Workmen To Abandon a Right which the Laws of Britain grant to every Subject. . . . Huddersfield, 1834.

O'BRIEN, JAMES BRONTERRE (1805–1864), ed., trans. *Buonarroti's History of Babeuf's Conspiracy for Equality.* London, 1836.
A Dissertation and Elegy on the Life and Death of the immortal Maximilian Robespierre, revealing for the First Time, the Causes and Authors of His Death. London, 1859.
European Letters and Tracts for the National Reform League. (No. 1, December 6, 1851; No. 2, December 13, 1851.) London, 1851.
Labour's Wrongs and Labour's Remedy: Address to the Trades of Great Britain and Ireland. London, 1868. [Extracts from J. F. Bray's *Labour's Wrongs and Labour's Remedy,* and J. B. O'Brien's *Political Instructor* of 1850.]

[O'BRIEN, JAMES BRONTERRE?] *Land Usurpers and Money Changers. Dedicated to the People by a National Reformer.* London [1870?].

O'BRIEN, JAMES BRONTERRE. *The Life and Character of Maximilian Robespierre.* London [1838. Numbered Vol. I, but no more published].
Mr. O'Brien's Vindication of his Conduct at the Late Birmingham Conference. . . . Birmingham, 1842.
Ode to Lord Palmerston. London [1856].
An Ode to Louis Napoleon Bonaparte. [London, 1857.]

[O'BRIEN, JAMES BRONTERRE?] *Propositions of the National Reform League, for the Peaceful Regeneration of Society.* [London, 1850.]

O'BRIEN, JAMES BRONTERRE. *The Rise, Progress, and Phases of Human Slavery: how it came into the World, and how it shall be made to go out.* London, 1885. [A posthumous compilation of O'Brien's writings. The first nineteen chapters are a reprint of the 21 letters under the same title in *Reynolds's Political Instructor,* 1850.]
State Socialism!! Propositions of the National Reform League. London [1885].
To the Distressed Classes, on the present Famine Prices of Bread and other Necessaries. London, 1855.

328

To the Oppressed and Mystified People of Great Britain. [London, 1851.]
A Vision of Hell; or, Peep into the Realms below, alias Lord Overgrown's Dream. . . . London, 1859.

Observations upon Currency and Finance . . . *with some Remarks upon* . . . *Mr. Owen's New System* . . ., *by a Looker On.* Philadelphia, Penn., 1826.

Observations on the Critique contained in the Edinburgh Review for October, 1819, of Owen's Plans for relieving the National Distress. Edinburgh, 1819.

O'DRISCOL, JOHN. *Views of Ireland; moral, political and religious.* 2 vols. London, 1823. [pp. 211–23, 'Mr. Owen's Plan'.]

On Co-operation. London, 1832. [Appeared originally in the *Monthly Repository,* July 1832, as a review of the Report of the Third Co-operative Congress, held in London in April 1832.]

On the best Means of improving the moral and physical Condition of the Working Classes; . . . [n.p.] 1830.

ORBISTON. *Articles of Agreement of the Orbiston Company, March 18, 1825.* [n.p., n.d.; broadsheet.]
Memorial and Abstract in Process of Ranking and Sale . . . *against the Orbiston Company, against Archibald James Hamilton of Dalzell,* . . . *15th February, 1830.* [n.p., n.d.]
[Trade advertisement sheet, showing various goods manufactured, and tradesmen employed by community. October 1826.]

OWEN, ROBERT DALE (1801–1877). [For a full bibliography, see R. W. Leopold, *Robert Dale Owen: a Biography.* Cambridge, Mass., 1940.]
Address on Free Inquiry; on Fear as a Motive of Action. London, 1840.
Address on the Hopes and Destinies of the Human Species. London, 1832. [And later edns.]
Address on the Influence of the Clerical Profession. New York, 1831.
[Another edn.] *To which is added, a Tract and a Warning; Truth and Error; on the Fear of God.* London 1840. [And later edns.]
Address to the Conductors of the New York Periodical Press (Popular Tracts, no. 3). New York, 1830.
Beyond the Breakers: a Story of the Present Day (*Village Life in the West*). Philadelphia, Penn., 1870.
Cause of the People (Popular Tracts, no. 5). New York, 1830.
Circular addressed to the Friends of Liberal Education. [Prospectus, New Harmony Manual Labor College. n.p., 1835.]
The Debatable Land between this World and the Next. London, 1871. [Another edn.] New York, 1872.
Divorce: being a Correspondence between Horace Greeley and Robert Dale Owen. New York, 1860.

Effects of Missionary Labours (Popular Tracts, no. 7). New York, 1830.

Footfalls on the Boundary of another World. Philadelphia, Penn., 1860.

[Another edn.] London, 1860.

The French Revolution (Popular Tracts, no. 9). New York, 1830.

Galileo and the Inquisition (Popular Tracts, no. 12). New York, 1830.

[Another edn., with] *Effects of Missionary Labours.* London, 1854.

Labor: its History and Prospects; an Address delivered before the Young Men's Mercantile Association of Cincinnati ... February 1, 1848. Cincinnati, Ohio, 1848

Lecture on Consistency. London, 1841.

[Another edn.] London, 1853.

Letters to William Gibbons. Philadelphia, Penn., 1830.

Moral Physiology; or, a brief and plain Treatise on the Population Question. New York, 1830.

[Numerous later edns.]

Neurology; an Account of some Experiments in Cerebral Physiology, by Dr. Buchanan. London, 1842.

New Harmony. London, 1842. [Issued with *Neurology.*]

An Outline of the System of Education at New Lanark. Glasgow, 1824.

[Another edn.] London, 1824.

[Another edn.] Cincinnati, Ohio, 1825.

[French edn.] *Esquisse du Système d'Éducation suivi dans les Écoles de New Lanark.* Traduit par M. Desfontains. Paris, 1825.

Pocahontas: a historical Drama in Five Acts; with an introductory Essay and Notes by a 'Citizen of the West'. New York, 1837.

Prossimo's Experience (Popular Tracts, no. 4). New York, 1830.

[And later edns.]

[OWEN, ROBERT DALE.] *The Rational Library.* London [1840?; six tracts by R. D. Owen].

OWEN, ROBERT DALE. *Reply to a Report of the New York Typographical Society.* New York, 1830.

A Sermon on Loyalty ... and a Sermon on Free Enquiry (Popular Tracts, no. 6). New York, 1830.

Situations: Lawyers, Clergy, Physicians, Men and Women (Popular Tracts, no. 10). New York, 1830.

Six Essays on Public Education. New York, 1830.

The System of Commercial Restriction. [Washington, D.C., 1846.]

A Tale of Old England (Popular Tracts, no. 1). New York, 1830.

Threading My Way. Twenty-seven Years of Autobiography. London, 1874.

[American edn.] *Twenty-seven Years of Autobiography: Threading My Way.* New York, 1874.

A Tract and a Warning (Popular Tracts, no. 13). New York, 1830.

Truth and Error (Popular Tracts, no. 2).   New York, 1830.
Wealth and Misery (Popular Tracts, no. 11).   New York, 1830.
[Another edn.]   Manchester, 1839.
[Other edns.]   London, 1840, 1846.
and ORIGEN BACHELER. *Discussion on the Existence of God and the Authenticity of the Bible between O. Bacheler and R. D. Owen*.   New York, 1831.
[Another edn.]   London, 1832.
and FRANCES WRIGHT. *Tracts on Republican Government and National Education. Addressed to the Inhabitants of the United States. . . .*   London [1839].
FRANCES WRIGHT and others. *Popular Tracts*.   New York, 1830. [14 vols. in 1.]
[Another edn.]   London, 1841–44.
[Another edn., 11 vols. in 1.]   London, 1851.
[Another edn.]   New York, 1854.

OWEN, WILLIAM (1802–1842). *The Diary of William Owen from November 10, 1824, to April 20, 1825*, ed. Joel W. Hiatt, in Indiana Historical Society *Publications*, IV, no. 1.   Indianapolis, Ind., 1906.

AN OWENIAN. *The Natural Mirror; or, Free Thoughts on Theology. . . .*   Manchester, 1839.

Owenism exposed: or, a Glance at the Rationality of the System by Common Sense.   Glasgow [c. 1839].

PAGET, AMEDÉE FÈLIX. *Introduction à l'Étude de la Science Sociale précédé d'un Coup d'Oeil . . . sur les Systèmes de Fourier, d'Owen, et de Saint-Simon. . . .*   Paris, 1839.
[2nd edn.]   Paris, 1841.

PALMER, EDWARD. *A Letter to those who think*.   Worcester, 1840.

Pamphlets advocating Socialism, pub. Abel Heywood (1810–1893).   Manchester, 1838–40. [32 pamphlets.]

PARE, WILLIAM (1805–1873). *An Address delivered at the Opening of the Birmingham Cooperative Society, November 17, 1828, by a Member. To which is added the Laws of the Society*.   Birmingham [1828].
An Address to the Working Classes of Liverpool, on the Formation of Co-operative Societies or Working Unions.   [n.p., 1829.]
The Claims of Capital and Labour: with a Sketch of practical Measures for their Conciliation. A Paper read before the Dublin Statistical Society.   London, 1854.
Co-operative Agriculture: a Solution of the Land Question, as exemplified in the History of the Ralahine Co-operative Agricultural Association, County Clare, Ireland.   London, 1870.

331

Equitable Commerce, as practised in the Equity Villages of the United States. . . . London, 1856. [Reprinted from the *Journal of the Statistical Society*, June, 1856.]

A Full and authentic Report of the Great Catholic Meeting, which took place in the Town Hall, Birmingham . . . *November the 23rd, 1835*. Birmingham [1835].

A Plan for the Suppression of the Predatory Classes: a Paper read before the Third Department of the 'National Association for the Promotion of Social Science', London Meeting, 1862 . . . *reprinted* . . . *with additional Matter from the Volume of 'Transactions of the Association'*. London, 1862.

PARSONS, REV. B. *Education, the Birthright of every Human Being, and the only Scriptural Preparation for the Millenium*. . . . London, 1845.

PAULDING, JAMES KIRKE. *Merry Tales of the Three Wise Men of Gotham*. New York, 1826.

PEARS, THOMAS. *New Harmony. An Adventure in Happiness. Papers of Thomas and Sarah Pears*, ed. Thomas C. Pears, Jr., in Indiana Historical Society *Publications*, XI, no. 1. Indianapolis, Ind., 1933.

PEARSON, REV. GEORGE. *The Progress and Tendencies of Socialism. A Sermon preached before the University of Cambridge, 17th November, 1839*. Cambridge, 1839.

PELHAM, WILLIAM (1759–1827). 'Letters of William Pelham, written in 1825 and 1826', in Harlow Lindley, ed., *Indiana as seen by early Travelers*. Indianapolis, Ind., 1916.

PEMBERTON, ROBERT. *An Address to the Bishops and Clergy of all Denominations* . . . *on Robert Owen's Proclamation of the Millenial State to commence this Year (1855)*. London, 1855 [4th edn.].

An Address to the People on the Necessity of Popular Education, in Conjunction with Emigration, as a Remedy for all our social Ills. London, 1859.

The Attributes of the Soul from the Cradle, and the Philosophy of the Divine Mother, detecting the false Basis, or fundamental Error, of the Schools, and developing the perfect Education of Man. London, 1849.

Explanation given . . . *of his Happy Colony, at the Public Meeting in St. Martin's Hall, London* . . . *proving that his Investigation of the Human Mind is in perfect Harmony with the Philosophy of Robert Owen*. London, 1855.

The Happy Colony, dedicated to the Workmen of Great Britain. London, 1854.

The Infant Drama: a Model of the Time Method of Teaching all Languages. London, 1857.

Report of the Proceedings at the Inauguration of Mr. Pemberton's New Philosophical Model Infant School, for Teaching Languages, native and foreign, on the Natural or Euphonic System, . . . August 22, 1857. London, 1857.

The Science of Mind-formation, and the Process of the Reproduction of Genius elaborated; involving the Remedy for all our social Evils. London, 1858.

Persecution not Christianity! A Letter to the Rev. W. J. Kidd, Incumbent of St. Matthew's, Manchester, on the Mode proposed by him for the Suppression of the Socialists. By a Member of the Church of England. Manchester [c. 1840].

PESTALOZZI, HENRY. *Letters on Early Education. Addressed to J. P. Greaves. Translated from the German . . . with a Memoir of Pestalozzi.* London, 1827.

PETRIE, GEORGE (–1836). *The Works of——, comprising Equality, a Poem, . . . with a Portrait and Biographical Memoir by R. E. Lee.* London [1836?; the poem 'Equality' is dedicated to Robert Dale Owen].

PHILIP, ROBERT. *The Royal Marriage; an Antidote to Socialism and Oxfordism; a Sermon preached at Maberly Chapel, 12th February, 1840.* London, 1840.

PHILLPOTTS, HENRY. *Progress of Socialism. The Bishop of Exeter's Speech in the House of Lords, . . . 24th January, 1840.* London, 1840.
[Also included in] *Reprint of the Debate in the Lords on Socialism, from 'The Times' of February 5th, 1840.* Leeds, 1840.
Socialism. Second Speech of the Bishop of Exeter, in the House of Lords, 4th February, 1840. London, 1840.
Speech in the House of Lords, 24 June, 1840. [London, 1840].

PHILLIPS, B. J. *A rational Invocation or Prayer; being the Sequel to a Lecture 'On the physical Advantages of Communities of United Interests'.* [n.p., n.d.]

PHILLIPS, GEORGE SEARLE [pseud. JANUARY SEARLE]. *Chapters in the History of a Life.* London, Leeds, 1849.
Emerson, his Life and Writings. London, 1855.
Essays, Poems, Allegories, and Fables: with an Elucidation and Analysis of the 'Bhagvat Geeta', by January Searle. London, 1851.
Essays. 2nd series. London, 1855.

PHILOPATRIUS [pseud.]. *Letter to Lord Melbourne, on his presenting Robert Owen, the Founder of the immoral, blasphemous and atheistical System, misnamed 'Socialism', to the Queen.* London, [1839].

PILGRIM, G. W. *Competition considered as a Principle in Human Nature; being an Introduction to a Debate on that Subject, in the Mutual Improvement Class of the Pottery Mechanics' Institution.* Newcastle [n.d.].

Plain Sense and Reason. Letters to the present Generation on the unrestrained Use of modern Machinery.... Norwich [1831?].

POLE, THOMAS. *Observations Relative to Infant Schools, designed to point out their Usefulness to the Children of the Poor, ... calculated to assist those who may benevolently incline to establish such Schools.* Bristol, 1823.

The Position of Women in Harmony. London, 1841.

POWELL, BENJAMIN F. *Bible of Reason; or, Scriptures of Ancient Moralists and of Modern Authors....* 3 parts. London, 1837–39.
Bible of Reason Supplement; or, Exhibition-Testament of 1851. London, [1851?]

POWELL, REV. THOMAS. *Socialism in its own Colours. A plain Tract on Socialism for Working Men.* London, 1840.

The Power of the People; or, the Way to Wealth, Prosperity, and Peace; a Social Pamphlet, showing how the Working Classes may become possessed of immense Landed Estates.... Leeds [1835?].

Prize Essay on the Comparative Merits of Competition and Cooperation, as the best Principle for the Basis of Society. Manchester [n.d.].

Production the Cause of Demand, being a brief Analysis of a Work [by John Gray] *entitled 'The Social System'....* Birmingham, 1832.

Prospects and Pleasures of Rationality: an Address delivered at the Opening of a Social Scientific Class in Scotland.... Manchester, 1842.

Prospectus and Plan of Operations of the Second Section of the Social Reformers' Cooperative Emigration Society. [23 November, 1843. Refers to the community of Equality, Wisconsin.]

Prospectus of a Plan for establishing an Institution on Mr. Owen's System in the Middle Ward of the County of Lanark. [n.p., 1822?]

Prospectus of the London Phalanx. London, 1841. [Compares Owenism with Fourierism.]

Public Warnings against Owen and Others; with an Account of the Death of Henry H. Hudson.... London, 1834 [in monthly numbers].

PUBLICOLA [pseud.]. *Socialism exposed, with its baneful Tendency and pernicious Effects ... and a brief History of Robert Owen, its Founder....* London, 1844.

PUFFEM, PETER [pseud.]. *Heaven on Earth; or, the New Lights of Harmony. An Extravaganza, in Two Acts.* Philadelphia, Penn., 1825.

RATIONAL SOCIETY. *Full Account of the Farewell Festival given to Robert Owen, on his departure for America.* London, 1844.

RATIONAL TRACT SOCIETY. *National Evils and National Remedies.* Ser. 3, nos. 1–6. London, 1843.

RAVENSTONE, PIERCY [pseud.?]. *A Few Doubts as to the Correctness of some Opinions generally entertained on the Subjects of Population and Political Economy.* London, 1821.
Thoughts on the Funding System and its Effects. [n.p.] 1824.

REECE, GEORGE. *Truth Without Mystery. A Few Facts regarding Mr. Owen and his Corresponding Secretary, Mr. Fleming, the principal Supporters of the Social System. In a Letter ... to the Operatives of Manchester.* Manchester, 1838.

REID, JAMES R. *Exposure of Socialism. A Refutation of the Letter on Harmony Hall, by 'One who has whistled at the Plough', which appeared in the Morning Chronicle of the 13th December Last; with an Appendix of Facts regarding Socialism. ...* London, 1843.

Rejected Address from the Concordists' Society at Ham Common, to the London Peace Society, presented at their Convention, 24th June, 1843, at the Freemason's Tavern (extracted from the 'New Age,' 1st July, 1843). [n.p.] 1843.

Relief of the Poor (from the 'Courier' of April 9). [n.p., 1817; broadsheet.]

Remarks on the Owen Plan to improve the Condition of the Working Classes. [n.p.] 1819.

Remarks on the Struggle between the Master and the Journeyman Builders. [Manchester?] 1833.

Resolutions intended to be proposed at the Public Meeting to be held on the 12th instant, at the Royal London Bazaar. [London, 1832?]

REY, JOSEPH. *Lettres sur le Système de la Co-opération mutuelle et de la Communauté de tous les Biens, d'après le Plan de M. Owen.* Paris, 1828.

REYBAUD, MARIE LOUIS. *Études sur les Réformateurs contemporains, ou Socialistes modernes, Saint-Simon, Charles Fourier, Robert Owen. ...* Paris, 1840.
[Later edns., 1841–44].

The Rise, Course, and Uses of Co-operation explained, in an Essay addressed to the First Norwich Co-operative Society, February 22, 1830. Norwich, London, 1830.

ROBERT OWEN CENTENARY COMMITTEE. *Programme of the Celebration of the Hundredth Anniversary of the Birthday of Robert Owen, the Philanthropist ... on ... May 16th, 1871.* [London, 1871.]
To the Reformers of Great Britain. [London, 1871.]

Robert Owen at New Lanark; with a Variety of interesting Anecdotes: being a brief and authentic Narrative of the Character and Conduct of Mr. Owen while Proprietor of New Lanark . . . by One formerly a Teacher at New Lanark. Manchester, 1839.

ROEBUCK, JOHN ARTHUR, ed. *Pamphlets for the People.* 2 vols. London, 1835.

ROEBUCK, REV. JOHN H. *Lectures. I. Anti-Owenism.* Glasgow, London [1840].
Lectures. II. Anti-Owenism. [n.p., 1840?]
Lectures and Sermons . . . with a Sketch of his Life. London, 1842.

ROSSER, CHARLES. *Intellect: its Nature, Rights and Duties. Being the Substance of a Lecture delivered to a Scientific Institution.* London, 1843.
Thoughts on the New Era of Society. A Lecture delivered at Mr. Owen's Institution, Burton Street, . . . 13th November, 1831, on the New Era of Society. London, 1831. [1st and 2nd edns.]
[3rd edn.] *Thoughts on the Progress and Prospects of Man, and on the New Era of Society.* London [1832?].

ST ANDRÉ, JULES LECHEVALIER. *Five Years in the Land of Refuge. A Letter on the Prospects of Co-operative Association in England, addressed to the Members of Council of the late Society for Promoting Working Men's Associations. . . .* London, 1854.

S., F. K. *Trades' Triumphant, or Unions' Jubilee! A Plan for the Consolidation of popular Power, and restoring to the People their long lost Rights.* [London] 1834.

SAINT-SIMON, HENRI COMTE DE. *New Christianity,* trans. James E. Smith. London, 1834. [Includes preface and notes by J. E. Smith.]

SANGSTER, JOHN. *The Rights and Duties of Property; with a Plan for paying off the National Debt.* London, 1857.

SARGANT, WILLIAM LUCAS. *Economy of the Labouring Classes.* London, 1857.
Social Innovators and their Schemes. London, 1858.

SATCHWELL, T. *Satchwell and Christianity versus Holyoake and atheistical Infidelity: Mr. Satchwell's Two Speeches delivered during his Discussion with Mr. G. J. Holyoake. . . .* Northampton, 1847.

SAXE WEIMAR-EISENACH, KARL BERNHARD, DUKE OF. *Travels through North America during the Years 1825 and 1826.* 2 vols. Philadelphia, Penn., 1828. [Includes account of visit to New Harmony.]
[Another edn., in] Harlow Lindley, *Indiana as seen by early Travelers.* Indianapolis, Ind., 1916.

Sayings and Doings about the New Moral World. [Leeds, 1840].

SCORESBY, WILLIAM. *Lectures on Socialism delivered in the Parish Church, Bradford....* London, 1839.

SCOTT, REV. A. J. *The Social Systems of the present Day, compared with Christianity. In Five Lectures....* London, 1841.

SEALSFIELD, CHARLES. *The Americans as they are.* London, 1828. [Includes description of New Harmony.]

SEARS, CHARLES. *Socialism and Christianity.* [n.p.] 1854.

SEEDAIR, STEPHEN. *Christian or true Constitution of Man, versus the pernicious Fallacies of Mr. Combe and other materialistic Writers.* Edinburgh, 1856.

SHEPHEARD, A. *Christianity and Socialism examined, compared, and contrasted, as Means for promoting Human Improvement and Happiness.* London, 1840.

SHORTER, THOMAS (1823–1899). *Confessions of a Truth-Seeker.* London, 1859.

SKENE, GEORGE ROBERT. *On the Condition of Land-Capitalists and Agriculturists ... reprinted from the Leamington Press.* [Leamington] 1834.

SKIDMORE, THOMAS. *Moral Physiology exposed and refuted.* New York, 1831.
The Rights of Man to Property: being a Proposition to make it equal among the Adults of the present Generation; and to provide for its equal Transmission to every Individual of each succeeding Generation.... New York, 1829.

[SMITH, C. M.]. *The Workingman's Way in the World: being the Autobiography of a Journeyman Printer.* London [1853].

SMITH, REV. HENRY. *The Destitution and Miseries of the Poor disclosed, and their Remedies suggested: being an Exposition of the Principles and Objects of the Church of England Self-supporting Village Society.* London, 1850.

SMITH, JAMES. *Notes taken during an Excursion in Scotland, in the Year 1820.* London, Liverpool, 1824.

SMITH, REV. JAMES ELISHAMA ('SHEPHERD') (1801–1857). *The Antichrist, or, Christianity reformed: in which is demonstrated from the Scriptures, ... that Evil and Good are from the same Source; ...* London, [1833].
The Coming Man. 2 vols. London, 1873. [A novel.]
The Divine Drama of History and Civilization. London, 1854.

Lecture on a Christian Community, delivered . . . *at the Surrey Institution.* London, 1833.

The Little Book; or, momentous Crisis of 1840; in which the Bishop of Exeter and Robert Owen are weighed in the Two Scales of One Balance, and a New Revelation of demonstrated Truth is announced to the World. London, 1840.

Mercury's Letters on Science, designed to suggest correct Modes of thinking and reasoning on scientific Subjects. London, 1853.

A Sermon in Refutation of the Doctrines of Robert Owen [by Rev. Dr. George Redford] . . . *to which is appended a Reply by the Rev. J. E. Smith.* . . . London, 1834.

SMITH, WILLIAM. *Scepticism and Infidelity, with Their tendencies.* Coventry [n.d.].

SMITH, WILLIAM HAWKES (1786–1840). *Birmingham and its Vicinity as a Manufacturing and Commercial District.* Birmingham, 1836.

The Errors of the Social System; being an Essay on wasted, unproductive, and redundant Labour. Birmingham, 1834.

Letters on Social Science. Birmingham, 1839.

Letters on the State and Prospects of Society. Birmingham, 1838.

On Cooperation. [n.p.] 1832. [Reprinted from *Monthly Repository*.]

[SMITH, WILLIAM HAWKES.] *A Radical mis-represented and truly re-presented; or, a Two-fold Character of Radicalism:—to which is added a brief History of the Rise and Fall of the Island of Peterloo.* London [1821?].

SMYLES, DR JOHN. *Emigration to the United States. A Letter addressed to Mr. Pitkethly of Huddersfield.* . . . London, 1842.

Social Hymns: for the Use of the Friends of the Rational System of Society. Manchester, 1835.

[Another edn.] Salford, 1838.

[Another edn.] Leeds, 1838.

[Authorized edn.] London, 1840.

[2nd edn.] Leeds, 1840.

SOCIAL MISSIONARY AND TRACT SOCIETY. *Exchange of Labour. Labour Banks. A Riddle. The Workings of Capital, at present represented by Money.* [n.p., n.d.; broadsheets.]

The Social Reformers' Almanack for 1842. Leeds, 1842.

SOCIAL SCIENCE LEAGUE. *Prospectus.* [n.p., 1857?]

The Social Science of the Constitution of Society, or the Cause and Cure of its present Evils. London, 1862.

Social Tracts, 1–7. [n.p., 1838?]

Socialism: What is Socialism? London, 1839.
[Another edn.] London, 1840.

The Socialist; a Tale of Philosophical Religion. Leeds, 1839.

SOCIETY FOR PROMOTING NATIONAL REGENERATION. *Rights of Industry, Catechism of the Society. . . .* Manchester, 1833.

[SOMERVILLE, ALEXANDER]. *Notes from the farming Districts. No. XVII. A Journey to Harmony Hall, in Hampshire, with some Particulars of the Socialist Community, to which the Attention of the Nobility, Gentry, and Clergy, is earnestly requested.* London, 1842. [Reprinted from the *Morning Chronicle* as a pamphlet.]
[Another edn., in] *The Whistler at the Plough.* Manchester, 1852.
The Working Man's Witness against the London Literary Infidels, no. 1. [n.p., 1858?]

The Source and Remedy of the National Difficulties, deduced from Principles of Political Economy in a Letter to Lord John Russell. [n.p.] 1821.

SOUTHEY, ROBERT. *Essays, Moral and Political.* 2 vols. London, 1832.
Sir Thomas More; or, Colloquies on the Progress and Prospects of Society. 2 vols. London, 1829.

SOUTHWELL, CHARLES (1814–1860). *Another 'Fourpenny Wilderness', in which may be found more Nails for the Coffin of Nonsense called Atheism, more Hints to Freethinkers, and a Reply to George Jacob Holyoake's Examination of . . . 'Impossibility of Atheism Demonstrated'.* London, 1852.
An Apology for Atheism. [n.p.] 1846.
The Confessions of a Freethinker. London [n.d.].
An Essay on Marriage. London, 1840.
The Impossibility of Atheism demonstrated; with Hints to nominal Atheists, in a Letter to the Freethinkers of Great Britain. London, 1852.
trans. *The Origin, Object and Organization of the Christian Religion,* by François Dupuis. London [n.d.].
Socialism made easy; or, a plain Exposition of Mr. Owen's Views. London, 1840.
Supernaturalism exploded, in a Review of Six Nights' Controversy between the Rev. Brewin Grant . . . and George Jacob Holyoake. London, 1853.
Superstition unveiled . . . abridged by the Author from his Apology for Atheism. London, 1854.
The Trial of Charles Southwell (Editor of the 'Oracle of Reason') for Blasphemy . . . reported by William Carpenter. London, 1842.
Twopennyworth of Truth about Owenism and the Owenites. London, 1845.

Spade Cultivation tried for Ten Years on an Estate in Wiltshire: in a Letter to the Rt. Hon. W. Sturges Bourne. By a Magistrate for the Counties of Hampshire and Wiltshire.   London, 1831. [2nd edn.]

SPIER, WILLIAM.   *The Causes and Cure of Social Unhappiness: a Lecture delivered in the Hall of Science, Glasgow.*   Glasgow, 1839.

Statement of the Master Builders of the Metropolis in Explanation of the Differences between them and the Workmen respecting the Trades Unions.   London, 1834.

Statement submitted to the most noble the Marquis of Normanby, . . . relative to the Principles and Objects of the Universal Community Society of Rational Religionists.   By the Branch A1 of that Society. London [1840].

STURMER, REV. FREDERICK.   *Socialism, its immoral Tendency; or, a plain Appeal to Common Sense.*   London, 1840.

SUDRE, ALFRED.   *Histoire du Communisme; ou Réfutation historique des Utopies Socialistes.*   Paris, 1849. [Includes Owen.]
   [Another edn.]   Brussels, 1849.
   [German edn.]   Berlin, 1882.

The Synopsis of the Rational System of Society.   London, 1834.

Table-Talk on the State of Society, Competition, and Co-operation, Labour and Capital, Morals and Religion.   Birmingham, 1832.

Talk about Socialism with an Old Shopmate.   London [1840?].

TAUNTON, WILLIAM.   *A Record of Facts: being an Exposure of the wilful Falsehoods and mean Hypocrisy of the Rev. John Sibtree . . . also an Account of the cowardly Conduct of the Rev. T. Milner. . . .*   Coventry, 1840.

TAYLOR, REV. CHARLES B.   *Edward; or, almost an Owenite.*   London, 1840.
   Jared; or, quite an Owenite.   London [1840].

TAYLOR, ISAAC.   *Man Responsible for his Dispositions, Opinions and Conduct. A Lecture . . . in the Mechanics' Institute, Southampton Buildings, 17 February, 1840.*   London, 1840.

THIERS, ADOLPHE.   *The Rights of Property; a Refutation of Communism and Socialism.*   London, 1848. [1st English edn.]

THIMBLEBY, JOHN.   *A Lecture on the Currency, in which is explained the represented Time Note Medium of Exchange, in Connexion with a universal System of Banking, delivered at the Barnet Institute.*   [n.p.] 1850.
   Monadelphia; or, the Formation of a New System of Society, without the Intervention of a circulating Medium.   Barnet, 1832.

What Is Money? or, Man's Birthright, 'Time' the only real Wealth; its Representative forming the true Medium of Exchange. [London? 1849].

THOMPSON, WILLIAM (1775–1830). *Appeal of One-half the Human Race, Women, against the Pretensions of the other Half, Men, to retain them in political, and thence in civil and domestic Slavery; in Reply to . . . Mr. Mill's celebrated 'Article on Government'.* London, 1825.

An Inquiry into the Principles of the Distribution of Wealth most conducive to Human Happiness; applied to the newly proposed System of Voluntary Equality of Wealth. London, 1824.

['A New Edition', by William Pare]. London, 1850.

[Another edn.] London, 1869.

[Reprint of 1st edn.] New York, 1963.

Labor Rewarded. The Claims of Labor and Capital conciliated: or, how to secure to Labor the whole Products of its Exertions. . . . London, 1827.

Practical Directions for the speedy and economical Establishment of Communities on the Principles of Mutual Co-operation, united Possessions and Equality of Exertions and of the Means of Enjoyments. London, 1830.

Practical Education for the South of Ireland. [n.p.] 1819.

THOMSON, WILLIAM. *The Age of Harmony; or, a new System of Social Economy eminently calculated to improve the Circumstances of the oppressed, enslaved, and impoverished Portion of the People of Great Britain and Ireland. . . .* Glasgow, 1834 [2nd edn.].

A Prospectus of Socialism, or, a Glimpse of the Millenium, showing its Plan and working Arrangements and How it may be brought about. London [n.d.].

THORNTON, WILLIAM THOMAS. *On Labour (its wrongful Claims and rightful Dues. Its actual Present and possible Future).* London, 1870.

Overpopulation and its Remedy. London, 1846.

A Plea for Peasant Proprietors. London, 1848.

Thoughts on the present State of Society, and on a Christian Community after the Manner of the early Disciples of Christ, by an Evangelical Reformer. [n.p., n.d.]

To the Friends of Robert Owen. Suggestions for the Formation of an Owen Institute. [n.p.] 1873.

The Town of New Harmony and the Rev. Benjamin Halsted; Being a Report of the Proceedings of a Meeting of the Inhabitants . . . at the New Harmony Hall . . . 13th April, 1842, To Take Into Consideration a Certain Communication Which Appeared in the 'Episcopal Recorder' of Philadelphia, Reflecting Upon the Character of the Town. [Evansville, Ind., 1842.]

TOWNLEY, HENRY, ed. *Report of a Public Discussion Carried on by Henry Townley . . . and George Jacob Holyoake . . . in the Scientific Institution, John Street, Fitzroy Square, London. . . .* London, 1852.

TRAVIS, HENRY (1807–1884). *The Coming Revolution. . . .* London [1872].
The Co-operative System of Society. . . . London, 1871.
Effectual Reform in Man and Society. London [1875].
The End of the Free-Will Controversy. London, 1875.
English Socialism. Parts I and II. London, Manchester, 1880.
Free Will and Law in perfect Harmony. London, 1868.
A Manual of Social Science for the Working Classes. London, 1877.
[Another edn.] London, 1877.
Moral Freedom, reconciled with Causation, by the Analysis of the Process of Self-Determination. The moral Basis of Social Science. With a Post-script on Co-operation. London, 1865.

TROLLOPE, FRANCES. *Domestic Manners of the Americans.* 2 vols. London, 1832. [Volume I includes account of Nashoba community.]

True Christianity, Atheism, and Infidelity defined and compared with Robert Owen's 'New Views of Society' and the Character of their Author. . . . Manchester [1839?].

A True Exposure of the noted Robert Owen! Concerning his late Visit to the Queen . . . with an Account of the Victims of Seduction, and his New Moral Marriage System. London, 1840.

TRUELOVE, EDWARD (1809–1899). *In the High Court of Justice. Queen's Bench Division, February 1, 1878. The Queen v. E. Truelove for publishing . . . Robert Dale Owen's 'Moral Physiology' and a Pamphlet entitled 'Individual, Family, and National Poverty'.* London, 1878.

Truth without Mystery, in Reply to F. Reece. Manchester [1839?].

Two Editions of the Apostles Creed; or, Which is the true One? Leeds [n.d.].

UNDERHILL, SAMUEL. *Campbell refuted; being a Correspondence between the Rev. Alexander Campbell . . . and Dr. . . . Underhill of Ohio; on the Subject of the Debate held in Cincinnati between the celebrated Robert Owen and Mr. Campbell.* [n.p.] 1831.

The Unique: a Series of Portraits of eminent Persons. With their Memoirs. No. 19: Robert Owen. London [1823].

UNIVERSAL COMMUNITY SOCIETY OF RATIONAL RELIGIONISTS. *Address to all Classes, Sects and Parties, containing an official Declaration of Principles, adapted for Practice by the Congress of the Universal Community Society . . ., held in Leeds, May, 1840: to which is added the Proclamation of the Congress. . . .* London, 1840.
Socialism set at Rest. . . . [Leeds] 1840.

A View of all Religions in the World.... Manchester [n.d.].

Views and Plans of a self-supporting Home Colony; with Description. London, 1841.

A Vindication of Mr. Owen's Plan for the Relief of the distressed Working Classes, in Reply to the Misconceptions of a Writer in No. 64 of the Edinburgh Review. London, 1820.

W., K. *Is Money beneficial or injurious to the People?* London, 1834.

W., N. *A Letter advocating the Establishment of Equitable Banks of Interchange; through which, by Means of Property Notes, ... an equitable Exchange of all Kinds of useful Goods and Services may be accomplished, independently of a scarce and costly metallic Currency.* London, 1847.

WALLACE, ALFRED RUSSEL. *My Life: a Record of Events and Opinions.* 2 vols. London, 1905.

WALPOLE, SPENCER. *The People armed against Priestcraft.* Manchester, 1840.

WALTER, EDWARD. *Does the Bishop of Worcester believe in Christ? The Question answered in a Letter to his Lordship.* London [n.d.].
How is Man's Character formed? The Question answered in a Letter to the Rev. Dr. Redford of Worcester. London, 1844 [2nd edn.].
Is the Bible true? The Question asked in a Letter to the ... Bishop of Worcester. London, 1844.
Why does not the Bishop answer the Question, 'Is the Bible true?' ... London, 1844.
and REV. GEORGE REDFORD. *A Reply to How is Man's Character Formed? ... with a Reply to the Same by Edward Walter.* London, 1844.

[WALTON, ALFRED A.] *Cooperative Self-Employment safely and systematically Arranged.* [n.p., c. 1865.]

[WARD, JOHN (ZION)] *Lord Melbourne's Chain unlinked, with which he intended through Robert Owen, to fetter the People for Ever. (Substance of a Discourse ... in Charles Town, Ashton-Under-Line, ... 3rd of January, the 12th Year).* Nottingham, 1840.

WARDEN, BENJAMIN. *Rewards of Industry. The Labour Exchange the only true Way to Wealth for the Working Classes.* [London, 1832?]

WARREN, JOSIAH (1798–1874). *Emancipation of Labor.* Cliftondale, Mass., 1864.
Equitable Commerce, a new Development of Principles as Substitutes for Laws and Government.... New York, 1835.
[Another edn.] New Harmony, Ind., 1846.

[Another edn.]   New York, 1852.
[Another edn.]   New York, 1858.
Equitable Villages in America. . . .   Cliftondale, Mass. [184?].
Explanation of the Design and Arrangements of the Co-operative Magazine which has recently been commenced.   Cincinnati, Ohio, [1827?].
Manifesto . . .   [n.p.] 1841. [Reprinted] Berkeley Heights, N.J., 1952.
Modern Government and its true Mission; a few Words for the American Crisis.   [n.p.] 1862.
Periodical Letters on true Civilization.   Princeton, Mass., 1852–73.
Practical Application of the elementary Principles of true Civilization.   Princeton, Mass., 1873.
The Quarterly Letter: devoted mainly to showing the practical Applications and Progress of 'Equity'. A Subject of serious Importance to all Classes, but most immediately to the Men and Women of Labor and Sorrow!   Cliftondale, Mass., 1867.
True Civilization an immediate Necessity, and the Last Ground of Hope for Mankind. . . .   Boston, Mass., 1863.
Written Music remodelled and invested with the Simplicity of an exact Science.   Boston, Mass., 1860.

WATTS, JOHN (1818–1887).   *The Alphabet of Political Economy.*   London, Manchester, 1847.
Catechism of Wages and Capital.   London, Manchester, 1867.
Cooperation considered as an economic Element in Society.   Manchester, 1887.
Co-operative Societies, productive and distributive: Past, Present, and Future.   Manchester [1861].
Ecroydism.   Manchester, 1882.
Facts and Fictions of Political Economists. . . .   London, Manchester, 1842.
The Facts of the Cotton Famine.   London, 1866.
Logic of Free Trade.   Manchester [n.d.].
Machinery: Its Influence on Work and Wages.   [n.p., 186?]
Metaphysical Parallels; or, Arguments in Juxtaposition for and Against the Existence of God. . . .   London, 1842.
Necessity and Importance of Economy in National Taxation.   Manchester, 1879.
On Strikes, and their Effects on Wages, Profits and Accumulations.   [n.p., n.d.; reprinted from *Journal of the Statistical Society of London*, XXIV (1861).]
On the Next Step in Primary Education.   [n.p., n.d.; reprinted from *Transactions of the Manchester Statistical Society*, 1878–79.]
Robert Owen 'The Visionary', a Lecture, on the third Anniversary of the Opening of the Manchester Hall of Science.   Manchester, 1843.
Trade Societies and Strikes: their good and evil Influences on the Members of Trades' Unions and on Society at Large.   Manchester, 1861.
What Are the Social Effects of Trades Unions, Strikes, and Lock-outs?   [n.p.] 1871.

Work of the First Manchester School Board. [n.p., 1873; reprinted from *Transactions of the Manchester Statistical Society*, 1873–74.]

The Working Man, a Problem: a Lecture. . . . Manchester, 1875.

and 'ICONOCLAST' [G. J. HOLYOAKE], eds. *Half-hours with Freethinkers.* London, 1864.

WAYLAND, T. *National Advancement and Happiness considered in Reference to the Equalization of Property, and the Formation of Communities.* London, 1832.

WHALLEY, R. *A Philosophical Refutation of the Theories of Robert Owen and his Followers . . . together with an Exposure of the remaining Inconsistencies.* . . . Manchester, 1840.

WHITWELL, STEDMAN. *Description of an architectural Model from a Design by——, for a Community upon a Principle of United Interests as advocated by Robert Owen.* . . . London, 1830.

[WILLIAMS, J. S.] *The Detriments of Civilization, and Benefits of Association; also Pledges and Rules for the Integral Phalanx . . . with Objections to the Common Property System of Owen, Rapp, and Others.* Cincinnati, Ohio, 1844.

WINKS, J. F. *Christianity and not Owenism, the Regenerator of the World.* Leicester, 1838.

WOODS, JOHN. *Two Years' Residence in the Settlement on the English Prairie, in the Illinois County, United States.* London, 1820.

[Another edn., in] Thwaites, Reuben Gold, ed., *Early Western Travels*, X. Cleveland, Ohio, 1904.

A WORKING MAN. *Strictures on the Lectures delivered by the Rev. Brewin Grant.* Keighley, 1853.

WRIGHT, FRANCES (1795–1852). [For a full bibliography, see William Randall Waterman, *Frances Wright* (New York, 1924); and A. J. G. Perkins and Theresa Wolfson, *Frances Wright, Free Enquirer* (New York, 1939).]

Address—containing a Review of the Times, as first delivered in the Hall of Science, New York, May 9, 1830. New York, 1830.

An Address to the industrious Classes . . . a Sketch of a System of National Education. New York, 1830.

An Address to young Mechanics, as delivered in the Hall of Science, 13th June, 1830. New York, 1830.

Altorf, a Tragedy. Philadelphia, Penn., 1819.

Biography, Notes, and political Letters. Dundee, 1844. [Reprinted from the Dundee *Northern Star.*]

[And later edns.]

Course of popular Lectures, as delivered . . . in the United States. With Three Addresses, on various public Occasions. And a Reply to the Charges against the French reformers of 1789.   New York, 1829.

[Another edn.]   London, 1829.

England the Civilizer—her History developed in its Principles.   London, 1848.

Fables.   New York, 1830.

A Few Days in Athens.   London, 1822.

Introductory Address, delivered by F. W., at the Opening of the Hall of Science, New York . . . April 26, 1829.   New York, 1829.

A Lecture on existing Evils and their Remedy; as delivered in the Arch Street Theatre, . . . Philadelphia, 2nd June, 1829.   New York, 1829.

Parting Address, as delivered in the Bowery Theater . . . New York, in June, 1830.   New York, 1830.

A Plan for the gradual Abolition of Slavery.   Baltimore, Md., 1825.

Tracts on Republican Government and National Education addressed to the Inhabitants of the United States. . . .   New York, 1832.

Views of Society and Manners in America—in a Series of Letters from that Country to a Friend in England, during the Years 1818, 1819, and 1820. By an Englishwoman.   New York, 1821.

[English edn.]   London, 1821.

WRIGHT, HENRY G.   *Marriage and its Sanctions.*   [n.p.] 1840.

and MISS ( ) WRIGHT.   *Exposition of an educative Effort at Alcott House, Ham Common, near Richmond, Surrey.*   [London] 1839.

[Another edn.]   *Retrospective Sketch of an educative Attempt at Alcott House. . . .*   London, 1840.

Y., W.   *Twelve Letters to young Men, on the Sentiments of . . . Robert Dale Owen. . . .*   [n.p.] 1830.

Young Germany, an Account of the Rise, Progress, and present Position of German Communism; with a Memoir of Wilhelm Weitling, its Founder; and a Report of the Proceedings at the Banquet given by the English Socialists, in the John Street Institution, London, 22nd September, 1844.   [London] 1844.

3 Owenite Periodicals

[This list includes only those periodicals which were conducted by Owenites or which at some time contained a substantial amount of material relative to the Owenite movement. It does not include the general radical and social reform press.]

The Advocate of the Working Classes. Edinburgh, 1826–27. [Ed. George Mudie.]

The Anti-Socialist Gazette, and Christian Advocate. Chester, October 1841–May 1842. [Ed. John Brindley.]
    [Continued as] *The Antidote. A Monthly Magazine for the Refutation of Modern Delusions, and for the Defence of Christian Truth*. July–December 1842.

The Apostle and Chronicle of the Communist Church. Isle of Man, 1848. No. 1, vol. 1, 1 August 1848. [Ed. Goodwyn Barmby.]

The Associate. London, nos. 1–9, January 1829–January 1830.
    [Continued as] *The Associate and Co-operative Mirror*. London, nos. 10–12, 1830.

The Beacon. New York, 3 vols., 1836–39 [old series]; 1839–44 [new series]. [Ed. Gilbert Vale.]

The Beacon. London [1843?].

The Bee. Liverpool, 1832–33. [Eds. John Finch and M. J. Falvey.]

The Belfast Co-operative Advocate. Belfast, 1830.

The Birmingham Co-operative Herald. Birmingham, nos. 1–19, April 1829–October 1830. [Ed. William Pare.]

The Birmingham Inspector. Birmingham, nos. 1–16, January–August 1817. [Ed. W. Hawkes Smith.]

The Birmingham Labour Exchange Gazette. Birmingham, nos. 1–5, January–February 1833.

The British Co-operator; or, Record and Review of Co-operative and Entertaining Knowledge. London, April–October 1830.

Bronterre's National Reformer, in Government, Law, Property, Religion, and Morals. London, vol. I, nos. 1–11, January–March 1837. [Ed. James Bronterre O'Brien.]

Carpenter's Monthly Political Magazine. London, September 1831–July 1832. [Ed. William Carpenter.]

Chester Co-operative Chronicle. Chester, nos, 1–6, July–October 1830.

The Circular of the Anti-Persecution Union. London, May–August 1845. [Ed. G. J. Holyoake.]

The Commonweal. London, 1845–46. [Ed. James Hill.]

The Communist Chronicle and Communitarian Apostle. London, 1843. [Ed. J. Goodwyn Barmby; a continuation of *The Promethean.*]

The Communitist. Mottville, New York, 1844–45. [Ed. John A. Collins.]

Co-operative Commercial Circular. London, nos. 1–17, November 1853–March 1855. [Under direction of the Executive Committee of the General Conference.]

Co-operative Magazine and Monthly Herald. London, vols. I–III, 1826–29. [Continued as] *London Co-operative Magazine.* [new series]. London, vol. IV, 1830.

The Co-operator. [Also known as the *Brighton Co-operator.*] Brighton, nos. 1–28, May 1828–August 1830. [Ed. William King.]
[Reprinted, 1922, as] *Dr. William King and the Co-operator, 1828–1830,* with introduction and notes by T. W. Mercer.

The Co-operator. A Record of Cooperative Progress: Conducted Exclusively by Working Men. Manchester, vols. I–XI, 1860–71. [Eds. E. Longfield (vol. I); Henry Pitman (vols. II–XI).]

The Cooperator. Utica, N.Y., April 1832–April 1833.

The Correspondent. New York, vols. I–V, January 1827–July 1829. [Ed. George Houston.]

The Crisis; or, the Change from Error and Misery, to Truth and Happiness. London, vols. I–IV, April 1832–August 1834. [Eds. Robert Owen, R. D. Owen, J. E. Smith.]

The Destructive and Poor Man's Conservative. London, February–December 1833. [Continued as] *The People's Conservative and Trades' Union Gazette.* London, December 1833–February 1834.

The Disseminator of Useful Knowledge. New Harmony, Ind., January 1828–March 1841. [Ed. William Maclure.]

The Divinearian. London, 1849. [Ed. James Duncan.]

The Economist; a Periodical Paper Explanatory of the New System of Society Projected by Robert Owen, . . . and of a Plan of Association for Improving the Condition of the Working Classes, . . . London, 2 vols., January 1821–March 1822. [Ed. George Mudie.]

The Educational Circular and Communist Apostle. London [new series] nos. 1–6, November 1841–May 1842. [Ed. Henry Fry.]

The English Republic. A Newspaper and Review. London, 4 vols., 1851–55. [Ed. William J. Linton.]

The Free Thinker's Information for the People. London, nos. 1–49, 1840–41.

The Halfpenny Magazine of Entertainment and Knowledge; conducted by the Author of various standard Works. London, nos. 1–50, 1840–41. [Ed. Henry Hetherington.]

The Healthian. A Journal of Human Physiology, Diet, and Regimen. London, nos. 1–14, January 1842–February 1843.

Herald of the New Moral World and Millenial Harbinger. Devoted to the Interests of the industrious and producing Classes, also to Science, Religion, and the Laws of the New Moral World. . . . New York, vol. I, no. 1, January 1841–vol. II, no. 8, August 1842. [Ed. J. M. Horner.]

Herald of Progress. London, nos. 1–16, October 1845–May 1846. [Ed. John Cramp.]

Herald of Redemption. Isle of Man, January–March 1847.
[Continued as] *The Herald of Cooperation and Organ of the Redemption Society,* April 1847–July 1848. [Ed. James Hole.]

The Herald of the Rights of Industry. Manchester, nos. 1–16, February–May 1834.

Herald to the Trades' Advocate and Cooperative Journal. Glasgow, nos. 1–36, September 1830–May 1831. [Ed. Alexander Campbell.]

The Investigator. London, nos. 1–28. [1843. Ed. Charles Southwell.]

The Lancashire Co-operator. Manchester, nos. 1–6, June–August 1831.
[Continued as] *The Lancashire and Yorkshire Co-operator: or, Useful Classes' Advocate.* Manchester, September 1831–February 1832. [Ed. E. T. Craig.]

The Lancashire Beacon. [c. 1849. Ed. Charles Southwell.]

Liberal Advocate. Rochester, N.Y., January 1832–November 1834.

The London Investigator: a Monthly Journal of Secularism. London, vols. 1–6, 1854–59. [Eds. Robert Cooper (vols. 1–3); 'Anthony Collins' [W. H. Johnson] (vol. 4); 'Iconoclast' [Charles Bradlaugh] (vols. 5 and 6).]

The London Social Reformer. London, vol. 1, nos. 1–2, May 1840.

The Magazine of Useful Knowledge and Co-operative Miscellany. London, October–November 1830.

Mechanics' Free Press. Philadelphia, Penn., April 1828–April 1831.

Midland Representative and Birmingham Herald. Birmingham, nos. 1–59, April 1831–June 1832. [Ed. James Bronterre O'Brien; incorporated with *The Birmingham Journal.*]

The Mirror of Truth. October–November 1817. [Ed. Robert Owen.]

The Model Republic, a Monthly Journal of Politics, Literature, and Theology. London, January–March 1843. [Ed. James Napier Bailey.]

The Monthly Messenger; a Repository of Information. . . . London, no. 1, 1840. [No more published. Ed. James Napier Bailey.]

The Movement: Anti-Persecution Gazette and Register of Progress. London, 2 vols., nos. 1–68, 1843–45. [Ed. G. J. Holyoake assisted by M. Q. Ryall; continued as] *The Circular of the Anti-Persecution Union.* London, nos. 1–4, May–August 1845. [Ed. G. J. Holyoake.]

The National: a Library for the People. London, nos. 1–26, January–June 1839. [Ed. W. J. Linton.]

The National Co-operative Leader. London, nos. 1–27, 1860–61. [Continued as] *The Cooperative Newspaper*, nos. 28–29, 1861.

The National Reformer, and Manx Weekly Review of Home and Foreign Affairs. Douglas, nos. 1–75, November 1844–May 1847. [Ed. James Bronterre O'Brien.]

The New Age, Concordium Gazette and Temperance Advocate. London, nos. 1–24, May 1843–December 1844.

The New Harmony Gazette. New Harmony, Ind., vols. I–III, October 1825–October 1828. [Ed. succ. by William Owen, Frances Wright, R. D. Owen, and R. L. Jennings.]
[Continued as] *The New Harmony and Nashoba Gazette or The Free Enquirer* [new series] vol. 1, October 1828–February 1829. [Eds. Frances Wright and R. D. Owen.]
[Continued as] *The Free Enquirer.* New York [new series] vols. I–IV, October 1828–June 1835.

The New Moral World . . . developing the Principles of the Rational System of Society. . . . London, vol. I, nos. 1–52, November 1834–October 1835. [Ed. 'Robert Owen and his Disciples'.]
[Continued as] *The New Moral World, or Millenium.* London, vol. II, nos. 53–104, October 1835–October 1836.
[Continued as] *New Moral World and Manual of Science.* London, vol. III, nos. 105–36, October 1836–June 1837; Manchester, nos. 137–56, June–October 1837.
Manchester, vol. IV, nos. 157–88, October 1837–June 1838; Birmingham, nos. 189–208, June–October 1838. [Ed. G. A. Fleming.]

[Continued as] *The New Moral World.* Birmingham, vol. V [new series], nos. 1–37, October 1838–July 1839.

[Continued as] *The New Moral World, or Gazette of the Universal Community Society of Rational Religionists.* Leeds, vol. VI [new series], nos. 38–62, July–December 1839.

Leeds, vol. VII [new series], nos. 63–88, January–June 1840.

Leeds, vol. VIII (vol. I, 3rd series), nos. 1–26, July–December 1840.

Leeds, vol. IX (vol. II, 3rd series), nos. 1–26, January–June 1841.

Leeds, vol. X (vol. III, 3rd series), nos. 1–16, July–October 1841; London, nos. 17–52, October 1841–June 1842.

London, vol. XI (vol. IV, 3rd series), nos. 1–52, July 1842–June 1843.

London, vol. XII (vol. V, 3rd series), nos. 1–52, July 1843–June 1844.

London, vol. XIII (vol. VI, 3rd series), nos. 1–32, June 1844–February 1845; Harmony, Hants., nos. 33–61, February–August 1845; London, nos. 62–64, August–September 1845. [Ed. James Hill.]

[Continued as] *The Moral World and Advocate of the Rational System of Society.* London, vol. I, nos. 1–11, August–November 1845. [Ed. G. A. Fleming.]

Official Gazette of the Trades' Unions. London, nos. 1–11, June–August 1834.

The Oracle of Reason. London, 2 vols., nos. 1–7, November 1841–January 1842 [ed. Charles Southwell]; nos. 8–36, February–August 1842 [ed. G. J. Holyoake]; nos. 37–85, September 1842–July 1843 [ed. Thomas Paterson]; nos. 86–103, August–December 1843 [ed. William Chilton].

The Peaceful Revolutionist. Cincinnati, Ohio, nos. 1–4, January–April 1833. [Ed. Josiah Warren.]

People's Review of Literature and Politics; edited by Friends of Order and Progress. London, nos. 1–3, February–April 1850. [Ed. G. J. Holyoake et al.]

The Philanthropist; or, Repository for Hints and Suggestions calculated to promote the Comfort and Happiness of Man. London, vols. I–VII, 1811–19. [Ed. William Allen et al.]

The Pioneer; or, Trades' Union Magazine. Birmingham, London, nos. 1–44, September 1833–July 1834.

[Continued as] *The Pioneer; or Grand National Consolidated Trades' Union Magazine.*

[Continued as] *The Pioneer and Official Gazette of the Associated Trades' Union* [new series] September 1834. [Ed. James Morrison.]

Political Economist and Universal Philanthropist. London, 1823. [Ed. George Mudie.]

The Poor Man's Advocate, and People's Library. Manchester, nos. 1–50, January 1832–January 1833. [Ed. John Doherty.]

The Poor Man's Guardian. London, nos. 1–238, January 1831–December 1835. [began as] *Penny Papers for the People, by the Poor Man's Guardian*, October–December 1830. [Eds. Henry Hetherington and James B. O'Brien.]

Potters' Examiner and Workman's Advocate. Shelton, 1843–45 [continued as] *Potters' Examiner and Emigrants' Advocate*, July 1848. [Ed. William Evans.]

The Promethean; or Communitarian Apostle. A magazine of Societarian Science. nos. 1–4, 1842. [Ed. Goodwyn Barmby.]

The Radical, and Advocate of Equality. Albany, N.Y., 1834. [Ed. Paul Brown.]

The Rational Reformer; or, Illustrations and Testimonies in Favour of the Rational Social System. London, vol. I, no. 1, October 1832.

The Rational Religionist, and Independent Inquirer into Social and Political Economy, Religion, Science and Literature. Manchester, nos. 1–3 [c. 1841; ed. R. Buchanan].

The Reasoner. London, vols. I–XXVI, nos. 1–788; June 1846–June 1861. [Ed. G. J. Holyoake. For continuing titles, see Goss, *Bibliography of G. J. Holyoake.*]

The Regenerator. London, nos. 1–5; June 1844. [Ed. Henry Hetherington.]

The Register for the First Society of Adherents to Divine Revelation at Orbiston. Edinburgh, Orbiston, 2 vols., nos. 1–34; November 1825–September 1827. [Ed. Abram Combe.]

Robert Owen's Journal. Explanatory of the Means to Well-place, Well-employ, and Well-educate the Population of the World. London, vols. I–IV; November 1850–October 1852. [Ed. Henry Travis.]

Robert Owen's Millenial Gazette. London, nos. 1–16, March 1856–July 1858. [Ed. Robert Owen.]

Robert Owen's Rational Quarterly Review and Journal. London, vol. I, 4 parts, 1853. [Ed. Robert Owen.]

The Shepherd, a London Weekly Periodical, illustrating the Principles of Universal Science. London, vol. I (August 1834–August 1835); vol. II (January–March 1837); vol. III (July 1837–March 1838). [Ed. Rev. J. E. Smith.]

The Shipwrights' Journal; a Periodical of General Literature, and Useful Information on the Social Condition of the Working Classes. . . . Sunderland, nos. 1–4, April–July 1858. [Ed. John Hopper.]

The Social Pioneer, and Herald of Progress. Boston, Mass., 1844.

The Social Pioneer; or, Record of the Progress of Socialism. Manchester, nos. 1–10, March–May 1839. [Ed. 'Epicurus'.]

The Social Reformer. London, nos.1–11, August–October 1849. [Eds. James B. O'Brien *et al.*]

Social Science Review. London, 2 vols., June 1862–December 1863. [new series] London, vols. I–VI, 1864–66. [Ed. B. W. Richardson.]

The Southern Star and London and Brighton Patriot. London, January–July 1840.

The Spirit of the Age; Journal of Political, Educational, and Industrial Progress. London, 2 vols., nos. 1–32, July 1848–March 1849. [Ed. Alexander Campbell; from November 1848, by G. J. Holyoake.]

The Spirit of the Times: or, the Social Reformer. London, 1847.

Star in the East. Wisbech, nos. 1–187, September 1836–April 1840. [Eds. E. T. Craig and James Hill.]

The Sunbeam. No. 1, July 1845. [Ed. J. E. Duncan.]

The Torch. No. 1, 1842. [Ed. J. N. Bailey.]

Trades Advocate or Scottish Trade Union Gazette. [Glasgow, 1833?; ed. Alexander Campbell.]

Trades Newspaper and Mechanics' Weekly Journal. London, nos. 1–106, July 1825–July 1827.
[Continued as] *Trades' Free Press*, nos. 107–63, July 1827–August 1828.
[Continued as] *Weekly Free Press*, nos. 164–299, August 1828–April 1831. [From December 1829, *... and Cooperative Journal.* [Ed. William Carpenter.]

The Trades Unions' Magazine, Devoted to the Advocacy of Peaceful Combination among the Operative Classes. ... Manchester, nos. 1–18, November 1850–May 1851. [Ed. Rev. Thomas G. Lee.]

The Tradesman. Glasgow (?), nos. 1–23, December 1833–May 1834. [Ed. Alexander Campbell.]

The Truth Seeker, in Literature, Philosophy, and Religion. ... London, vols. I–III, 1846–48. [Eds. F. R. Lees and G. S. Phillips.]
[Continued, in 2nd series, as] *The Truth Seeker and Present Age: a Catholic Review of Literature, Philosophy and Religion.* London, 2 vols., 1849–50. [Ed. F. R. Lees.]

The Union: a Monthly Record of Moral, Social and Educational Progress. London, nos. 1–10, April 1842–January 1843. [Ed. G. A. Fleming.]

The Union Exchange Gazette. By the Union Exchange Society. . . . London, 1829.

The Union Pilot and Co-operative Intelligencer. Manchester, March–May 1832.

The United Trades' Co-operative Journal. Manchester, March–October 1830. [Ed. John Doherty.]

The Voice of the People. By an Association of Working Men. Manchester, January–September 1831.

The Voice of the West Riding. Huddersfield, vol. I, nos. 1–53; June 1833–June 1834. [Ed. Joshua Hobson.]

Weekly Letters to the Human Race. London, nos. 1–17, 1850. [Ed. Robert Owen.]
  [2nd edn.] *Letters to the Human Race on the Coming Universal Revolution.* London, 1850.

The Working Bee and Herald of the Hodsonian Community Society. Manea Fen, nos. 1–46, July 1839–May 1840.

  [New series] vol. I, nos. 1–28, June 1840–January 1841. [Eds. William Hodson and John Green.]

The Working Man's Friend; and Political Magazine. London, nos. 1–33, December 1832–August 1833. [Ed. James Watson.]

The Yorkshire Tribune; a Monthly Journal of Democracy and Secularism, for the People. London, July 1855–September 1856. [Ed. William Mitchell.]

4 Rules, Reports and Proceedings

ASSOCIATION FOR THE INTERNAL COLONISATION OF ARTISANS AND THE POOR, BY MEANS OF A NEW SYSTEM OF MUTUAL LABOUR. *Rules and Regulations with a Plan of the Organisation and Colonisation of the Settlements.* London, 1837.

ASSOCIATION OF ALL CLASSES OF ALL NATIONS. *The Constitution and Laws of the Association . . . as revised by the Congress of May, 1838.* [Laws and Regulations first appeared Manchester, 1835.]
Manual of the Association of All Classes of All Nations founded May 1, 1835. London, nos. 1 and 2, 1835–36.
Liverpool Branch. *Minutes of the Proceedings* (5 December 1837–17 May 1839).

ASSOCIATION TO REMOVE THE CAUSE OF IGNORANCE AND POVERTY. *An Outline of the Proceedings at the Public Meeting.* London [1831?].

BIRMINGHAM COOPERATIVE SOCIETY. *Rules.* Birmingham, 1828.

BRITISH AND FOREIGN PHILANTHROPIC SOCIETY. *Proceedings of the First General Meeting . . . held at the Freemasons Hall, Great Queen Street, London . . . 1st June, 1822.* London, 1822.
A Report . . . with Other Statements and Calculations explanatory of Mr. Owen's Plan for the Relief of Ireland. . . . Dublin, 1823.
Summary of Mr. Owen's Plan for the permanent Relief of the Working Classes. London, 1822.

BRITISH ASSOCIATION FOR THE PROMOTION OF COOPERATIVE KNOWLEDGE. *Report of the Committee and Proceedings:* 3rd Quarterly Meeting (7 January 1830), 4th Quarterly Meeting (8 April 1830), 6th Quarterly Meeting (October 1830). [See also Society for the Promotion of Cooperative Knowledge.]

CONGRESS OF THE ADVANCED MINDS OF THE WORLD. *Report of the Meeting of——, convened by Robert Owen, held in St. Martin's Hall, Long Acre, and in the Literary and Scientific Institution, John Street, . . . 12th to the 15th of May, 1857.* London, 1857.

COOPERATIVE CONGRESS—FIRST. [No formal Report of First Congress, but following items relate to it, in Goldsmiths' Library, vol. *Cooperative Congresses: Reports and Papers, 1831–32.*]
Circular Letter from the 'Manchester Association for the Spread of the Principles and Practice of Cooperation.'
Resolutions passed at the First Meeting of the Cooperative Congress, held in Manchester . . . May, 1831.
Address of the Delegates, 27 May, 1831.

Important Meeting of the Working Classes, Delegates from the Fifty Co-operative Societies.
Cooperative Congress—List of Delegates.

COOPERATIVE CONGRESS—SECOND. *Proceedings of ... held in Birmingham, October 4, 5, and 6, 1831, and composed of Delegates from the Cooperative Societies of Great Britain and Ireland.* Birmingham [1831].

COOPERATIVE CONGRESS—THIRD. *Proceedings of ... held in London, ... on the 23rd of April, 1832, and edited, by Order of the Congress, by William Carpenter.* London, 1832.

COOPERATIVE CONGRESS—FOURTH. *Proceedings of ... held in Liverpool on ... 1st October, 1832, and by Adjournment on Each of the Five following Days. Reported ... by W. Pare. ...* Salford, Manchester, 1832.

COOPERATIVE CONGRESS HELD AT MANCHESTER ... 15TH AND 16TH AUGUST, 1853, AT COOPER STREET INSTITUTE. *Report, with Appendices.* London, 1853.

COOPERATIVE LEAGUE. *Plan of the Cooperative League.* London, 1847.

COOPERATIVE LEAGUE TO PROMOTE SCIENTIFIC INVESTIGATION OF THE PRINCIPLES OF COOPERATIVE ACTION. *Transactions.* London, 1852 [3 parts.]

FESTIVAL IN COMMEMORATION OF THE CENTENARY BIRTHDAY OF ROBERT OWEN. *Report of ... to Which Is Added Mr Owen's 'Outline of the Rational System of Society'.* London, 1871.

GRAND NATIONAL CONSOLIDATED TRADES' UNION. *Rules and Regulations of ..., instituted for the Purpose of the more effectually enabling the Working Classes to Secure, Protect, and Establish the Rights of Industry.* London, 1834.

LONDON ASSOCIATION FOR THE PROMOTION OF COOPERATIVE KNOWLEDGE. *Rules of. ...* London, 1829. [Broadsheet.]

LONDON CO-OPERATIVE SOCIETY. *Articles of Agreement for the Formation of a Community on the Principles of Mutual Cooperation, within Fifty Miles of London.* London, 1825.
[Another edn.] London, 1826.
Rules for the Observance of. ... London, 1825.

LONDON CO-OPERATIVE TRADING FUND ASSOCIATION. *Address and Regulations.* London, 1828.

Minutes of Proceedings of Friends to the Rational System of Society, founded by Robert Owen. Commencing at Liverpool, 15th October, 1837. [n.p., n.d.].

NATIONAL COMMUNITY FRIENDLY SOCIETY. *Rules, as revised by the Delegates assembled in Congress, May, 1838.* London [n.d.].
Rules to be observed for the Government and Management of the Community Friendly Society, . . . London, 1836.

NATIONAL EQUITABLE LABOUR EXCHANGE. *Report of the Committee appointed by a Public Meeting held on the 24th September, 1832, at the Equitable Labour Exchange,* . . . *for the Purpose of taking into Consideration the increasing Distress of the non-productive and industrous Classes, and to devise efficient Means for their permanent Relief.* London, 1832.
Rules and Regulations. . . . London, 1832.
Birmingham Branch. *Laws of.* . . . Birmingham, 1832.

PHILOSOPHICAL CO-OPERATIVE LAND ASSOCIATION. *Articles.* [n.p.] 1832.

PRACTICAL SOCIETY. *Second Report of the Economical Committee of the Practical Society, 13th February, 1822.* Edinburgh, 1822.
Third Report of the Economical Committee of the Practical Society, 13th April, 1822. [Edinburgh, 1822.]

RATIONAL SICK AND BURIAL ASSOCIATION. *General Laws.* Manchester, 1844.
Laws for the Government of the Rational Sick and Burial Association, instituted January 1st, 1837. Manchester, 1845.

SOCIAL UNITED INTEREST COLONISATION SOCIETY. *An Address, with Rules and Regulations of* . . .*; showing the great Advantages of immediate Emigration; and that Community, as recommended by Robert Owen, may be commenced by raising a Fund of Fourteen Guineas for each Individual.* Manchester, 1839.

SOCIETY FOR THE PROMOTION OF COOPERATIVE KNOWLEDGE. *Report of the Proceedings at the Second Quarterly Meeting* . . . *October 8th, 1829.* London [1829].
[Continued as the] British Association for the Promotion of Cooperative Knowledge.

UNIVERSAL COMMUNITY SOCIETY OF RATIONAL RELIGIONISTS. *Address of the Congress of the Rational Society, held in Harmony Hall, from the 9th to the 19th of May, 1842, to the Chartists of Great Britain and Ireland* [with an] *Address* . . . *to the Trades Unions of Great Britain and Ireland.* [London?] 1842.
Address to All Classes, Sects and Parties, containing an official Declaration of Principles adapted for Practice by the Congress of the Universal Community Society . . . *held in Leeds, May, 1840. To which is added the proclamation of the Congress.* . . . London, 1840.

The Constitution and Laws of. . . .   London, 1839.
[1st and 2nd supplements].   London, 1840.
[3rd and 4th supplements].   London, 1841.
[Another edn.]   . . . *As agreed to at the Annual Congress, held at Harmony Hall, Hampshire, 10th May, 1843.*   London, 1843.
Declaration of Principles, and Proclamation of the Congress Held at Leeds, May 1840.   [n.p., n.d.]
Proceedings of the Third Congress of the Association of All Classes of All Nations, and the First of the National Community Friendly Society . . . held in Manchester, in May 1838.   Birmingham, London, 1838.
Proceedings of the Fourth Congress . . . held in Birmingham, in May 1839.   Birmingham, 1839.
Full Report of the Proceedings of the Fifth Annual Congress . . . Holden in Leeds, 1840.   [n.p., n.d.]
Proceedings of the Sixth Congress of the Association of all Classes. . . .   Birmingham, London, 1841.
Proceedings of the First to Fourth Congresses. . . .   Birmingham, 1838–41.
Report of the Proceedings of the Eighth Annual Congress of the Rational Society . . . held in Harmony Hall, Hampshire, May, 1843, and composed of Delegates from Branches of the Society in England and Scotland.   London, 1843.

5 Secondary Works
(i) *Unpublished*

ANDRUS, J. RUSSELL. 'The Economics of the Utopian Socialists, 1800–1850' (Ph.D. thesis, University of California, Berkeley, 1934).

BALDWIN, SISTER JULIANA. 'Constitutional History of the New Harmony Experiment' (Ph.D. thesis, University of Oklahoma, 1937).

BLACK, A. 'Owenite Education, 1839–1857, with particular Reference to the Manchester Hall of Science' (Dip.Ed. dissertation, University of Manchester, 1953).

BLACK, ARCHIBALD MUIR. 'The Educational Work of Robert Owen' (Ph.D. thesis, St Andrews University, 1949).

BURGESS, CHARLES ORVILLE. 'The Educational State in America: selected Views on Learning as the Key to Utopia, 1800–1924' (Ph.D. thesis, University of Wisconsin, 1962).

CARR, H. J. 'A critical Exposition of the social and economic Ideas of John Francis Bray, and an Estimate of his Influence upon Karl Marx' (Ph.D. thesis, London University, 1943).

COOK, DONALD R. 'Reverend James Elishama Smith: Socialist Prophet of the Millenium (a Study of socio-religious Radicalism in the British Working Class Movement of the 1830s)' (M.A. thesis, State University of Iowa, 1961).

ELLIOTT, HELEN. 'Development of the New Harmony Community with Special Reference to Education' (M.A. thesis, Indiana University, 1933).

GRANT, ALASTAIR CAMERON. 'George Combe and His Circle: with Particular Reference to His Relations with the United States of America' (Ph.D. thesis, Edinburgh University, 1960).

IRVIN, MARY LOUISE. 'Contemporary American Opinion of the New Harmony Movement' (M.A. thesis, University of Illinois, 1932).

JANES, EILEEN MARGOT. 'The Quest for the New Moral World; Changing Patterns of Owenite Thought, 1817–1870' (M.A. thesis, University of Wisconsin, 1963).

KNIPE, JOHN RICHARD. 'Owenite Ideas and Institutions, 1828–1834' (M.A. thesis, University of Wisconsin, 1967).

MORRIS, DAVID CARADOG. 'The History of the Labour Movement in England, 1825–1852. The Problem of Leadership and the Articulation of Demands' (Ph.D. thesis, London University, 1952).

NEIMAN, FRASER. 'William J. Linton, 1812–1897' (Ph.D. thesis, Harvard University, 1938).

OLIVER, W. H. 'Organizations and Ideas Behind the Efforts To Achieve a General Union of the Working Classes in England in the Early 1830's' (D.Phil. thesis, Oxford University, 1954).

PESSEN, EDWARD. 'The Social Philosophies of Early American Leaders of Labor' (Ph.D. thesis, Columbia University, 1954).

PLUMMER, A. 'The Life of James Bronterre O'Brien' (B.Litt. thesis, Oxford University, 1928).

SALT, JOHN. 'Isaac Ironside and Education in the Sheffield Region in the first half of the nineteenth century' (M.A. thesis, Sheffield University, 1960).

SEVER, J. 'James Morrison of "The Pioneer". Notes on his Life and Background'. (Typograph copy, 1963). [Copies in British Museum, Bodleian, Cambridge University Library, and the Newcastle, Birmingham, and Manchester Public Libraries.]

STORCH, ROBERT D. 'Owenite Communitarianism in Britain' (M.A. thesis, University of Wisconsin, 1964).

THOMPSON, KEITH HEATHCOTE. 'The Educational Work of Robert Dale Owen' (Ph.D. thesis, University of California, 1948).

(ii) *Books and Pamphlets*

ADAMS, W. E. *Memoirs of a Social Atom.* 2 vols. London, 1903.

ALBJERG, VICTOR L. *Richard Owen.* Lafayette, Ind., 1964.

ARMYTAGE, W. H. G. *Heavens Below: Utopian Experiments in England, 1560–1960.* London, 1961.

ARNDT, KARL J. R. *George Rapp's Harmony Society, 1785–1847.* Philadelphia, Penn., 1965.

BAILIE, WILLIAM. *Josiah Warren, the First American Anarchist.* Boston, Mass., 1906.

BARKER, AMBROSE G. *Henry Hetherington, 1792–1849.* London [1938].

BEALES, H. L. *The Early English Socialists.* London, 1933.

BEER, MAX. *A History of British Socialism.* 2 vols. London, 1919. [Another edn., in 1 vol.] London, 1940.

BENNETT, C. A. *History of Manual and Industrial Education up to 1870.* Peoria, Ill., 1926.

BESTOR, ARTHUR EUGENE, Jr. *Backwoods Utopias: the Sectarian and Owenite Phases of Communitarian Socialism in America, 1663–1829.* Philadelphia, Penn., 1950.

BLAUG, MARK. *Ricardian Economics: a Historical Study.* New Haven, Conn., 1958.

BROWN, WILLIAM HENRY. *Brighton's Cooperative Advance, 1828–1938* (*With the Jubilee History of the Brighton Equitable Cooperative Society, Ltd., 1888–1938*). Manchester [1938].
A Century of Liverpool Cooperation. Liverpool [1929].
Hepworth's Hundred Years of Cooperative Adventure. [Manchester, 1948.]

[BUCHANAN, BARBARA ISABELLA]. *Buchanan Family Records: James Buchanan and His Descendants.* Capetown, South Africa, 1923.

COLE, GEORGE DOUGLAS HOWARD. *Attempts at General Union: A Study in British Trade Union History, 1818–1834.* London, 1953. [Also published in *International Review of Social History*, IV (1939), 359–462.]
A Century of Cooperation. Manchester [1944].
History of Socialist Thought: Vol. I, The Forerunners. London, 1953.

COMMONS, JOHN R., ed. *Documentary History of American Industrial Society*, vol. VII (*The Labor Movement*). Cleveland, Ohio, 1910.
et al. History of Labour in the United States. Vol. 1. New York, 1936.

CO-OPERATIVE UNION LTD. *The Robert Owen Memorial Committee.* Manchester, 1902.

CRIMES, TOM. *Edward Owen Greening: a Maker of Modern Cooperation.* Manchester, 1923.

CULLEN, ALEXANDER. *Adventures in Socialism: New Lanark Establishment and Orbiston Community.* London, Glasgow, 1910.
Robert Owen and the Orbiston Community . . . a Paper Read before the Members of the United Young Men's Christian Associations of Motherwell, at Orbiston, 12th September, 1896. Hamilton, 1896.

DE LA HUNT, THOMAS JAMES. *History of the New Harmony Workingmen's Institute . . . 1838–1927.* Evansville, Ind., 1927.

DENT, J. *The Cooperative Ideals of Dr. William King.* Manchester, 1921.

GARNETT, R. G. *The Ideology of the Early Cooperative Movement.* First Kent Cooperative Endowment Lecture, University of Kent, Canterbury, 1966.

GIDE, CHARLES. *Communist and Co-operative Colonies.* New York, 1931.

GUGGISBERG, KURT. *Philipp Emanuel von Fellenberg und sein Erziehungsstaat.* 2 vols. Bern, Switzerland, 1953 [pp. 481–6, 'Owen und Fellenberg'].

HAMPTON, ERNEST WALTER. *Early Cooperation in Birmingham and District.* Birmingham, 1928.

HARRIS, DAVID. *Socialist Origins in the United States: American Forerunners of Marx, 1817–1832.* Assen, Netherlands, 1966.

HARRISON, J. F. C. *Social Reform in Victorian Leeds: the Work of James Hole, 1820–1895.* Thoresby Society, Leeds, 1954.
   ed. *Utopianism and Education: Robert Owen and the Owenites.* New York, 1968. [Introductory essay and selections from Owenite writings on education.]

HASBACH, MARIE. William Thompson. Jena, 1922 [in German].

HENDRICKSON, WALTER BROOKFIELD. *David Dale Owen, Pioneer Geologist of the Mid-West.* Indianapolis, Ind., 1943.

HERTZLER, JOYCE O. *History of Utopian Thought.* New York, 1923.

HILLQUIT, MORRIS. *History of Socialism in the United States.* New York, 1903.

HIMES, NORMAN E. 'Robert Dale Owen', in *Encyclopaedia of the Social Sciences*, XI. New York, 1933.

HINDS, WILLIAM ALFRED. *American Communities.* Oneida, N.Y., 1878.
[2nd edn., revised.] 1902.
[3rd edn.] Chicago, Ill., 1908.

HOLLOWAY, MARK. *Heavens on Earth: Utopian Communities in America, 1680–1880.* New York, London, 1951.

JACKSON, EDWARD. *A Study in Democracy: Being an Account of the Rise and Progress of Industrial Co-operation in Bristol.* Manchester, 1911.

JAY, HARRIETT. *Robert Buchanan.* London, 1903.

JONES, BENJAMIN. *Co-operative Production.* 2 vols. Oxford, 1894.

KAUFMANN, REV. M. *Utopias; or, Schemes of Social Improvement, from Sir Thomas More to Karl Marx.* London, 1879.

KIMBALL, JANET. *The Economic Doctrines of John Gray, 1799–1883.* Washington, D.C., 1948.

LEES, FREDERIC. *Dr. F. R. Lees, a Biography.* London, 1904.

LEOPOLD, R. W.   *Robert Dale Owen.*   Cambridge, Mass., 1940.

LICHTENBERGER, ANDRÉ.   *Le Socialisme Utopique, Études sur Quelques Précurseurs Inconnues du Socialisme.*   Paris, 1898.

LOCKWOOD, GEORGE BROWNING.   *The New Harmony Communities.* Marion, Ind., 1902.
[Revised and republished as]   *The New Harmony Movement.*   New York, 1905.

LOWENTHAL, ESTHER.   *The Ricardian Socialists.*   New York, 1911.

McCABE, JOSEPH.   *Life and Letters of George Jacob Holyoake.*   2 vols. London, 1908.

MARWICK, W. H.   *The Life of Alexander Campbell.*   Glasgow, 1964.

MAXWELL, WILLIAM.   *The History of Cooperation in Scotland; Its Inception and Its Leaders.*   Glasgow, 1910.

MENGER, ANTON.   *The Right to the Whole Produce of Labour . . .* trans. M. E. Tanner.   London, 1899.
[Reprinted]   New York, 1962.

MERCER, T. W.   *Cooperation's Prophet, the Life and Letters of Dr. William King of Brighton.*   Manchester, 1947.
Towards the Cooperative Commonwealth.   Manchester, 1936.

MORTON, ARTHUR L.   *The English Utopia.*   London, 1952.

MULLER, HANS.   'Dr. William King and His Place in the History of Cooperation', in *Year Book of International Cooperation, 1913.*   London, Zurich, 1913.

MUMFORD, LEWIS.   *The Story of Utopias.*   Gloucester, Mass., 1959.

NORDHOFF, CHARLES.   *The Communistic Societies of the United States. . . .* London, New York, 1875.
[Another edn.]   New York, 1900.
[Reprinted.]   New York, 1960, 1961.

OWEN, HAROLD.   *The Staffordshire Potter.*   London, 1901.

OWEN, ROSAMUND DALE.   *My Perilous Life in Palestine.*   London, 1928.
[Autobiography of daughter of Robert Dale Owen. Includes references to Robert Owen, New Harmony, and Owen family.]

OWEN, WALTER R. D.   *A Glimpse of the Early History of New Harmony.* Evansville, Ind., 1898.

PANCOAST, ELINOR, and ANNE E. LINCOLN.   *The Incorrigible Idealist: Robert Dale Owen in America.*   Bloomington, Ind., 1940.

PANKHURST, RICHARD K. P. *William Thompson (1775–1833). Britain's Pioneer Socialist, Feminist, and Cooperator.* London, 1954.
The Saint Simonians, Mill and Carlyle. [London, 1957].

PERKINS, A. J. G., and THERESA WOLFSON. *Frances Wright: Free Enquirer.* New York, 1939.

POLLARD, SIDNEY. *Dr. William King of Ipswich: a Co-operative Pioneer.* Co-operative College Papers, No. 6. April, 1959. Loughborough, 1959.
'Nineteenth Century Cooperation: from Community Building to Shopkeeping', in Briggs, Asa, and John Saville, *Essays in Labour History.* London, 1960.

POST, ALBERT. *Popular Freethought in America, 1825–1850.* New York, 1943.

POSTGATE, RAYMOND W. *The Builders' History.* London, 1923.
Out of the Past. London, 1922.

QUACK, H. P. G. *De Socialisten.* 6 vols. Amsterdam, Netherlands, 1899–1901.

REEVES, JOSEPH. *A Century of Rochdale Cooperation.* London, 1944.

RUNCIE, CONSTANCE OWEN. *Divinely Led; or, Robert Owen's Granddaughter.* New York, 1887.

RUSK, ROBERT R. *History of Infant Education.* London, 1933.
[2nd edn.] London, 1951.

SCHNECK, J., and RICHARD OWEN. *The History of New Harmony, Indiana.* Evansville, Ind., 1890.

SILVER, HAROLD. *The Concept of Popular Education: a Study of Ideas and Social Movements in the early nineteenth Century.* London, 1965. [A study of Owen and education.]

SMITH, WILLIAM ANDERSON. *'Shepherd' Smith the Universalist; the Story of a Mind. Being a Life of the Rev. James E. Smith.* London, 1892.

SNEDEKER, CAROLINE DALE [*née* Owen]. *The Beckoning Road.* New York, 1930. [A novel.]
Seth Way: a Romance of the New Harmony Community. Boston, New York, 1917. [A novel.]
The Town of the Fearless. New York, 1931.

SOTHERAN, CHARLES. *Horace Greeley and other Pioneers of American Socialism.* New York, 1892.

THOMAS, ALBERT. *Quelques Notes sur Robert Owen et la Législation internationale de Travail.* Strasbourg, 1924.

THOMPSON, EDWARD P. *The Making of the English Working Class.* London, 1963.

WASHBURTON, W. H. *The History of Trade Union Organization in the North Staffordshire Potteries.* London, 1931.

WATERMAN, WILLIAM R. *Frances Wright.* New York, 1924.

[WEBB] POTTER, BEATRICE. *The Cooperative Movement in Great Britain.* London, 1891.
[2nd edn.] London, 1893.

WEBB, CATHERINE, ed. *Industrial Cooperation: the Story of a Peaceful Revolution. Being an Account of the History, Theory, and Practice of the Co-operative Movement in Great Britain and Ireland.* Manchester, 1904.
Lives of Great Men and Women . . . Friends of Co-operation. Manchester, 1912. [2nd edn.]

WEBB, SIDNEY. *Socialism in England.* London, 1890.
[Another edn.] London, 1899.
and BEATRICE. *The History of Trade Unionism.* London, 1894.
[And later edns.]

WEBBER, EVERETT. *Escape to Utopia; the Communal Movement in America.* New York, 1959.

WICKWAR, WILLIAM H. *The Struggle for the Freedom of the Press, 1819–1932.* London, 1928.

WILLIAMS, AARON. *The Harmonists, or the New Harmony Society.* Pittsburgh, Penn., 1866.

WILLIAMS, GWYN A. *Rowland Detrosier, a Working Class Infidel, 1800–1834.* Borthwick Papers, no. 28. York, 1965.

WILSON, WILLIAM E. *The Angel and the Serpent: the Story of New Harmony.* Bloomington, Ind., 1964.

WOOLSEY, THEODORE D. *Communism and Socialism in Their History and Theory: a Sketch.* New York, 1880.

YOUNG, MARGUERITE. *Angel in the Forest: a Fairy Tale of Two Utopias.* New York, 1945.

(iii) *Articles*

ABRAHAMS, ALECK. 'No. 277, Gray's Inn Road', *Antiquary* (April 1908). [Equitable Labour Exchange.]

ALBERTSON, RALPH. 'A Survey of Mutualistic Communities in America', *Iowa Journal of History and Politics*, XXXIV (October 1936).

ARMYTAGE, WILLIAM H. G.   'The Early Utopists and Science in England', *Annals of Science*, XII, no. 4 (December 1956).

'George Mudie: Journalist and Utopian', *Notes and Queries*, CCII (1957).

'John Minter Morgan, 1782–1854', *Journal of Education*, LXXXVI (1954).

'John Minter Morgan's Schemes, 1841–1845', *International Review of Social History*, III (1958).

'The Journalistic Activities of J. Goodwyn Barmby between 1841 and 1848', *Notes and Queries*, CCI (1956).

'Manea Fen; an Experiment in Agrarian Communitarianism, 1838–1841', *Bulletin of the John Rylands Library*, XXXVIII, no. 2 (March 1956).

'Nashoban Narrative. An Account of Frances Wright's Scheme of Slave Emancipation in Indiana', *Dalhousie Review*, XXXIII, no. 2 (1953).

'Pant Glas: a Communitarian Experiment in Merionethshire', *Journal of the Merioneth Historical Records Society*, II (1955).

'William Maclure, 1763–1840: a British Interpretation', *Indiana Magazine of History*, XLVII (1951).

BANTA, RICHARD E.   'New Harmony's Golden Years', *Indiana Magazine of History*, XLIV (March 1948).

BESTOR, ARTHUR E. JR.   'The Evolution of the Socialist Vocabulary', *Journal of the History of Ideas*, IX (June 1948).

'Patent Office Models of the Good Society: Some Relationships between Social Reform and Westward Expansion', *American Historical Review*, LVIII (1953).

Review of *Diaries of Donald Macdonald, 1824–26*, *New York History*, XXIV (1943).

BLACK, A.   'Education before Rochdale: First Attempts Helped to Keep Movement Alive', *Cooperative Review*, XXVIII, no. 6 (June 1954).

'Education before Rochdale: (2) the Owenites and the Halls of Science', *Cooperative Review*, XXIX, no. 2 (February 1955).

BROWN, ANNA.   'A Dream of Emancipation', *New England Magazine*, new series, XXX (June 1904).

BROWNE, C. A.   'Some Relations of the New Harmony Movement to the History of Science in America', *Scientific Monthly*, XLII (June 1936).

BUSHEE, F. A.   'Communistic Societies in the United States', *Political Science Quarterly*, XX (1955).

CARR, H. J.   'John Francis Bray', *Economica*, new series, VII, no. 28 (November 1940).

EDWARDS, JOHN.   'John Francis Bray', *Socialist Review* (December 1916).

ELLIOTT, HELEN.   'Frances Wright's Experiment with Negro Emancipation', *Indiana Magazine of History*, XXXVI (1939).

ELLIOTT, JOSEPHINE MIRABELLA. 'The Owen Family Papers', *Indiana Magazine of History*, LX, no. 4 (December 1964).

EMERSON, O. B. 'Frances Wright and her Nashoba Experiment', *Tennessee Historical Quarterly*, VI (December 1947).

ESTABROOK, ARTHUR. 'The Family History of Robert Owen', *Indiana Magazine of History*, XIX (March 1923).

FARRELL, EMMA L. 'The New Harmony Experiment, an Origin of Progressive Education', *Peabody Journal of Education*, XV (1938).

FOX, WENDALL P. 'The Kendal Community', *Ohio Archaeological and Historical Quarterly*, XX (April–July 1911).

GARNETT, RONALD GEORGE. 'E. T. Craig: Communitarian, Educator, Phrenologist', *The Vocational Aspect of Secondary and Further Education*, XV (Summer 1963).
'A Housing Association for New Lanark', *Amateur Historian*, VI, no. 4 (Summer 1964).
'Owen's Descendant at New Lanark', *Cooperative Review* (December 1963).
'William Pare: a non-Rochdale Pioneer', *Cooperative Review* (May 1964).

HARRISON, J. F. C. 'The Steam Engine of the New Moral World: Owenism and Education, 1817–1829', *Journal of British Studies*, VI, no. 2 (May 1967).

HENDRICKSON, W. B. 'An Owenite Society in Illinois', *Indiana Magazine of History*, XLV (June 1949).

HIMES, NORMAN E. 'The Place of John Stuart Mill and Robert Owen in the History of English Neo-Malthusianism', *Quarterly Journal of Economics* (May 1928).
'Robert Dale Owen, the Pioneer of American Neo-Malthusianism', *American Journal of Sociology*, XXXV, no. 4 (January 1930).

HOLYNSKI, ALEXANDRE. 'Le Communisme en Amérique', *Revue Socialiste*, XII–XVI (September 1890–September 1892).

HOLYOAKE, GEORGE JACOB. 'Unpublished Correspondence of the Robert Owen Family', *Cooperative News*, nos. 16–32 (16 April–6 August 1904).

HURST, R. A. 'The New Harmony Manuscript Collections', *Indiana Magazine of History*, XXXVII (March 1941).

JOLLIFFE, M. F. 'Fresh Light on John Francis Bray', *Economic History*, III, no. 14 (February 1939).
'John Francis Bray', *International Review of Social History*, IV (1939).

JORDAN, DAVID S., and AMOS BUTLER. 'New Harmony', *Scientific Monthly*, XXV (November 1927).

MCINTOSH, MONTGOMERY E. 'Co-operative Communities in Wisconsin', Wisconsin State Historical Society, *Proceedings, 1903*, LI (1904).

MCKINLEY, KENNETH W. 'A Guide to the Communistic Communities of Ohio', *Ohio State Archaeological and Historical Quarterly*, XLVI (January 1937).

MALLOCK, W. H. 'A Century of Socialistic Experiments', *Dublin Review*, CXLV (July 1909).

MOORE, J. PERCY. 'William Maclure—Scientist and Humanitarian', American Philosophical Society, *Proceedings*, XCI (1947).

MORRISON, JOHN. ' "The 'Toon o' Maxwell"—an Owen Settlement in Lambton County, Ontario', Ontario Historical Society, *Papers and Records*, XII (1914).

MUSSON, A. E. 'The Ideology of early Cooperation in Lancashire and Cheshire', *Transactions*, Lancashire and Cheshire Antiquarian Society, LXVIII (1958).

OLIVER, W. H. 'The Consolidated Trades' Union of 1834', *Economic History Review*, 2nd series, XVII, no. 1 (August 1964).
'The Labour Exchange Phase of the Cooperative Movement', *Oxford Economic Papers*, new series, X (October 1958).

PANKHURST, RICHARD K. P. 'Anna Wheeler: a Pioneer Socialist and Feminist', *Political Quarterly*, XXV, no. 2 (April–June 1954).

PARKS, EDD WINFIELD. 'Dreamer's Vision: Frances Wright at Nashoba (1825–1830)', *Tennessee Historical Magazine*, 2nd series, II (January 1932).

PLUMMER, A. 'The Place of Bronterre O'Brien in the Working Class Movement', *Economic History Review*, II (1929–30).

POLLARD, SIDNEY. 'The Factory Village in the Industrial Revolution', *English Historical Review*, LXXIX (1964).
'Factory Discipline in the early nineteenth Century', *Economic History Review*, 2nd series, XVI, no. 2 (1963).

REINDERS, ROBERT C. 'T. Wharton Collens: Catholic and Christian Socialist', *Catholic Historical Review*, LII, no. 2 (July 1966).

ROSE, R. B. 'John Finch, 1784–1857: a Liverpool Disciple of Robert Owen', *Transactions*, Historic Society of Lancashire and Cheshire, CIX (1958).

SALT, JOHN. 'Isaac Ironside and the Hollow Meadows Farm Experiment', *Yorkshire Bulletin of Economic and Social Research*, XII (1960).

SCHUSTER, EUNICE M. 'Native American Anarchism', Smith College *Studies in History*, XVII, nos. 1–4 (1931–32).

SELIGMAN, E. R. A. 'Robert Owen and the Christian Socialists', *Political Science Quarterly*, I (1886);
[Also published in] Seligman, *Essays in Economics* (New York, 1925), chap. 2.

SIMONS, RICHARD. 'A Utopian Failure', *Indiana History Bulletin*, XVIII (February 1941).

STEARNS, BERTHA-MONICA. 'Reform Periodicals and Female Reformers, 1830–1860', *American Historical Review*, XXXVII (July 1932).

WALKER, B. 'The Birmingham Town Hall and its Architect', *Central Literary Magazine*, XXVIII (1927–28).

WARD, J. T. 'Centenary of Lawrence Pitkeithley's Death: he Fought with Oastler for shorter Hours in Mills', *Huddersfield Daily Examiner*, 2 June 1958.

WILLIAMS, HENRY B. 'Syndicalism: History of the Movement in Birmingham: the Work of Robert Owen'. [Newspaper cuttings, 1914, in Birmingham Public Library.]

WILLIAMS, MENTOR L. 'Paulding Satirizes Owenism', *Indiana Magazine of History*, XLIV (December 1948).

Index

Both text and footnotes are indexed, but not the bibliography. Separate titles, in shortened form, are listed in alphabetical order under author. Newspapers and journals are indexed under title.